Information Quality Management:
Theory and Applications

Latif Al-Hakim
University of Southern Queensland, Australia

IDEA GROUP PUBLISHING
Hershey • London • Melbourne • Singapore

Acquisition Editor:	Michelle Potter
Senior Managing Editor:	Jennifer Neidig
Managing Editor:	Sara Reed
Development Editor:	Kristin Roth
Copy Editor:	April Schmidt
Typesetter:	Marko Primorac
Cover Design:	Lisa Tosheff
Printed at:	Yurchak Printing Inc.

Published in the United States of America by
    Idea Group Publishing (an imprint of Idea Group Inc.)
    701 E. Chocolate Avenue
    Hershey PA 17033
    Tel: 717-533-8845
    Fax: 717-533-8661
    E-mail: cust@idea-group.com
    Web site: http://www.idea-group.com

and in the United Kingdom by
    Idea Group Publishing (an imprint of Idea Group Inc.)
    3 Henrietta Street
    Covent Garden
    London WC2E 8LU
    Tel: 44 20 7240 0856
    Fax: 44 20 7379 3313
    Web site: http://www.eurospan.co.uk

Copyright © 2007 by Idea Group Inc. All rights reserved. No part of this book may be reproduced in any form or by any means, electronic or mechanical, including photocopying, without written permission from the publisher.

Product or company names used in this book are for identification purposes only. Inclusion of the names of the products or companies does not indicate a claim of ownership by IGI of the trademark or registered trademark.

Library of Congress Cataloging-in-Publication Data

Information quality management : theory and applications / Latif Al-Hakim, editor.
    p. cm.
  Summary: "This book provides insights and support for professionals and researchers working in the field of information and knowledge management, information quality, practitioners and managers of manufacturing, and service industries concerned with the management of information"--Provided by publisher.
  ISBN 1-59904-024-7 (hardcover) -- ISBN 1-59904-025-5 (softcover) -- ISBN 1-59904-026-3 (ebook)
  1. Information resources management. 2. Information technology--Management. I. Al-Hakim, Latif, 1946-
  T58.64.I5287 2006
  658.4'038--dc22
                      2006019119

British Cataloguing in Publication Data
A Cataloguing in Publication record for this book is available from the British Library.

Information Quality Management: Theory and Applications is part of the Idea Group Publishing series named *Information Quality Management Series*.

All work contributed to this book is new, previously-unpublished material. The views expressed in this book are those of the authors, but not necessarily of the publisher.

Introducing IGI's

INFORMATION QUALITY MANAGEMENT SERIES

Latif Al-Hakim, Editor-in-Chief
University of Southern Queensland, Australia

Challenges of Managing Information Quality in Service Organizations
IGP imprint
1-59904-420-X (h/c) ISBN
1-59904-421-8 (s/c) ISBN
© 2007
$94.95 (h/c) * $79.95 (s/c)

Global E-Government: Theory, Applications and Benchmarking
IGP imprint
1-59904-027-1 (h/c) ISBN
1-59904-029-8 (s/c) ISBN
© 2007
$94.95 (h/c) * $79.95 (s/c)

Information Quality Management: Theory and Applications
IGP imprint
1-59904-024-7 (h/c) ISBN
1-59904-025-5 (s/c) ISBN
© 2007
$94.95 (h/c) * $79.95 (s/c)

It's Easy to Order! Order online at www.idea-group.com or
call 717/533-8845 x10 —
Mon-Fri 8:30 am-5:00 pm (est) or fax 24 hours a day 717/533-8661

IDEA GROUP PUBLISHING
Hershey • London • Melbourne • Singapore

An excellent addition to your library!

Information Quality Management:
Theory and Applications

Table of Contents

Section I: Processing Issues in IQ

> *John Talburt, University of Arkansas at Little Rock, USA*
> *Richard Wang, Massachusetts Institute of Technology, USA*
> *Kimberly Hess, CASA 20th Judicial District, USA*
> *Emily Kuo, Massachusetts Institute of Technology, USA*

> *Laure Berti-Équille, IRISA, France*

> *M. Mehdi Owrang O., American University, USA*

Section V: Applications in Developing Countries

Foreword

As modern society becomes increasingly information driven, the capability and maturity of an organization to manage the quality of its information can mean the difference between success and failure. Information quality is becoming the competitive advantage for many companies. In banking and finance, even a small percentage improvement in data quality when applied to millions of transactions can add significantly to the bottom line. Unfortunately, experience has also shown that when critical decisions, such as launching a space vehicle or approving the safety of a drug, rely upon inaccurate, incomplete, outdated, or inconsistent information, bad things can happen.

From my perspective, I believe that information quality has finally reached a critical mass, and is rapidly maturing as a distinct and important discipline. Year by year, researchers and practitioners are adding to its theory and practice, and I see the documentation of this development through scholarly publication as particularly important. This book contributes to that effort and continues the legacy of Don Ballou, Shobha Chengular-Smith, Beverly Kahn, Yang Lee, Stu Madnick, Harold Pazer, Leo Pipino, Tom Redman, Diane Strong, Giri Tayi, Rich Wang, and other pioneering researchers whose early papers helped define information quality as we now understand it.

I think it is particularly auspicious that this book will be appearing in the same year that the first graduate degree in this area will be offered, a Master of Science in Information Quality at the University of Arkansas at Little Rock, USA. I am honored to have had the opportunity share ideas with several of the contributing authors, many of whom I have met through the annual International Conference on Information Quality (ICIQ) at MIT. I hope that by reading this book you will benefit from their work as well.

John R. Talburt
Acxiom Chair of Information Quality
University of Arkansas at Little Rock, USA

Preface

Abstract

This preface addresses the book Information Quality Management: Theory and Applications. *It discusses the importance of information quality (IQ) and presents examples of IQ documented problems. The preface discusses the importance of information quality (IQ) and IQ dimensions. It presents examples of documented IQ problems and relates these problems to IQ dimensions. It itemises with brief descriptions the structure of this book. This book comprises 12 chapters organised into five sections covering various theoretical and practical issues. It provides insights and support for academic professionals as well as for practitioners concerned with the management of information.*

Overview

The current era is associated with widespread and successive waves of technology-driven innovations in information technology (IT). Technologies, such as the Internet, electronic commerce, World Wide Web (WWW), and mobile commerce, bring with them ubiquitous connectivity, real-time access, and overwhelming volumes of data and information. More and more electronically captured information needs to be processed, stored, and distributed through IT-based business systems. Information is shared amongst various decision makers within organisations and between supply chain partners not only to benchmark, amend, or formulate competitive strategies but also to control day-to-day operations and to solve problems on a real-time basis (Al-Hakim, 2003). The world has experienced a transition from an industrial economy to an information economy. Data and information have become as much a strategic necessity for an organisation's well being and future success as oxygen is to human life (Eckerson, 2002). IT allows organisations to collect great volumes of data. Vast databases holding terabytes of data and information are becoming commonplace (Abbott, 2001).

The literature emphasises that enterprises have far more data than they can possibly use. Yet, at the same time, they do not have the data they actually need (Abbott, 2001; Eckerson, 2002). Furthermore, the stored data and information may be obsolete, ambiguous, inaccurate, or incomplete. In other words, enterprises have achieved "quantity" of data and information but not necessarily the "quality" of either (Pierce, 2005). In 1999, Bill Gates, the founder of Microsoft, stated:

The most meaningful way to differentiate your company from your competitors, the best way to put distance between you and the crowd, is to do an outstanding job with information. How you can gather, manage and use information will determine whether you win or lose.

Gates' statement implies there are some issues that traditional information management systems have not addressed. One critical issue in particular is the quality of information an organisation should gather, manage, and use. The literature suggests that information quality (IQ) problems are becoming increasingly prevalent. The growth of data warehouses and communication and information technologies has increased the need for, and awareness of, high IQ management in organisations. IQ has been rated a top concern to data and information consumers and has been reported as a major factor affecting the success of information systems. There is strong evidence to suggest that IQ has become a critical concern of organisations (Al-Hakim & Xu, 2004; Lee, Strong, Kahn, & Wang, 2002; Redman, 2001; Wand & Wang, 1996). Firms become so critically dependent on information that IQ problems must be identified and treated as urgently as possible. Poor quality of data and information can have a deleterious impact on decision making and therefore on the overall effectiveness of an enterprise. Incorrect and misleading information associated with an enterprise's production and service provision jeopardise both customer relationships and customer satisfaction and ultimately have a negative effect on revenue. Poor information quality is not only prevalent in manufacturing and service organisations; it can also be at the root of many issues of national and international importance which dominate the news (Redman, 2004). Table 1 illustrates some well documented problems associated with poor information quality.

Information and Data

Turban, Aronson, and Liang (2005) provide the following commonly accepted view of the terms information and data:

- **Data:** Items about things, events, activities, and transactions are recorded, classified, and stored but are not organised to convey any specific meaning. Data items can be numeric, alphanumeric, figures, sounds, or images.
- **Information:** Data that has been organised in a manner that gives meaning for the recipient. They confirm something the recipient knows, or may have "surprise" value by revealing something not known.

These definitions clarify the relationship between data and information. They are consistent with the concept of information product (Ballou et al., 1998; Huang et al., 1999) in which information is a product of an information manufacturing system. The input for this information manufacturing system is data. Similar to a product manufacturing system, an information manufacturing system is hierarchical in that information output from a certain stage can be considered data for the next stage of the information manufacturing system.

From this perspective, the term information can be used to refer to both data and information (Strong, Lee, & Wang, 1997). However, the reverse is not always applicable; that is, data collected and stored in a data warehouse cannot be considered information as these data are not yet organised and processed to give meaning for a recipient. Wang urges organisations to manage information as they manage products if they want to increase productivity. Wang finds an analogy between quality issues in product manufacturing and those in information manufacturing and asserts that information manufacturing can be viewed as processing system acting on raw data to produce information products. There are differences between product manufacturing and information manufacturing that can be classified under five main headings: intangibility, input, users, consumption, and handling (Table 2). However, the differences listed in Table 2 will not affect the main idea behind the analogy proposed by Wang between product and information (Al-Hakim, 2004).

Earlier literature dealing with information quality as well as some recent publications use information quality (IQ) and data quality (DQ) interchangeably. While information quality as the quality of the information product implies data quality or the quality of its

Table 1. Examples of some documented problems associated with IQ

Field	Problem	Reason	IQ Dimension
Space Industry	The spacecraft launched by NASA on December 11, 1998, to observe the seasonal climate changes on Mars was lost upon arrival at the planet on September 23, 1999.	It is found that the "root cause" of the loss of the spacecraft was the "the failed translation of English units into metric units in a segment of ground-based, navigation-related mission software" (Isbell & Savage, 1999). The IQ problem here is the use of two different types of information obtained from two measurement systems.	Consistency of representation, compatibility, coherency.
Mine Safety and Health	On July 24, 2002, miners working underground in the Quecreek coal mine in Western Pennsylvania (USA) accidentally broke into an adjacent abandoned mine, which unleashed millions of gallons of water and trapped nine men for three days.	The report of the Mine Safety and Health Administration (MSHA) found that the primary cause of the water inundation was use of undated information obtained from old mine map (MSHA, 2003).	Timeliness, free-of-error.
Bosnian War	On May 8, 1999, NATO forces accidentally bombed the Chinese Embassy in Belgrade.	The bombing instruction was based on outdated data. The data regarding the movement of the location of the Chinese Embassy in 1996 was undated in the NATA database and on their maps (Lehrer, 1999).	Timeliness.

Table 1. continued

Legal System - Death Penalty	In March 2000, a judge acquitted Mr. Green from the 1992 murder of a Starke woman. Mr. Green became one of 21 inmates released from death row in Florida (Kestin, 2000).	A study conducted by Columbia Law School found that during a period of 23 years, the overall rate of prejudicial errors in the American capital punishment system was 68% (Columbia News, 2000). The three most common errors are: (1) incompetent lawyers (37%); (2) suppression of evidence of innocence (19%); and (3) faulty instruction to jurors (20%).	Accuracy, believability, coherency, completeness, ease of understanding, relevancy, reputation.
Terrorism	On September 11, 2001, a series of terrorist attacks destroyed the twin towers of the World Trade Center and severely damaged the Pentagon.	The 9/11 Commission Report depicted a failure to effectively share terrorism warning information and to link the collective knowledge of the agents in the field of national priority (The 9/11 Commission Report, 2004).	Coherency, objectivity, value-added.
Weapons of Mass Destruction	The United States government asserted that [the former Iraqi dictator] Saddam Hussein had reconstituted his nuclear weapons program, had biological weapons and mobile biological weapon production facilities, and had stockpiled and was producing chemical weapons.	The final report of a special commission confirms that "not one bit of it could be confirmed when the war was over." The Commission concludes that "our study of Iraq found several situations where key information failed to reach those who needed it" (Commission WMD, 2005).	Timeliness, free-of-error, completeness, coherency.
Health - Surgery	Two women with the same first name attended a hospital in the same day to have a breast biopsy. One had breast cancer. One did not. The woman with the breast cancer died after nine months.	It was discovered that the biopsy information results had been mixed up. The woman with the breast cancer died after nine months and the patient without breast cancer had endured months of chemotherapy and was minus a breast (Pirani, 2004).	Accuracy, interpretability, free-of-error, conciseness of representation.
Industry - Refinery	On March 23, 2005, the BP Texas City refinery in the U.S. suffered a huge blast. The blast claimed 15 lives and injured 170 (BBC, 2005a).	The interim report into the tragedy has found that failure to follow the proper procedure (which is one type of information) contributed to the explosion, that is, IQ problem.	Accessibility, ease of understanding, interpretability.

Table 1. continued

Finance - Share Market	On December 9, 2005, brokers at Mizuho Securities tried to sell 610,000 shares at 1 yen (0.8 US cents) each. The company had meant to sell one share for 610,000 yen – US$5,065 (BBC, 2005b).	Mizuho said the brokerage had purchased the majority of the phantom shares it sold, but the error has so far caused the company a loss of 27 billion yen or US$21.6 billion. It is announced that this chaos into Japan market trading was a result of a "typing error" (BBC, 2005b), that is, problem in information quality.	Free-of-error, interpretability, objectivity.
Media & Mine Safety	On January 2, 2006, an explosion at the Sago mine (West Virginia, USA) trapped 13 workers. Shortly before midnight on Tuesday, a statement that 12 miners had been found alive was made on several national TV stations and the broadcast prompted jubilant scenes as friends and relatives celebrated. But the euphoria was short lived. Just hours after the banner headlines announced that the 12 miners were safe, rescue workers found their bodies (Associated Press, 2006).	Only one miner out of the 13 miners survived. The sole survivor was taken to the hospital where doctors said his condition was critical. Ben Hatfield, president of mine owner, International Coal Group, blamed the earlier report on "miscommunication."	Accuracy, accessibility, believability, reputation.

raw material "data," the reverse is not always true. Good IQ implies good DQ and poor DQ causes poor IQ. However, good DQ may not necessarily lead to good IQ. Poor IQ may be caused by errors within the process of transforming data into information. A researcher or analyst may collect accurate, complete, and timely data but may conclude from them poor quality information. IQ implies DQ and the term information quality reflects both "information quality" and "data quality." The focus of authors speaking only about DQ is primarily on the issue of data as raw material for example issues related to quality of data for data warehousing. The editor of this book has successfully oriented the authors of this book to use DQ when their research is oriented to data only and to use IQ when they deal with IQ.

Table 2. Main differences between product manufacturing and information manufacturing

Item	Difference
Intangibility	Product manufacturing system produces tangible, visible, or physical products whereas information is intangible. The quality of product can be measured with physical measures such as design specifications. The measures for quality of information are subjective and mainly based on the user's opinion and expectation.
Inputs	Product process requires raw material, experience/knowledge, and technology; while information process requires four inputs: data, experience, technology, and time.
End user	The users of the end product are undefined in the former, whereas they are clearly defined in the latter (Sen, 2001). The user of an information system is part of the system, whereas products are produced away from the users.
Consumption	The raw materials used in information manufacturing are data which can be consumed by more than one consumer without depletion, not like raw materials in product manufacturing that can only be used for single physical products. Further, information can be produced and consumed simultaneously, while products need to be produced before consumption.
Handling	Unlike products, same data and information can be transported to an undefined number of consumers simultaneously via physical carrier, for example, disk, or through an intangible way, for example, e-mail. However, both information and products can be stored and inspected before delivery to the customers. This makes information quality similar to product quality but different from service quality as the service quality cannot be stored and inspected before the delivery (Evans & Lindsay, 2005).

IQ Dimensions

Evans and Lindsay (2005) stress that quality can be a confusing concept. They provide two main reasons for this assertion: (1) people view quality using different perspectives and dimensions based on their individual roles, and (2) the meaning of quality continues to evolve as the quality profession grows and matures. Similar to product quality, IQ has no universal definition. To define IQ, it is important to comprehend both the perspective from which IQ is viewed and its dimensions. The Cambridge Dictionaries Online (2005) define perspective as "a particular way of considering something" and dimension as "a measurement of something."

Individuals have different ways of considering the quality of information as they have different wants and needs, hence, different quality standards which lead to a user-based quality perspective (Evans & Lindsey, 2005). Information users can view IQ from various

Table 3. Definitions of the common IQ dimensions used in literature and their categories (adapted from several research works)

Dimension	Definition	Category		
		Wang and Strong (1996)	Wang et al. (1995)	Lee et al. (2002)
Accessibility	The degree to which information is available, easily obtainable, or quickly retrievable when needed. Accessibility depends on the customer's circumstances.	Accessibility	Internal + External -Data / system related	Usable
Accuracy	The degree to which information represents a real-world state.	Intrinsic	Internal -Data related	Sound
Amount of Information	This dimension measures the appropriateness of volume of information to the user or task at hand.	Contextual	Internal/ External -Data related	Useful
Believability	This dimension measures the user assessment of trueness and credibility of information.	Intrinsic	Internal/ External - Data/system related	Usable
Coherency	This measures how information "hangs together" and provides one meaning to different users.	Intrinsic + contextual	Internal - Data related	Sound
Compatibility	The level to which information can be combined with other information to form certain knowledge.	Intrinsic + Contextual	Internal - Data related	Useful
Completeness	The degree to which information is sufficient enough to depict every state of the task at hand or the represented system, that is, assesses the degree of missing information.	Contextual	Internal - Data related	Sound
Conciseness of Representation	The compactness of information representation.	Represent'nal	External - Data related	Sound

Table 3. continued

Consistency of Representation	The degree of similarity and compatibility of information representation format.	Represent'nal	Internal - Data related	Sound
Ease of Manipulation	The applicability of information to different tasks.	Intrinsic	Internal - Data related	Useful
Ease of Understanding	The degree of comprehension of information.	Represent'nal	Internal - Data/system related	Useful
Free-of-error	The degree to which information is correct. This dimension measures the number, percent, or ratio of incorrect or unreliable information.	Intrinsic	Internal - Data/system related	Sound
Interpretability	The appropriateness and clarity of information language and symbols to the user.	Represent'nal	Internal - Data related	Useful
Objectivity	This dimension measures the information impartiality including information is unbiased and unprejudiced.	Intrinsic	External - Data related	Useful
Relevancy	Relevancy indicates weather information addresses the customer's needs. It reflects the level of appropriateness of information to the task under consideration.	Contextual	External - Data related	Useful
Reputation	The degree of respect and admiration of both information source and information content.	Intrinsic	External - Data related	Usable
Security	It indicates the level of either restriction on access of information or appropriateness of information back-up — protecting information from disasters.	Accessibility	Internal/ External - System related	Dependable

Table 3. continued

Timeliness	This dimension measures how up-to-date information is with respect to customer's needs or the task at hand. It reflects also how fast the information system is updated after the state of the represented real-world system changes.	Contextual	Internal/ External - Data/system related	Dependable

perspectives; as "fitness for intended use," "conformance to specifications," or "meeting or exceeding customer expectations." While these perspectives capture the essence of IQ, they are very broad definitions and are difficult to use in the measurement of quality. There is a need to identify the dimensions that can be used to measure IQ.

IQ is multidimensional. This means that organisations must use multiple measures to evaluate the quality of their information or data. Several researchers have attempted to identify the IQ dimensions. Wang, Storey, and Firth (1995) list 26 IQ dimensions, which in turn are classified into either internal view (design operation) or external view (use and value). Each of these classifications is divided into two subcategories: data-related and system-related (Wand & Wang, 1996). Wang and Strong (1996) conducted an empirical two-phase sorting study and provide the most comprehensive list of IQ attributes. Their list comprises 118 attributes. The 118 attributes are reduced to 20 dimensions, which in turn are grouped into four categories: accuracy, relevancy, representation, and accessibility. Wang and Strong (1996) reexamine their four initial categories and relabeled the first two categories and the four categories became: intrinsic, contextual, representation, and accessibility. It should be noted here that Wang and Strong use the term DQ (rather than IQ) to represent both DQ and IQ. Recently, Lee et al. (2002) developed a two-by-two conceptual model for describing IQ. The model comprises 16 dimensions, which are classified into four categories: sound information, dependable information, useful information, and usable information. Table 3 provides definitions of the most common IQ dimensions used in the literature and illustrates their categories. The last column of Table 1 links the IQ problems with IQ dimensions.

Structure of the Book

This book deals with the theoretical aspects of IQ as well as the IQ applications. It provides insights and support for:

• Professionals and researchers working in the field of information and knowledge management in general and in the field of IQ in particular
• Practitioners and managers of manufacturing and service industries concerned with the management of information

This book comprises 12 chapters organised into five sections covering various theoretical and practical issues. The following is a brief description of each section and the chapters included in them.

Section I: Processing Issues in IQ. The first section of the book comprises three chapters that cover issues associated with IQ processing including IQ metrics for entity resolution, query processing, and attributes of symbolic representation. **Chapter I**, "An Algebraic Approach to Data Quality Metrics for Entity Resolution Over Large Datasets" by John Talburt, Richard Wang, Kimberly Hess, and Emily Kuo, introduces abstract algebra as a means of understanding and creating data quality metrics for entity resolution. Entity resolution is a particular form of data mining that is basic to a number of applications in both industry and government. The chapter describes current research into the creation and validation of quality metrics for entity resolution, primarily in the context of customer recognition systems. It discusses the difficulty of applying statistical cluster analysis to this problem when the datasets are large and propose an alternative index suitable for these situations. The chapter reports preliminary experimental results and outlines areas and approaches to further research in this area.

The second chapter of this section, **Chapter II**, is "Quality-Extended Query Processing for Mediation Systems" by Laure Berti-Équille. It deals with the extension and adaptation of query processing for taking into account constraints on quality of distributed data and presents a novel framework for adaptive query processing on quality-extended query declarations. This chapter attempts to find the best trade-off between the local query cost and the result quality. It discusses that quality of data and quality of service can be advantageously conciliated for tackling the problems of quality-aware query processing in distributed environments and, more generally, that opens innovative research perspectives for quality-aware adaptive query processing.

Current database technology involves processing a large volume of data in order to discover new knowledge. **Chapter III**, titled "Discovering Quality Knowledge from Relational Databases" by M. Mehdi Owrang O., deals with the quality of knowledge discovery and stresses that relational databases create new types of problems for knowledge discovery since they are normalized to avoid redundancies and update anomalies, which make them unsuitable for knowledge discovery. The chapter emphasises that a key issue in any discovery system is to ensure the consistency, accuracy, and completeness of the discovered knowledge. The chapter describes the aforementioned problems associated with the quality of the discovered knowledge and provides some solutions to avoid them.

Chapter IV, titled "Relativity of Information Quality: Ontological vs. Teleological, Internal vs. External View" by Zbigniew Gackowski, presents a qualitative inquiry into the universe of quality attributes of symbolic representation such as data and information values. It offers a rationale for a move from the internal toward the external, from the ontological to the teleological perspective. The focus is on approaches that derive attributes from established theories. The chapter illustrates four cases to offer examples of top-down, dataflow-up examination of quality attributes to demonstrate the potential of the teleological perspective.

Section II: IQ Assessment and Improvement. This section includes two chapters that deal with the challenge of assessment and improvement of information quality. **Chapter V**, titled "The Development of a Health Data Quality Programme" by Karolyn Kerr and Tony Norris, stresses that successful DQ improvement programs require viewing data quality from a holistic perspective — going beyond only the assessment of quality dimensions such as accuracy, relevance, timeliness, comparability, usability, security, and privacy of data.

The chapter emphasises that the core components of a data quality program are quality determinants, assessment framework, and implementation strategy. The chapter discusses the theoretical background of each component in order to formulate a framework for the health care sector. The chapter describes the development of a data quality evaluation framework (DQEF) and an underpinning strategy for the Ministry of Health in New Zealand and outlines the process to "institutionalise" Total Data Quality Management throughout the whole of the health sector.

Chapter VI is "Assessment and Improvement of Data and Information Quality" by Ismael Caballero and Mario Piattini. This chapter provides the theoretical background for assessing and improving information quality at organisations. It introduces IQ assessment and improvement framework through the concept of information management process (IMP). An IMP is assessed according to an information quality maturity model by using an assessment and improvement methodology. The chapter claims that the framework provides a consistent roadway for coordinating efforts and resources to manage information quality with a strategic perspective. The chapter presents a case study to illustrate the applicability of the approach.

Section III: IQ Process Mapping. To be able to effectively manage the quality of information products, professionals can employ several information management tools. However, there does not seem to be sufficient tools in place to assist the information system professionals in understanding the production process that transforms data collected by the organization into the intermediate component data and information that are then formed into the final information products that are distributed to the consumers in the organization. The third section of the book deals with data and information mapping and features two chapters. The first chapter of this section, **Chapter VII**, titled "Integrating IP-Maps with Business Process Modeling" by Elizabeth Pierce, introduces the concept of information production map (IP-Map). The chapter takes the basic constructs of the IP-Map diagram and demonstrates how they can be combined with the event-driven process chain methodology's family of diagrams. This extended family of diagrams can be used to more fully describe the organizational, procedural, informational, and communication structure of a business process while at the same time highlighting the manufacture of the information products used by that business process. The chapter concludes with a review of requirements for a software package that will allow analysts to model and explore their business processes with an emphasis on improving the quality of the organisation's information products.

This second chapter of this part, **Chapter VIII**, "Procedure for Mapping Information Flow: A Case of Surgery Management Process" by Latif Al-Hakim, proposes a procedure to map information and uses the surgery management process (SMP) as a case to illustrate the steps of the procedure. The chapter discusses the issues that make information mapping of SMP a challenging task and explains the difficulties associated with traditional process mapping techniques in mapping information and determining the interdependencies of various elements of SMP activities. The proposed procedure integrates a structured process mapping technique known as IDEF0 with another structured technique referred to as dependency structured matrix (DSM) to map the information of the process. The chapter indicates that it is possible to reduce feedback from other activities that affect the performance of SMP by administratively controlling the information flow through certain activities of SMP.

Section IV. IQ Applications in Manufacturing and Management. The fourth section of the book presents two chapters that deal with issues related to engineering management, product information quality (PIQ), and engineering asset management.

Chapter IX, "A Methodology for Information Quality Assessment in the Designing and Manufacturing Processes of Mechanical Products" by Ying Su and Zhanming Jin, concentrates on IQ related to designing and manufacturing a product, that is, product information quality (PIQ). It emphasises that PIQ is critical in manufacturing enterprises. Yet, the IQ field lacks comprehensive methodologies for PIQ evaluation. The chapter develops such a methodology, which is called activity-based measuring and evaluating of PIQ (AMEQ) to form a basis for PIQ measurement and evaluation. The methodology is illustrated through a business case.

Chapter X, titled "Information Quality in Engineering Asset Management" by Andy Koronios and Shien Lin, discusses the criticality and important issues of information quality associated with the management of engineering assets. They argue that it is essential to ensure the quality of data in monitoring systems, control systems, maintenance systems, procurement systems, logistics systems, and range of mission support applications in order to facilitate effective asset management. The chapter's authors hope that a better understanding of the current issues and emerging key factors for ensuring high quality asset management data will not only raise the general information quality awareness in engineering asset management organisations, but also assist managers and IT professionals in obtaining an insightful and overall appreciation about what information quality problems are in engineering asset management and why they have emerged.

Section V. IQ Applications in Developing Countries. This section comprises two chapters that provide insight information about IQ application in China and Malaysia.

China is experiencing a significant reform in its decision mechanisms, and this is causing a change in the quality requirement for information and the necessity of total quality management for information. **Chapter XI**, "Quality Management Practices Regarding Statistical and Financial Data in China" by Zhenguo Yu and Ying Wang, presents a survey into quality management practices regarding statistics and financial data in China. The chapter stresses the needs for total information quality management in China and stresses that Chinese people understand the quality of the information based on multidimensional metrics. It explores IQ management organizations in China and the legislations against information fraud and information disclosures.

The last chapter in this book, **Chapter XII**, titled "The Effects of Information Quality on Supply Chain Performance: New Evidence from Malaysia" by Suhaiza Zailani and R. Premkumar, presents a study conducted in Malaysia. It introduces how information quality plays an important role in a supply chain performance. This chapter examines the factors influencing information quality and investigates the influences of information quality on supply chain performance in Malaysia. The chapter finds that the extent of information quality will increase supply chain performance and the extent of information quality is influenced by technological, organizational, and environmental characteristics.

References

Abbott, J. (2001). Data data everywhere: And not a byte of use? *Qualitative Market Research, 4*(3), 182-192.

Al-Hakim, L. (2003). Web-based supply chain integration model. In J. Mariga (Ed.), *Managing e-commerce and mobile computing technologies* (pp. 183-207). Hershey, PA: IRM Press.

Al-Hakim, L. (2004). Information quality function deployment. In *Proceedings of the 9th International Conference on Information Quality.* Cambridge: Massachusetts Institute of Technology.

Al-Hakim, L., & Xu, H. (2004). On work alignment: Do IT professionals think differently? In A. Sarmanto (Ed.), *Issues of human computer integration* (pp. 291-320). Hershey, PA: IRM Press.

Associated Press. (2006, January 5). Joy turn to grief for trapped miners' families. South *China Morning Post, LXII*(5).

Ballou, D., Wang, R., Pazer, H., & Tayi, H. (1998). Modeling information manufacturing systems to determine information product quality. *Management Science, 44*(4), 462-484.

BBC. (2005a). Errors led to BP refinery blast. *BBC News.* Retrieved April 17, 2006, from http://news.bbc.co.uk/2/hi/business/4557201.stm

BBC. (2005b). Probe into Japan share error. *BBC News.* Retrieved April 17, 2006, from http://news.bbc.co.uk/2/hi/business/4512962.stm

Cambridge Dictionaries Online. (2005). Retrieved April 17, 2006, from http://dictionary.cambridge.org/

Columbia News. (2000). *Landmark study find capital punishment system "fraught with error."* Retrieved April 17, 2006, from http://www.columbia.edu/cu/news/00/06/lawStudy.html

Commission WMD — Commission on the Intelligent Capabilities of the United States Regarding Weapons of Mass Destruction. (2005). *Report to the president.* Retrieved April 17, 2006, from http://www.wmd.gov/report/report.html#chapter9

Eckerson, W. W. (2002). *Data quality and bottom line: Achieving business success through high quality data* (TDWI Report Series). Seattle, WA: The Data Warehousing Institute.

English, L. (2005). Information quality and increasing regulation. *News and Resources.* Retrieved April 17, 2006, from http://support.sas.com/news/feature/05may/iqcompliance.html

Evans, J. R., & Lindsay, W. M. (2005). *The management and control of quality* (6th ed.). Cincinnati, OH: South-Western, Thomson Learning.

Gates, B. (1999). *Business @ the speed of thought: Using a digital nervous system.* London: Penguin Books.

Huang, K.-T., Lee, Y. W., & Wang, R. Y. (1999). *Quality information and knowledge.* Upper Saddle River, NJ: Prentice Hall PTR.

Isbell, D., & Savage, D. (1999). *Mars climate orbiter failure board releases report: Numerous NASA actions underway in response.* Retrieved April 17, 2006, from http://www.spaceref.com:16080/news/viewpr.html?pid=43

MSHA. (2003). *MSHA issues Quecreek investigation report.* U.S. Department of Labor: Mine Safety and Health Administration. Retrieved April 17, 2006, from http://www.msha.gov/Media/PRESS/2003/NR030812.htm

Kestin, S. (2000). *State's death penalty error rate among highest in nation.* Retrieved April 17, 2006, from http://www.helpvirginia.com/6-19-00.htm

Lee, Y. W., Strong, D. M., Kahn, B. K., & Wang, R. Y. (2002). AIMQ: A methodology for information quality assessment. *Information & Management, 40*, 133-146.

Lehrer, J. (1999). The wrong target. *Online News Hour.* Retrieved April 17, 2006, from http://www.pbs.org/newshour/bb/europe/jan-june99/bombing_5-10.html

Pierce, E. M. (2005). Introduction. In R. Wang, E. Pierce, S. Madnick, & C. Fisher (Eds.), *Information quality* (pp. 3-17). Armonk, NY: M.E. Sharpe, Inc.

Pirani, C. (2004, January 24-25). How safe are our hospitals. *The Weekend Australian.*

Redman, T. C. (2001). *Data quality: The field guide.* Boston: Digital Press.

Redman, T. C. (2004, August). Data: An unfolding quality disaster. *DM Review Magazine.* Retrieved April 17, 2006, from http://www.dmreview.com/article_sub.cfm?articleId=1007211

Sen, K. (2001). Does the measure of information quality influence survival bias? *International Journal of Quality and Reliability Management, 18*(9), 967-981.

SerachTechTarget. (2005). Data. *SearchDataManagement.Com definition.* Retrieved April 17, 2006, from http://searchdatamanagement.techtarget.com/sDefinition/

Strong, D. M., Lee, Y. W., & Wang, R. Y. (1997). Data quality on context. *Communication of the ACM, 40*(5), 103-110.

The 9/11 Commission Report. (2004). *Final report of the National Commission on Terrorist Attacks upon the United States* (Executive Summary). Washington, DC: US Government Printing Office. Retrieved April 17, 2006, from http://a257.g.akamaitech.net/7/257/2422/22jul20041147/www.gpoaccess.gov/911/pdf/execsummary.pdf

Turban, E., Aronson, J. E., & Liang, T. P. (2005). *Decision support systems and intelligent systems* (7th ed.). Upper Saddle River, NJ: Prentice Hall.

Wand, Y., & Wang, R. Y. (1996). Anchoring data quality dimensions in ontological foundations. *Communications of ACM, 39*(11), 86-95.

Wang, R. Y. (1998). A product perspective on total data quality management. *Communications of the ACM, 41*(2), 58-65.

Wang, R. Y., Pierce, E. M., Madnick, S. E., & Fisher, C. W. (Eds.). (2005). *Information quality.* Armonk, NY: M.E. Sharpe, Inc.

Wang, R. Y., Storey, V. C., & Firth, C. P. (1995). A framework for analysis of data quality research. *IEEE Transactions Knowledge and Data Engineering, 7*(4), 623-640.

Wang, R. Y., & Strong, D. M. (1996). Beyond accuracy: What data quality means to data consumers. *Journal of Management Information Systems, 12*(4), 5-34.

Acknowledgments

The editor is grateful to all those who have assisted him with the completion of this work. In particular, the editor would like to acknowledge his deepest appreciation to many reviewers for their time and effort. Amendments suggested by them were incorporated into the manuscripts during the development process and significantly enhanced the quality of the work.

The editor wants to thank Dr. Mehdi Khosrow-Pour, the executive director of Idea Group Inc., and Jan Travers, the managing director, who provided needed support and co-ordination. Appreciation also goes to Kristin Roth, Michelle Potter, and Jessie Weik who gave their time willingly to describe many issues related to the preparation of this work and share their experiences with me. A special thanks to the staff of the University of Southern Queensland for all of their assistance in seeing this work completed.

List of Reviewers

Laure Berti-Équille   Universitaire de Beaulieu, France
Monica Bobrowski   Pragma Consultores, Argentina
Mikhaila S E Burgess   Cardiff University, UK
Ismael Caballero   University of Castilla-La Mancha, Spain
Zbigniew J. Gackowski   California State University, Stanislaus, USA
Heather Maguire   University of Southern Queensland, Australia
Kimberly Hess   Acxiom Corporation, USA
Karolyn Kerr   Simpl, New Zealand
Andy Koronios   University of South Australia, Australia
Shien Lin   University of South Australia, Australia
Daniel Maier   Credit Suisse, Switzerland
Helinä Melkas   Helsinki University, Finland
Felix Naumann   Humboldt-Universität zu Berlin, Germany

Tony Norris	Massey University, New Zealand
M. Mehdi Owrang	American University, USA
Elizabeth M. Pierce	Indiana University of Pennsylvania, USA
Barbara Roberts	University of Southern Queensland, Australia
Mary Roth	IBM Silicon Valley Lab, USA
Ying Su Tsinghua	University, China
John R. Talburt	Acxiom Corporation, USA
Michael B. Twidale	University of Illinois at Urbana-Champaign, USA
Sabrina Vazquez Soler	Pragma Consultores, Argentina
Jon R. Wright	AT&T Labs-Research, USA
Zhenguo Yu	Zhejiang University City College, China
Suhaiza Zailani	Universiti Sains Malaysia, Malaysia

Section I

Processing Issues in IQ

Chapter I

An Algebraic Approach to Data Quality Metrics for Entity Resolution Over Large Datasets

John Talburt, University of Arkansas at Little Rock, USA

Richard Wang, Massachusetts Institute of Technology, USA

Kimberly Hess, CASA 20th Judicial District, USA

Emily Kuo, Massachusetts Institute of Technology, USA

Abstract

This chapter introduces abstract algebra as a means of understanding and creating data quality metrics for entity resolution, the process in which records determined to represent the same real-world entity are successively located and merged. Entity resolution is a particular form of data mining that is foundational to a number of applications in both industry and government. Examples include commercial customer recognition systems and information sharing on "persons of interest" across federal intelligence agencies. Despite the importance of these applications, most of the data quality literature focuses on measuring the intrinsic quality of individual records than the quality of record grouping or integration. In this chapter, the authors describe current research into the creation and validation of quality metrics for entity resolution, primarily in the context of customer recognition systems. The approach is based on an algebraic view of the system as creating a partition of a set of

Copyright © 2007, Idea Group Inc. Copying or distributing in print or electronic forms without written permission of Idea Group Inc. is prohibited.

entity records based on the indicative information for the entities in question. In this view, the relative quality of entity identification between two systems can be measured in terms of the similarity between the partitions they produce. The authors discuss the difficulty of applying statistical cluster analysis to this problem when the datasets are large and propose an alternative index suitable for these situations. They also report some preliminary experimental results and outline areas and approaches to further research in this area.

Introduction

Traditionally, data quality research and practice have revolved around describing and quantifying the intrinsic quality of individual data records or rows in a database table. However as more and more organizations continue to embrace the strategies of customer relationship management (CRM), new issues are raised related to the quality of integrating or grouping records, especially as it related to the process of entity resolution.

Most current approaches to data integration quality are rooted in the evaluation of traditional data matching or duplicate detection techniques, such as precision and recall graphs (Bilenko & Mooney, 2003). However, these techniques are inadequate for modern knowledge-based entity resolution techniques where two records for the same entity may present entirely different representations, and can only be related to each other through a priori assertions provided by an independent source of associative information.

The authors propose that casting data integration problems in set theoretic terms and applying well-developed definitions and techniques from abstract algebra and statistics can lead to productive approaches for understanding and addressing these issues, especially when applied to very large datasets on the order of 10 to 100 million records or more. The chapter also describes the application of algebraic techniques for defining metrics for grouping accuracy and consistency, including measurement taken on real-world data.

Background

Entity resolution is the process in which records determined to represent the same real-world entity are successively located and merged (Benjelloun, Garcia-Molina, Su, & Widom, 2005). It can also be viewed as a special case of heterogeneous system interoperability (Thuraisingham, 2003). The attributes that are used to determine whether records related to two entities are the same are called "indicative information." A basic problem is that the indicative information for same entity can vary from record to record, and therefore does not always provide a consistent way to represent or label the entity. Although the specific techniques used to implement a particular entity resolution system will vary, in almost all cases the end result is that the system assigns each entity a unique "token," a symbol or string of symbols that is a placeholder for the entity. Token-based entity resolution systems fall into two broad classes, based on how the tokens are created: hash tokens and equivalence class tokens.

Copyright © 2007, Idea Group Inc. Copying or distributing in print or electronic forms without written permission of Idea Group Inc. is prohibited.

Hash Tokens

The simplest method for associating a token with an entity is to use an algorithm to calculate or "derive" a value for the token from the primary indicative information for the entity. The derived value is called a "hash token." For example, if the indicative information for a customer were "Robert Doe, 123 Oak St.," then the underlying binary representation of this string of characters can be put through a series of rearrangements and numeric operations that might result in a string of characters like "r7H5pK2."

The use of hash tokens for entity resolution has two drawbacks: hash collisions and lack of consistency. Hash collisions occur when the hash algorithm operating on two different arguments creates the same hash token, thus creating a many-to-one mapping from indicative information to the token representations. There are a number of mitigations for hash collisions, and this does not present a major obstacle for entity resolution.

On the other hand, a more serious problem related to the use of hash tokens is their lack of consistency. Hash algorithms are notoriously sensitive to very small changes in the argument string. For example, even though "Robert Doe, 123 Oak St." and "Bob Doe, 123 Oak St." may represent the same customer, most hash algorithms will produce very different hash values for each. Although some systems go to great lengths to "standardize" the argument string before the algorithm is applied (Frederich, 2005) such as changing "Bob" to "Robert," in the real world the indicative information for the same entity can often change dramatically. For example, "Jane Doe, 123 Pine St." can marry John Smith and move to a new address, resulting in "Jane Smith, 345 Elm St." as valid indicative information for the same person. In cases like this, no amount of name and address standardization could enable these two records to produce the same hash token.

Equivalence Class Tokens

One way to improve the consistency of token assignments for these kinds of situations is to use a knowledge base approach (Morgan, McLaughlin, et al., 2000; Morgan, Talley, et al., 2003). As knowledge the is acquired that indicative information for an entity has

Table 1. Two equivalence classes

	Token	Representation
Equivalence Class xH45nT	xH45nT	Jane Doe, 123 Pine St.
	xH45nT	Jane Smith, 345 Elm St.
	xH45nT	J S Smith, 345 Elm St.
Equivalence Class y7Bw6	y7Bw6	Robert Doe, 123 Oak St.
	y7Bw6	Bob Doe, 123 Oak St.

Copyright © 2007, Idea Group Inc. Copying or distributing in print or electronic forms without written permission of Idea Group Inc. is prohibited.

changed, the new representation is stored along with other valid representations in a list, called an "equivalence class." Each equivalence class is assigned an arbitrary, but unique, token value that is not derived from a particular representation of the entity. Table 1 shows how both examples described earlier can easily be accommodated using an equivalence class approach.

If we consider all of the possible entity representations as the underlying set S, then the rule that "two representations are assigned the same token if, and only if, they represent the same entity" defines an equivalence relation on S that partitions S into equivalence classes, that is, all representations associated with the same token. Equivalence classes, equivalence relations, partitions, and other concepts from abstract algebra are not only descriptive, but they also provide important new analysis tools for problems related to data integration and entity resolution (Talburt, Kuo, Wang, & Hess, 2004).

Customer Recognition

An important commercial application of entity resolution is customer recognition, where the entities in question are the customers of a business, usually an individual or a business (Hughes, 2005). For several years, businesses have realized that in a highly competitive environment they must not only gain market share, but they must also retain and maximize the value of the customers they have. A company will have multiple interactions with the same customer at different times, locations, or lines of business. Each failure to make these connections is a lost opportunity to discover knowledge about a customer's behavior — knowledge that can make these and future interactions more profitable for the business and more satisfying for the customer. The collection of strategies around maximizing the value of these customer interactions is called customer relationship management, or CRM (Lee, 2000)

Most modern businesses interact with their customers through several channels that carry transactions to and from internal systems. Channels may represent different lines of business (homeowners vs. auto for an insurance company), different sales channels (inbound telephone sales vs. online sales for a retailer), or different geographic locations. It is common for each channel to have its own form of internal customer recognition based on one or more items of identification information. The identification information in the transaction may include some type of internally assigned customer key specific to that particular channel. Even within a single channel, key-based recognition is not perfect. The same customer may be assigned different identifying keys for a number of reasons. The white paper, "Customer-Centric Information Quality Management" (Talburt, Wang, et al., 2004), published through the MITIQ program gives a more complete discussion of the factors that impact the quality of customer recognition.

In a multichannel business the problem is further compounded by the need to recognize and profile customers across channels and synchronize the keys assigned by different channels. Figure 1 shows a typical configuration for a customer recognition system that manages recognition across channels. Note that in this diagram and discussion, the indicative attributes are called "ID fields."

In Figure 1, the customer transactions coming through the channels include one or more items of identifying information. The two channels are connected to a recognition

Copyright © 2007, Idea Group Inc. Copying or distributing in print or electronic forms without written permission of Idea Group Inc. is prohibited.

Figure 1. Block diagram of a multichannel recognition system

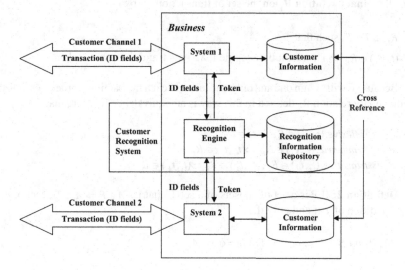

engine, which has access to a repository of recognition information that has been collected from both channels. The information in the repository is organized in such a way that the transactions belonging to the same customer are assigned a unique token as shown in the diagram. The token represents the customer's single, enterprise identity, and is used to bring together the various internal (system) keys the customer may have been assigned at different times or through different channels. For this reason, customer recognition tokens are sometime referred to as "cross-reference identifiers."

Despite the fact that customer recognition is a critical factor in successful CRM solutions, there is little guidance in the literature on metrics specific to entity resolution in general, and customer recognition quality in particular. This chapter attempts to describe a formal approach to quality metrics for entity resolution similar to what has been done by Wang, Lee, and others to develop a data quality algebra for database systems (Wang, Ziad, & Lee, 2001) and information products in general (Huang, Lee, & Wang, 1999).

An Algebraic Model for Entity Resolution

Despite the complexity involved in an actual entity resolution system implementation, its function can be described relatively simply in terms of "equivalence relation" from basic abstract algebra. In this model there are three critical elements. Let $T = \{t_1, t_2, \ldots, t_n\}$ represent a finite set of "n" entity transactions that have been processed in a particular order through a given resolution engine. As shown in Figure 1, the engine will assign to each transaction a token.

Copyright © 2007, Idea Group Inc. Copying or distributing in print or electronic forms without written permission of Idea Group Inc. is prohibited.

Definition 1: For a given resolution engine E, and a given order of the transactions T, define the **binary relation R$_E$** on the set of transactions **T** by:

$R_E \subset T \times T$, such that

$(t_i, t_j) \in R_E \Leftrightarrow$ The resolution engine E assigns t$_i$ and t$_j$ the same token.

Because E will assign one and only one token to each transaction it processes, it follows that the binary relation R$_E$ defined in this way is an equivalence relation, that is:

1. R_E is reflexive, $(t_i, t_i) \in R_E \;\; \forall t_i \in T$
2. R_E is symmetric, $(t_i, t_j) \in R_E \Rightarrow (t_j, t_i) \in R_E$
3. R_E is transitive, $(t_i, t_j) \in R_E, (t_j, t_k) \in R_E \Rightarrow (t_i, t_k) \in R_E$

Definition 2: If P is a set of subsets of a set T, that is, $A \in P \Rightarrow A \subseteq T$, then P is said to be a partition of T if and only if:

$A \in P$ and $B \in P \Rightarrow$ either $A \cap B = \phi$ or $A = B$,

and, $\bigcup_{A \in P} A = T$

Because the binary relation R$_E$ defined on particular ordering of T by a Resolution Engine E is an equivalence relation, the set of all equivalence classes of R is a partition P$_R$ of T, that is, if $P_i = \{t_j \,|\, (t_j, t_i) \in R\}$, then $P_E = \{P_i \,|\, 1 \le i \le n\}$ is a partition of T.

Each equivalence class P$_i$ represents all of the transactions belonging to the same entity as determined by the resolution engine.

Definition 3: If E is an entity resolution engine, T is a set of transactions, α is a particular ordering of T, and P$_E$ is the partition of T generated by the equivalence relation R$_E$, then {E, T, α, P$_E$} is an entity resolution model.

Different resolution engines, different transactions sets, or even different orderings of the same transaction set will produce different models. However, the models are considered equivalent if they produce the same partition of the transaction set.

Definition 4: Two entity resolution models, {R, T, α, P$_R$} and {S, T, β, P$_S$}, are equivalent over the same transaction set T if and only if P$_R$ = P$_S$.

Note that Definition 4 requires the models be defined over the same set of transactions. However, different engines and different orderings of the transactions comprise different models, which may or may not be equivalent.

As a simple example, suppose that R assigns an incoming entity transaction a token that is the same as the first previously processed transaction where the last names are no more than one character different, and the street numbers are the same.

Table 2 shows that the four transactions processed in the order shown would be clas-

Copyright © 2007, Idea Group Inc. Copying or distributing in print or electronic forms without written permission of Idea Group Inc. is prohibited.

Table 2. Classification into two partition classes

Order (α)	Transactions (T)	Token
T₁	(Smithe, 101 Oak St.)	A
T₂	(Smith, 101 Elm St.)	A
T₃	(Smith, 202 Oak St.)	B
T₄	(Smythe, 101 Pine St.)	A

Table 3. Classification into three partition classes

Order (β)	Transactions (T)	Token
T₄	(Smythe, 101 Pine St.)	A
T₃	(Smith, 202 Oak St.)	B
T₂	(Smith, 101 Elm St.)	C
T₁	(Smithe, 101 Oak St.)	A

sified into two partition classes: $\{T_1, T_2, T_4\}$ and $\{T_3\}$. The first transaction would be assigned a token of "A". The second transaction would be compared to the first, and because "Smithe" and "Smith" are only one character different, and the street numbers are the same, it would also be assigned "A". The third transaction has a street number that does not match either the first or second transaction, and would therefore receive a different token of "B". Finally, the fourth transaction would be assigned "A" because when compared to the first transaction, "Smythe" is only one character different than "Smithe" and the street numbers are the same.

On the other hand, Table 3 shows the outcome of processing the same set of transactions with the same resolution rules, but reversing the order of processing. In this case, the four transactions are classified into three partition classes: $\{T_1, T_4\}$, $\{T_2\}$, and $\{T_3\}$. In this processing order, the third transaction processed (T_2) does not match the first transaction (T_4) because "Smythe" and "Smith" differ by two characters, and does not match the second transaction (T_3) because the street numbers are different.

Definition 5: A resolution engine R is said to be order invariant over a set of transactions T if and only if R produces the same partition for every ordering of T.

Partition Similarity

Definition 4 relates the equality (equivalence) of two resolution models to the equality of the partitions they produce. In the same way, the relative similarity of two resolution models can be based on the relative similarity of the partitions they produce. However in this case, the definition of similarity between partitions is less clear. A number of similarity "indices" have been developed in statistics in connection with cluster analysis. The primary

Copyright © 2007, Idea Group Inc. Copying or distributing in print or electronic forms without written permission of Idea Group Inc. is prohibited.

consideration in selecting a particular index for an application is the extent to which it provides adequate discrimination (sensitivity) for a particular application. As a starting point in the initial research, the authors have chosen to test three indices, the Rand index (Rand, 1971) and the adjusted Rand index (Yeung & Ruzzo, 2001), in the initial research, and the TW index developed by the authors and described in this chapter.

The Talburt-Wang index was designed by the authors to provide an easily calculated baseline measure. The Rand index and adjusted Rand index have been taken from the literature on cluster analysis and recommended for cases where the two partitions have a different number of partition classes (Hubert & Arabie, 1985). These indices have a more complex calculation than the Talburt-Wang index, involving the formula for counting the combinations of n things taken two at a time, C(n,2). Because transaction sets can be on the order of hundreds of thousands or even millions of records, the combination calculations for the Rand and adjusted Rand indices can exceed the limits of single precision for some statistical packages. Moreover, the lack of symmetry in the calculations for these indices requires that either a very large amount of main memory be available to make all of the calculations in a single pass of the transactions, or that the transactions be sorted and processed twice.

Talburt-Wang Index

Definition 6: If A and B are two partitions of a set T, define $\Phi(A,B)$, the partition overlap of A and B, as follows:

$$\Phi(A,B) = \sum_{i=1}^{|A|}\left|\left\{B_j \in B \mid B_j \cap A_i \neq \phi\right\}\right|$$

For a given partition class of partition A, it counts how many partition classes of partition B have a non-empty intersection with it. These are summed over all partition classes of A.

Theorem 1: If A and B are two partitions of a set T, then $\Phi(A,B) = \Phi(B,A)$.

Proof: It is easy to see that the definitions of $\Phi(A,B)$ and $\Phi(B,A)$ are symmetric.

Definition 7: If A and B are two partitions of a set T, define $\Delta(A,B)$, the Talburt-Wang index between A and B, as follows:

$$\Delta(A,B) = \frac{|A| \cdot |B|}{\left(\Phi(A,B)\right)^2}$$

Figure 2 shows a 5-by-5 array of 25 points that represents an underlying set T. The four partition classes of partition A are represented as rectangles labeled A_1 through A_4, and the six partition classes of partition B are represented by the oval shapes labeled B_1 through B_6.

Copyright © 2007, Idea Group Inc. Copying or distributing in print or electronic forms without written permission of Idea Group Inc. is prohibited.

Figure 2. Array diagram of two partitions A and B

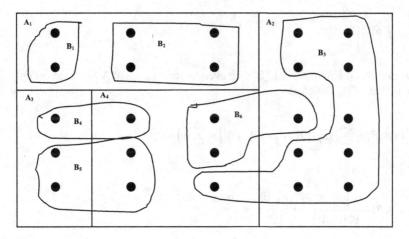

The calculation of the overlap of A and B for this example is:

$\Phi(A, B)$

$= \left|\left\{B_j \in B \mid B_j \cap A_1 \neq \phi\right\}\right| + \left|\left\{B_j \in B \mid B_j \cap A_2 \neq \phi\right\}\right| + \left|\left\{B_j \in B \mid B_j \cap A_3 \neq \phi\right\}\right|$

$\quad + \left|\left\{B_j \in B \mid B_j \cap A_4 \neq \phi\right\}\right|$

$= \left|\left\{B_1, B_2\right\}\right| + \left|\left\{B_3, B_6\right\}\right| + \left|\left\{B_4, B_5\right\}\right| + \left|\left\{B_3, B_4, B_5, B_6\right\}\right|$

$= 2 + 2 + 2 + 4 = 10$

Therefore,

$$\Delta(A, B) = \frac{|A| \cdot |B|}{\left(\Phi(A,B)\right)^2} = \frac{4 \cdot 6}{10^2} = 0.24$$

Corollary 1: If A and B are partitions of the set T, then $\Delta(A, B) = \Delta(B, A)$.

Definition 8: If A and B are partitions of the set T, partition A is said to be a "refinement" of partition B, if and only if

$A_i \in A \Rightarrow A_i \subseteq B_j \text{ for some } j, 1 \leq j \leq |B|$;

that is, every partition class of partition A is a subset of some partition class of partition B.

Copyright © 2007, Idea Group Inc. Copying or distributing in print or electronic forms without written permission of Idea Group Inc. is prohibited.

Theorem 2: If A and B are partitions of the set T, and A is a refinement of B, then:

$$\Delta(A,B) = \frac{|B|}{|A|}$$

Proof: If A is a refinement of B, then every partition class of A will intersect only one partition class of B. Therefore:

$$\Phi(A,B) = \sum_{i=1}^{|A|}\left|\left\{B_j \in B \mid B_j \cap A_i \neq \phi\right\}\right| = \sum_{l=1}^{|A|}(1) = |A|$$

and

$$\Delta(A,B) = \frac{|A|\cdot|B|}{\left(\Phi(A,B)\right)^2} = \frac{|A|\cdot|B|}{|A|^2} = \frac{|B|}{|A|}$$

From Definition 6, it is easy to see that:

$$\Phi(A,B) \geq \max\left(|A|,|B|\right).$$

Consequently, by Definition 7:

$$\Delta(A,B) \leq 1.$$

The following theorem shows that the Talburt-Wang index is equal to one, only when the partitions are identical.

Theorem 3: A and B are identical partitions of T, if and only if $\Delta(A,B) = 1$.

Proof: Suppose the A and B are identical partitions of T. Then A must be a refinement of B. By Theorem 2:

$$\Delta(A,B) = \frac{|B|}{|A|}.$$

However, because A and B are identical, |A| = |B|. Consequently, $\Delta(A,B) = 1$.
The converse can be demonstrated by observing that Definition 6 requires that:

$$\Phi(A,B) \geq \max\{|A|,|B|\}.$$

Any difference between partitions A and B will mean that either $\Phi(A,B) > |A|$ or $\Phi(A,B) > |B|$ and, consequently:

Copyright © 2007, Idea Group Inc. Copying or distributing in print or electronic forms without written permission of Idea Group Inc. is prohibited.

$$\Delta(A, B) = \frac{|A| \cdot |B|}{\left(\Phi(A, B)\right)^2} < 1.$$

Corollary 2: If A is any partition of T, and B is the "trivial partition" of T, that is, B = {T}, then:

$$\Delta(A, B) = \frac{1}{|A|}.$$

Proof: Every partition is a refinement of the trivial partition. Therefore by Theorem 2:

$$\Delta(A, B) = \frac{|B|}{|A|} = \frac{1}{|A|}.$$

Corollary 3: If A is the "point partition" of T, that is, A = {{t_1}, {t_2},...,{t_n}} where each partition class of A contains only one element of T, and B is any partition of T, then:

$$\Delta(A, B) = \frac{|B|}{|T|}.$$

Proof: The "point partition" is a refinement of every partition. Again by Theorem 2:

$$\Delta(A, B) = \frac{|B|}{|A|} = \frac{|B|}{|T|}.$$

Corollary 4: If A is the "point partition" of T, and B is the trivial partition of T, then:

$$\Delta(A, B) = \frac{1}{|T|}.$$

Proof: Apply Corollaries 2 and 3 together.

Although the Talburt-Wang index will always be greater than zero, Corollary 4 shows that it approaches zero for the point partition of an arbitrarily large set T. Therefore, the Talburt-Wang index takes on values in the half open interval (0,1].

Rand Index and Adjusted Rand Index

The Rand index (Rand, 1971) and the adjusted Rand index (Yeung & Ruzzo, 2001) are both commonly used indices to compare clustering results against external criteria (Hubert

Copyright © 2007, Idea Group Inc. Copying or distributing in print or electronic forms without written permission of Idea Group Inc. is prohibited.

Table 4. Intersection matrix for partitions A and B

A\B	B_1	B_2	...	B_n	Sums
A_1	C_{11}	C_{12}	...	C_{1n}	S_{1*}
A_2	C_{21}	C_{21}	...	C_{2n}	S_{2*}
...	...	...		...	...
A_m	C_{m1}	C_{m2}	...	C_{mn}	S_{m*}
Sums	S_{*1}	S_{*2}	...	S_{*n}	S_{mn}

& Arabie, 1985). The computation of these indices is best explained using a tabular representation of the overlap between two partitions.

If A and B are two partitions of the set T, the overlap between A and B can be represented in Table 4.

In Table 4, the row and column entry C_{ij} represents the count of elements in the intersection between partition class A_i of partition A and the partition class B_j of partition B. Each row sum S_{i*} is equal to the number of elements in the partition class A_i, and the column sum S_{*j} is equal to the number of elements in the partition class B_j. The sum S_{mn} is equal to the number of elements in the underlying set T.

The calculation of both the Rand index and adjusted Rand index can be expressed in terms of four values: x, y, z, and w, defined as follows:

$$x = \sum_{i,j} \binom{C_{ij}}{2}, \text{ where } \binom{N}{2} = \frac{N \cdot (N-1)}{2}$$

$$y = \sum_i \binom{S_{i*}}{2} - x$$

$$z = \sum_j \binom{S_{*j}}{2} - x$$

$$w = \binom{S_{mn}}{2} - x - y - z$$

Based on these values:

$$\text{Rand index} = \frac{x+w}{x+y+z+w}$$

Copyright © 2007, Idea Group Inc. Copying or distributing in print or electronic forms without written permission of Idea Group Inc. is prohibited.

Table 5. Intersection matrix for the partitions of Figure 2

A\B	B_1	B_2	B_3	B_4	B_5	B_6	Sums
A_1	2	4	0	0	0	0	6
A_2	0	0	9	0	0	1	10
A_3	0	0	0	1	2	0	3
A_4	0	0	1	1	2	2	6
Sums	2	4	10	2	4	3	25

$$\text{adjusted Rand index} = \frac{x - \left(\dfrac{(y+x)\cdot(z+x)}{x+y+z+w}\right)}{\dfrac{(y+z+2x)}{2} - \left(\dfrac{(y+x)\cdot(z+x)}{x+y+z+w}\right)}$$

The primary difference is that the adjusted Rand takes on a wider range of values thus increasing its sensitivity.

Transforming the example of Figure 1 into tabular form yields Table 5.

Based on these counts:

$x = 1 + 6 + 36 + 1 + 1 + 1 = 46$
$y = 15 + 45 + 3 + 15 - 46 = 32$
$z = 1 + 6 + 45 + 1 + 6 + 3 - 46 = 16$
$w = 300 - 46 - 32 - 16 = 206$
Rand index = $(46+206)/(46 + 32 + 16 + 206) = 0.84$
adjusted Rand index = $(46 - (78*62)/300)/((78 + 62)/2 - (78*62)/300) = 0.5546$

By contrast:

Talburt-Wang index = 0.24

An important aspect of the preliminary research is to determine which one, or which possible combination, of these indices provides an appropriate level of discrimination in comparing the partitions actually generated by entity resolution applications involving large volumes of transactions.

Entity Resolution Quality Metrics

Given that entity resolution system outcomes can be represented as partitions, and that an appropriate index has been selected to assess the degree of difference between partitions, the next step is to investigate the use of the index to create data quality metrics relevant to

Copyright © 2007, Idea Group Inc. Copying or distributing in print or electronic forms without written permission of Idea Group Inc. is prohibited.

entity resolution systems. Having measurements appropriate for critical touch points in a data process flow is an important aspect of any total data quality strategy (Campbell & Wilhoit, 2003). For purposes of this discussion, we will simply refer to it as the "similarity index." The following suggests how a partition similarity index could be applied.

Metric for Entity Resolution Consistency

The following describes three contexts in which a similarity index could provide a type of consistency metric for cases where the entity resolution is customer recognition. The first is a comparison between two different recognition systems, and the second is an assessment of changes to a single recognition system. In both cases we hold the transaction set fixed. Experiments 1 and 2 illustrate these two applications, respectively. A third example (Experiment 3) considers the case where the engine is held fixed and the transaction set changes in quality.

Experiment 1: Different Engines

In this experiment, the first recognition system R is a CDI product based on traditional "merge/purge" approximate string matching technology, and the second system S is a newer customer data integration (CDI) product using both matching and a knowledge base of external information about occupancy associations. Both R and S are used as the recognition engine in Customer Recognition applications. T is a fixed set of ordered customer transaction.

Tables 6 and 7 show a comparison of the partitions A and B created by R and S respectively.

Table 6. Results of Experiment 1

Statistic	A	B
Record Cnt	673,003	673.003
Class Cnt	175,527	136,795
Single Cnt	112,857	62,839
Avg Class	3.83	4.92
Max Class	110	80

Table 7. Similarity index results

Index	Value
Talburt-Wang	0.4339
Rand	0.9998
Adj Rand	0.8104

Copyright © 2007, Idea Group Inc. Copying or distributing in print or electronic forms without written permission of Idea Group Inc. is prohibited.

In this experiment, the second partition B shows more grouping, in that it has fewer partition classes than the partition A created by engine R that relies entirely on string matching. On average the partition classes created by the knowledge-assisted engine S are larger, and there are fewer singleton classes. These all indicate that the knowledge-assisted recognition engine S groups more transactions. Presumably this can be attributed to the additional knowledge that allows some of the "match only" classes of R to be consolidated into a single class using external knowledge. For example, partition A may contain two classes: one with two transactions, {"John Jones, 123 Main", "J. Jones, 123 Main"}, and another with one transaction {"John Jones, 345 Oak"}. However if external knowledge indicates that "John Jones" has moved from "123 Main" to "345 Oak", then these three transactions would be in the same class of partition B, that is, the class {"John Jones, 123 Main", "J. Jones, 123 Main", "John Jones, 345 Oak"}.

Although this may be an expected result, the indices only indicate the degree to which R and S generate different partitions, with the profile showing that R makes fewer associations (on average) than S. The measurement does not indicate which, if either, makes more correct associations. Furthermore, the three indices vary widely on the degree of similarity with the Rand indicating a rather strong similarity, the Talburt-Wang index a fairly strong difference, and the adjusted Rand somewhere in the middle.

Experiment 2: Changes to the Same Engine

Having a way to measure the impact of changes to the recognition engine can also be very useful in assessing recognition quality, especially in the initial phases of a system implementation. In this scenario, the input transactions are held fixed, and the grouping is performed twice, once before the change (R), and once after the change (S). The similarity index provides a metric for assessing the change in groupings that can be attributed to the change in the recognition engine.

In this experiment, R is the April release of a knowledge-based CDI product that is released monthly and used in customer recognition applications. S is the May release of the same product. T is a fixed set of ordered customer transactions.

Tables 8 and 9 show a comparison of the partitions A and B created by R and S, respectively.

Table 8. Results of Experiment 2

Statistic	A	B
Record Cnt	17,778	17,778
Class Cnt	3,218	3,223
Single Cnt	1,271	1,222
Avg Class	5.53	5.52
Max Class	63	63

Copyright © 2007, Idea Group Inc. Copying or distributing in print or electronic forms without written permission of Idea Group Inc. is prohibited.

Table 9. Similarity index results

Index	Value
Talburt-Wang	0.9972
Rand	0.9999
Adj Rand	0.9989

Although the partition of the new release (B) shows increased clustering in terms of fewer singleton classes and fewer classes overall, the average class size has slightly decreased. This would be an expected result if we believe that in a knowledge-based approach, knowledge about the entities in a fixed set of transactions increases over time; that is, there is a time-latency in knowledge gathering. Under this assumption and given that the transactions are held fixed in time, one could expect that knowledge about these transactions (customers) will increase over time, and that the engine's ability to connect transactions for the same customer will improve. In this particular measurement, all three indices point to a very high degree of similarity (consistency) between the partitions produced by the two releases, and the second release brings together slightly more transactions. However this measurement only points to stability between the two releases and does not prove that the second release is more or less accurate in grouping than the first.

Experiment 3: Changes in Input Quality

Here the Recognition Engine is held fixed and the transaction set is intentionally degraded in quality. For experimental purposes, the change (error) can be introduced at a fixed rate.

In this experiment, R is a knowledge-based CDI product used in customer recognition applications and is held fixed. R identifies individual customers based on name and address (occupancy). First, R processes the ordered transaction set T to create the partition A. Next, the quality of T is deliberately degraded by removing all vowels from the names in 800 of

Table 10. Results of Experiment 3

Statistic	A	B
Record Cnt	17,788	17,788
Class Cnt	3,218	3,332
Single Cnt	1,271	1,675
Avg Class	5.53	5.34
Max Class	63	60

Copyright © 2007, Idea Group Inc. Copying or distributing in print or electronic forms without written permission of Idea Group Inc. is prohibited.

Table 11. Similarity index results

Index	Value
Talburt-Wang	0.6665
Rand	0.9998
Adj Rand	0.8782

the 17,788 transaction records (4.5%), and R processes the degraded transactions to create the second partition B.

Tables 10 and 11 show a comparison of the partitions A and B created by R and S respectively.

In this scenario, the effect of quality degradation is evident. Even though more classes are created from the degraded transactions, the number of singleton classes has increased dramatically. These represent records that were formerly integrated into larger classes, but due to degradation, cannot be matched and become outliers. The average size of the classes has also decreased significantly. Again, the Talburt-Wang index is the most sensitive to this change, whereas the Rand indicates almost complete similarity.

Metric for Customer Recognition Accuracy

If A and B are both partitions of the same ordered transaction set T, and if A represents the "correct partition of T" (i.e., is a benchmark), and B represents the partition of T imposed by some recognition system R, then the similarity index can provide a quantifiable and objective measure of the accuracy of the recognition system R. Because all of the indices described previously have the characteristic of taking on the value of 1 when the partitions are identical, and values less than 1 as the partitions become dissimilar, then the value of the similarity index times 100 (or some normalized transformation of the similarity index) can be used as an accuracy metric.

Even though it is evident how one could create an accuracy metric for customer recognition using a similarity index, it is less obvious how to create the benchmark of correct groupings. In practice, this can be very difficult to do. The authors have experience in using the following methods to create a benchmark.

In the case of recognition systems that rely only on matching, it is possible to create correct groupings by manually inspecting the records and making an expert judgment about which records belong in each class. The primary limitation of this method is the effort required to create a benchmark of any significant size. In addition, experts do not always agree, and this method may require some type of arbitration, such as a voting scheme.

However in the case of knowledge-based recognition systems using equivalence class tokens, manual inspection is not enough. For example, the mere inspection of two occupancy records, such as "Jane Smith, 123 Oak" and "Jane Jones, 456 Elm," cannot establish if they should or should not be in the same class without a priori knowledge that these represent the same customer who has married and moved to a new address. In this situation, creating a benchmark requires accurate information about changes in addresses and changes in

Copyright © 2007, Idea Group Inc. Copying or distributing in print or electronic forms without written permission of Idea Group Inc. is prohibited.

names that is best obtained from the customers. Such a benchmark can be both expensive and difficult to create, even for a relatively small sample (Talburt & Holland, 2003). Even attempts to create these by having company employees volunteer this information have been largely abandoned due to privacy and legal concerns.

Future Trends

Although there are a number of interesting problems related to the quality of entity resolution, two have the most importance: grouping accuracy and the time-to-failure problem, also known as the system entropy problem.

Grouping Accuracy Problem

As discussed earlier, the problem in determining accuracy of a particular grouping is the difficulty in establishing the correct benchmark. To overcome this problem, at least two approaches have been suggested: verification of match exceptions and synthetic data generation.

Match Exceptions Approach

This is an approach that could apply to those entity resolution systems in which the majority of associations between entity records are established through matching. However, this is often the case in commercial applications such as customer recognition. Consider the example of a knowledge-based customer recognition system where the indicative information is customer name and address. A typical grouping generated by the system would predominately comprise records of the same name and same address within the tolerance of a given set of matching rules. For example, the matching rules might allow for single edit differences such as a missing letter or transposed characters. It also might allow for aliases and abbreviations, such as Bob for Robert, or St for Street.

Because the system is knowledge based, there may also be some classes that contain associations where the name and/or the address are different. This basis of approach would be to factor out the matching associations and focus only on the smaller number of cross-name and cross-address associations. For a large dataset, it would still be necessary to work with only a sample of these cases.

The objective is to reduce the amount of verification to manageable amount of time and effort. The assumptions would be that the records established through matching are essentially correct, and the error found in the verification of the cross-name and cross-address sample can be extrapolated to the entire dataset.

Because this method begins by looking at the correctness of associations that have already been made, it is biased against estimating errors for failing to make associations. What is lacking here is any empirical understanding of the expected rate of cross-name and cross-address association for a particular kind of dataset.

This approach is more complex, but somewhat akin to the estimation of a population mean through sampling. In this case, there is a correct, but unknown, partition of the dataset, and we assume that the given partition is an approximation of the correct partition. Is

Copyright © 2007, Idea Group Inc. Copying or distributing in print or electronic forms without written permission of Idea Group Inc. is prohibited.

it possible to develop a methodology to estimate how similar the given partition is to the correct partition from the known errors of association found in some sample of the partition classes?

Synthetic Data Approach

An alternative approach is to generate a correct partition with supporting associations, extract a partial transaction set, resolve the transaction set into a partition, then apply the similarity index to measure the accuracy of the resolution engine. The issue here is how closely the target population of entities can be simulated. The use of synthetically generated occupancy information has been used in the context of partitioning data over nodes in a grid application where the validation of performance optimization is dependent upon the data reflecting real-world name and address characteristics (White & Thompson, 2005).

Again using the example of a knowledge-based customer recognition system, the generation of the synthetic data would have to account for numerous factors that could affect the performance of the resolution system, such as distribution of name frequencies, rates of change in address individually and by household, and rates of change in name from marriage and divorce.

After the synthetic entity population has been created, the second step is to extract a set of transactions to process through the resolution engine. The partition created from the extracted transactions can then be compared to the correct partition to determine the accuracy of resolution.

This approach is a direct test of the performance of the resolution engine and leads to a number of interesting experiments. If the transaction set used is the entire synthetic dataset including associative transactions, then the resolution engine should recreate exactly the correct partition. Another series of experiments can be set up that will test the sensitivity of the resolution engine to error and omissions, or even the order of processing, of the transaction set.

For example, if the assumption is that only 80% of individual moves can typically be found through associative sources, then extracting only 80% of the change-of-address assertion from the full universe into the transaction set would indicate the amount of error in the resolution attributable to this cause. Using a degraded extraction of the correct dataset to create the transaction dataset could be used to assess the impact of types of errors and incompleteness in the transaction dataset.

Time-to-Failure Problem

In physics the Law of Entropy states that a system left on its own will spontaneously tend toward disorder; that is, "entropy", the measure of disorder, will increase. Energy must be expended to increase the system's organization, that is, decrease entropy. An automobile is a highly organized, statistically improbable configuration of materials that requires a great deal of energy to produce. Accidents and everyday wear and tear tend to make it less like its original "new" configuration, and at some point, unusable. Energy, in the form of repairs, must be expended to move it back toward its original configuration. In general we do not expect cars to spontaneously look new again. Everything that happens tends to make it less organized, that is, less like a new car.

Copyright © 2007, Idea Group Inc. Copying or distributing in print or electronic forms without written permission of Idea Group Inc. is prohibited.

Figure 3. Change in quality over time for three systems

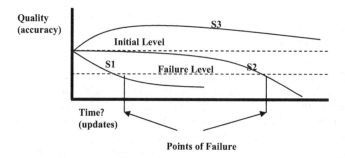

The concept of entropy can also be applied to an entity resolution system, in particular to the configuration of its identification repository. The question becomes whether updates to the system cause the entropy to increase (be less organized) or the entropy to decrease (become more organized). Given that the measure organization is the correct association of transactions, increasing entropy is manifest as decreasing accuracy of the system and vice versa.

A commonly occurring failure of many entity resolution implementations is typified by what is often observed in commercial customer recognition systems. They often initially perform well based on the set of transactions available during setup, but then steadily degrade in accuracy as new update requests are received. Degradation of customer recognition accuracy over time is perhaps the most overlooked and the least understood point of failure in CRM implementations.

Figure 3 illustrates the changes in quality as a function of time of three hypothetical recognition systems: S1, S2, and S3. In this case, time implies change through update requests that change the configuration of the systems' repositories. System S1 shows a rapid degradation in quality with a short time to failure, that is, accuracy below a given threshold. S2 has a longer time to failure, and S3 shows a system where quality improves as updates are processed.

Metrics and case studies of entity resolution quality over time are virtually nonexistent and are fertile ground for further study and research.

Conclusion

The algebraic approach of characterizing entity resolution systems as partitions of ordered transaction sets is proving to be useful in creating metrics for quality assessment. In addition to providing an easily understood model, it also opens the door to utilizing the research literature already available related to cluster analysis.

Although the preliminary experiments indicate that the Talburt-Wang index provides even more discrimination than the Rand or adjusted Rand indices, and is easier to calculate,

Copyright © 2007, Idea Group Inc. Copying or distributing in print or electronic forms without written permission of Idea Group Inc. is prohibited.

further testing on a broader range of recognition outcomes needs to be done before abandoning these or other techniques. In the end, the quality of entity resolution outcomes will probably best be expressed in terms of a number of key metrics, of which the Talburt-Wang index is only one.

There are many fertile areas of research related to the quality of entity resolution, and clearly better answers are needed to assist companies and government agencies dealing with the implementations of these systems.

References

Benjelloun, O., Garcia-Molina, H., Su, Q., & Widom, J. (2005, March 3). *Swoosh: A generic approach to entity resolution* (Technical report). Stanford InfoLab.

Bilenko, M., & Mooney, R. J. (2003, August 27). On evaluation of training-set construction for duplicate detection. In *Proceedings of the ACM SIGKDD-03 Workshop on Data Cleaning, Record Linkage, and Object Consolidation,* Washington, DC (pp. 7-12).

Campbell, T., & Wilhoit, Z. (2003, November 7-9). How's your data quality? A case study in corporate data quality strategy. In *Proceedings of the International Conference on Information Quality* (pp. 112-124). Massachusetts Institute of Technology.

Frederich, A. (2005, May). *IBM DB2 Anonymous Resolution: Knowledge discovery without knowledge disclosure* (IBM White Paper). Retrieved March 27, 2006, from http://faculty.washington.edu/kayee/pca/supp.pdf

Huang, K., Lee, Y. W., & Wang, R. Y. (1999). *Quality information and knowledge.* Upper Saddle River, NJ: Prentice Hall.

Hubert, L., & Arabie, P. (1985). Comparing partitions. *Journal of Classifications*, 193-218.

Hughes, A. M. (2005). *Building customer loyalty by recognition.* Database Marketing Institute. Retrieved March 27, 2006, from http://www.local6.com/news/4643968/detail.html

Lee, D. (2000). *The customer relationship management survival guide.* San Diego, CA: HYM Press.

Morgan, C. D., McLaughlin, G. L., Fogata, M. G., Baker, J. L., Cook, J. E., Mooney, J. E., et al. (2000, June 6). *Method and system for the creation, enhancement, and update of remote data using persistent keys* (U.S. Patent No. 6,073,140). Washington, DC: U.S. Patent and Trademark Office.

Morgan, C. D., Talley, T., Talburt, J. R., Bussell, C., Kooshesh, A., Anderson, W., et al. (2003, February 18). *Data linking system and method using tokens* (U.S. Patent No. 6,523,041). Washington, D.C : U.S. Patent and Trademark Office.

Rand, W. M. (1971). Objective criteria for the evaluation of clustering methods. *Journal of the American Statistical Association, 66*, 846-850.

Talburt, J. R., & Holland, G. (2003). A shared system for assessing consumer occupancy and demographic accuracy. In *Proceedings of the International Conference on Information Quality* (pp. 166-177). Massachusetts Institute of Technology.

Talburt, J. R., Kuo, E., Wang, R., & Hess, K. (2004, November 5-7). An algebraic approach to data quality metrics for customer recognition. In *Proceedings of the 9th International Conference on Information Quality (ICIQ-2004)* (pp. 234-247). Cambridge, MA.

Copyright © 2007, Idea Group Inc. Copying or distributing in print or electronic forms without written permission of Idea Group Inc. is prohibited.

Talburt, J. R., Wang, R. Y., et al. (2004). *Customer-centric information quality management* (MITIQ White Paper). Retrieved March 27, 2006, from http://mitiq.mit.edu/Documents/CCIQM/CCIQM%20White%20Paper.pdf

Thuraisingham, B. (2003). *Web data mining and applications in business intelligence and counter-terrorism*. Boca Raton, FL: CRC Press.

Wang, R. Y., Ziad, M., & Lee, Y. W. (2001). *Data quality*. Norwell, MA: Kluwer Academic Publishers.

White, J., & Thompson, D. R. (2005, June 20-23). Load balancing on a grid using data characteristics. In *Proceedings of the 2005 International Conference on Grid Computing and Applications* (pp. 184-188). Las Vegas, NV.

Yeung, K. Y., & Ruzzo, W. L. (2001). Details of the adjusted Rand index and clustering algorithms, supplement to the paper "An empirical study on principal component analysis for clustering gene expression data". *Bioinformatics, 17*(9), 763-774.

Copyright © 2007, Idea Group Inc. Copying or distributing in print or electronic forms without written permission of Idea Group Inc. is prohibited.

Chapter II

Quality-Extended Query Processing for Mediation Systems

Laure Berti-Équille, IRISA, France

Abstract

For noncollaborative distributed data sources, quality-driven query processing is difficult to achieve because the sources generally do not export data quality indicators. This chapter deals with the extension and adaptation of query processing for taking into account constraints on quality of distributed data. This chapter presents a novel framework for adaptive query processing on quality-extended query declarations. It proposes an expressive query language extension combining SQL and QML, the quality of service modeling language proposed by Frølund and Koistinen (1998) for defining, in a flexible way, dimensions, and metrics on data, source, and service quality. The originality of the approach is to include the negotiation of quality contracts between the distributed data sources competing for answering the query. The principle is to find dynamically the best trade-off between the local query cost and the result quality. The author is convinced that quality of data (QoD) and quality of service (QoS) can be advantageously conciliated for tackling the problems of quality-aware query processing in distributed environments and, more generally, open innovative research perspectives for quality-aware adaptive query processing.

Copyright © 2007, Idea Group Inc. Copying or distributing in print or electronic forms without written permission of Idea Group Inc. is prohibited.

Introduction

For classical mediator/wrapper architectures, the access to distributed information sources is carried out in a declarative way. The mediator processes the queries of the users at the global level and optimizes the query plans according to the wrappers that reach respectively their underlying data sources. In this type of distributed environment, the sources are usually noncollaborative and do not export information describing the local costs of query processing, neither indicators of their quality of service (e.g., resource accessibility, reliability, security, etc.) nor information describing the quality of their content[1] (e.g., data accuracy, freshness, completeness, etc.). However, this information is useful and has to be dynamically computed and periodically updated. Efficient and effective query processing is particularly difficult to achieve because of the growing number and the ever-changing structure of the queried distributed data sources. Although there are several approaches that deal with the assessment and management of quality metadata, the dual problem of fixing the query cost and optimizing the result quality, or fixing the result quality and optimizing the query cost, still remains. Querying simultaneously several data sources with different degrees of quality and trust in a dynamic and distributed environment raises several interesting problems and open issues:

- **Selecting dynamically appropriate sources:** Different information sources may answer a global query with different response times, query costs, and various levels of result quality. How do we define strategies for selecting adaptively the most appropriate sources for answering the whole or some parts of the global query with the appropriate quality at a given time? What are the criteria to select dynamically the sources with "the best relative quality"?

- **Defining semantically and qualitatively correct distributed query plans:** The result of a global query is built according to the particular order for execution of subquery plans. This must combine in a coherent way both information and quality meta-information from the various sources; but data quality levels are often unknown, heterogeneous from one source to another (intersource data quality heterogeneity), and locally nonuniform (intrasource data quality nonuniformity). In this context, the aim is to control and merge data quality indicators in a consistent and meaningful way for both correctly integrating data and quality metadata.

- **Making trade-offs between the cost of the query and the perceived quality of the result (including both the quality of service and the quality of content):** Because we may accept a query result of lower quality (if it is cheaper or has a shorter response time than if the query cost is higher), it is necessary to adapt query costs to users' quality requirements (and tolerance thresholds). The objective is to measure and optimally reduce the query cost and bargain query situations where the system searches for solutions that "squeeze out" more gains (in terms of result quality) than the classical query without specified quality constraints.

- **Developing concrete cost models to evaluate whether the expected benefits from the improved (or quality-extended) query plan compensate for the cost of collecting and evaluating feedbacks from the environment during query execution time:** The difficulty here is to adapt existing query processing techniques to environments where resource availability, allocation, quality, and cost are not, by definition, decidable or known at compile time.

Copyright © 2007, Idea Group Inc. Copying or distributing in print or electronic forms without written permission of Idea Group Inc. is prohibited.

For these open questions, some solutions have been proposed in the literature (e.g., Ballou & Pazer, 2002; Missier & Embury, 2005; Naumann, 2002; Naumann, Leser, & Frey-tag, 1999) but, to the best of our knowledge, very few approaches combine the techniques of quality of service together with those of quality of data for adapting distributed query processing.

In this context, our objectives are (1) to extend a generic SQL query language for describing and manipulating in a flexible way data and source quality contracts and (2) to propose a novel query processing framework for selecting sources dynamically and negotiating quality based on the requirements expressed in the quality-extended queries.

This chapter describes our project, entitled *XQuaL*, that defines a quality-extended query language and the associated query processing with its corresponding mediation architecture. We also propose a quality negotiation that finds the best trade-off between the query cost and the result quality as part of the query processor. While our general approach to query processing is typical, a number of factors associated with quality constraints specification and negotiation complicate the problem. The challenges have been to define an appropriate formalism for specifying in a flexible and declarative way quality metadata (dimensions, constraints, and metrics) and to devise methods for quality-extended query processing, including the quality-based negotiation algorithm.

The chapter is organized as follows. In the next section we present previous work in the areas of quality of service and mainly quality of data relevant to our approach. In the third section we describe our twofold contribution on adaptive quality-extended query processing: first, we describe the specification and syntax of our query language extension; then, we present the definitions and the negotiation algorithm for quality-extended query processing. Moreover we present an illustrative example. The fourth section provides the concluding remarks for the chapter. The last section presents future and emerging trends from the perspective of quality-aware query processing.

Background

In this section we first highlight the convergence of two areas of research, namely the quality of service (*QoS*) and the quality of data (*QoD*). Several solutions and techniques of QoS can be advantageously used and adapted for tackling some issues of quality-aware query processing. Then, we present some related work on data quality research, and next we focus on quality-extended languages and quality-aware processing techniques that have been proposed in the literature.

When QoS Meets QoD

Quality of service (*QoS*) has gained much attention in the field of distributed multimedia applications where it covers essentially the notion of end-to-end guarantees associated with the communication of multimedia contents over networks and their processing on computing nodes (Vogel, Bochmann, Disallow, Geckos, & Kerherve, 1994). A considerable amount of work has been done in this area to introduce models and architectures supporting such QoS guarantees (Aurrecoechea, Campbell, & Hauw, 1998). This narrow vision of QoS (generally centered on the concept of performance) has been generalized to extrafunctional properties

Copyright © 2007, Idea Group Inc. Copying or distributing in print or electronic forms without written permission of Idea Group Inc. is prohibited.

of distributed systems. And the traditional acceptance of quality of service for distributed information systems has been revised with a broader definition raising new problems (Bochmann, & Hafid, 1997; Frølund & Koistinen, 1999). Traditional quality of service categories and dimensions (such as execution time or cost) can be extended to integrate the concepts of data quality and source quality as well as quality of provided services (such as searching techniques, optimization strategies, data transfer, adaptation, or presentation). In this context, the *QML* language (*Quality of Service Modeling Language*) has been proposed by Frølund and Koistinen (1998) in order to deal with the quality of service of software components in a systematic and declarative manner, allowing flexible definition of quality dimensions, quality contracts, and profile constraints. As will be described further, we found relevance in borrowing the syntax of the *QML* language for extending SQL queries with constraints on the various dimensions of data and source quality.

Related Work on Quality of Data

Data quality is a multidimensional, complex, and morphing concept (Dasu & Johnson, 2003). In a decade (Wang, Storey, & Firth, 1995), there has been a significant emergence of work in the area of information and data quality management initiated by several research communities (i.e., statistics, database, information system, workflow and project management, knowledge engineering, and knowledge discovery from databases), ranging from various techniques in assessing information quality to the design of large-scale data integration systems over heterogeneous data sources (Clavanese, DeGiacomo, Lenzerini, Nardi, & Rosati, 1997; Naumann et al., 1999) and in improving data quality in databases (Dasu & Johnson, 2003), in information systems (Ballou & Pazer, 2002; Fox, Letivin, & Redman, 1994; Pipino & Lee, 2002; Redman, 1996, 2001; Wang, 1998, 2002) or in cooperative information systems (Batini, Catarci, & Scannapieco, 2004), for example, the *DaQuinCIS* project (Scannapieco, Virgillito, Marchetti, Mecella, & Baldoni, 2004), and in data warehouse systems, for example, the *Data Warehouse Quality (DWQ)* project (Clavanese et al., 1997; Vassiliadis, 2000). Various data quality definitions, metrics, models, methodologies, cleaning, and *extraction-transformation-loading (ETL)* tools have been proposed by practitioners and academics with the aim of tackling the following main classes of data quality problems:

1. **Duplicate detection and record matching**, also known as record linkage, merge/purge problem (Hernandez & Stolfo, 1998), duplicate elimination (Ananthakrishna, Chaudhuri, & Ganti, 2002; Low, Lee, & Ling, 2001), or entity resolution (Benjelloun, Garcia-Molina, Su, & Widom, 2005)
2. **Instance conflict resolution** using heuristics, domain-specific rules, data source selection (Mihaila, Raschid, & Vidal, 2001; Naumann, 2002), or data cleaning and *ETL* techniques (Rahm & Do, 2000; Winkler, 2004)
3. **Missing values and incomplete data** (Little & Rubin, 1987; Schafer, 1997)
4. **Staleness of data** (Bouzeghoub & Peralta, 2004; Theodoratos & Bouzeghoub, 2001)

Several surveys and empirical studies have shown the importance of quality in the design of information systems. Many works in the fields of information systems and software engineering address quality control and assessment for the information and for the

Copyright © 2007, Idea Group Inc. Copying or distributing in print or electronic forms without written permission of Idea Group Inc. is prohibited.

processes which produce this information (Bobrowski, Marré, & Yankelevich, 1999; Pipino & Lee, 2002).

The most frequently mentioned data quality dimensions in the literature are accuracy, completeness, timeliness, and consistency with various definitions depending on the authors:

- Accuracy is the extent to which collected data are free of error measurements (Liu & Chi, 2002) or can be measured by the quotient of the number of correct values in a source and the number of the overall number of values (Naumann, 2002).
- Completeness is measured by the quotient of the number of non-null values in a source and the size of the universal relation (Naumann, 2002).
- Timeliness is the extent to which data are sufficiently up-to-date for a task (Liu & Chi, 2002); definitions of freshness, currency, and volatility are reported in Bouzeghoub and Peralta (2004).
- Consistency is the coherence of the same data represented in multiple copies or different data with respect of integrity constraints and rules (Batini et al., 2004).

Many other dimensions, metrics, and measurement techniques have been proposed in the literature (Fox et al., 1994; Kahn, Strong, & Wang, 2002; Naumann, 2002; Redman, 1996, 2001; Wang, 1998, 2002; Wang et al., 1995). Various works tackled the problem of the evaluation of data quality. In Pipino and Lee (2002), the authors present a set of quality dimensions and study various types of metrics and the ways of combining the values of quality indicators. In Naumann and Rolker (2000), various strategies to measure and combine values of quality are described. In Ballou and Pazer (2002), a methodology to determine the quality of information is presented with various ways of measuring and combining quality factors like freshness, accuracy, and cost. The authors also present guidelines that exploit the quality of information to carry out the reverse engineering of the system, so as to improve the trade-off between information quality/cost. The use of metadata for evaluation and improvement of data quality was recommended by Rothenberg (1996) where information producers were encouraged to carry out the verification, the validation, and the certification (*VV&C*) of their data.

The general trend is the use of artificial intelligence methods (training, knowledge representation schemes, management of uncertainty, etc.) for data validation (Maletic & Marcus, 2000). The use of machine learning techniques for data validation and correction was first presented by Parsaye and Chignell (1993): rules inferred from the database instances by machine learning methods were used to identify outliers in data and facilitate the data validation process. Another similar approach was proposed by Schlimmer (1991, 1993). Most of the approaches for quality control and evaluation are centered on various methods of imputation such as inferring missing data from statistical patterns of available datasets (Dasu & Johnson, 2003; Winkler, 2004), inferring data quality (Pon & Cardenas, 2005), predicting accuracy of the estimates based on the given data, data edits (automatic detection and handling of errors and outliers in data), error control (Paradice & Fuerst, 1991), or data cleaning using belief propagation (Chu, Wang, Parker, & Zaniolo, 2005). Various methods were developed to measure the data quality provided to the users in conformance to their quality constraints (Missier & Embury, 2005) or by comparison with a referential database (Redman, 1996).

Copyright © 2007, Idea Group Inc. Copying or distributing in print or electronic forms without written permission of Idea Group Inc. is prohibited.

Utilization of statistical techniques for improving the correctness of the databases and introduction of a new kind of statistical integrity constraints were proposed by Hou and Zhang (1995). Statistical constraints are derived from the database instances using conventional statistical techniques (sampling, regression). In this trend, *exploratory data mining (EDM)*, described in Dasu and Johnson (2003), is a set of statistical techniques providing summaries that characterize data with typical values (such as medians and averages), variance, range, quantiles, and correlations. Used as a first pass, EDM methods can be advantageously employed for data preprocessing before carrying out more expensive analyses. EDM aims to be widely applicable while dealing with unfamiliar datasets; it has quick response time, and results are easy to interpret, to store, and to update. EDM can either be driven by the model to facilitate the use of parametric methods (model log-linear, for example) or to be driven by the data without any prior assumptions about the interrelationship between data with well-known nonparametric techniques for exploring multivariate distributions such as clustering, hierarchical, or neural networks. The EDM summaries (e.g., averages, standard deviations, medians, or other quantiles) are used to characterize the data distribution, the correlations between attributes, and to quantify and describe the dispersion of the values of an attribute (form, density, symmetry, etc.).

Other techniques are used to detect suspected data such as missing values, improbable outliers, and incomplete values. Concerning the techniques of analysis on missing data, the method of imputation through regression described by Little and Rubin (1987) is very much used. Other methods, such as Markov Chain Monte Carlo *(MCMC)* (Schafer, 1997), are used to simulate data under the multivariate normal distribution assumption. Concerning the isolated data (outliers), the techniques of detection employed are mainly control charts and various techniques respectively based on (1) a model, (2) geometrical methods for distance measurement in the dataset (called geometric outliers), and (3) the distribution (or the density) of data population. Other tests of "goodness-of-fit," such as Chi^2, check the independence of the attributes. These univariate tests are still useful to validate the analysis techniques and the assumptions on the used models. Other complex and multivariate tests can be used (such as the test of Mahalanobis for distances between multivariate averages). We invite the interested reader to read the survey of Pyle (1999, Section 11.3), in particular, for the use of entropy as a preliminary data characterization measure and Dasu and Johnson (2003) for an illustrative description of these techniques useful to characterize data quality and define relevant metrics.

Quality-Extended Languages and Quality-Aware Query Processing

Various propositions concern the definition of declarative language extensions for:

*   Specifying, querying, and controlling quality metadata (e.g., *Q-Data* proposed by Sheth, Wood, & Kashyap, 1993)
*   Applying data transformations necessary to data cleaning tasks, for example, *AJAX* (Galhardas, Florescu, Shasha & Simon, 2001), ARKTOS (Vassiliadis, Vagena, Skiadopoulos, & Karayannidis, 2000), Potter's Wheel (Raman & Hellerstein, 2001), Tailor (Elfeky, Verykios, & Elmagarmid, 2002)

Copyright © 2007, Idea Group Inc. Copying or distributing in print or electronic forms without written permission of Idea Group Inc. is prohibited.

The prototype *Q-Data* proposed by Sheth, Wood, and Kashyap (1993) checks if the existing data are correct: the authors call it data validation and cleanup by using a logical database language (*LDL++*). The system employs data validation constraints and data cleanup rules. AJAX (Galhardas et al., 2001) is an SQL extension for specifying each data transformation (such as record matching, merging, mapping, or clustering operations) necessary to the data cleaning process. These transformations standardize the data formats when possible and find pairs of records that most probably refer to the same object (for entity resolution). The duplicate-elimination step is applied if approximate duplicate records are found and multitable matching computes similarity joins between distinct data flows and consolidates them.

Recently, the Trio project (started in 2005) at Stanford University (Widom, 2005) provides a novel enhanced database architecture that manages not only data, but also the accuracy and lineage of the data based on their related previous work (Cui & Widom, 2001). The goals of the Trio project are (1) to combine previous work on uncertain and fuzzy data into a simple and usable model; (2) to design a query language as an understandable extension to SQL; and (3) to build a working system that augments conventional data management with both accuracy and lineage as an integral part of the data.

The problem of designing multisource information systems (e.g., mediation systems, data warehouses, or Web portals), taking into account information about quality, has been addressed by several approaches that propose methodologies or techniques to select the data sources, by using metadata on their content and quality (Mihaila et al., 2000; Naumann et al., 1999).

Among the projects that have been proposed for considering data quality in distributed query processing, HiQIQ B&B (high quality branch and bound algorithm) proposed by Naumann (2002), is a distributed query planning algorithm that enumerates query plans in such a way that it usually finds the best N query plans after computing only a fraction of the total number of query plans. Upper quality bounds for partial query plans are constructed and thereby nonpromising subplans are early pruned in the search tree. This integrates the source and plan quality-based selection phases to a query planning algorithm that finds the top N plans for a query distributed over several quality-heterogeneous sources.

In ObjectGlobe (Braumandl, Keidl, Kemper, et al, 2001) the query processing follows a multistep strategy. First, a lookup service locates data from each source that are relevant to the query by consulting a metadata repository. It also gathers statistical cost information. In the second step, the optimizer enumerates alternative query execution plans using a system-R-like dynamic algorithm and an optimal plan is built based on a cost model using the previously gathered information. In the last step, the query execution plan is distributed and executed using an iterator model. Users can specify quality constraints on the execution of their query. Constraints are defined on results (e.g., size of the result), cost (i.e., how much the user is ready to pay), and time (e.g., time to first results). Quality of service management is introduced as part of the query processor. The quality constraints are treated in all the phases of querying processing. If they cannot be fulfilled, the query plan is dynamically adapted or the query is aborted. Based on that QoS concept, the optimizer's goal is to maximize the percentage of successful queries and abort any query that cannot fulfill its QoS constraints as soon as possible.

As will be described further, our approach offering a declarative language extension for specifying quality constraints and a quality negotiation mechanism is very complementary to these two last approaches: the first one (HiQIQ) uses different classes of quality criteria

Copyright © 2007, Idea Group Inc. Copying or distributing in print or electronic forms without written permission of Idea Group Inc. is prohibited.

to select relevant sources and rank alternative query plans; the other (ObjectGlobe) allows users to specify quality constraints on the execution of queries. These constraints may be related to the expected results, cost of the query, or time for the first results or complete execution. These QoS constraints are then enforced during the execution of the query.

Adaptive Processing of Quality-Extended Query

In mediation systems, we argue that database techniques, such as having an expressive internal data model and query language, together with a metainformation repository and metainformation analysis techniques, constitutes a necessary foundation for a mediator system. In order to alleviate the problem of information overload and confusion when various results of a query are presented, the classical solution is to rank the results according to consistent relevance assessments. Our approach is to include quality specifications for sources and send them with the query extending de facto the select-from-where query (SFW-query) with quality constraints. Such functionality for retrieval and integration of information must be supported by an easily extensible, scalable, and customizable architecture for addressing a wide range of applications. In this context, we proposed the multisource architecture depicted in Figure 1. The key concepts of our approach are the notions of:

- **Quality contract type** (and instances) that describes respectively the set of constraints (and instances of constraints per source) defined on several quality dimensions with specific aspects;
- **Quality profile** that describes the set of the required quality contracts assigned to one or several sources or functionalities included in the declaration of the query extension.

The next subsections will describe these concepts in detail.

From the application layer of Figure 1, the user can create quality contract types and profiles and submit a global quality-extended query (noted SFW-Qwith query) to the mediator which sends the query and quality requirements to the sources' wrappers. The wrappers send the corresponding quality-extended query to their respective source. Information sources may be cross-referenced, structured or not, and with or without a metainformation repository. They respond to their wrapper with the query result and a contract instance. The mediator then negotiates with the sources for finding the best trade-off between result quality and query cost, and it combines the query results for data recommendation to the user.

The underlying approach is orthogonal to this three-layer architecture and can be divided into three steps (shown in Figure 2): the first step consists of the quality declaration (i.e., quality contract types and profiles extending the query); the second step consists of the instantiation of the contract types for each data source. This step is performed by each wrapper that computes the quality metrics specified in the contract types and checks the satisfaction of quality constraints. At the mediation layer, the third step consists of the quality-adaptive query processing divided into two subtasks: (1) the control that the quality of each source is in conformance with (or better than) the quality requirements declared in the profile of the extended-query and (2) the negotiation on quality contracts for finding the best trade-off between result quality and query cost.

Copyright © 2007, Idea Group Inc. Copying or distributing in print or electronic forms without written permission of Idea Group Inc. is prohibited.

Figure 1. Overview of XQuaL architecture

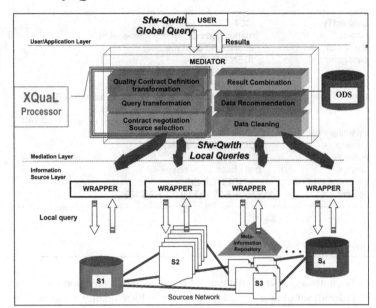

Figure 2. Main steps of XQuaL approach

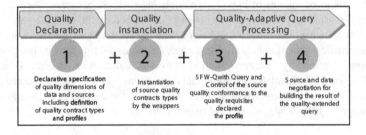

Combining SQL and QML for Defining the Quality-Constrained Query Language XQuaL

The syntax of the quality-extended query language XQuaL is adapted from QML proposed by Frølund and Koistinen (1998). We refer the reader to this paper for more information on the syntax and applications of this QoS modeling language. The complete syntax of XQuaL is presented in the appendix. As we will present in the next sections, this language extension is a *data description language* (*DDL*) that can be used to create contract type declarations and also a *data manipulation language* (*DML*) that can be used to query data under various quality constraints.

Copyright © 2007, Idea Group Inc. Copying or distributing in print or electronic forms without written permission of Idea Group Inc. is prohibited.

Figure 3. Syntax of quality contract type

```
contractType ::=        CONTRACT { dimensions } ;
dimensions ::=          dimensions dimension | dimension
dimension ::=           dimName : dimType ;
dimName ::=             IDENTIFIER
dimType ::=             dimSort | dimSort unit
items ::=               items , IDENTIFIER | IDENTIFIER
dimSort ::=             ENUM { items } | relSem ENUM { items } WITH order
                        | SET { items } | relSem SET { items }
                        | relSem SET { items } WITH order | relSem NUMERIC
relations ::=           relations , relation | relation
relation ::=            IDENTIFIER < IDENTIFIER
order ::=               ORDER { relations }
unit ::=                unit / base-unit | base-unit
base-unit ::=           % | IDENTIFIER
relSem ::=              DECREASING | INCREASING
```

Quality Metadata Description

A quality contract is a set of constraints that are defined as relations on an enumerated (potentially ordered) set of user-specified dimensions. Each quality contract is an instance of a complex contract type whose syntax is given in Figure 3.

Figure 4 gives examples of contract type declarations for the following dimensions: Reliability, Freshness, Completeness, and Credibility that are defined as contract types.

The Reliability contract type (classically defined in QoS specifications) has four dimensions (noted d1,…,d4 as comments of Figure 4), namely failureMasking, serverFailure, numberOf-Failures, and availability. Dimension failureMasking is defined by the possible values among omission, lostResponse, noExecution, and so on, and the relation (decreasing) is interpreted such as the smallest sets of values are the preferable values for this dimension. Dimension serverFailure is defined by an enumeration of individual values with no order. Dimensions numberOfFailures and availability are numerical dimensions. The number of failures per year as the unit of numberOfFailures is nf/year. The other quality contract types, such as Freshness, Completeness, and Credibility, are defined respectively by:

- Three dimensions for Freshness: the age of data, the percentage of the records most recently updated, and the mean frequency of updates
- Two dimensions for Completeness: the percentage of null values, and the evolution of number of null values per query
- One dimension for Credibility: the reputation rate of the data source

Quality can be defined in a flexible way as a specific ordered combination of contract types on data and source quality representing the relative importance of the different quality contract types.

Figure 5 presents an example for the creation of a complex contract type using the syntax of XQuaL. It defines the quality as an ordered set of the previously defined contract types in Figure 4.

Copyright © 2007, Idea Group Inc. Copying or distributing in print or electronic forms without written permission of Idea Group Inc. is prohibited.

Figure 4. Examples of quality contract types

```
type Reliability = contract {
        failureMasking : decreasing set {omission, lostResponse,
                                noExecution, response, responseValue, stateTransition } ;    //d1
        serverFailure : enum { halt, initialState, rolledBack } ;                            //d2
        numberOfFailures : decreasing numeric nf / year ;                                    //d3
        availability : increasing numeric ;                                                  //d4
} ;
type Freshness = contract {
        dataAge : decreasing numeric seconds;                                                //d5
        PercentageOfLastUpdate : increasing numeric % ;                                      //d6
        updateMeanFrequency : numeric uf / month ;                                           //d7
} ;
type Completeness = contract {
        percentageOfNullValues : decreasing percentile number %;                             //d8
        numberOfNullValuesPerQuery : decreasing numeric nnv / query ;                        //d9
} ;
type Credibility = contract {
        reputation : enum {veryGood, good, bad, veryBad, unknown } ;                          //d10
} ;
```

Figure 5. Example of quality contract creation

```
CREATE TYPE Quality = CONTRACT {
  sourceQuality : INCREASING SET {Reliability,Freshness,Completeness,Credibility }
      WITH ORDER {Reliability<Completeness, Completeness< Freshness, Freshness <
  Credibility}
    } ;
```

Quality Contract Instantiation

Figure 6 presents four instances corresponding to the contract types declared in Figure 4 such as S_Reliability, S_Freshness, S_Completeness, and S_Credibility. These instances may have been computed by a wrapper associated to a source or manually created with the CREATE operator of XQuaL.

Quality Metadata Manipulation

A quality-extended query (Qwith-query) is a select-from-where query followed by a Qwith operator used to declare or invoke a quality profile declaration (profileDeclaration) — see the appendix for the detailed syntax. A quality profile is the set of the required contracts that are associated to one (or several) data sources or to the source functionalities. The declaration of profiles is useful to associate specific and user-defined quality constraints to sources interfaces (or their wrappers). More precisely, a profile declaration (profileDeclara-

Copyright © 2007, Idea Group Inc. Copying or distributing in print or electronic forms without written permission of Idea Group Inc. is prohibited.

Figure 6. Examples of quality contract instances

```
S_Reliability = Reliability contract {
   failureMasking < { noExecution, response };
   serverFailure == initialState ;
   numberOfFailures < 10 nf / year ;
   availability > 0.8 ;
} ;
S_Freshness = Freshness contract {
   dataAge < 4200 seconds;
   PercentageOfLastUpdate > 3 %;
   updateMeanFrequency == 3 uf / month;
};
S_Completeness = Completeness contract {
   PercentageOfNullValues < 8 %;
   NumberOfNullPerQuery < 2 nnv/query;
};
S_Credibility = Credibility contract {
   reputation == veryGood ;
};
```

tion) is defined with the identifier of the profile, the identifier of the interface, and a series of expressions (profileExpression) requiring the satisfaction of contracts by the entities of the targeted interfaces/wrappers (requisites) — see the syntax in Figure 7.

The profile declaration makes it possible to associate existing quality contracts as constraints with targeted source interfaces or their specific services or methods. Figure 8 presents the creation of a profile declaration, namely Source_Profile applied to the source S1 that, in its first part, assigns constraints defined as contract instances in Figure 6 for freshness, completeness, and credibility and, in its second part, specifically applies the quality contract S_Reliability as constraint on the method query_answer_method of S1.

The clause REQUIRE binds all the interface/wrapper entities to a list of contracts, whereas the clause FROM... REQUIRE... specifically identifies a list of interface entities to which the list of contracts definitions will be associated in the following clause require.

Negotiation for Quality-Extended Query Processing

In the last step of our approach, the contribution is to include the principle of quality contract negotiation over the distributed sources and to adapt the query processing.

Definitions

Negotiation can range over a number of quantitative and qualitative dimensions. Each successful negotiation requires a range of such dimensions to be resolved to the satisfaction of both parties (i.e., the querying and the queried systems). Making trade-offs between the cost of query and the quality of result is required in order to come to an agreement for "the

Copyright © 2007, Idea Group Inc. Copying or distributing in print or electronic forms without written permission of Idea Group Inc. is prohibited.

Figure 7. Syntax of quality profile

```
profileDeclaration ::=    IDENTIFIER FOR IDENTIFIER = profileExpression
profileExpression ::=     profile | IDENTIFIER REFINED BY { requisites }
profile ::=               PROFILE { requisites }
requisites ::=            requisites requisite ;
requisite ::=             REQUIRE contractList | FROM entityList REQUIRE contractList
contractList ::=          contractList , contractElem | contractElem
contractElem ::=          IDENTIFIER | contractExpression
entityList ::=            entityList , entity | entity
entity ::=                IDENTIFIER | IDENTIFIER . IDENTIFIER | RESULT OF IDENTIFIER
```

Figure 8. Example of source profile for source S1

```
CREATE Source_Profile FOR S1 = PROFILE {
    REQUIRE S_Freshness, S_Completeness, S_Credibility ;
    FROM S1.query_answer_method REQUIRE S_Reliability CONTRACT ;
} ;
```

best quality" query results. The structure of negotiation is based almost directly on the quality contract used to regulate agreements, which is fairly rich and may cover content quality, service quality, and metaservice attributes. Let us now outline the definitions and the formal basis of our quality-extended query negotiation model in a comprehensible way.

Let i ($i \in [1..n]$) represent the data sources and j ($j \in [1..k]$) be the dimensions of quality contracts under negotiation (e.g., dataAge, failureMasking, serverFailure, availability, numberOfNullValuesPerQuery, etc.). Let $x_{ij} \in [min_{ij}, max_{ij}]$ be a value for the quality dimension j that is acceptable to the user for querying the source i. At the given time t, each source has a scoring function $score_{ij}(t)$: $[min_{ij}, max_{ij}] \to [0,1]$ that gives the score of the source i assigned to a value of the dimension j in the range of its acceptable values. For convenience, scores are kept in the interval $[0, 1]$. The relative importance that the user assigns to each dimension under negotiation is modeled as a weight, noted w_{ij}, that gives the importance of the dimension j for the source i. We assume the weights are normalized:

$$\sum_{1 \leq j \leq k} w_{ij} = 1 \ \forall i \in [1..n], \forall j \in [1..k] \tag{1}$$

The multidimensional space of quality dimensions is noted $x = (x_1, ..., x_k)$ representing the k quality dimensions declared in the contract types and instantiated for each source by its associated wrapper. An aggregate quality scoring function of the source i is defined at the given time t in the multidimensional quality space x as:

$$Score_i(x,t) = \sum_{1 \leq j \leq k} w_{ij}.score_{ij}(x_j,t) \tag{2}$$

Copyright © 2007, Idea Group Inc. Copying or distributing in print or electronic forms without written permission of Idea Group Inc. is prohibited.

For analytical purposes, we restrict our study to an additive and monotonically increasing or decreasing value scoring function.

During the query processing, negotiation consists in finding trade-offs between the requisites of the quality profile declared in the Qwith clause of the quality-extended query and the instances of quality contracts computed for each source.

Definition 1. Aspirational quality: Given a quality-extended query q, at the given time t, the *aspirational quality level* noted $\theta\,(q,t)$ represents the "most preferable" quality score that is declared in the Qwith clause of the query q (as quality profile) on the various dimensions of the quality space x.

$\theta_j(q,t)$ is the "ideal" score value for the quality dimension j of the query q at the given time t.

The aim of the trade-off mechanism is to find the quality contract instance that is the closest to the most preferable quality profile (i.e., the aspirational quality) and that minimizes the query cost. This instance lies on the *aspirational iso-curve* we define as follows:

Definition 2. Aspirational quality iso-curve: Given the aspirational quality level θ, the aspirational quality iso-curve is defined as the set of values of quality dimensions that are the most similar (with the minimal distance) to θ:

$$iso(\theta(q,t)) = \{x_j \mid min(distance_j\,(score_{ij}(x_j,t),\theta_j(q,t)))\ \forall i \forall j\} \tag{3}$$

The heuristic we employ is to select the contract that is the most "similar" to the negotiator's last proposal (since this may be more acceptable to the user in terms of quality requirements).

The distance function $distance_j$ in the multidimensional space x, returns the distance between two of the k-dimensional vectors. We assume the distance function $distance_j$ to be a weighted L_p metric (i.e., for a given value of p); the distance between two k-dimensional vectors T^1 and T^2 in x is given by:

$$distance_j\left(T^1,T^2\right) = \left[\sum_{j=1}^{k}\mu_j\left(\left|T_j^1-T_j^2\right|\right)^p\right]^{1/p} \tag{4}$$

where μ_j denotes weight associated with the jth dimension of the space x ($1 \geq \mu_j \geq 0, \sum_{j=1}^{k}\mu_j = 1$).

Note that this assumption is general since the most commonly used distance functions (e.g., Manhattan distance, Euclidean distance, bounding box distance) are special cases of the Lp metric. D_q specifies which L_p metric to use (i.e., the value of p) and the values of the dimension weights.

For the sake of simplicity, we currently use Euclidean distance for $distance_j$ for all the dimension of the quality space x.

The *trade-off* is defined locally for each source as follows:

Definition 3. Local trade-off: Given a quality-extended query q, the local trade-off of the source i at the given time t in the quality space x is defined as follows:

Copyright © 2007, Idea Group Inc. Copying or distributing in print or electronic forms without written permission of Idea Group Inc. is prohibited.

$$TradeOff_i(q,x,t) = \frac{Score_i(x,t)}{Cost_i(q,t)} \tag{5}$$

In practice, the cost of a query q at a given time t is never null, $Cost_i(q,t) \in]0,1]$.

The database community devoted significant attention to efficient plans of executing a given query (through a static optimization phase, generally cost-based and calibration-based), and intelligent methods for choosing, among several such query execution plans, the one that best meets a given performance goal. Various solutions to cost estimate problems have been proposed in the past for distributed query processing (Apers, Hevner, & Yao, 1983; Bernstein, Goodman, Wong, Reeve, & Rothnie, 1981; Naacke, Gardarin, & Tomasic, 1998; Yu & Chang, 1984) and the quality of cost estimators still is one of the burning issues in query optimization but this topic is beyond the scope of this chapter. We will not describe here the cost formula that is very similar to the one provided by Naacke et al. (1998) in the DISCO project at INRIA, and we refer the reader to Tomasic, Raschid, and Valduriez (1996).

Negotiation Strategy

Intuitively, the principle of the negotiation strategy is based on an adaptation of the simulated annealing process (Kirkpatrick, Gerlatt, & Vecchi, 1983). Simulated annealing mimics the annealing process for crystalline solids, where a solid is cooled very slowly from an elevated temperature, with the hope of relaxing toward a low-energy state (objective function value). The principle is as follows: we define a system state as the query execution cost and the quality of the source at a given time. Then, we search for the well-balanced state (i.e., the trade-off) that is the state with the lowest cost and the best quality in conformance with the quality requirements defined into the profiles (i.e., in the Qwith clause of the extended query). Our objective is to find the trade-off state out off a local minimum state. The pseudocode of the negotiation is given in Figure 9. First, we choose randomly a candidate source among the sources. We evaluate its cost and quality. We examine other query plans over the sources answering the query and put them into the candidate list even if their costs are greater than the best current one. We accept cost increasing when quality also increases for getting out of the local minimum and converge to the global minimum of cost for the global maximum of quality. If no trade-off is found, we modify slightly the quality contracts required in the profile and the Qwith clause (i.e., we soften a constraint) and restart the process with new costs and new quality scores.

The algorithm starts from a valid solution and randomly generates new states for the problem and calculates the associated cost and quality function. Simulation of the annealing process starts at high fictitious temperature (noted T). A new state is randomly chosen and the differences in cost and in quality function are calculated. If $\Delta Cost \leq 0$, that is, the cost is lower and the quality is monotone or increasing, then this new state is accepted. This forces the system toward a state corresponding to a local or a possibly global minimum. However, most large optimization problems have many local minima and the optimization algorithm is therefore often trapped in a local minimum. To get out of a local minimum, an increase of the cost function is accepted with a certain probability. For each temperature, the system must reach the equilibrium (i.e., a number of new states must be tried before the temperature is reduced typically by 10%). It can be shown that the algorithm will find, under certain conditions, the global minimum and not get stuck in local minima. The source that provides the trade-off is selected for answering the query.

Copyright © 2007, Idea Group Inc. Copying or distributing in print or electronic forms without written permission of Idea Group Inc. is prohibited.

Figure 9. Pseudocode for negotiation

```
Negotiation(SourceSet, Query, Aspirational_Quality_Θ)
Initialization(Current_State, T)
     // Random selection of a current state
     //Initialization of Temperature T

Calculation Current_State(Current_Cost,Current_Quality_Score)

while T ≠ 0
while no trade-off
   Calculation New_State(New_Cost,New_Quality_Score)
   Δcost = Current_Cost - New_Cost
   Δquality = Current_Quality_Score - New_Quality_Score
   if Δquality ≥ 0 :
       ifΔcost ≤ 0 : Current_State = New_State
          else if e^(-Δcost/T) > Random(0,1)
          then Current_State = New_State
       Else no trade-off
       Else
       No trade-off
       Renegotiate quality contract
              with New_Aspirational_Quality_Θ
End-while
decrease T
End-while: T ≤ 1 and New_State doesn't change 4 times
```

An Illustrative Example

"Nowadays flexibility and profitability in the banking and finance industry depends on the availability of ready, actual, and accurate information at the working place of every single employee" (Peinl & Störl, 2005, p. 257). To illustrate our approach in the banking context, this section presents a realistic but simplified example.

Consider the everyday life of your financial advisor who works with online streaming NASDAQ quotes, offers his experience for tracking your personal portfolio, has good ideas for investments based on real-time quotes, on his past experiences, and on his acute knowledge of the companies in the marketplace. Let us suppose your financial advisor uses four main data sources:

- **S1:** data of your bank account
- **S2:** the everyday market report with outlook, statistics diary, and daily spotlights
- **S3:** connections to the usual broker's PDA and smart phone,
- **S4:** the real-time U.S. and international indices of every market and stock exchange

Let us now assume a global query sent to these four sources and consider the following scenarios:

Copyright © 2007, Idea Group Inc. Copying or distributing in print or electronic forms without written permission of Idea Group Inc. is prohibited.

- **Focus 1:** Every transaction on your bank account updates data of S1; S2 updates data everyday; S3 updating is variable between 1 and 20 times per day; and S4 updates data every 15 minutes. In this case, the global query time may determine from which data source the most up-to-date data are retrieved. But the freshness of data neither implies credible data nor complete data.
- **Focus 2:** S3 is the PDA of the broker who has high credibility according to your financial advisor. S2 data may sometimes have parsing errors and may come from other Web sites.
- **Focus 3:** S3 and S2 cover more specific sectors than S4. Information of S2 is usually less complete and less accurate than in S3 for what concerns your portfolio.
- **Focus 4:** S1, S2, and S4 are highly available and reliable sources with very few failures compared to S3 (due to intermittent connections).

These scenarios briefly show that the way of how and when the local data sources are queried plays an important role for the integrated result quality of the global queries. They also present source dependencies and data quality dimensions such as freshness, accuracy, credibility or reliability.

Actually, a user might be interested in data freshness, and another one might be rather interested in the most complete data. In both cases, it is necessary for these users to take into account, in a declarative and a flexible way, their requirements of data and source quality into the global query declaration. Let us now keep on our example at a higher abstraction level and consider several global queries restricted to one universal relational table with five attributes (A1, ..., A5) in the case where these four information sources can answer the whole or some parts of the global queries (see the structure of the sources in Table 1). We assume that all the structural conflicts on the source schema are solved.

Several SQL queries (Q1,...,Q4), whose SQL-like algebra is given in Table 2, are sent to the four sources.

Table 1. Source simplified schema

Sources	Attributes			
S1	A1	A2	A3	A4
S2	A1	A2	A3	A4
S3	A1	A2<50		A4
S4	A1	A2>40	A3	

Table 2. List of algebraic queries

Sfw-query#	Algebraic Expression	Candidate Sources
q1	Select(A1, λa1, true)	S1,S2,S3,S4
q2	Select(A2, λa2, a2>30)	S1,S2,S3,S4
q3	Project(A3, λa3, Join(q1,q2, λa1, a2, (a1=a2)))	S1,S2,S4
q4	Project(A4, λa4, Join(q1,q2, λa1, a2, (a1=a2)))	S1,S2,S3

Copyright © 2007, Idea Group Inc. Copying or distributing in print or electronic forms without written permission of Idea Group Inc. is prohibited.

We consider the 10 quality dimensions (d1,…,d10) previously defined in the contract types of Figure 4. Every global query is extended with the following quality statement presented in Figure 10.

sfw-query# is the variable representing the query number in Table 2. Reliability, Freshness, Completeness, and Credibility have been previously defined as contract types in Figure 4 and are invoked in the profile of the Qwith operator, and Source_Set = { S1, S2, S3, S4}.

Each wrapper will instantiate the quality contract types on its underlying source. Figure 11a represents the quality dimensions values computed for each source. The aspirational quality level required initially is represented with the red dotted line. Figure 11b represents the cost variations of each source in temporal window for the query q1.

The negotiation processing computes the trade-off between minimal query cost and maximal quality gain over the 10 quality dimensions with renegotiating quality contracts and decomposes the subqueries to route to the most appropriate sources.

For each query, the negotiation processing computes the trade-off that minimizes the query cost and maximizes the quality over the four sources with eventually renegotiating

Figure 10. Example of quality-extended query

```
sfw-query#
Qwith Source_Profile FOR Source_Set = PROFILE {REQUIRE S_Reliability,
                                S_Freshness,
                                S_Completeness,
                                S_Credibility};
```

Figure 11. (a) Quality of sources: S1, S2, S3, and S4; (b) Cost of the query q1: For S1, S2, S3, and S4

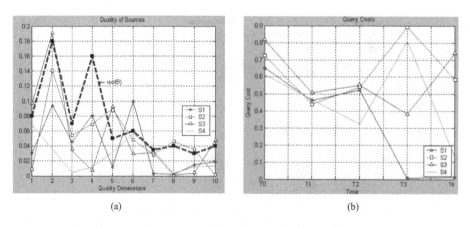

(a)   (b)

Copyright © 2007, Idea Group Inc. Copying or distributing in print or electronic forms without written permission of Idea Group Inc. is prohibited.

Figure 12. Reaching the global minimum trade-off for the quality-extended query q1

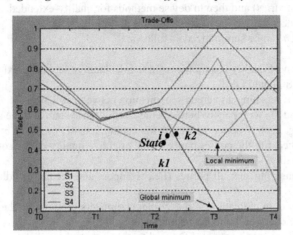

quality contracts to find the best trade-off. The negotiator module of the XQuaL architecture decides to make a trade-off action when it does not wish to decrease the aspirational quality level (θ) for a given quality-extended query. Thus, the negotiator module first computes the quality differential between the effective quality of the sources and the required quality represented by the curve of aspirational quality level θ. And it also generates the contract that lies on the iso-value curve for θ.

For the sake of brevity of the example, the negotiation mechanism is illustrated in Figure 12, starting in state *i*, the new state *k1* (provided by source S4) is accepted, but the new state *k2* (provided by source S1) is only accepted with a certain probability. The probability of accepting a worse state is high at the beginning and decreases as the temperature decreases. Finally the global minimum of trade-off is found and is provided by source S1 that will be queried first for answering the query *q1* among the potential sources.

Conclusion

This chapter presents a novel and comprehensible framework for processing quality-extended query declarations and describes our project, entitled *XQuaL — QML-Extended Query Language*, a query language extension that combines SQL and QML languages and that includes declarations of quality contracts and profiles for querying multisource mediation systems. Its declarative nature allows the expression of complex quality-constrained queries in a precise and simple way. We present the algorithm of quality-driven negotiation for adapting the query processing. While our general approach to query processing is typical, a number of factors associated with quality constraints specification and negotiation complicate the problem at runtime. The challenges have been first to define an appropriate

Copyright © 2007, Idea Group Inc. Copying or distributing in print or electronic forms without written permission of Idea Group Inc. is prohibited.

formalism for specifying in a flexible and declarative way quality constraints and metadata (dimensions and metrics) and then to devise methods for quality-extended and quality-negotiated query processing.

Our approach can be summarized as follows:

1.   Specification of quality requirements in the declarative language extension XQuaL combining SQL and QML
2.   **Negotiation:** reaching an agreed specification between all parties (e.g., between the mediator and the wrappers or between the integration system and the sources)
3.   **Monitoring:** each wrapper measuring the quality actually provided by its source
4.   **Control:** checking the conformance of the effective quality of the sources with the required quality
5.   **Policing:** ensuring that all parties (i.e., wrappers and mediator) adhere to quality contracts
6.   **Maintenance:** modification of the system parameters to maintain the best trade-off between the query cost and the result quality
7.   **Renegotiation:** modification of the quality contracts and requisites

The contribution of the work reported in this chapter is threefold. First, we propose a declarative language for specifying and querying data as well as quality metadata: we take advantage of QML (Frølund & Koistinen, 1998) in the domain of quality of service for flexibly extending the SQL query language with constraints on quality of service and on quality of distributed data sources. Second, past work on query processing has largely ignored the issue of source quality negotiation between query costs and result quality gains: our approach introduces trade-offs into the query processing taking into account the multidimensional constraints on data and service quality. Finally, negotiation constitutes the originality of the approach. The principle is to find continuously the best trade-off between the cost of the query and the quality of the result from several distributed sources.

The aim of our framework is to take as input a quality-extended query and adapt the processing to:

1.   **User preferences on quality requirements and declarations:** Adapting to user preferences includes cases where users are interested in obtaining some partial results of the query quickly with specific constraints on data quality and source quality of service. In order to meet such needs, the XQuaL query processor may, for instance, produce results incrementally, as they become available. The user may classify the output elements depending on the importance of specific quality dimensions and, in that case, the query evaluator has to adapt its behavior in order to produce more or better quality results earlier. Thus, the query processor has to consider potential input from the user, such as priority ratings and quality declarations for different parts of the result.
2.   **Data source statistics:** In some cases, it is not possible at compile time to gather accurate statistics about the content and the quality of available data sources. A solution to this problem is to collect such statistical information at runtime through wrappers, thereby ensuring that they are valid for the current circumstances, and to adapt query execution based on it. Techniques that adopt this policy may change the query plan when the actual statistics become available.

Copyright © 2007, Idea Group Inc. Copying or distributing in print or electronic forms without written permission of Idea Group Inc. is prohibited.

Moreover our work is focused on the definition of appropriate database statistics and a cost model, and we describe plan enumeration including heuristics and different strategies for quality negotiation. The purpose of our future work is to study the quality-adaptive query processing problem from the perspective of multiobjective optimization. Another important aspect of our future work is the automatic generation of wrappers that are XQuaL-compliant.

Future Trends

As highlighted by this chapter, providing efficient access to interconnected information sources has received a sustained interest for several decades, but an interesting research direction in optimizing queries over multisource data integration and mediation systems is the use of information quality. Few approaches have been proposed to deal with the various issues of quality-aware query processing in distributed environments, for example, HiQIQ (Naumann, 2002) and ObjectGlobe (Braumandl et al., 2001). These issues are particularly challenging due to the characteristics of the sources, including autonomy, volatility, amounts of data, large heterogeneity spectrum (both on data type, e.g., multimedia, XML, relational records, etc., on database schema and data quality). The main motivation is that the quality constraints and parameters reflect the user's needs better in such environments. Quality constraints are of crucial importance for some applications. A major issue is how to get related information from semistructured sources (e.g., XML data) and sources scattered on the Web. Furthermore, due to the "subjective" nature of some of these constraints, the query optimizer may not always succeed in finding the best plans.

The main future direction we identify is to build *a quality-aware query processing infrastructure*. Building such an infrastructure requires addressing several research issues:

- **QoD and QoS-based query languages:** Devise a declarative service-based query language that targets quality of data and quality of service with the advantage that the same quality-constrained query specification holds whatever underlying information is available.
- **Computation model:** The resolution of any quality-extended query may involve an iterative process between the different distributed systems within the infrastructure. We need to devise a *computation model* for the interaction of the different (sub)systems (e.g., wrapper/mediator systems, sources/data warehouse, peers, Web portals, Web services, Web providers, etc.).
- **Optimization model:** Performance has prime importance in successfully deploying a quality-aware query processing infrastructure over distributed systems. It mainly relates to query optimization. One challenge is to define appropriate metrics to characterize and measure QoS and QoD depending on the application domain, the systems capabilities and the required performance. The different query planning strategies focus generally on finding feasible and optimal subgoal orderings based on available bindings and supported conditions at the information sources. Proposed techniques assume full knowledge of the query capabilities of every participating source. They rely heavily on the way that information sources are described and the objective function of the optimizer (e.g., number of sources, response time). Using the same source

Copyright © 2007, Idea Group Inc. Copying or distributing in print or electronic forms without written permission of Idea Group Inc. is prohibited.

description and quality description models may not always be possible across a large spectrum of information sources. The optimization of quality-aware query processing on structured data (i.e., relational records) as well as on semi-structured data (XML) has to be considered. XML quality-aware query processing is still in its infancy and constitutes a very interesting trend in the near future.

- **Optimization heuristics:** General randomized search heuristics are a popular tool for query optimization. Besides simulated annealing (we used in our approach), *evolutionary algorithms* and other kinds of algorithms such as *randomized hill-climbing, Tabu search* (that uses memory to guide the search towards optimal/near-optimal solutions, by dynamically managing a list of forbidden moves) or *genetic algorithms* (that emulate the evolutionary behavior of biological systems to create subsequent generations that guide the search toward optimal/near-optimal solutions) can be used and adapted for quality-aware query optimization in distributed environments. In most of the real-world applications, it is quite natural that quality-extended query should meet a number of different and conflicting quality dimensions. Optimizing a particular objective function may sacrifice optimization of another dependent and conflicting objective. An interesting perspective is the study of the quality-driven query processing problem from the perspective of multiobjective optimization.

- **Quality-aware adaptive query processing:** Another interesting trend is the use of adaptive or dynamic approaches in dealing with quality-aware query optimization. This is motivated by the intrinsic dynamics of the distributed and autonomous sources where unpredictable events may occur during the execution of a query. The types of actions that are considered in these approaches fall into one of the following cases: (1) change the query execution plans in order to privilege data quality of query results, (2) change the scheduling of operations in the same query execution plan or in different concurrent query plans, (3) introduce new operators to cater for unpredictable events, or (4) modify the order of inputs of binary operators. Adaptive techniques have yet to demonstrate their applicability to various real applications with large numbers of information sources. There is also a need to show how they react under heavy quality of data and quality of service fluctuations.

References

Ananthakrishna, R., Chaudhuri, S., & Ganti, V. (2002). Eliminating fuzzy duplicates in data warehouses. In *Proceedings of the 28th International Conference on Very Large Data Bases (VLDB '02)*, Hong Kong, China.

Apers, P., Hevner, A. R., & Yao, S. B. (1983). Optimization algorithms for distributed queries. *IEEE Transactions on Software Engineering, 9*(1), 57-68.

Aurrecoechea, C., Campbell, A. T., & Hauw, L. (1998, May). A survery of QoS architectures. *Multimedia Systems, 6*(3), 138-151.

Ballou, D. P., & Pazer, H. (2002). Modeling completeness versus consistency tradeoffs in information decision contexts. *IEEE Transactions on Knowledge and Data Engineering, 15*(1), 240-243.

Copyright © 2007, Idea Group Inc. Copying or distributing in print or electronic forms without written permission of Idea Group Inc. is prohibited.

Batini, C., Catarci, T., & Scannapiceco, M. (2004, November). *A survey of data quality issues in cooperative information systems.* Tutorial presented at the 23rd International Conference on Conceptual Modeling, (ER2004), Shanghai, China.

Benjelloun, O., Garcia-Molina, H., Su, Q., Widom, J. (2005, March). *Swoosh: A generic approach to entity resolution* (Technical report). Stanford Database Group. Retrieved March 28, 2006, from http://dbpubs.stanford.edu/pub/2005-5

Bernstein, P. A., Goodman, N., Wong, E., Reeve, C. L., & Rothnie J. B. (1981). Query processing in a system for distributed databases (SDD-1). *ACM Transactions on Database Systems (TODS), 6*(4), 602-625.

Bobrowski, M., Marré, M., & Yankelevich, D. (1999). A hogeneous framework to measure data quality. In *Proceedings of the 4th International Conference on Information Quality (IQ'99)*, (pp. 115-124). Massachusetts Institute of Technology, Cambridge.

Bochmann, G., & Hafid, A. (1997). Some principles for quality of service management. *Distributed Systems Engineering Journal, 4,* 16-27.

Bouzeghoub, M., & Peralta, V. (2004, June). A framework for analysis of data freshness. In *Proceedings of the 1st ACM International Workshop on Information Quality in Information Systems (IQIS 2004)*, Paris, (pp. 59-67).

Braumandl, R., Keidl, M., Kemper, A., Kossmann, D., Kreutz, A., Seltzsam, S., & Stocker, K. (2001). ObjectGlobe: Ubiquitous query processing on the Internet. *The VLDB Journal, 10*(1), 48-71.

Chu, A., Wang, Y., Parker, D. S., & Zaniolo, C. (2005). Data cleaning using belief propagation. In *Proceedings of the 2nd ACM International Workshop on Information Quality in Information Systems (IQIS 2005)*, Baltimore, Maryland, (pp. 99-104).

Clavanese, D., DeGiacomo, G., Lenzerini, M., Nardi, D., & Rosati, R. (1997, Ocotober). *Source integration in datawarehousing* (Tech. Rep. No. DWQ-UNIROMA-002). Università di Roma "La Sapienza", DWQ Consortium.

Cui, Y., & Widom, J. (2001). Lineage tracing for general data warehouse transformation. In *Proceedings of the 27th International Conference on Very Large Data Bases (VLDB'01)*, Rome, Italy (pp. 471-480).

Dasu, T., & Johnson, T. (2003). *Exploratory data mining and data cleaning.* Hoboken, NJ: John Wiley & Sons Inc.

Elfeky, M. G., Verykios, V. S., & Elmagarmid, A. K. (2002). Tailor: A record linkage toolbox. In *Proceedings of the 18th International Conference on Data Engineering (ICDE'02)*, San Jose, CA, (pp. 17-28).

Fox, C., Levitin, A., & Redman, T. (1994). The notion of data and its quality dimensions. *Information Processing and Management, 30*(1), 9-20.

Frølund, S., & Koistinen, J. (1998). *QML: A language for quality of service specification* (Tech. Rep. No. HPL-98-10). Hewlett-Packard Software Technology Laboratory.

Frølund, S., & Koistinen, J. (1999). Quality of service aware distributed object systems. In *Proceedings of the 5th USENIX Conference on Object-Oriented Technologies and Systems (COOTS)*, San Diego, CA, (pp. 69-84).

Galhardas, H., Florescu, D., Shasha, D., & Simon, E. (2000). An extensible framework for data cleaning. In *Proceedings of the 16th International Conference on Data Engineering (ICDE'00)*, San Diego, CA, (p. 312).

Copyright © 2007, Idea Group Inc. Copying or distributing in print or electronic forms without written permission of Idea Group Inc. is prohibited.

Hernandez, M., & Stolfo, S. (1998). Real-world data is dirty: Data cleansing and the merge/purge problem. *Data Mining and Knowledge Discovery, 2*(1), 9-37.

Hou, W. C., & Zhang, Z. (1995). Enhancing database correctness: A statistical approach. In *Proceedings of the International Conference ACM SIGMOD*, San Jose, CA (pp. 223-232).

Kahn, B. K., Strong, D. M., & Wang, R. Y. (2002). Information quality benchmarks: Product and service performance. *Communications of the ACM, 45*(4), 184-192.

Kirkpatrick, S., Gerlatt, C. D., Jr., & Vecchi, M. P. (1983). Optimization by simulated annealing. *Science, 220*, 671-680.

Liu, L., & Chi, L. (2002, November). Evolutionary data quality. A theory-specific view. In *Proceedings of the 7th International Conference on Information Quality (IQ'02)* (pp. 292-304). Cambridge: Massachusetts Institute of Technology.

Little, R. J., & Rubin, D. B. (1987). *Statistical analysis with missing data.* New York: Wiley.

Low, W. L., Lee, M. L., & Ling, T. W. (2001). A knowledge-based approach for duplicate elimination in data cleaning. *Information System, 26*(8), 585-606.

Maletic, J., & Marcus, A. (2000). Data cleansing: Beyond integrity analysis. In *Proceedings of the 5th International Conference on Information Quality (IQ'00)* (pp. 200-209). Cambridge: Massachusetts Institute of Technology.

Mihaila, G. A., Raschid, L., & Vidal, M. (2000). Using quality of data metadata for source selection and ranking. In *Proceedings of the 3rd International Workshop on World Wide Web and Databases (WebDB 2000),* Dallas, TX (pp. 93-98).

Missier, P., & Embury, S. (2005). Provider issues in quality-constrained data provisioning. In *Proceedings of the 2nd ACM International Workshop on Information Quality in Information Systems (IQIS 2005) in conjunction with the International ACM 2005 PODS/SIGMOD Conference*, Baltimore, MD (pp. 5-15).

Naacke, H., Gardarin, G., & Tomasic, A. (1998). Leveraging mediator cost models with heterogeneous data sources. In *Proceedings of the 14th International Conference on Data Engineering (ICDE'98)*, Orlando, FL (pp. 351-360).

Naumann, F. (2002). *Quality-driven query answering for integrated information systems* (LNCS 2261).

Naumann, F., Leser, U., & Freytag, J. (1999). Quality-driven integration of heterogeneous information systems. In *Proceedings of the 25th International Conference on Very Large Data Bases (VLDB'99),* Edinburgh, Scotland (pp. 447-458).

Naumann, F., & Rolker, C. (2000). Assessment methods for information quality criteria. In *Proceedings of the 5th International Conference on Information Quality (IQ'00)*, (pp. 148-162). Cambridge: Massachusetts Institute of Technology.

Parsaye, K., & Chignell, M. (1993). *Intelligent database tools and applications.* John Wiley & Sons Inc.

Paradice, D. B., & Fuerst, W. L. (1991). An MIS data quality management strategy based on an optimal methodology. *Journal of Information Systems, 5*(1), 48-66.

Peinl, P., & Störl, U. (2005). Information dissemination in modern banking applications. In *Data Management in a Connected World* (LNCS 3551, pp. 257-276).

Pipino, P., & Lee, Y. W. (2002). Data quality assessment. *Communications of the ACM, 45*(4), 211-218.

Copyright © 2007, Idea Group Inc. Copying or distributing in print or electronic forms without written permission of Idea Group Inc. is prohibited.

Pon, R. K., & Cardenas, A. F. (2005). Data quality inference. In *Proceedings of the 2nd ACM International Workshop on Information Quality in Information Systems (IQIS 2005)*, Baltimore, MD (pp. 105-111).

Pyle, D. (1999). *Data preparation for data mining*. Morgan Kaufmann.

Rahm, E., & Do, H. (2000). Data cleaning: Problems and current approaches. *IEEE Data Engineering Bulletin, 23*(4), 3-13.

Raman, V., & Hellerstein, J. M. (2001). Potter's Wheel: An interactive data cleaning system. In *Proceedings of the 27th International Conference on Very Large Data Bases (VLDB'01)*, Rome, Italy (pp. 381-390).

Redman, T. (1996). *Data quality for the information age*. Artech House Publishers.

Redman, T. (2001). *Data quality: The field guide*. Digital Press (Elsevier).

Rothenberg, J. (1996, April). Metadata to support data quality and longevity. In *Proceedings of the 1st IEEE Metadata Conf*erence.

Scannapieco, M., Virgillito, A., Marchetti, C., Mecella, M., & Baldoni, R. (2004). The DaQuinCIS Architecture: A platform for exchanging and improving data quality in cooperative information systems. *Information System, 29*(7), 551-582.

Schafer, J. L. (1997). *Analysis of incomplete multivariate data*. Chapman & Hall.

Schlimmer, J. (1991). Learning determinations and checking databases. In *Proceedings of the AAAI-91 Workshop on Knowledge Discovery in Databases*.

Schlimmer, J. (1993). Self-modeling databases. *IEEE Expert, 8*(2), 35-43.

Sheth, A., Wood, C., & Kashyap, V. (1993). *Q-Data: Using deductive database technology to improve data quality* (pp. 23-56). Kluwer Academic Press.

Theodoratos, D., & Bouzeghoub, M. (2001). Data currency quality satisfaction in the design of a data warehouse. *Special Issue on Design and Management of Data Warehouses, International Journal of Cooperative Information Systems, 10*(3), 299-326.

Tomasic, A., Raschid, L., & Valduriez, P. (1996, May). Scaling heterogeneous database and the design of DISCO. In *Proceedings of the 16th International Conference on Distributed Computing Systems (ICDCS96)*, Hong Kong, China (pp. 449-457).

Vassiliadis, P. (2000). *Data warehouse modeling and quality issues*. Doctoral thesis, Department of Electrical and Computer Engineering, National Technical University of Athens, Greece.

Vassiliadis, P., Vagena, Z., Skiadopoulos, S., & Karayannidis, N. (2000). ARKTOS: A tool for data cleaning and transformation in data warehouse environments. *IEEE Data Engineering Bulletin, 23*(4), 42-47.

Vogel, A., Bochmann, G. V., Disallow, R., Geckos, J., & Kerhervé, B. (1995). Distributed multimedia applications and quality of service: A survey. *IEEE Multimedia, 2*(2), 10-19.

Wang, R. (1998). A product perspective on total data quality management. *Communications of the ACM, 41*(2), 58-65.

Wang, R. (2002). Journey to data quality. *Advances in Database Systems, 23*. Boston: Kluwer Academic Press.

Wang, R., Storey, V., & Firth, C. (1995). A framework for analysis of data quality research. *IEEE Transactions on Knowledge and Data Engineering, 7*(4), 670-677.

Wang, R., Ziad, M. & Lee, Y. (2002). *Data quality*. Cambridge: Kluwer Academic Publishers.

Copyright © 2007, Idea Group Inc. Copying or distributing in print or electronic forms without written permission of Idea Group Inc. is prohibited.

Widom, J. (2005). Trio: A system for integrated management of data, accuracy, and lineage. In *Proceedings of the 2nd Biennial Conference on Innovative Data Systems Research (CIDR '05)*, Asilomar, CA (pp. 262-276).

Winkler, W. (2004). Methods for evaluating and creating data quality. *Information Systems, 29*(7), 531-550.

Yu, C. T., & Chang, C. C. (1984). Distributed query processing. *ACM Computing Surveys, 16*(4), 399-433.

Endnote

[1]   To clarify the object of the research described further, we are tackling specific aspects of information quality in relation to data processing and we voluntarily use the terms "data quality."

Copyright © 2007, Idea Group Inc. Copying or distributing in print or electronic forms without written permission of Idea Group Inc. is prohibited.

Appendix: Syntax of XQuaL

Qwith-query ::=	query QWITH profileDeclaration | CREATE declarations
query ::=	(query) | query set-op query | query bool-op query | NOT query
	| query constraintop query | query IN query | COUNT (query)
	| constant | var | sfw-query | EXISTS var query : query
	| FORALL var query : query
set-op ::=	UNION | INTERSECT | MINUS
bool-op ::=	AND | OR
constant ::=	integer literal | real literal | quoted string literal | true | false
var ::=	IDENTIFIER | $IDENTIFIER | @IDENTIFIER
sfw-query ::=	sfw-query WHERE query | SELECT projs-list FROM ranges-list
projs-list ::=	projs-list, var | * | var
ranges-list ::=	ranges-list, one-range | one-range
one-range ::=	var query | path-expr
path-expression ::=	path-elem.path-expression | path-elem
path-elem ::=	[from-to]query | query | path-elem[from-to]
from-to ::=	from-to:query | var
declarations ::=	declarations declaration ;
declaration ::=	contractTypeDeclaration | contractDeclaration |
profileDeclaration	
contractTypeDeclaration ::=	TYPE IDENTIFIER = contractType
contractType ::=	CONTRACT { dimensions } ;
dimensions ::=	dimensions dimension | dimension
dimension ::=	dimName : dimType ;
dimName ::=	IDENTIFIER
dimType ::=	dimSort | dimSort unit
items ::=	items , IDENTIFIER | IDENTIFIER
dimSort ::=	ENUM { items } | relSem ENUM { items } WITH order
	| SET { items } | relSem SET { items }
	| relSem SET { items } WITH order | relSem NUMERIC
relations ::=	relations , relation | relation
relation ::=	IDENTIFIER < IDENTIFIER
order ::=	ORDER { relations }
unit ::=	unit / base-unit | base-unit
base-unit ::=	% | IDENTIFIER
relSem ::=	DECREASING | INCREASING
contractDeclaration ::=	IDENTIFIER = contractExpression
contractExpression ::=	IDENTIFIER contractDefinition
	| IDENTIFIER REFINED BY {constraints}
contractDefinition ::=	CONTRACT { constraints }
constraints ::=	constraints constraint | constraint ;
constraint ::=	dimName constraintOp dimValue | dimName { aspects }
constraintOp ::=	== | >= | <= | > | < | LIKE | !=
dimValue ::=	literal unit | literal
literal ::=	IDENTIFIER | { items } | NUMBER
aspects ::=	aspects aspect;
aspect ::=	PERCENTILE NUMBER constraintOp dimValue
	| MEAN constraintOp dimValue | VARIANCE constraintOp dimValue
	| FREQUENCY freqRange constraintOp NUMBER %
freqRange ::=	dimValue | lRangeLimit dimValue , dimValue rRangeLimit

continued on following page

Copyright © 2007, Idea Group Inc. Copying or distributing in print or electronic forms without written permission of Idea Group Inc. is prohibited.

```
lRangeLimit ::=              [ | (
rRangeLimit ::=              ] | )
profileDeclaration ::=  IDENTIFIER FOR IDENTIFIER = profileExpression
profileExpression ::=   profile | IDENTIFIER REFINED BY { requisites }
profile ::=          PROFILE { requisites }
requisites ::=        requisites requisite ;
requisite ::=        REQUIRE contractList | FROM entityList REQUIRE contractList
contractList ::=        contractList , contractElem | contractElem
contractElem ::=      IDENTIFIER | contractExpression
entityList ::=        entityList , entity | entity
entity ::=          IDENTIFIER | IDENTIFIER . IDENTIFIER | RESULT OF IDENTIFIER
```

Copyright © 2007, Idea Group Inc. Copying or distributing in print or electronic forms without written permission of Idea Group Inc. is prohibited.

Chapter III

Discovering Quality Knowledge from Relational Databases

M. Mehdi Owrang O., American University, USA

Abstract

Current database technology involves processing a large volume of data in order to discover new knowledge. However, knowledge discovery on just the most detailed and recent data does not reveal the long-term trends. Relational databases create new types of problems for knowledge discovery since they are normalized to avoid redundancies and update anomalies, which make them unsuitable for knowledge discovery. A key issue in any discovery system is to ensure the consistency, accuracy, and completeness of the discovered knowledge. We describe the aforementioned problems associated with the quality of the discovered knowledge and provide some solutions to avoid them.

Copyright © 2007, Idea Group Inc. Copying or distributing in print or electronic forms without written permission of Idea Group Inc. is prohibited.

Introduction

Modern database technology involves processing a large volume of data in databases to discover new knowledge. Knowledge discovery is defined as the nontrivial extraction of implicit, previously unknown, and potentially useful information from data (Adriaans & Zantinge, 1996; Agrawal, Imielinski, & Swami, 1993; Berry & Linoff, 2000; Brachman & Anand, 1996; Brachman, Khabaza, Kloesgen, Piatetsky-Shapiro, & Simoudis, 1996; Bradley, Gehrke, Ramakrishnan, & Srikant, 2002; Fayad, 1996; Fayad, Piatetsky-Shapiro, & Symth, 1996a, 1996b, 1996c; Fayyad & Uthurusamy, 2002; Frawley, Piatetsky-Shapiro, & Matheus, 1992; Han & Kamber, 2000; Hand, Mannila, & Smyth, 2001; Inmon, 1996; Simoudis, 1996; Uthurusamy, 1996; Keyes, 1990).

Databases contain a variety of patterns, but few of them are of much interest. A pattern is interesting to the degree that it is not only accurate but that it is also useful with respect to the end user's knowledge and objectives (Brachman et al., 1996; Bradley et al., 2002; Hand et al., 2001; Berry & Linoff, 2000; Piatetsky-Shapiro & Matheus, 1994; Silberschatz & Tuzhilin, 1995). A critical issue in knowledge discovery is how well the database is created and maintained. Real-world databases present difficulties as they tend to be dynamic, incomplete, redundant, inaccurate, and very large. Naturally, the efficiency of the discovery process and the quality of the discovered knowledge are strongly dependent on the quality of data.

To discover useful knowledge from the databases, we need to provide clean data to the discovery process. Most large databases have redundant and inconsistent data, missing data fields, and values, as well as data fields that are not logically related and are stored in the same data relations (Adriaans & Zantinge, 1996; Parsaye & Chingell, 1999; Piatetsky-Shapiro, 1991; Savasere et al. 1995). Subsequently, the databases have to be cleaned before the actual discovery process takes place in order to avoid discovering incomplete, inaccurate, redundant, inconsistent, and uninteresting knowledge. Different tools and techniques have been developed to improve the quality of the databases in recent years, leading to a better discovery environment. There are still problems associated with the discovery techniques/schemes which cause the discovered knowledge to be incorrect, inconsistent, incomplete, and uninteresting.

Most of the knowledge discovery has been done on operational relational databases (Sarawagi et al., 1998). Operational relational databases, built for online transaction processing, are generally regarded as unsuitable for rule discovery since they are designed for maximizing transaction capacity and typically have a lot of tables in order not to lock out users. In addition, the goal of the relational databases is to provide a platform for querying data about uniquely identified objects. However, such uniqueness constraints are not desirable in a knowledge discovery environment. In fact, they are harmful since, from a data mining point of view, we are interested in the frequency with which objects occur (Adriaans & Zantinge, 1996; Berry & Linoff, 2000; Bradley & Gehrke, 2002; Hand et al., 2001). Subsequently, knowledge discovery in an operational environment could lead to inaccurate and incomplete discovered knowledge. The operational data contains the most recent data about the organization and is organized as normalized relations for fast retrieval as well as avoiding update anomalies. Summary and historical data, which are essential for accurate and complete knowledge discovery, are generally absent in the operational databases. Rule discovery based on just the detailed (most recent) data is neither accurate nor complete.

Copyright © 2007, Idea Group Inc. Copying or distributing in print or electronic forms without written permission of Idea Group Inc. is prohibited.

A data warehouse is a better environment for rule discovery since it checks for the quality of data more rigorously than the operational database. It also includes the integrated, summarized, historical, and metadata which complement the detailed data (Bischoff & Alexander, 1997; Bradley & Gehrke, 2002; Hand et al., 2001; Inmon, 1996; Berry & Linoff, 2000; Meredith & Khader, 1996; Parsaye, 1996). Summary tables can provide efficient access to large quantities of data as well as help reduce the size of the database. Summarized data contains patterns that can be discovered. Such discovered patterns can complement the discovery on operational/detail data by verifying the patterns discovered from the detailed data for consistency, accuracy, and completeness. In addition, processing only very recent data (detailed or summarized) can never detect trends and long-term patterns in the data. Historical data (i.e., sales product 1982-1991) is essential in understanding the true nature of the patterns representing the data. The discovered knowledge should be correct over data gathered for a number of years, not just the recent year. The goals of this chapter are twofold:

1. To show that anomalies (i.e., incorrect, inconsistent, and incomplete rules) do exist in the discovered rules due to:
   a. An inadequate database design
   b. Poor data
   c. The vulnerability/limitations of the tools used for discovery
   d. Flaws in the discovery process (i.e., the process used to obtain and validate the rules using a given tool on a given database)
2. To define mechanisms (algorithms or processes) in which the above anomalies can be detected or avoided.

Our discussions focus on the discovery problems caused by the flaws in the discovery process as well as the inadequacy of the database design and, to some extent, by the limitations of the discovery tool (i.e., tool able only to discover from a single relational table).

Knowledge Discovery Process

The KDD (knowledge discovery in databases) process is outlined in Figure 1. The KDD process is interactive and iterative (with many decisions made by the user), involving numerous steps, and summarized as data (Adriaans & Zantinge, 1996; Agrawal et al., 1993; Brachman & Anand, 1996; Brachman et al., 1996; Bradley & Gehrke, 2002; Fayad, 1996; Fayad et al., 1996a; Hand et. al, 2001; Berry & Linoff, 2000; Simoudis, 1996; Uthurusamy, 1996; Smyth et al. 2002). The KDD process includes the following steps:

1. **Learning the application domain:** includes relevant prior knowledge and the goals of the application.
2. **Creating a target dataset:** includes selecting a dataset or focusing on a subset of variables or data samples on which discovery is to be performed (John & Langley, 1996; Parsaye, 1998.
3. **Data cleaning and preprocessing:** includes basic operations such as removing noise or outliers if appropriate, collecting the necessary information to model or account for

Copyright © 2007, Idea Group Inc. Copying or distributing in print or electronic forms without written permission of Idea Group Inc. is prohibited.

Figure 1. Overview of the steps constituting the KDD process

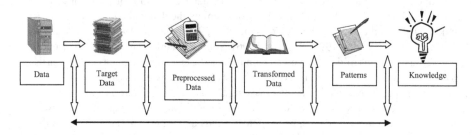

noise, deciding on strategies for handling missing data fields, and accounting for time sequence information and known changes, as well as deciding DBMS issues such as data types, schema, and mapping of missing and unknown values.

4. **Data reduction and projection:** includes finding useful features to represent the data, depending on the goal of the task, and using dimensionality reduction or transformation methods to reduce the effective number of variables under consideration or to find invariant representations for the data.

5. **Choosing the function of data mining:** includes deciding the purpose of the model derived by the data mining algorithm (e.g., summarization, classification, regression, and clustering).

6. **Choosing the data mining algorithm(s):** includes selecting method(s) to be used for searching for patterns in the data, such as deciding which models and parameters may be appropriate (e.g., models for categorical data are different from models on vectors over reals) and matching a particular data mining method with the overall criteria of the KDD process (e.g., the user may be more interested in understanding the model than in its predictive capabilities).

7. **Data mining:** includes searching for patterns of interest in a particular representational form or a set of such representations, including classification rules or trees, regression, clustering, sequence modeling, dependency, and line analysis.

8. **Interpretation:** includes interpreting the discovered patterns and possibly returning to any of the previous steps, as well as possible visualization of the extracted patterns, removing redundant or irrelevant patterns, and translating the useful ones into terms understandable by users.

9. **Using discovered knowledge:** includes incorporating this knowledge into the performance system, taking actions based on the knowledge, or simply documenting it and reporting it to interested parties, as well as checking for and resolving potential conflicts with previously believed (or extracted) knowledge (Adriaans & Zantinge, 1996; Han & Kamber, 2000; Hand et al., 2001).

Our work in this chapter is related to step 8 of the KDD process in which we try to interpret the discovered knowledge (rule) and understand the quality of the discovered rule. Of course, the first step is to understand that if (and why) we have incorrect, incomplete, and inconsistent discovered rules. Our proposed schemes are intended to illustrate this aspect of the interpretation step of the KDD. Other issues including the interestingness/usefulness

Copyright © 2007, Idea Group Inc. Copying or distributing in print or electronic forms without written permission of Idea Group Inc. is prohibited.

of the discovered rules are studied in Ganti, Gebrke, and Ramakrishnan (1999); Piatetsky-Shapiro and Matheus (1994); and Silberschatz and Tuzhilin (1995).

Data Warehouses

Most of the knowledge discovery has been done on operational relational databases. However, such knowledge discovery in an operational environment could lead to inaccurate and incomplete discovered knowledge. The operational data contains the most recent data about the organization and is organized for fast retrieval as well as for avoiding update anomalies (Date, 2000). Summary data are not generally found in the operational environment. In addition, metadata (i.e., description of the data) are not complete. Rule discovery does not mean analyzing details of data alone. To understand and discover the deep knowledge regarding the decision-making process for expert system development, it is critical that we perform pattern analysis on all sources of data, including the summarized and historical data.

Without first warehousing its data, an organization has lots of information that is not integrated and has little summary information or history. The effectiveness of knowledge discovery on such data is limited. The data warehouse provides an ideal environment for effective knowledge discovery. Basically, data warehousing is the process of extracting and transforming operational data into informational data and loading them into a central data store or warehouse. A data warehouse environment integrates data from a variety of source databases into a target database that is optimally designed for decision support. A data warehouse includes integrated data, detailed and summary data, historical data, and metadata (Barquin & Edelstein, 1997; Berry & Linoff, 2000; Bischoff & Alexander, 1997; Inmon, 1996; Meredith & Khader, 1996; Parsaye, 1996). Each of these elements enhances the knowledge discovery process.

- **Integrated data:** When data are moved from the operational environment into the data warehouse, they assume a consistent coding convention (i.e., gender data are transformed to "m" and "f"). Without integrated data, we have to cleanse the data before the process of knowledge discovery could be effective. That is, keys have to be reconstituted, encoded values reconciled, structures of data standardized, and so forth. Integrated data could remove any redundancies and inconsistencies that we may have on data, thus reducing the change of discovering redundant and inconsistent knowledge.
- **Detailed and summarized data:** Detailed data (i.e., sales detail from 1992-1993) is necessary when we wish to examine data in their most granular form. Very low levels of detail contain hidden patterns. At the same time, summarized data ensure that if a previous analysis is already made, we do not have to repeat the process of exploration. Summary data (highly summarized monthly sales by product line 1981-1993; lightly summarized-weekly sales by subproduct 1985-1993) are detail data summarized for specific decision-support requirements. Summary tables can provide efficient access to large quantities of data as well as help reduce the size of the database. Summarized data contain patterns that can be discovered. Such discovered patterns can complement the discovery on operational/detail data by verifying the patterns discovered from the detailed data for consistency, accuracy, and completeness.

Copyright © 2007, Idea Group Inc. Copying or distributing in print or electronic forms without written permission of Idea Group Inc. is prohibited.

- **Historical data:** Processing only very recent data (detailed or summarized) can never detect trends and long-term patterns in the data. Historical data (i.e., sales product 1982-1991) are essential in understanding the true nature of the patterns representing the data. The discovered knowledge should be correct over data gathered for a number of years, not just the recent year.
- **Meta data:** The means and methods for providing source information with semantic meaning and context is through the capture, use, and application of metadata as a supplement. The possibility exists that the same data may have different meanings for different applications within the same organization. Basically, metadata are used to describe the content of the database, including:
    - What the data mean: description of the data contents, including tables, attributes, constraints, dependencies among tables/attributes, units of measure, definitions, aliases for the data, and detail of how data were derived or calculated
    - Data transformation rules such as profit = income-cost
    - Domain knowledge such as "male patients cannot be pregnant"

In addition, metadata are used to define the context of the data. When data are explored over time, context becomes as relevant as content. Raw content of data becomes very difficult for exploration when there is no explanation for the meaning of the data. Metadata can be used to identify the redundant and inconsistent data (when data are gathered from multiple data sources), thereby reducing the chance of discovering redundant and inconsistent knowledge. There are several benefits in rule discovery in a data warehouse environment.

1. Rule discovery process is able to examine all the data in some cohesive storage format. There is a repository or directory (metadata) of enterprise information. This will enable the users or tools to locate the appropriate information sources. To allow an effective search of data, it is important to be aware of all the information and the relationships between them stored in the system. Rules discovered from only part of a business data produce potentially worthless information. Rule discovery tools actually need to be able to search the warehouse data, the operational data, the legacy data, and any distributed data on any number of servers.
2. A major issue in rule discovery in operational database environment is whether the data are clean. As we explained before, the data have to be verified for consistency and accuracy before the discovery process. In a data warehouse environment, however, the validation of the data is done in a more rigorous and systematic manner. Using metadata, many data redundancies from different application areas are identified and removed. In addition, a data cleansing process is used in order to create an efficient data warehouse by removing certain aspects of operational data, such as low-level transaction information, which slow down the query times (Barquin & Edelstein, 1997; Berry & Linoff, 2000; Bischoff & Alexander, 1997; Hand et al., 2001; Inmon, 1996; Meredith & Khader, 1996; Parsaye, 1996). The cleansing process will remove duplication and reconcile differences between various styles of data collection.
3. Operational relational databases, built for online transaction processing, are generally regarded as unsuitable for rule discovery since they are designed for maximizing transaction capacity and typically have a lot of tables in order not to lock out users (Han & Kamber, 2000; Hand et al., 2001). Also, they are normalized to avoid update anomalies. Data warehouses, on the other hand, are not concerned with the update

Copyright © 2007, Idea Group Inc. Copying or distributing in print or electronic forms without written permission of Idea Group Inc. is prohibited.

Figure 2. A framework of knowledge discovery in a data warehouse environment

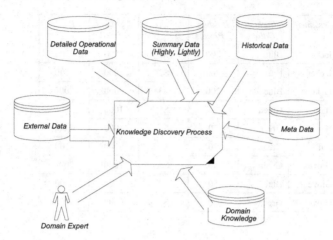

anomalies since update of data is not done. This means that at the physical level of design, we can take liberties to optimize the access of data, particularly in dealing with the issues of normalization and physical denormalization. Universal relations can be built in the data warehouse environment for the purposes of rule discovery, which could minimize the chance of undetecting hidden patterns.

Figure 2 shows a general framework for knowledge discovery in a data warehouse environment. External data, domain knowledge (data not explicitly stored in the database; that is, male patient cannot be pregnant), and domain expert are other essential components to be added in order to provide an effective knowledge discovery process in a data warehouse environment.

In this chapter, we assume that we are given a data warehouse for a domain (i.e., medicine, retail store, etc.) and we are performing the KDD process on data represented as a relational database. Even with the improved data quality in a data warehouse (compared to the data quality in an operational database), we still could discover inaccurate, incomplete, and inconsistent knowledge (rules) from databases. Such anomalies might be caused by applying a particular data selection scheme (i.e., summarization) or by the criteria (general or detailed) used for a particular discovery case. In the following, we show how and why these anomalies could occur and how we detect them.

Incorrect Knowledge Discovery

Incorrect Knowledge Discovery from Detailed Data

In general, summary data (aggregation) is never found in the operational environment. Without discovery process on summary data, we may discover incorrect knowledge

Copyright © 2007, Idea Group Inc. Copying or distributing in print or electronic forms without written permission of Idea Group Inc. is prohibited.

Table 1. Sample sales data

Product	Product Color	Product Price	Store	Store Size	Profit
Jacket	Blue	200	S1	1000	-200
Jacket	Blue	200	S2	5000	-100
Jacket	Blue	200	S3	9000	7000
Hat	Green	70	S1	1000	300
Hat	Green	70	S2	5000	-1000
Hat	Green	70	S3	9000	-100
Glove	Green	50	S1	1000	2000
Glove	Blue	50	S2	5000	-300
Glove	Green	50	S3	9000	-200

from detailed operational data. Discovering a rule based just on current detail data may not depict the actual trends on data. The problem is that statistical significance is usually used in determining the interestingness of a pattern (Giarrantanto & Riley, 1989). Statistical significance alone is often insufficient to determine a pattern's degree of interest. A "5% increase in sales of product X in the Western region," for example, could be more interesting than a "50% increase of product X in the Eastern region." In the former case, it could be that the Western region has a larger sales volume than the Eastern region, and thus its increase translates into greater income growth.

In the following example (Matheus, Chan, & Piatetsky-Shapiro, 1993), we show that we could discover incorrect knowledge if we only look at the detailed data. Consider Table 1, where the goal of discovery is to see if product color or store size has any effect on the profits. Although the dataset in the table is not large, it shows the points.

Assume we are looking for patterns that tell us when profits are positive or negative. We should be careful when we process this table using discovery methods such as simple rules or decision trees. These methods are based on probabilities that make them inadequate for dealing with influence within aggregation (summary data). A discovery scheme based on probability may discover the following rules from Table 1:

Rule 1: IF Product Color=Blue Then Profitable=No CF=75%

Rule 2: IF Product Color=Blue and Store Size> 5000 Then Profitable=Yes CF=100%

The results indicate that blue products in larger stores are profitable; however, they do not tell us the amounts of the profits which can go one way or another. Now, consider Table 2, where the third row in Table 1 is changed. Rules 1 and 2 are also true in Table 2. That is, from a probability point of view, Tables 1 and 2 produce the same results.

However, this is not true when we look at the summary Tables 3 and 4, which are the summary tables based on Tables 1 and 2, respectively. Table 3 tells us that Blue color product is profitable and Table 4 tells us it is not. That is, in the summary tables, the probability behavior of these detailed tables begins to diverge and thus produces different results. We

Copyright © 2007, Idea Group Inc. Copying or distributing in print or electronic forms without written permission of Idea Group Inc. is prohibited.

Table 2. Sample sales data

Product	Product Color	Product Price	Store	Store Size	Profit
Jacket	Blue	200	S1	1000	-200
Jacket	Blue	200	S2	5000	-100
Jacket	Blue	200	S3	9000	100
Hat	Green	70	S1	1000	300
Hat	Green	70	S2	5000	-1000
Hat	Green	70	S3	9000	-100
Glove	Green	50	S1	1000	2000
Glove	Blue	50	S2	5000	-300
Glove	Green	50	S3	9000	-200

Table 3. Summary sales table based on Table 1

Product Color	Profit
Blue	6400
Green	1000

Table 4. Summary sales table based on Table 2

Product Color	Profit
Blue	-500
Green	1000

should be careful when we analyze the summary tables since we may get conflicting results when the discovered patterns from the summary tables are compared with the discovered patterns from detailed tables. In general, the probabilities are not enough when discovering knowledge from detailed data. We need summary data as well.

Incorrect Knowledge Discovery from Summary Data

In knowledge discovery, we believe that it is critical to use summary tables to discover patterns that could not be otherwise discovered from operational detailed databases. Knowledge discovery on detailed data is based on statistical significance (uses probability), which may not detect all patterns, or may produce incorrect results as we noted in the previous

Copyright © 2007, Idea Group Inc. Copying or distributing in print or electronic forms without written permission of Idea Group Inc. is prohibited.

Table 5. Summary sales table based on Table 1

Product	Product Color	Profit
Glove	Blue	-300
Glove	Green	1800
Hat	Green	-800
Jacket	Blue	6700

Table 6. Summary sales table based on Table 1

Product	Product Color	Profit
Glove	Blue	2000
Hat	Green	300
Jacket	Blue	-200

Table 7. Summary sales table based on Table 1

Product	Product Color	Profit
Glove	Blue	-300
Glove	Green	-200
Hat	Green	-1100
Jacket	Blue	6900

section. Knowledge discovery on summary tables could improve the overall data mining process and prevent incorrect knowledge discovery. Summary tables have hidden patterns that can be discovered. For example, Table 3 tells us that Blue products are profitable. Such discovered patterns can complement the discoveries from the detailed data (as part of the validation of the discovered knowledge, explained later).

In general, for any given detailed data, there are numerous ways to summarize them. Each summarization or aggregation can be along one or more dimensions, as shown in the Tables 3 and 4. Accurate knowledge, however, cannot be discovered just by processing the summary tables. The problem is that the summarization of the same dataset with two summarization methods may result in the same result, and the summarization of the same dataset with two methods may produce two different results. Therefore, it is extremely important that the users be able to access metadata (Adriaans & Zantinge, 1996) that tells them exactly how each type of summarized data was derived, so they understand which dimensions have been summarized and to what level. Otherwise, we may discover inaccurate patterns from different summarized tables. For example, consider Tables 5 through 7, summarized/aggregated tables based on Table 1, which provide different and conflicting results.

Copyright © 2007, Idea Group Inc. Copying or distributing in print or electronic forms without written permission of Idea Group Inc. is prohibited.

These tables show different results for Green Hat product. In fact, it is the Green Hat in small stores (Store Size <=1000) that makes profit (Table 6) and it is the Green Hat product in large stores (Store Size > 1000) that loses money. This fact can only be discovered by looking the different summary tables and knowing how they are created (i.e., using the metadata to see the SQL statements used to create the summarized/aggregated tables). Alternatively, we can combine the patterns discovered from the detailed data and the summary data to avoid discovering contradictory knowledge (as explained in the following discussion).

As we noted, summary tables greatly enhance the performance of information retrieval in a large volume database environment (Barquin & Edelstein, 1997). There are, however, several problems associated with creating and maintaining the summary tables. First, in most databases, it is physically impossible to create all the summary tables required to support all possible queries. For the general case, given N items (or columns) on an axis of a cross-tabular report, there are 2 N-1 possible ways of combining the items. The number of aggregate rows required depends on the number of valid combinations of item values, and the situation is complicated further when the items are in a multilevel hierarchy (i.e., with Month rolling up to Quarter and Year). However, there are pruning techniques that can be employed. For example, by specifying which combinations of dimensions or levels do not make business sense to combine (using metadata and available domain knowledge gathered from domain expert), and by not aggregating at all levels, allowing some minimal aggregation from a lower level, where required. Second, there is also a possibility that information is lost or distorted as summary tables are created. For example, consider a retail data warehouse where Monday to Friday sales are exceptionally low for some stores, while weekend sales are exceptionally high for others. The summarization of daily sales data to weekly amounts will totally hide the fact that weekdays are "money losers," while weekends are "money makers" for some stores. In other words, key pieces of information are often lost through summarization, and there is no way to recover them by further analysis. Finally, another key issue is the maintenance of the summary tables to keep them up to date, and ensuring that the summary tables are consistent with each other and the detailed data. Once the summary tables have been created, they need to be refreshed at regular intervals as the base data (detailed data) gets refreshed. We need to use an incremental scheme for maintaining summary tables efficiently (Barquin & Edelstein, 1997; Bischoff & Alexander, 1997).

Validating Possible Incorrect Discovered Knowledge

As we showed in the previous section, knowledge discovery based on just the detailed tables may lead to incorrect discovery since the discovered knowledge is based on statistical significance. Such statistical significance represents the probability that is based on the occurrences of the records in which certain attributes satisfy some specific conditions. Summary tables have hidden patterns that can be discovered. Such patterns provide the relationships between certain attributes based on their actual values as well as on the statistical significance. Therefore, we propose to use the patterns discovered from the summary tables to validate the discovered knowledge from the detailed tables. Our proposed scheme identifies the following cases for validating possible incorrect/correct discovered rules.

- **Case 1:** If the discovered pattern from the summary tables completely supports the discovered knowledge from the detailed tables, then we have more confidence on

Copyright © 2007, Idea Group Inc. Copying or distributing in print or electronic forms without written permission of Idea Group Inc. is prohibited.

Table 8. Sample sales data

Product	Product Color	Product Price	Store	Store Size	Profit
Jacket	Blue	200	S1	1000	-200
Jacket	Blue	200	S2	5000	-100
Jacket	Blue	200	S3	9000	-100
Hat	Green	70	S1	1000	300
Hat	Green	70	S2	5000	-1000
Hat	Green	70	S3	9000	-100
Glove	Green	50	S1	1000	2000
Glove	Blue	50	S2	5000	-300
Glove	Green	50	S3	9000	-200

Table 9. Summary sales table based on Table 1

Product Color	Profit
Blue	-700
Green	1000

the accuracy of the discovered knowledge. For instance, consider Table 8, where the third row in Table 2 is changed such that profit = -100. From Table 8 we can discover that:

If Product Color = Blue Then Profitable =No CF=100% (4 records out of 4)

By looking at Table 9, which is a summary table based on Table 8, we can discover that Blue color product provides no profit (negative profit). So, the detailed and summary tables produce the same results. Subsequently, we have more confidence in the discovered knowledge.

- **Case 2:** The patterns discovered from the detailed and summary tables support each other, but they have different confidence factors. For example, from Table 2, we discover that:

If Product Color = Blue Then Profitable = No CF=75% (3 records out of 4).

From Table 4, we discover that Blue color product is not profitable (CF = 100%, Profit = -500). Since the discovered patterns on the summary tables are based on the actual values, they represent more reliable information compared to the discovered patterns from

Copyright © 2007, Idea Group Inc. Copying or distributing in print or electronic forms without written permission of Idea Group Inc. is prohibited.

the detailed tables which are based on the occurrences of the records. In such cases, we cannot say that the discovered pattern is incorrect, but rather it is not detailed enough to be considered as an interesting pattern. Perhaps the hypothesis for discovering the pattern has to be expanded to include other attributes (i.e., Product or Store Size or both) in addition to the Product Color.

- **Case 3:** The patterns discovered from the detailed and summary tables contradict each other. For example, from Table 1, we discover that:

    If Product Color = Blue Then Profitable = No CF=75% (3 records out of 4).

    From Table 3, we discover that the Blue color product is profitable (CF = 100%, Profit = 6400). The explanation is the same as the one provided for case 2.

Incomplete Knowledge Discovery

The traditional database design method is based on the notions of functional dependencies and lossless decomposition of relations into third normal forms. However, this decomposition of relation is not useful with respect to knowledge discovery because it hides dependencies among attributes that might be of some interest (Adriaans & Zantinge, 1996). To provide maximum guarantee that potentially interesting statistical dependencies are preserved, knowledge discovery process should use the universal relation (Chiang, Barron, & Storey, 1994; Date, 2000; Maier, 1983; Parsaye & Chignell, 1999) as opposed to normalized relations. In the following example, we show that knowledge discovery on a normalized relations may not reveal all the interesting patterns.

Consider the relations Sales and Region (Adriaans & Zantinge, 1996) in Figure 3 which are in third normal form. Figure 4 shows the universal relation which is the join of the two tables in Figure 3. From Figure 4, we can discover a relationship between the Average Price of the House and the type of Products Purchased by people. Such relationship is not that obvious on the normalized relations in Figure 3. This example shows that knowledge discovery on "well designed" (i.e., 3NF) databases, according to the normalization techniques, could lead to incomplete knowledge discovery.

Figure 3. Relational database in third normal form

Sales

Client Number	Zip Code	Product Purchased
1111	11111	Wine
2222	22222	Bread
3333	11111	Wine
4444	33333	Wine
5555	44444	Wine

Region

Zip Code	City	Average House Price
11111	Paris	High
22222	Peking	Low
33333	New York	High
44444	Moscow	High

Copyright © 2007, Idea Group Inc. Copying or distributing in print or electronic forms without written permission of Idea Group Inc. is prohibited.

Figure 4. Universal relation, join of the tables in Figure 3

Sales / Region

Client Number	Zip Code	City	Average House Price	Product Purchased
11111	11111	Paris	High	Wine
22222	22222	Peking	Low	Bread
33333	11111	Paris	High	Wine
44444	33333	New York	High	Wine
5555	44444	Moscow	High	Wine

Validating Possible Incomplete Discovered Knowledge

Every decomposition involves a potential information loss that has to be analyzed and quantified, and traditional techniques from statistics and machine learning (minimum description length) can be used (Adriaans & Zantinge, 1996). The chance of having complete/incomplete knowledge discovery depends on the discovery process. If knowledge the discovery process uses the universal relation, then we could provide maximum guarantee that potentially interesting statistical dependencies are preserved. In case of the normalized relations, it depends on how the discovery process is performed on multiple relations. For instance, if the discovery process works on relations independently, then we may never discover a relationship between Average House Price and the Product Purchased in the relations of Figure 3.

For validating the completeness/incompleteness of the discovered knowledge, we propose to analyze the discovered rules (known as statistical dependencies) with the available functional dependencies (known as domain knowledge). If new dependencies are generated that are not in the set of discovered rules, then we have an incomplete knowledge discovery. For example, processing the Sales relation in Figure 3, we may discover that if Zip Code=11111 then Product Purchased = Wine with some confidence. We call this a statistical dependency that indicates a correlation (with some confidence) between the Zip Code and the Product Purchased by people. Now, consider the Region relation in Figure 3, where the given dependencies are Zip Code → City and City → Average House Price which gives the derived new functional dependency Zip Code → Average House Price due to the transitive dependency. By looking at the discovered statistical dependency and the new derived (or a given dependency in general), one may deduce a relationship between the Average House Price and the Product Purchased (with some confidence). If our discovery process does not generate such a relationship, then we have an incomplete knowledge discovery that is the consequence of working on normalized relations as opposed to universal relations. The main issue in the validation process is then to generate all the statistical dependencies. Foreign key detection algorithms used in reversed engineering of databases along with a special query mechanism can be used to detect statistical dependencies (Adriaans & Zantinge, 1996).

As we noted, to provide maximum guarantee that potentially interesting statistical dependencies are preserved, the knowledge discovery process should use the universal relation (Chiang et al., 1994) as opposed to normalized relations. However, we should be careful

Copyright © 2007, Idea Group Inc. Copying or distributing in print or electronic forms without written permission of Idea Group Inc. is prohibited.

when processing a universal relation since it could mistakenly lead to discovering a known fact (i.e., a functional dependency, or FD). Note that, when we denormalize the relations (join them) to create the universal relation, we will have redundancies due to the functional dependencies among attributes. For example, consider the universal relation Sales/Regions in Figure 4. A discovery system may discover that:

>*If Zip Code = 11111 Then City = Paris*
>*If City = Paris Then AverageHousePrice = High*

The above rules indicate relationships between Zip Code and City, and between City and AverageHousePrice. These relationships, however, do not represent new discovery since they are in fact the given functional dependencies which are true.

Using Historical Data for Knowledge Discovery

Knowledge discovery from operational/detailed or summary data alone may not reveal trends and long-term patterns in data. Historical data should be an essential part of any discovery system in order to discover patterns that are correct over data gathered for a number of years as well as the current data. For example, we may discover from current data a pattern indicating an increase in student enrollment in the universities in the Washington, DC area (perhaps due to good Economy). Such a pattern may not be true when we look at the last five years of data.

There are several schemes that could be identified in using historical data in order to improve the overall knowledge discovery process. In the following, we propose schemes that could help us to detect undiscovered patterns from detailed and summary data, and to validate the consistency/accuracy/completeness of the discovered patterns from the detailed/summary data.

1.   **Validate discovered knowledge from detailed/summary data against historical data:** We can apply the discovered rules from detailed and/or summary data to the historical data to see if they hold. If the rules are strong enough, they should hold on the historical data. A discovered rule is inconsistent with the database if examples in the database exist that satisfy the condition part of the rule, but not the conclusion part (Giarrantanto & Riley, 1989; Keller, 1994). A knowledge base (i.e., set of discovered rules from detailed and summary data) is inconsistent with the database if there is an inconsistent rule in the knowledge base. A knowledge base is incomplete with respect to the database if examples exist in the database that do not satisfy the condition part of any consistent rule.

If there are inconsistent rules, we have some historical data that contradict the rules discovered from detailed/summary data. It means we may have anomalies in some of the historical data. This is the case where any knowledge from external data, domain expert, and/or domain knowledge could be used to verify the inconsistencies. Similarly, if we have an incomplete knowledge base, some historical data could represent new patterns or some anomalies. Again, additional information (i.e., domain expert) is necessary to verify that.

Copyright © 2007, Idea Group Inc. Copying or distributing in print or electronic forms without written permission of Idea Group Inc. is prohibited.

2. **Compare the rules discovered from detailed/summary data with the ones from historical data:** We perform the knowledge discovery on the historical data and compare the rules discovered from the historical data (call it H_RuleSet) with the ones discovered from detailed/summary data (call it DS_RuleSet). There are several possibilities:

    a. If H_RuleSet $\cap$ DS_RuleSet $= \varnothing$, then none of the rules discovered from detailed/summary data hold on the historical data.

    b. If H_RuleSet $\cap$ DS_RuleSet $= X$, then:

        •   If DS_RuleSet - X $= \varnothing$, then all of the rules discovered from detailed/summary data hold on the historical data.

        •   If X $\subset$ DS_RuleSet, then there are some rules discovered from detailed/summary data that do not hold on the historical data (i.e., N_RuleSet - X). We can find the data in the historical data that do not support the rules discovered from the detailed/summary data by finding the data that support the rules in N-RuleSet and subtract them from the entire historical data. This data can then be analyzed for anomalies.

    c. If H_RuleSet - DS_RuleSet $!= \varnothing$ (or DS_RuleSet $\subset$ X), then there are some rules discovered from historical data that are not in the set of rules discovered from the detailed/summary data. This means we discovered some new patterns.

Conclusion and Future Direction

Current database technology involves processing a large volume of data in databases in order to discover new knowledge. Most of the knowledge discovery process has been on the operational (most recent) data. Knowledge discovery on just the detailed/recent data does not reveal all patterns that exist in the organizational data nor could it be consistent/accurate.

We showed that rule discovery in operational relational databases could lead to incomplete and inaccurate discovery. Relational databases are normalized in order to prevent update anomalies. In addition, operational databases contain mainly the most recent/detailed data. We need an environment where the detailed data as well as the summary and historical data are provided in order to have an effective discovery process. We showed how the discovered patterns from summary data can be used to validate the discovered patterns from the detailed operational data. Also, we described the process for using the discovered patterns from the historical data to validate the patterns discovered from the detailed/summary data.

We have done some manual testing of the proposed schemes for detecting the anomalies on the discovered rules. The IDIS (2000) knowledge discovery tool was used on a PC on dataset related to the accident with fatality (we used the data available in the U.S. Department of Transportation). We used the detailed data as well as the summarized data. We should note that the IDIS tool discovered a lot of trivial, inaccurate, inconsistent rules on both the detailed and summarized data. We manually checked the results from the two sets of data. The initial results indicate that we are able to detect anomalies on the discovered rules using the schemes provided in this chapter. Once implemented, this validation tool can be connected to a discovery tool. Then, the generated rules from the discovery tool are given to our validation tool for further processing. The results from the validation tool can be made available to the discovery tool to refine its discovery process.

Copyright © 2007, Idea Group Inc. Copying or distributing in print or electronic forms without written permission of Idea Group Inc. is prohibited.

There are several issues/concerns that need to be addressed before we could have an effective knowledge discovery process in databases. The following are some of the main issues.

1.   A major issue is the size of the databases, which are getting bigger and bigger (Chattratichat, Darlington, & Ghahem, 1997). The larger a database, the richer its patterns; and as the database grows, the more patterns it includes. However, after a point, if we analyze "too large" a portion of a database, patterns from different data segments begin to dilute each other and the number of useful patterns begins to decrease (Parsaye, 1997). To find useful patterns in a large database, we could select segments to data that fit a particular discovery objective, prepare it for analysis and then perform data discovery. As we segment, we deliberately focus into a subset of the data (i.e., a particular medication for a disease), sharpening the focus of the analysis. Alternatively, data sampling can be used for faster data analysis (Kivinen & Mannila, 1994). However, when we sample data, we lose information because we throw away data not knowing what we keep and what we ignore. Summarization may be used to reduce data sizes; although, it can cause problems too, as we noted. Currently, we are trying to define criteria which one could use to manage the large volume of data in the KDD process.

2.   Traditionally, most of the data in a database has come from internal operational systems such as order entry, inventory, or human resource data. However, external sources (i.e., demographic, economic, point-of-sale, market feeds, and Internet) are becoming more and more prevalent and will soon be providing more content to the data warehouse than the internal sources. The next question is how we process these external sources efficiently to retrieve relevant information and discover new knowledge that could explain the behavior of the internal data accurately. We are investigating this aspect of the KDD.

3.   While promising, the available discovery schemes and tools are limited in many ways. A major restriction of these tools/techniques is that most of them operate on a single data relation to generate the rules. Many existing databases, however, are not stored as single relations, but as several relations for reasons of nonredundancy or access efficiency. For databases with several interrelated relations, the relevant data relations are to be joined in order to create a single relation, called a universal relation (UR) (Date, 2000; Maier, 1983). As we mentioned before, a UR could reveal more interesting patterns. However, from a data mining point of view, this could lead to many issues such as universal relations of unmanageable sizes, infiltration of uninteresting attributes, and inconveniences for distributed processing. Currently, we are considering the problem of knowledge discovery in multirelation databases (Ribeiro, Kaufman, & Kerschberg, 1995; Wrobel, 1997; Yoon & Kerschberg, 1993; Zhong & Yamashita, 1998).

4.   Finally, current discovery tools, such as IDIS (2000), produce rules that are at times inaccurate, incomplete, inconsistent, and trivial. Our future plan is to study the implementation of the processes (algorithms) defined in this chapter for validating (or detecting) the consistency, accuracy, and completeness of the discovered rules.

Copyright © 2007, Idea Group Inc. Copying or distributing in print or electronic forms without written permission of Idea Group Inc. is prohibited.

References

Adriaans, P., & Zantinge, D. (1996). *Data mining.* Reading, MA: Addison-Wesley.

Agrawal, R., Imielinski, T., & Swami, A. (1993). Database mining: A performance perspective. *IEEE Transactions on Knowledge and Data Engineering, 5*(6), 914-925.

Barquin, R., & Edelstein, H. A. (1997). *Building, using, and managing the data warehouse.* Upper Saddle River, NJ: Prentice Hall PTR.

Berry, M., & Linoff, G. (2000). Mastering data mining. New York: John Wiley & Sons.

Bischoff, J., & Alexander, T. (1997). *Data warehouse: Practical advise from the expert.* Upper Saddle River, NJ: Prentice Hall.

Brachman, R. J., & Anand, T. (1996). The process of knowledge discovery in databases. In U. M. Fayyad, G. Piatetsky-Shapiro, & P. Symth (Eds.), *Advances in knowledge discovery and data mining* (pp. 37-57). Menlo Park, CA: AAAI Press/The MIT Press.

Brachman, R. J., Khabaza, T., Kloesgen, W., Piatetsky-Shapiro, G., & Simoudis, E. (1996). Mining business databases. *Communications of the ACM, 39,* 42-28.

Bradley, P., Gehrke, J., Ramakrishnan, R., & Srikant, R. (2002). Scalling mining algorithms to large databases. *Communications of the ACM, 45*(8), 38-43.

Chattratichat, J., Darlington, J., & Ghahem, M. (1997, August 14-17). Large scale data mining: Challenges and responses. In *Proceedings of the 3rd International Conference on Knowledge Discovery and Data Mining,* Newport Beach, CA (pp. 143-146).

Chiang, R. H. L., Barron, T. M., & Storey, V. C. (1994, July 31-August 4). Extracting domain semantics for knowledge discovery in relational databases. In *Proceedings of the AAAI Workshop on Knowledge Discovery in Databases*, Seattle, WA (pp. 299-310).

Date, C. J. (2000). *An introduction to database systems* (7th ed.). Reading, MA: Addison-Wesley.

Fayyad, U. (1996). Data mining and knowledge discovery: Making sense out of data. *IEEE Expert, 11,* 20-25.

Fayyad, U., Piatetsky-Shapiro, G., & Symth, P. (1996a). The KDD process for extracting useful knowledge from volumes of data. *Communications of the ACM, 39,* 27-33.

Fayyad, U., Piatetsky-Shapiro, G., & Symth, P. (1996b, August 2-4). Knowledge discovery and data mining: Towards a unifying framework. In *Proceedings of the Second International Conference on Knowledge Discovery and Data Mining,* Portland, OR (pp. 82-88).

Fayyad, U., Piatetsky-Shapiro, G., & Symth, P. (1996c). From data mining to knowledge discovery: An overview. In U. Fayyad, G. Piatetsky-Shapiro, & P. Symth (Eds.), *Advances in knowledge discovery and data mining* (pp. 1-34). Menlo Park, CA: AAAI/MIT Press.

Fayyad, U., & Uthurusamy, R. (2002). Evolving data mining into solution for insights. *Communications of the ACM, 45*(8), 28-31.

Frawley, W. J., Piatetsky-Shapiro, G., & Matheus, C. J. (1992). Knowledge discovery in databases: An overview. *AI Magazine, 14*(3), 57-70.

Ganti, V., Gebrke, J., & Ramakrishnan, R. (1999). Mining very large databases. *IEEE Computer, 32*(8), 38-45.

Giarrantanto, J., & Riley, G. (1989). *Expert systems: Principles and programming.* Boston: PWS-Kent Publishing Company.

Copyright © 2007, Idea Group Inc. Copying or distributing in print or electronic forms without written permission of Idea Group Inc. is prohibited.

Groth, R. (1998). *Data mining: A hands-on approach for business professionals.* Englewood Cliffs, NJ: Prentice Hall.

Han, J., & Kamber, M. (2000). *Data mining: Concepts and techniques.* San Francisco: Morgan Kaufmann.

Hand, D., Mannila, H., & Smyth, P. (2001). *Principles of data mining.* Cambridge, MA: MIT Press.

IDIS. (2000). *The information discovery system user's manual.* Los Angeles: Intelligence-Ware.

Inmon, W. H. (1996). The data warehouse and data mining. *Communications of the ACM, 39,* 49-50.

John, G. H., & Langley, P. (1996, August 2-4). Static versus dynamic sampling for data mining. In *Proceedings of the 2nd International Conference on Knowledge Discovery and Data Mining,* Portland, OR (pp. 367-370).

Keller, R. (1994). *Expert system technology: Development and application.* New York: Yourdon Press.

Keyes, J. (1990, February). Branching to the right system: Decision-tree software. *AI EXPERT,* 61-64.

Kivinen, J., & Mannila, H. (1994, May). The power of sampling in knowledge discovery. In *Proceedings of the 1994 ACM SIGACT-SIGMOD-SIGACT Symposium on Principles of Database Theory (PODS'94),* Minneapolis, MN (pp. 77-85).

Maier, D. (1983). *The theory of relational databases.* Potamac, MD: Computer Science Press.

Matheus, C. J., Chan, P. K., & Piatetsky-Shapiro, G. (1993). Systems for knowledge discovery in databases. *IEEE Transactions on Knowledge and Data Engineering, 5*(6), 903-913.

Meredith, M. E., & Khader, A. (1996, June). Designing large warehouses. *Database Programming & Design, 9*(6), 26-30.

Parsaye, K. (1996, September). Data mines for data warehouses. *Database Programming & Design, 9*(Suppl).

Parsaye, K. (1997, February). OLAP & Data mining: Bridging the gap. *Database Programming & Design, 10*(2), 31-37.

Parsaye, K. (1998, September). Small data, small knowledge: The pitfalls of sampling and summarization. *Information Discovery Inc.* Retrieved April 6, 2006, from http://www.datamining.com/datamine/ds- start1.htm

Parsaye, K., & Chignell, M. (1999). *Intelligent database tools and applications: Hyperinformation access, data quality, visualization, automatic discovery.* New York: John Wiley & Sons.

Piatetsky-Shapiro, G. (1991). Discovery, analysis, and presentation of strong rules. *Knowledge Discovery in Databases, 229-247.* Menlo Park, CA: AAAI Press.

Piatetsky-Shapiro, G., & Matheus, G. (1994, July). The interestingness of deviations. In *Proceedings of the AAAI-94 Workshop on KDD,* Seattle, WA (pp. 25-36).

Ribeiro, J. S., Kaufman, K. A., & Kerschberg, L. (1995, June 7-9). Knowledge discovery from multiple databases. *IASTED/ISMM International Conference, Intelligent Information Management Systems,* Washington, DC.

Sarawagi, S., Thomas, S., & Agrawal, R. (1998). Integrating association rule mining with relational database systems: Alternatives and implications. *ACM SIGMOD Record, 27*(2), 343-354.

Copyright © 2007, Idea Group Inc. Copying or distributing in print or electronic forms without written permission of Idea Group Inc. is prohibited.

Savasere, A., Omiecinski, E., & Navathe, S. (1995). An efficient algorithm for mining association rules in large databases. In *Proceedings of the 21ˢᵗ International Conference on Very Large Data Bases* (pp. 432-444). San Fransisco: Morgan Kaufmann.

Silberschatz, A., & Tuzhilin, A. (1995, August 20-21). On subjective measures of interestingness in knowledge discovery. In *Proceedings of the 1ˢᵗ International Conference on Knowledge Discovery and Data Mining,* Montreal, Quebec, Canada.

Simoudis, E. (1996). Reality check for data mining. *IEEE Expert, 11*, 26-33.

Smyth, P., Pregibon, D., & Faloutsos, C. (2002). Data driven evolution of data mining algorithms. *Communications of the ACM, 45*(8), 33-37.

Uthurusamy, R. (1996). From data mining to knowledge discovery: Current challenges and future directions. In U. M. Fayyad, G. Piatetsky-Shapiro & Symth, P. (Ed.), *Advances in knowledge discovery and data mining* (pp. 561-569). Menlo Park, CA: AAAI Press/The MIT Press.

Wrobel, S. (1997). An algorithm for multi-relational discovery of subgroups. In J. Komorowsk &. J. Zytkow (Eds.), *Principles of data mining and knowledge discovery* (LNAI 1263, pp. 367-375). Springer-Verlag.

Yoon, J. P., & Kerschberg, L. (1993). A framework for knowledge discovery and evolution in databases *IEEE Transactions on Knowledge and Data Engineering, 5*(6), 973-979.

Zhong, N., & Yamashita, S. (1998, May 27-30). A way of multi-database mining. In *Proceedings of the IASTED International Conference on Artificial Intelligence and Soft Computing*, Cancun, Mexico (pp. 384-387).

Ziarko, W. (1991). The discovery, analysis, and presentation of data dependencies in databases. *Knowledge Discovery in Databases*, 195-209. Menlo Park, CA: AAAI/MIT Press.

Copyright © 2007, Idea Group Inc. Copying or distributing in print or electronic forms without written permission of Idea Group Inc. is prohibited.

Chapter IV

Relativity of Information Quality:
Ontological vs. Teleological, Internal vs. External View

Zbigniew J. Gackowski, California State University Stanislaus, USA

Abstract

This chapter presents a qualitative inquiry into the universe of quality attributes of symbolic representation such as data and information values. It offers a rationale for a move from the internal toward the external, from the ontological to the teleological perspective. The focus is on approaches that derive attributes from established theories. The special relativity of quality as applied to information values is discussed at various levels of viewing those attributes within business-decision contexts. Four cases offer examples of top-down, dataflow-up examination of quality attributes to demonstrate the potential of the teleological perspective. A rationale for a broader use of qualified names for quality attributes is given. The evolutional, by Liu and Chi (2002), and the purpose-focused, by Gackowski (2004, 2005a,

Copyright © 2007, Idea Group Inc. Copying or distributing in print or electronic forms without written permission of Idea Group Inc. is prohibited.

2005b), views of operations quality offer new potential for integrating the present theoretical contributions into a more complete, cohesive, and pragmatic model. Examples begin with the quantity and utility value of information, the direct primary attributes of quality, some of the direct secondary attributes, and end with samples of indirect attributes.

Introduction

This chapter presents a qualitative inquiry into the universe of operations quality requirements of information and the corresponding research directions. There is an urgent need to recognize the undeniable relativity of quality within the context of business applications and decision-making and, subsequently, to move from the solely internal toward the external, from the ontological toward the teleological perspective of quality.

In the literature review, Liu and Chi (2002) categorized different approaches as intuitive, empirical, and theoretical. Initially, the intuitive and the empirical approaches were most prevalent, but they lack theoretical foundations about how these attributes are defined and grouped. They identified four theories: mathematical theory of communications, information economics, ontological mappings, and operations research. Nevertheless, they concluded, "Existing theoretical approaches are limited in their ability to derive a full-fledged measurement model," and a "generally accepted model has not yet appeared" (p. 292). In their response, they proposed a concept of evolutional and theory-specific information quality that evolves along the stages of data collection, organization, presentation, and application.

This inquiry stays within the theoretical approaches, which promise results that are of a more lasting validity. The theoretical approaches derive attributes from established theories. There are also frequent references to quality attributes derived from operations research, management science, and decision science in the purpose-focused view presented by Gackowski (2004, 2005a, 2005b). A discussion of the merits of both approaches is presented.

The special relativity of operations quality requirements that pertains to data and information values is discussed at the two major levels of information support: operations and management. A rationale for a top-down, dataflow-up examination of operations quality requirements is given. Four case-based examples (news media, one-time strategic business opportunity, simple business transaction processing, and an inventory-control information system that supports inventory management) illustrate the applicability and the potential of the teleological perspective of operations quality. Examples begin with a discussion of the controversial *quantity or amount of information* and *utility value of information*. They are followed by short discussions of the direct primary tentatively universal operations quality requirements, the direct secondary attributes, whether mandatory or not; and some examples of the indirect attributes that affect the direct primary and direct secondary ones, as defined by Gackowski (2004, 2005a, 2005b). There is a by-product of this discussion: a rationale for changing the naming convention of some of the basic operations quality attributes. One needs a broader use of qualified names to better reflect the multiple aspects of those attributes.

To develop a full-fledged qualitative framework of operations quality, one must reach beyond the empirical survey-based assessment of frequently loosely and haphazardly defined attributes of operations quality. This happens easily when they are not defined within the context of their actual use. The correctness and completeness of the empirical results

Copyright © 2007, Idea Group Inc. Copying or distributing in print or electronic forms without written permission of Idea Group Inc. is prohibited.

cannot be proven via fundamental principles; therefore, empirical studies are not discussed here. From the pure science view, the energy spent on those studies is lost for research of broader and more lasting effects. However, empirical studies may yield immediate practical improvements. Similarly, efforts spent on developing better, but not well founded, metrics for assessment of empirically derived quality attributes are secondary to the importance of a stronger qualitative framework for assessing the basic quality attributes in their multiple aspects. The evolutional, by Liu and Chi (2002), and the purpose-focused, by Gackowski (2004, 2005a, 2005b), views offer new potential for integrating the present theoretical contributions into a more complete, cohesive, and pragmatic model.

The main objective of this chapter is to demonstrate:

- The special relativity of operations quality of any symbolic representations
- The absolute dominance of the external over the internal view of operations quality
- The use of data is not and should not be outside the information system designers' control
- The need for moving from the ontological to the teleological perspective
- How the perspective of operations quality dramatically changes when moving from the operational to the management support level
- The need for qualified names for operations quality requirements that can reflect their multifaceted aspects

Literature Review

In 1949, within the mathematical theory of communications,[2] Shannon and Weaver defined the amount of information (A_I) transmitted as a function of its probability (p_I); that is, $A_I = -\log_2 p_I$. The formula yields a number that indicates the rarity or the surprise effect associated with an object, event, or state represented by the received signal or value. Other attributes of information encoding can be derived from this one: encoding capacity of communication channels or data fields, absolute and relative information encoding efficiency and redundancy, and so forth. It also enables calculation of the cost effectiveness of storing and processing data and information. Two decades later, Mazur (1970) developed a generalized qualitative communication theory that eliminated the assumptions of probabilities and arrived at the same results, thus providing the ultimate rational proof of its validity. In science, use of probabilities indicates that the internal mechanics of the phenomenon is not yet fully known. How abstract the definition of amount of information sounds, it plays a direct role in news services and news media[3] such as the press, radio, and TV.

In 1968, in information economics, Kofler defined the utility value of information as the difference between the value of results of actions or business operations while acting with and without it. The assumptions are that the decision makers, while making decisions and acting accordingly, use some data (**D**) known to them. An incoming piece of information (**I**) may change the decision situation from what they know represented by state **D** to state **D + I**. Then, the *utility value of information V(I),*[4] or its impact on business results, is the difference between the value of results V_R of actions or business operations while acting with $V_R(D + I)$ and without it $V_R(D)$. It can be calculated only under the assump-

Copyright © 2007, Idea Group Inc. Copying or distributing in print or electronic forms without written permission of Idea Group Inc. is prohibited.

tion that *the results of business operations can be measured and evaluated* although not necessarily in monetary units. The same formula covers the utility value of a lost piece of a previously available data item that significantly affects the outcomes. From this definition, other related attributes can be derived, such as its net utility value, and simple and expected cost effectiveness. Most authors of MIS textbooks do not pay attention to these attributes, or they pay lip service only. It is amazing that Alter, the author of an MIS textbook (2002), ironically describes this simple and highly pragmatic definition of utility value of information as "more elegant than practical" (p. 162).

In 1996, based on ontological foundations, Wand and Wang (1996) proposed four quality attributes (complete, unambiguous, meaningful, and correct). Within the confines of the assumptions used,[5] Liu and Chi (2002, p. 294) write, "those attributes have crystal-clear definitions and theoretically sound justification, but they constitute only a small subset of known attributes leaving the rest unspecified." There is, however, another problem. These attributes were labeled intrinsic to data, but they are intrinsic to information system design and operations. They were derived from design and operations deficiencies, not the data content deficiencies. Casual readers of secondary sources, in particular, are lured into believing that, for instance, "incompleteness" of data has been defined, whereas actually the designer of an information system did not provide enough states for proper representation of the selected states of reality. All of the proposed attributes are logical or engineering requirements of an information system that assure its *correct* internal functioning. They are necessary but insufficient requirements for a successful business information system. Their ultimate success depends on a purpose-focused selection of those real-world states that needs to be reckoned with in decision making. Thus, results come only from a sufficient combination of necessary requirements defined from both the teleological and the ontological perspective. Within the purpose- and content-focused, and impact-determined, taxonomy by Gackowski (2004, 2005a, 2005b), by the law of relativity there is no room for operations quality requirements that are intrinsic to the data content or value. The system design and system operations quality requirements are a precondition of an accurate representation of reality, hence a precondition of proper data accuracy (meant here as free from errors) and precision (meant here as the number of significant digits or dots per inch) that are contributing to credibility of any symbolic representation.

Despite careful explanations provided by the authors, the remaining attributes are similarly confusing to usually unsuspecting business-oriented individuals. Simply, they are *only* design requirements for *complete, unambiguous, meaningful,* and *correct mapping of real-world states into information-system states*. Their definitions suggest very little of what casual business users would expect from complete, unambiguous, correct, and meaningful data used in operations viewed from the external perspective. A proposed remedy for this unintended confusion is the qualified naming of those attributes, such as *complete mapping, unambiguous mapping, correct mapping,* and so forth. This comment is the first attempt to address the issue that the currently prevalent generic names of quality attributes are insufficient to reflect their multiple aspects. Their unqualified names cause unintended confusion, which is not limited to this case. Other examples will follow.

In 2002, in an evolutional and theory-specific approach to data quality, Liu and Chi tried to overcome the weaknesses of the product-analogy-based approach and the narrowness of the ontological approach, which is limited to the internal view only. They claim that data have meaning only through a theory. As data evolve through the stages of the data-evolution life cycle (DELC), they undergo a sequence of transformations and exist

Copyright © 2007, Idea Group Inc. Copying or distributing in print or electronic forms without written permission of Idea Group Inc. is prohibited.

independently as different morphons (captured data, organized data, presented data, and utilized data). Each transformation introduces independent errors such as measurement errors during data collection, data-entry errors during data organization, and interpretation biases in data presentation. Different theories apply to different stages of the DELC; hence, different definitions to measure the quality of those morphons are needed. Instead of a single universal concept of DQ, four hierarchical quality views are used for data collection, organization, presentation, and application. They measure, respectively, the quality of collected data, stored data, presented data, and utilized data. The evolutionary nature of the four views implies that the quality of data at earlier stages of DELC contribute to the data quality at later stages. The authors suggest a monotonically increasing order of specificity of the four hierarchical views of DQ.

Liu and Chi developed two complementary approaches to derive attributes and develop semantically valid measurement models for collection, organization, presentation, and application quality. The first is concerned with data errors during data evolution. A fishbone diagram shows the causes that contribute to poor quality. The causes were identified from literature surveys and brainstorming sessions. Some of them were grouped into parsimonious categories. Then the authors explained the causes, derived corresponding measurement attributes, and developed measurement models.

Certainly, the concept of evolutional and theory-specific data quality (ETSDQ) is a landmark. It addresses new issues, never or rarely discussed before, but it is also burdened with serious drawbacks. One may argue that data derive their meaning, relevance, and utility value from their use for task-specific purposes only. A theory may only explain it for us. Another drawback is that the data is not treated as other resources that require similar attention as the 4 Ms (methods, machines, materials, and manpower). They all, in their own way, serve the same operations' purposes. Why incur the cost of acquisition, storing, presentation, and utilization of data for no defined purposes of higher value? Data collection should be guided by the specific purposes they are designed to serve. It is a postulate of sound business economics. Sound systems analysis teaches also that the hierarchical examination of quality should be top down and dataflow up; the requirements of data-application quality should determine the requirements for data-presentation quality, in turn, the data-organization quality, and finally, the data-collection or acquisition quality.

There are many issues, less with the concept itself and more with the way it is presented.

- Assuming the authors' definition of theory, one may say that the collection quality is determined by the pertinent data-collection theory, which, however, cannot ignore the requirements of theories used for data application, presentation, and organization.
- Data-collection quality may be impaired by falsifications, observation biases, and measurement errors. The authors discuss them, however, from the least to the most dangerous. If outright falsification cannot be excluded, there is no point in worrying about the subtleties of bias or random measurement errors.
- The evolutional concept of data quality suggests a monotonically increasing *complexity* rather than specificity (Liu & Chi, 2002).
- Completeness is considered a function of collection theory only. Completeness should be viewed mainly from the point of the data application's purpose. One may argue that the role of collection theories is rather to fine-tune the data collection, for instance, to become more cost effective by using proper sampling.

Copyright © 2007, Idea Group Inc. Copying or distributing in print or electronic forms without written permission of Idea Group Inc. is prohibited.

- In its current version, the evolutional approach leads also to a myopic view of data quality. When discussing the data-organization quality, the authors express concern about missing data values. They are right, but they do it from the pure formal technical viewpoint only, whether a relational model or XML is used for storing data. Where is the importance of completeness for business applications?[6]
- Under data-application quality, the authors discuss relevance and the proper amount of information (probably meant as number of data values, not as it is defined in communications theory) as separate fundamental criteria to all theories. However, there are two sides to the issue. What is not relevant is irrelevant. Does it affect only application quality? Should we not eliminate irrelevant data from the data-collection process from the very beginning? By definition, when one identifies all information values that are relevant or of significant impact, one cannot add anything more, as it must be irrelevant. Similarly, one cannot ignore any of the relevant or of the significant-impact values; otherwise, they become incomplete for the task.
- Interpretability, defined here as data with clear meaning, is discussed very late under presentation quality. Is it not too late to worry about the clear meaning of data during their presentation only, and not during their collection? Within the purpose-focused teleological view (Gackowski, 2004, 2005a, 2005b), interpretability is rightly considered the *first* direct primary tentatively universal operations quality requirement. If this condition is not met, one should cease examining all the remaining quality attributes of such a questionable value.

In 2004, anchoring the concept of data/information quality in operations research, management science, and decision science, Gackowski (2004, 2005a, 2005b) proposed a purpose-focused perspective derived from operations purposes. It is done in four steps:

1. Development of a relatively complete qualitative cause/effect diagram, known as a fishbone diagram, to identify the major factors impacting the desired business results
2. Impact analysis and evaluation of the relative strength of each factor identified before
3. Development of a symbolic model of the decision situation by taking inventory of what is already known (*data values*) and what is unknown (*information values*), and must be acquired by business intelligence, and then ranking each value by its impact on the operational outcomes by any agreed measures[7]
4. Examination of each representation value with regard to the operations quality requirements

This approach enables a hierarchical impact-determined taxonomy of the entire universe of operations quality requirements into those that are direct and indirect, the direct into primary and secondary ones and the primary into universal and situation specific ones. It defines the necessary and sufficient conditions of effective usability of information values and two levels of their usefulness, that is, the general and the economical or cost-effective usefulness (Gackowski, 2005a, 2005b). It also facilitates a simplified, time-saving, and economical examination sequence of the direct primary tentatively universal quality requirements.

This approach views representation values (data, information) within a universal pragmatic context, which illuminates their specific role and significance. It is applicable

Copyright © 2007, Idea Group Inc. Copying or distributing in print or electronic forms without written permission of Idea Group Inc. is prohibited.

not only at the operational, but also at the strategic levels of management. Where necessary, it requires a clear distinction of data (the known, given, or assumed) and information (the unknown to be yet acquired) defined by its utilitarian functions when it qualitatively changes the decision situation itself and/or changes the actions that implement the decisions made, and/or quantitatively changes the results. It is, however, still a research in progress. Nevertheless, the soundness of the presented rationale for this kind of approach to quality has not yet been challenged. The latter may elevate the assessment of IQ from mainly the operational level to the *strategic level* of applications in business and administration, including applications related to national security.

Relativity of Operations Quality

Accepting the widely adopted definition of *quality* as "fitness for use," one notices that it is the *use* of values that determines what *fits*. Thus, quality is determined by the use of data or information (Wand & Wang, 1996). Some authors see it as a problem, others as an advantage. It is a problem when one limits the view of the information system designers' view and the faithful representation of the known aspects of the world within an information system only (Wand & Wang, 1996). This may be proper, to a limited degree, in the design of general-purpose systems. In business and in public administration, system analysts and designers usually custom tailor their designs to meet specific needs of the organizations that the information systems serve. Otherwise, off-the-shelf systems would cover the majority of needs.

The assessment of how well values fit their intended use is determined by the prevalent view of what is important in their use. Such a view acts like a force field that *determines* all aspects of quality *of whatever is used*, not only of data and information. Analogous to motion in physics, the use of symbolic representations changes with its purpose (in physics, the observation point) and the circumstances (in physics, the frame of reference) and thus changes the assessment of any operations quality requirements for whatever is used.

The *special relativity of operations quality of representation values (data or information)* means here that it is always determined by the purpose and the circumstances of the operations where the values are used. It pertains to all types of representations of the real-world states. (The qualifier, "special," denotes that this chapter discusses relativity of quality as applicable exclusively to symbolic representations such as data, information, and knowledge (meant as rules of reasoning) in contrast to the general relativity of operations quality of anything used (products, raw materials, services, human skills, etc.). By this law, *no operations quality attributes can be intrinsic* to the symbolic representation values, per se. Some of them may be intrinsic to something else, for instance, to the system design, but not to the data values. One cannot deny that the required design-intrinsic completeness of representations is always ultimately determined by the needs of their use. If delivery systems of nanoprecision do not yet exist, they will be designed and delivered, because otherwise they could not meet the quality requirements of their intended use. It seems at present that no intrinsic quality attribute of any symbolic representation has yet been identified.

In tightly run, cohesively bonded organizations, views focused on strategic business purposes dominate. Otherwise, the local and particular views, whether individual or group,

Copyright © 2007, Idea Group Inc. Copying or distributing in print or electronic forms without written permission of Idea Group Inc. is prohibited.

have the upper hand. The latter are guided by local interests and preferences. When this happens, a gradual disintegration of organizations begins.

This does not mean that limited approaches to quality are entirely without merit, particularly in research. Severe limitations in viewing quality enabled Wand and Wang (1996) to define rigorously, for example, the system design and operations intrinsic attributes of complete, unambiguous, meaningful, and correct mapping of reality into states of the information system. Confusion arises when others refer to those attributes without properly qualifying the names.

After successes within the realm of pure engineering requirements and database-management systems in particular (Nauman & Roth, 2004), it is time to move upward toward a broader definition of quality that can also be used in specifications of user requirements. It means a move from a purely internal to a broader external view of quality, from a purpose- and use-independent view to one that is purpose and use dependent. The internal view leads toward defining only the engineering requirements of quality, which are under the exclusive control of designers. The external view leads toward defining user requirements of quality that are under the control of users and belong to the realm of management disciplines. For a correct assessment of quality, both views are important, but they are not of the same weight. One may strongly argue that the external view carries the dominant weight, for it is derived from the ultimate purpose of information systems applications. This can be explained well when one realizes the different levels of viewing quality.

Levels of Viewing Operations Quality and Research Priorities

One can distinguish several perspectives of viewing the operations quality of data and information. On one hand, there is the internal view of the designers, which is system centric. This view is clearly independent of the data use and purpose. On the other hand, there is the external view that is use centric, application centric, or better, purpose centric. The internal view is delivery system centric focused on a correct and reliable implementation of the mapping requirements (complete, unambiguous, meaningful, and correct), secure storing and processing of data, and making them available to authorized users. The external view is focused on the purpose of operations to be served, the acquisition of the necessary information, its convenient presentation, and cost-effective use.

Any full-fledged research framework should reflect the relative nature of quality. In MIS, there is a general accepted (O'Brien, 2003, 2004) categorization of information systems into operations support information systems and management (support) information systems (MIS). The latter support is distinctively different at different levels of management: (a) strategic or executive, (b) tactical or middle, and (c) operational or supervisory.

These distinctions provide a helpful insight into the potential problems with quality. For simplicity, the discussion of the operations support systems is limited to transaction-processing systems (TPS) and excludes process-control systems (PCS), computer-aided design (CAD), computer-aided manufacturing (CAM), and enterprise collaboration systems (ECS) (O'Brien, 2003, 2004). Transaction-processing systems provide a real *foundation* for practically all the remaining types of business-information systems. No other business-information system can be developed and operated when routine, daily business transaction processing

Copyright © 2007, Idea Group Inc. Copying or distributing in print or electronic forms without written permission of Idea Group Inc. is prohibited.

has not been successfully implemented. The rationale for considering TPS as fundamental lies in the fact that *transaction-processing systems* capture, store, process, and retrieve transaction data for input to other types of business-information systems. MIS requires and depends heavily on properly functioning transaction-processing systems. (They were the main domains of traditional data-processing systems.) The way of developing higher level MIS is to begin with the deployment of transaction-processing systems first.

In their pure version, transaction-processing systems should faithfully keep track of the current state of the business reality and account for all the changes that took place. They use as input simple deterministic data that are documented consistently with the general accepted accounting principles (GAAP). At the operational level, there is rarely a need for distinguishing data from information. In routine applications, one does not yet ask inquisitive questions about why the data are needed, how they will be used, or to what business purpose they contribute. Simply, they are required to satisfy GAAP. Those principles also determine data-quality requirements, including their credibility, precision, auditing procedures, and so forth

At the level of business or administrative transaction processing, the internal view is adequate. Similarly, the empirical approaches are helpful in efforts of continuous quality improvements. This also explains why most of transaction processing can be accomplished with off-the-shelf application software packages.

However, the same assumptions for assessing data/information quality, when applied to situations pertinent to management-support information systems, are grossly inadequate. At this level, a qualitative change in thinking about quality is necessary to face the completely different situations. Any upward movement toward the management-support information systems that assist in attaining business goals requires a bold paradigm shift in thinking from the (1) ontological toward the teleological view; (2) internal toward the external view; (3) survey-based toward the theory-based and theory-specific view; (4) engineering requirements' toward the user requirements' view; (5) design intrinsic to the situation-specific operations quality requirements; and (6) simple generic attribute names toward the more refined qualified naming of quality attributes that represent their situation-specific aspects.

While developing management-support information systems, one must analyze the top-down and flow-up quality of data/information at different stages of the system development cycle (SDLC):

1. The desired purposes, outcomes, and strategies of attaining them
2. The decision situations, related theories, decision-making processes, and decision makers
3. The data and information about all factors of significant impact on the outcomes
4. A cost-effective presentation of the required data/information in a form and format preferred by the current end users
5. Cost-effective computer applications that generate the required presentations
6. A cost-effective delivery system of the required data/information (entry, storage, and retrieval)
7. A cost-effective gathering of the required input data/information

The form and format of data/information presentation is usually differentiated for end users at different levels of decision making, such as the nonmanagerial, supervisory, tactical, and strategic. When viewing quality attributes from different levels of decision making,

Copyright © 2007, Idea Group Inc. Copying or distributing in print or electronic forms without written permission of Idea Group Inc. is prohibited.

one immediately notices a strong shift in emphasis on different groups of quality attributes. At the strategic level, when using the purpose-focused approach, the operations triggering completeness[8] of actionably credible[9] information on the most urgent threats are the most important of the direct primary quality attributes. At the tactical level, the most important quality attributes are likely significance of impact, operationally and timely availability, and operations triggering completeness. At the lowest level, however, all the direct secondary attributes, which mainly *quantitatively* affect the business results, are everyone's everyday concern.

With regard to stages 4, 5, and 6 of the SDLC, the system intrinsic requirements or, in other words, the engineering quality requirements, are strictly under the designers' control. Here, however, one must again take exception with the position taken by some authors that the quality of data generated by information systems depends on their design (Wand & Wang, 1996). It depends, but only partially. It depends much more on the user specifications that the designers must follow. Designers may deliver a perfectly functioning system, which, however, from the viewpoint of the desired business outcomes, may be a poor or useless system.

The same authors also stated that the actual use of data is outside of designers' control (Wand & Wang, 1996). Again, this is only partially true. It depends on how the scope of the information systems was defined, viewed, and treated, whether it ends with technical printouts or displays only, or whether the design actually supports the attainment of the stated purposes. Too many designers of business-information systems act as if their responsibility ends with the computer-generated outputs — called outright products. This purely technical attitude, proper in the development of general-purpose software, is not what business owners and managers expect. However, even in accredited schools of business or management, the systems analysis and design courses are mostly taught by young, inexperienced instructors. They may have the proper terminal doctoral degree; however, in most cases, they never managed information-system development, never participated in such projects, and never had any intimate contact with a business environment where such systems are used. Therefore, they limit themselves to teaching techniques and technical aspects of information-system analysis and design only.

In contrast, instructors with practical experience know that in business environments the system designers' responsibilities are broader. They know how to design a report or message with a built-in feedback, which literally forces the addressee to read it and, even more, to act upon it. They may insist that the users document and notify the system about the corrective actions they actually triggered. If the feedback does not meet the requirements of the organizational policies, then in effect, the system may also be designed to automatically notify the immediate higher level of management. Notification may be about absence of action, excessively delayed action, inadequate or ineffective action, and so forth. In addition, they may build in stringent auditing requirements, which, if not satisfied, may again trigger other notifications and alerts. Experienced and conscientious designers with proper business experience may incorporate many subtle tricks into their designs. Those features may nearly enforce the use of the output generated by information systems.

In schools of business or management, less in engineering schools, in research and teaching, there is a real need for moving beyond the internal view of information systems. Information systems designed and functioning correctly are the necessary preconditions of quality. Nevertheless, quality defined this way is unrelated to the desired business results, which should be the main point. The inherent relativity of operations quality or symbolic

Copyright © 2007, Idea Group Inc. Copying or distributing in print or electronic forms without written permission of Idea Group Inc. is prohibited.

representations demands that the quality must be assessed from the natural viewpoint of defined business purposes. Data and information to be of quality must fit the business purpose, and only then does it make sense to consider the quality of their presentation, their processing, and their delivery system. This implies that one must also be aware of which stages determine the quality of data/information at other stages. It seems that:

- Business purposes, strategies to attain them, and desired outcomes (stage 1), decision situations, decision-making processes, the related theories (stage 2), and those individuals responsible for the implementation of the strategy determine what they need to know, what data/information (with pertinent quality requirements) are needed (stage 3), and how they should be presented (stage 4).
- Presented outputs (stage 4) determine the computer applications that generate them (stage 5) with the pertinent quality requirements.
- Information-system applications (stage 5) determine, in turn, the quality requirements for the data/information delivery system (stage 6).
- Information system applications (stage 5) and the data/information delivery system (stage 6) determine the final operations quality requirements for the gathering data/information (stage 7).

The next question is how to prioritize the research at those levels. Only the purpose-focused impact-determined taxonomy or operations quality requirements (Gackowski, 2004, 2005a, 2005b) suggests some solid answers to this question. In general, one may argue:

1.   Attributes that *qualitatively* affect decision situations certainly deserve the *highest priority*. These are the direct primary tentative universal quality attributes (acquisition interpretable, of significant impact, operationally and timely availability, actionably credible, and operations triggering complete) for the data/information input (stage 7).
2.   Attributes that mainly *quantitatively* affect business outcomes deserve *second level priority*. These are the direct secondary quality attributes (economically acquisition interpretable, operationally and timely available, actionably credible, presentation interpretable, and economically operationally complete) that are focused on cost effectiveness of data/information presentation (stage 4), processing (stage 5), and delivery (stage 6).
3.   Attributes that only *indirectly* affect any of the direct quality attributes deserve *third level priority*.

When conducting research and planning, one must take into consideration additional questions, such as where the researchers' interests lie, where the resources are, where funding is available, where the immediate interests of business or administrative entities are backed by willingness of funding such research, and so forth. If thinking along these lines is approximately acceptable, it may offer a starting point for identifying and planning new research directions on quality in order to widen its present scope. The remaining part of the chapter consists of four business cases that illustrate the relativity of operations quality requirements.

Copyright © 2007, Idea Group Inc. Copying or distributing in print or electronic forms without written permission of Idea Group Inc. is prohibited.

Business Cases on Relativity of Quality Requirements

Discussion of Selected Theory-Based Attributes of Quality

In a discussion of theory-based attributes of data/information, one must make a rigorous distinction between data and information that in other situations might not be required. Here, this distinction is made within the context of decision situations. Decision makers or acting agents already know some aspects of the situation, but some other aspects remain unknown. Within this chapter, the *data values* are symbolic representations of aspects of reality that are known, given, or assumed true. *Reality* encompasses business organizations and their environments. Within reality, one distinguishes *entities*, which are objects or events represented symbolically by their identifiers and values of their attributes. *Information values* are symbolic representations of things, events, and unknown states that are yet to be acquired, and which change the decision situations by themselves, and/or change the operations results, and/or change the actions that implement the decisions made. From the viewpoint of the theory of communications, any symbolic representation already known contains or conveys zero (0) bits of information. Shannon and Weaver's (1949) formula for the amount of information ($A_I = -\log_2 p_I$) associates A_I bits of information with any symbolic representation of reality that is yet unknown as a function of its probability p_I. The amount of information measures the rarity or the surprise effect associated with the object, event, or state. Thus, symbolic representations of objects, events, or states, which are very unlikely, with probability (p_I) close to zero, is associated with nearly an infinite amount of information for their recipients ($A_I = -\log_2 0 = -\log_2 (1/\infty) = \log_2 \infty \approx \infty$ [bits]).

Amount of Information and Other Quality Attributes in the News Media

Within communications theory, the amount of information is used mainly for calculating the capacity of communication channels and efficiency of encoding. However, it also measures an important aspect of news for the news media. Nothing generally known or obvious makes good news. It must be extraordinary, rare, and unlikely to be considered good news. For the news media, the more unlikely an event is, the more useful it is. Reporting of rare events increases ratings, circulation, and visibility. It attracts high-paying advertisers. In addition, the higher the general appeal of the rare event to the public, the higher utility value it acquires. Its impact on business results of media may be very high. It is a business case when a *high amount of information translates into high utility value of the information*.

Users do not feel informed when the information-gathering process yields only what they already know. It never changes the outcomes of business operations. Users receive zero amount of information of zero utility value. There must be at least some amount of information to carry any utility value. Thus, between the two, there is only a qualitative

Copyright © 2007, Idea Group Inc. Copying or distributing in print or electronic forms without written permission of Idea Group Inc. is prohibited.

relationship — no direct quantitative relationship. The formulas that define the amount of information and the utility value of information are completely independent and are derived from different sets of assumptions. No direct or intrinsic relationship between the two attributes has been discovered.

The purpose-focused view of quality (Gackowski, 2005a, 2005b) emphasizes the impact an information value makes on the desired business results. In a news service, however, there is another important direct primary and mandatory requirement that enables effective translation of the amount of information into utility value for the publishers. The information value must be operationally and timely available with the exclusion of other competing actors; otherwise, it loses or has substantially diminished utility value. Everybody seems to agree that availability of data or information is a serious issue. Inconsistent with the CPA's terminology, several authors interpret timeliness as timely updated or as an aspect of information aging, instead of using a better label, "currency." Nevertheless, timely availability has at least three aspects; therefore, one needs to qualify this term also. In this case, information must be exclusively and timely available. In other words, it must be of restricted availability. The other two — operationally and timely available and economically operationally timely available — were identified before (Gackowski, 2005a, 2005b). This leads to the conclusion that at least some quality attributes currently considered simple attributes, in reality are multifaceted attributes. More examples follow.

In the news media, there is an unending race for exclusively operationally and timely available information. The most frequent casualty of this race is credibility or believability and completeness of the information. Even worse, credibility of news is frequently compromised by a strong dose of political bias by media owners, editors, and the journalists themselves who more and more represent their agenda and views than objectively report the news (reporting mixed with opinionating). Under the pressure of sensationalism or political expediency, for example, to be the very first to report something unusual, there is not much time and not much interest in checking for veracity and other mitigating circumstances. Even worse, the pressure to sensationalize the news literally leads to its invention, thus to disinformation. Many journalists succumb to the pressure to attain the highest utility value for them personally and for the editors at any cost, even when it is detrimental to their personal and their company's reputations.[10] Both attributes are never fully attainable. Both are measured by a continuum of degrees (0, 100%). If 100% is not attainable, there must be at least an acceptable minimum that triggers operations. Thus, in reality, one needs qualified terms such as *actionably credible* and *operations triggering completeness*. They are always mandatory. From the external view, they are well defined, but from the decision-makers' view, they are subjective, for they will be different for decision makers of different personalities.

Alas, the evolutional theory-based approach (Liu & Chie, 2002) omits completely the issues of the amount of information in the meaning derived from communications theory and the utility value as defined in information economics as well. It also addresses the issues of falsification, bias, accuracy, and completeness of information. These issues are important but not on their own. These questions should be asked only when the concerned data/information has been declared of significant impact. Logically, the latter two should be addressed in reverse order, for deficiencies in completeness hide much worse consequences than for instance deficiencies in accuracy.

Copyright © 2007, Idea Group Inc. Copying or distributing in print or electronic forms without written permission of Idea Group Inc. is prohibited.

Amount and Utility Value of Information in Strategic Business Decisions

This case represents the other extreme in the relation between the amount and utility value of information. This is a historical business case when enormous business opportunities hinge on a single variable of only two, possibly three values that represent the potential outcome of the event. It demonstrates how limited the present ways of thinking about quality attributes are.

In 1815, in one of the 20 most decisive battles in world history, the British, in alliance with Prussia, faced Napoleon's last-ditch effort to change the course of history, not only in Europe but also in Britain. Innumerable business opportunities, among them the pricing of assets (deposits, stocks, bonds, real estate, etc.) of the Rothschild Bank in London, hinged on any decisive outcome of the Battle of Waterloo in Belgium. The outcome may be represented by a binary variable, which cannot yield more than one bit of information (the maximum amount of information possible in this situation). If one takes into account three options (an outright victory, an outright defeat, or an inconclusive outcome), the maximum amount of information cannot exceed 1.6 bits, according to Shannon and Weaver (1949). The actual amount of information was less. From historical experience, the outcome of battles waged by Napoleon was not 50/50, associated with the maximum amount of information. Most people still favored Napoleon. At that time, a decisive outcome would change the pricing of most assets in Britain. Rothschild decided to learn about the outcome as the first businessperson in London. He sent observers to Waterloo equipped with carrier pigeons to be dispatched with the encoded result.[11]

The informational model of the situation consists of one variable of unknown value that must be acquired. In this case, however, the amount of less than 1.6 bits of information is associated with an enormous utility value. Rothschild was a shrewd businessperson, too. Once he received the valuable information about the victorious outcome of the battle, he started selling assets, sending all the prices into a tailspin, and later he started buying everything at depressed prices, using concealed representatives. He implicitly disinformed the public first, and then multiplied his fortune.

This is a classic case where utility value of information of enormous magnitude depended on about one bit of the amount of information. This information, however, had to be of proper quality, hence, with many requirements attached so that it was fit for use. The outcome of the battle must be accurately interpreted, encoded, transmitted, received, properly interpreted by the receiver, and, finally, shrewdly acted upon. All of this was uncertain, as it usually is when stakes are high. Even redundancy had to be added; for example, many observers deployed, many encoding schemas used, and many carrier pigeons dispatched because some might perish. The information might have arrived in an unrecognizable form so that it could not be interpreted properly. Many things might have gone wrong. The requirement of exclusivity applies here as well; hence, all types of security precautions must be taken.

The first conclusion from this case is that the previously mentioned research in progress (Gackowski, 2004, 2005a, 2005b) about purpose-focused assessment of quality illuminates immediately the potentially most important quality requirements that must be considered for a successful acquisition. This research, even in its incomplete form, without the promised mapping of mutual interdependencies among quality attributes, provides an examiner

Copyright © 2007, Idea Group Inc. Copying or distributing in print or electronic forms without written permission of Idea Group Inc. is prohibited.

with an insight into what is important, what is mandatory, and what is of secondary rank without resorting to survey-based research. The latter is practically infeasible with high-stake business opportunities. The purpose-focused view does not exclude brainstorming sessions with experts.

Similarly, the recommended preliminary sequence of economic examination of the direct primary quality attributes within the purpose-focused view (Gackowski, 2004) turns out to be helpful, too.

- First, whatever information arrives, whether from the battlefield or anywhere else, it must be interpretable. It is the first direct primary tentative universal quality requirement.
- Second, it must be of significant impact on the desired business results. For instance, an indecisive outcome of the battle would probably be of no practical use.
- Third, the information must be not only available, but also exclusively and operationally timely available; for example, sufficiently in advance so that any required action can be triggered successfully before anybody else becomes aware of the same opportunity. It also logically suggests that all pertinent security measures must be taken for preventing information sharing. The operational timely availability is a tentative universal requirement, but exclusivity, although mandatory also, is only a situation specific quality requirement; otherwise, the impact the information value would be nullified or unacceptably diminished.
- Fourth, it is desirable that the information is not simply credible but actionably credible, again a tentative universal quality requirement; otherwise, it would be foolish to act upon it. Of course, what constitutes actionable credibility must be operationally defined within the context of a specific situation; for instance, when received from two independent sources that are experienced enough to correctly interpret the outcome of the battle and sufficiently trustworthy to rely on them.
- Fifth, it must also be effectively complete to trigger a state transition in operations to act or not, which, in this simplified case, is not a problem.

If any one of the five direct primary tentative universal requirements of information quality could not be met, the potential business opportunity is lost. This precludes considering any of the other 179+ quality attributes identified by Wang and Strong (1996). When it comes to the direct secondary attributes, they usually affect only the cost effectiveness of using information. In a case of high stakes, cost considerations are rather tertiary. Thus, the operations-based purpose-focused view (Gackowski, 2004, 2005a, 2005b) facilitates examining data/information quality derived from various theories and used in different situations.

Again, the evolutional approach (Liu & Chi, 2002) addresses neither the amount of information nor the most important issue of quality of all — the utility value of the information under consideration. By ignoring this most important all-pervasive, factor, it does not provide any hints about how much attention to pay to different information values while rathering, storing, presenting, and using them. When combined, however, with the purpose-focused approach and applied in reverse sequence (top-down, flow-up), the evolutionary approach may become much more useful than in its current version.

Copyright © 2007, Idea Group Inc. Copying or distributing in print or electronic forms without written permission of Idea Group Inc. is prohibited.

Two Cases of Quality in Transaction-Processing and Inventory-Control Systems

There is a qualitative difference in assessing quality at different levels of operations support and management support by information systems. A simple example illustrates the differences:

- At the inventory *transaction-processing* level, one can see clearly that the limitations imposed by the assumption of the internal view are adequate. The ontological approach by Wand and Wang (1996) to data quality excludes issues related to what the data represent, why they are needed, how they are used, and what their value is.
- At the *inventory-control* level, only *one notch* higher, the limitations imposed by the internal system design view only are intolerable.

Therefore, this example actually represents two cases of inventory applications in retailing sporting goods. The mission of an inventory transaction processing system may be defined such that it represents faithfully and cost effectively the inventoried assets, and accounts for their changes according to the theory-specific generally accepted accounting principles (GAAP). GAAP determine what data must be collected and stored, including the quality requirements with regard to their credibility, which comprises values definition, objectivity, accuracy, precision, and currency. From the external perspective, business users expect the system to be cost effective. A convenient measure of it may be the ratio of the inventory transaction processing related cost divided by the number of transactions, or the ratio's reciprocal. The main issue is meeting the accounting requirements. No decisions are expected or made except for taking corrective actions when the transaction processing deviates from the established principles. For traditional pure data-processing systems, everything is relatively simple. Within this domain, they reflect the current states of business organizations and account for their changes. Once one ascends one notch higher — into the realm of real information systems that support management in contrast to data-processing systems that support business operations — *qualitative* changes take place.

The mission of an *inventory-control system* should be purpose focused and results oriented; for instance, minimize the inventory-control related costs per sales dollar. Now, as rightly explained by Liu and Chi (2002), other potential theory-specific approaches come into play. Inventory control does not affect sales volume in dollars, with one major exception: when out-of-stock conditions cause loss of sales. The way inventory control is conducted, however, affects its operating cost and the cost of financial assets engaged in keeping the minimum stock on hand. The function of inventory-control systems is to maintain the amount of stock between the MinimumStock = SafetyStock and the MaximumStock = SafetyStock + EconomicOrderQuantity (EOQ). In addition, reordering must be properly timed. Reordering is triggered when the actual amount of stock falls below the ReorderPoint = SafetyStock + LeadTime * AverageDailyDepletionRate. Without going into details, those formulas determine the additional data that this inventory-control model requires in excess of what transaction processing requires. According to the purpose-focused view of quality (Gackowski, 2004), they constitute the data component of the model.

To make it work, the inventory controllers must receive printed exception reports or displayed messages whenever the actual amount of stock crosses those control points — an

Copyright © 2007, Idea Group Inc. Copying or distributing in print or electronic forms without written permission of Idea Group Inc. is prohibited.

information value. Inventory controllers are assigned to specific product groups according to their professional experiences and familiarity with those products. The actual warnings (type of exception, level of its urgency, level of its importance, which and where an inventory item is affected) convey some amount of information as defined in the theory of communication. Those values constitute the actual information component of the model (Gackowski, 2004). The amount of information may be computed, but it does not matter here. In this case, only the utility value of information associated with the warnings issued by the system really matters. The utility value is determined by the impact on business results when the warnings are not issued or remain unheeded; hence, no actions are triggered, or they are triggered with a significant delay. (Of course, respective exception reports must contain all the auxiliary data that facilitate decision making and triggering the corresponding corrective actions. When the absence of some data hampers those actions, the impact of this fact on the business results can be assessed in the same way.) The amount of information associated by Shannon and Weaver (1949) with those warnings according to their probabilities is not the information some authors of MIS textbooks define as processed data, while others kindly add "useful" processed data. It is time to put the issue to rest: On one hand, data are data; useful data are useful data and nothing more; however, data are not information. On the other hand, information is information and remains information even when it is not useful, as Callaos and Callaos (2002) gently remind us. Decision situations with a defined purpose determine usefulness of data and information.

The experienced designer will build in feedback requirements from the responsible controllers about the actions they triggered (purchase-order requests, cancellations of previous orders, internal-transfer orders from locations with surpluses to locations with shortages, etc.). In addition, the designers may build in monitoring of compliance and performance of inventory controllers and/or automatically generated reminders of necessary audits. Such warnings or reminders are not data; they are not given. Within defined decision situations, they are unknown values that still need to be acquired either by observation or by calculation each time the level of inventory changes. Hence, the relevant questions here include what data are required, how they are used, the type of warning information needed, and when they should be supplied to concerned decision makers (here inventory controllers), to enable them to act to meet the stated business objectives. The latter, if well defined, should be contributing factors to defined common business purposes. The above questions should be asked and considered by all full-blooded business-aware analysts and designers of information systems that really are out there to support management in decision making. Otherwise, one deals with IT technicians devoid of the indispensable business background.

Information systems do not only represent the real world as pure data-processing systems do. If well designed, they assist in *changing* business results for the better. The *teleological* perspective is required in the design of management information systems. Hence, the assessment of the quality of data/information used must be done from the same perspective, whether at all and how much those systems contribute to the desired business results.

Now, one may note:

1. On one hand, the theory-specific view of quality (Liu & Chi, 2002), when applied top-down and flow-up as suggested here, literally guides the analyst in identifying what data/information are needed, including the questions about their quality requirement that pertain to the situation under consideration.

Copyright © 2007, Idea Group Inc. Copying or distributing in print or electronic forms without written permission of Idea Group Inc. is prohibited.

2.   On the other hand, the purpose-focused view of quality (Gackowski, 2004, 2005a, 2005b) suggests an economic sequence of asking those questions, and the relative amount of attention to pay to each data/information value as derived from their perceived impact on the business results. It is according to the tentative universal principle of pervasiveness of the significant impact of data/information value on all other quality attributes of the same value.

When staying with Liu and Chi's (2002) use of theory "for any technique, method, approach or model that is employed" (p. 295), one easily can see that the selected method for controlling inventory immediately determines what additional data are required. When data are required, they are relevant and "fit the need of a task" (Liu & Chi, 2002, p. 300). By Gackowski (2005a, p. 110), however, those data must be of significant impact first. A specific method of inventory control is selected because the analysts and/or designers expect to attain a significant difference in business results. Hence, all the data values required by the method also must be "of significant impact." Without them, the method would not work. Thus, the question about an "appropriate amount of information" is redundant at best. It seems that here also, the term "effective operations state transition triggering completeness," fits the situation better.

Once all relevant data are identified, the next direct primary tentative universal quality requirement is "operationally timely available" (Gackowski, 2005a, p. 110). If it is not, why bother asking questions about other quality requirements? In this case, however, serious doubts may arise whether Economic Order Quantities (EOQ), Safety Stocks, and Depletion Rates for all inventory values will be "operationally timely available" — that is, before the system's deployment deadline. There are other legitimate questions asked by Liu and Chi (2002), such as about privacy (the extent to which a task has permission to access the data) and security (the extent to which a task has secured access to the data). They are, however, factors that only contribute to the attribute operationally timely available discussed before (Gackowski, 2005a, p. 110). Within taxonomy by Gackowski (2004), there is a place for them among the "indirect quality attributes" (p. 132). They do not stand on their own merit, but they may negate a direct primary mandatory attribute when they are a determining factor. Here, the need for a map of important logical and functional interdependencies within the universe of all quality attributes is evident.

The next direct primary tentative universal quality requirement identified as "actionably credible" (Gackowski, 2004, p. 111) is not an issue in this case. All the required data come from internal sources. It is unlikely that they will be misrepresented. The last of the direct primary tentative universal quality requirement "effective operations state transition triggering completeness," can certainly be met as long the "operationally timely availability" is assured.

Once all the direct primary tentative universal quality requirements are met, only then should the direct secondary quality requirements such as economical level of acquisition interpretability, operationally timely availability, actionably credibility, presentation interpretability, and effective operations triggering completeness be considered, if questions in this respect arise. Because they contribute to the economy of data/information use, their impact is independent and additive. Thus, the sequence of their examination is irrelevant. This is not the case, however, in a business environment where usefulness of data/information is assessed by its cost effectiveness. If this is so, the direct secondary requirements of quality, which are of an economic nature, automatically become mandatory requirements

Copyright © 2007, Idea Group Inc. Copying or distributing in print or electronic forms without written permission of Idea Group Inc. is prohibited.

too. When any of those secondary requirements cannot be economically met, it renders useless the corresponding data/information value when viewed from the purpose-focused perspective (Gackowski, 2005a, 2005b).

Liu and Chi (2002), under the title "presentation quality" (p. 299), and other authors concerned with quality of presentations on Web pages (Moustakis, Litos, Dalivigas, & Tsironis, 2004), developed presentation-specific quality criteria, which are and should be thoroughly empirically tested, as those criteria heavily depend on individual user preferences. They are difficult to determine a priori. They can be tested only statistically. Probably the highest clarity on the design intrinsic quality requirement has been attained with regard to databases (Nauman & Roth, 2004). Although databases must be designed, keeping foremost in mind the external user requirements, in this area, a wide body of logical and technical criteria that belong to the category of engineering requirements has been developed and well tested.

The weakest point in Liu and Chi's (2002) "data collection quality" is that it is completely unrelated to application requirements. The listed criteria are reasonable, but when applied in abstract, following only the data-collection theory-specific requirements, they may become costly and still insufficient. One might suggest that all the collection quality requirements of any commonly shared data/information values should be *minimaxed,* that is, they should be kept at the lowest level required by the most sensitive application in which they are designated to be used.

Besides the quality attributes explicitly discussed, there is a plethora of literally other quality attributes identified by researchers and listed under different names. Most of them seem to be indirect attributes that do not directly affect the business results but are preconditions or contributing factors to some of the direct quality attributes. To facilitate their examination and applicability within the context of real-world information systems, a use diagram in Unified Modeling Language (UML), a process chart, and respective entity-relationship diagrams that represents all important logical interdependencies among them (Gackowski, 2004) should be developed with a glossary and index of generally accepted definitions of quality attributes.

Conclusion

This chapter presents a compelling rationale for paying sufficient attention to all the numerous consequences of the relativity of the operations quality of any type of symbolic representations presented here as a special case of the general relativity of quality of anything else in use. It calls for an extension of the current research on quality toward the theory-based approaches that promise research results of a more lasting validity. It requires a decisive move of viewing the operations quality of representations from the:

- Ontological toward the teleological perspective
- Internal toward the external perspective
- Survey-based toward the theory-based and theory-specific perspective
- Design intrinsic toward the situation-specific perspective
- Static toward the evolutional perspective
- Simple generic naming of quality attributes toward adequately refined and qualified naming conventions that better represent their multifaceted aspects

Copyright © 2007, Idea Group Inc. Copying or distributing in print or electronic forms without written permission of Idea Group Inc. is prohibited.

It seems also that the:

- Evolutional and theory-specific view of quality attributes, as proposed by Liu and Chi (2002), could be considerably improved, when used during the SDLC in reverse order, that is, top-down and dataflow-up order.
- Purpose-focused view of quality, as proposed by Gackowski (2004, 2005a, 2005b), has the potential of integrating the present theory-based contributions into a more complete, cohesive, and pragmatic model of viewing, categorizing, and examining those attributes. To facilitate the examination of its applicability within the context of real-life information systems, a use diagram in UML, process chart, and entity-relationship diagrams that represents all the important logical interdependencies among the quality attributes should be developed with a glossary and index of their generally accepted definitions.

References

Alter, S. (2002). *Information systems: Foundation of e-business*. Upper Saddle River, NJ: Prentice Hall.

Callaos, N., & Callaos, B. (2002). Toward a systemic notion of information: Practical consequences. *Informing Science, 5*(1), 106-115.

Gackowski, Z. J. (2004). Logical interdependence of data/information quality dimensions: A purpose-focused view on IQ. In *Proceedings of the 9th International Conference on Information Quality (ICIQ 2004)*, Cambridge, Massachusetts Institute of Technology (MIT). Retrieved April 8, 2006, from http://www.iqconference.org/Documents/IQ Conference 2004/Papers/LogicalInterdependence.pdf

Gackowski, Z. J. (2005a). Informing systems in business environment: A purpose-focused view. *Informing Science Journal, 8*, 101-122. Retrieved April 8, 2006, from http://inform.nu/Articles/Vol8/v8p101-122Gack.pdf

Gackowski, Z. J. (2005b). Operations quality of data and information: Teleological operations research-based approach, call for discussion. In *Proceedings of the 10th Anniversary International Conference on Information Quality (ICIQ-05)*, Cambridge, Massachusetts Institute of Technology (MIT).

Kofler, E. (1968). *O wartosci informacji* [On value of information]. Warsaw, Poland: Panstwowe Wydawnictwa Naukowe (PWN).

Liu, L., & Chi, L. N. (2002). Evolutional data quality: A theory-specific view. In *Proceedings of the 7th International Conference on Information Quality (ICIQ-02)* (pp. 292-304), Cambridge, MA. Retrieved April 8, 2006, from http://www.iqconference.org/iciq/iq-download.aspx?ICIQYear=2002&File=EvolutionalDataQualityATheorySpecificView.pdf

Mazur, M. (1970). *Jakosciowa teoria informacji* [Qualitative theory of information]. Warsaw, Poland: Panstwowe Wydawnictwa Techniczne (PWT).

Moustakis, V. S., Litos, C., Dalivigas, A., & Tsironis, L. (2004). Website quality assessment criteria. In *Proceedings of the 9th International Conference on Information Quality (ICIQ-04)*, Cambridge, MA (pp. 59-73). Retrieved April 8, 2006, from http://www.

Copyright © 2007, Idea Group Inc. Copying or distributing in print or electronic forms without written permission of Idea Group Inc. is prohibited.

iqconference.org/iciq/iqdownload.aspx?ICIQYear=2004&File=WebsiteQualityAsse
ssmentCriteria.pdf

Nauman, F., & Roth, M. (2004). Information quality: How good are off-the-shelf DBMS? In *Proceedings of the 9th International Conference on Information Quality (ICIQ-04)*, Cambridge, MA.

O'Brien, J. A. (2003). *Introduction to information systems* (11th ed.). New York: McGraw-Hill/Irwin.

O'Brien, J. A. (2004). *Management information systems* (6th ed.). New York: McGraw-Hill/Irwin.

Shannon, C. E., & Weaver, W. (1949). *The mathematical theory of communication.* Urbana: University of Illinois Press.

Wand, Y., & Wang, R. Y. (1996). Anchoring data quality dimensions in ontological foundations. *Communications of the ACM, 39*(11), 86-95.

Endnotes

[1]   Most authors use the terms *data* and *information* interchangeably; however the purpose-focused, operations-research-based perspective requires considering data and information as two disjunctive sets of symbolic representations with common quality attributes but distinctively different quality problems.

[2]   The theory deals with the *quantity of information* and problems arising in transmission of messages, which usually consist of one or more values.

[3]   This measure is important not only in analyzing the efficiency of information transmission, but also carries a practical and monetary weight in the news media. The anecdotal saying, "Dog bites man does not make news, but man bites dog makes news," illustrates the above statement.

[4]   The utility value of a special information service about road conditions, for instance.

[5]   *"The Internal View assumptions:* Issues related to the external view, such as why the data are needed and how they are used, is not part of the model. We confine our model to system design and data production aspects by *excluding issues related to use and value of the data"* (Wand & Wang, 1996, p. 89) (emphasis added).

[6]   According to the press, computer security officers at UC Berkeley Computing Center several times reported to the FBI that they discovered seemingly minor, unaccounted use of computer resources. They were told not to worry too much about such fractional losses. After setting up traps, major security breaches were discovered that originated with hackers in Germany. This illustrates that some missing data values may be more worrisome from the application viewpoint than from the storing models' view.

[7]   Examples: net income after taxes, retained earnings, return on investment, return on equity, cost effectiveness of services, and so forth

[8]   Generally, according to *the tentative universal principle of task-specific effective operational completeness,* an activity-specific cluster of indispensable usable/information values to be effectively operationally complete must consist of one or more task-specific benefit-adding values and all their mandatory usable companion values. The *effective operations state transition triggering completeness* of data/information

Copyright © 2007, Idea Group Inc. Copying or distributing in print or electronic forms without written permission of Idea Group Inc. is prohibited.

is more demanding; it requires that all benefits and costs computed as functions of the data and information values used for the completed activities over the entire operations project or campaign become motivationally sufficiently effective to trigger the operations under consideration.

[9]   *Actionable credibility* of information can be defined for practical purposes as the degree of credibility at which the target of informing is willing to take action in response to it (Gackowski, 2005b).

[10]   Note: CBS's far reaching debacle with the credibility of their reporting during the last presidential election campaign.

[11]   As historical reports show, at those times, one could watch a battle without being unduly harassed as a noncombatant and nonparticipating observer.

Copyright © 2007, Idea Group Inc. Copying or distributing in print or electronic forms without written permission of Idea Group Inc. is prohibited.

Section II

IQ Assessment
and Improvement

Chapter V

The Development of a Health Data Quality Programme

Karolyn Kerr, Simpl, New Zealand

Tony Norris, Massey University, New Zealand

Abstract

Data quality requirements are increasing as a wider range of data becomes available and the technology to mine data shows the value of data that is "fit for use." This chapter describes a data quality programme for the New Zealand Ministry of Health that first isolates the criteria that define "fitness" and then develops a framework as the basis of a health sector-wide data quality strategy that aligns with the sector's existing strategies and policies for the use of health information. The framework development builds on existing work by the Canadian Institute for Health Information, and takes into account current data quality literature and recognised total data quality management (TDQM) principles. Strategy development builds upon existing policy and strategy within the New Zealand health sector, a review of customer requirements, current sector maturity and adaptability, and current literature to provide a practical strategy that offers clear guidelines for action. The chapter ends with a summary of key issues that can be employed by health care organisations to develop their own successful data quality improvement programmes.

Copyright © 2007, Idea Group Inc. Copying or distributing in print or electronic forms without written permission of Idea Group Inc. is prohibited.

Introduction

The New Zealand health sector data quality improvement programme attempts to provide a structure for managing data to prevent data quality errors at the source of collection and to maintain the meaning of the data as they move throughout the health sector. This approach requires viewing data quality from a holistic perspective — going beyond a one-dimensional assessment of quality based only on accuracy — and assessing other dimensions (Ballou & Tayi, 1999) such as relevance, timeliness, comparability, usability, security, and privacy of data.

As data quality affects everyone in the health sector, the whole sector is responsible for maintaining and improving data quality. The role of the New Zealand Ministry of Health is one of leadership and support, whilst data collectors need to employ all possible processes to ensure only high quality data are collected, using agreed national and international standards, where available. Data quality needs to be the responsibility for high-level managers in an organisation to ensure the entire organisation makes the required changes for improvement. "All too often data quality is seen as something that is the responsibility of informatics staff alone and is often seen with disinterest by clinicians and managers, despite being so critical to the quality of the decisions they make" (Data Remember, UK National Health Service, 2001; UK Audit Commission, 2002).

This chapter describes the development of a data quality evaluation framework (DQEF) and underpinning strategy for the Ministry of Health in New Zealand and outlines the process to "institutionalise" total data quality management throughout the whole of the health sector.

The Importance and Elements of Data Quality Programmes

Bill Gates (1999) states:

The most meaningful way to differentiate your company from your competition, the best way to put distance between you and the crowd, is to do an outstanding job with information. How you gather, manage and use information will determine whether you win or lose.

Organisations are becoming more and more dependent on information. Virtually everything the modern organisation does both creates and depends upon enormous quantities of data. A comprehensive data management programme is therefore essential to meet the needs of the organisation (Pautke & Redman, 2001). Many authors, for example, Levitin and Redman (1993), also draw attention to the importance of data quality in managing information as a resource of the organisation.

The first step in setting up a data quality (improvement) programme is therefore to decide the determinants that define quality. A framework is then required to apply these determinants and their associated metrics that can assess the level of data quality and establish processes such as collection, storage, access, and maintenance that lead to quality

Copyright © 2007, Idea Group Inc. Copying or distributing in print or electronic forms without written permission of Idea Group Inc. is prohibited.

improvements where they are necessary. Finally, whilst a data quality framework models the data environment, it must be underpinned and supported by a strategy that is broader in scope. This strategy establishes the business purpose and context of data and aims to make the framework a routine tool and part of day-to-day operations.

These three elements, quality determinants, assessment framework, and implementation strategy are the core components of a data quality programme and we now look at these stages in more detail.

Data Quality Determinants

Strong, Lee, and Wang (1997) take a consumer (people or groups who have experience in using organisational data to make business decisions) focused view that quality data are "data that are fit for use," and this view is widely adopted in the literature (Wang, Strong, & Guarascio, 1996). Redman (2001) comes to the following definition based on Juran and Godfrey (1999):

> *Data are of high quality if they are fit for their intended uses in operations, decision-making, and planning. Data are fit for use if they are free of defects and possess desired features.*

Clearly, however, fitness for purpose depends upon the purpose and so the set of data quality determinants will vary according to the application. In addition, modern views of data quality have a wider frame of reference and many more features than the simple choice of attributes such as accuracy and currency. There are therefore multiple approaches to designing and applying data quality systems as well as competing terminologies to trap the unwary (Canadian Institute for Health Information, 2005; Eppler & Wittig, 2000). The approach we have adopted here is based on a hierarchical system (see next section) developed by the Canadian Institute for Health Information (CIHI) (2003a, 2005). At the uppermost level are the familiar attributes such as accuracy, relevance, and so forth. These attributes are referred to in the scheme as "dimensions." Each dimension is defined in context by appropriate determinants known as "characteristics." For example, characteristics of the accuracy dimension might include the tolerated level of error and the population to which the data accuracy must apply. Characteristics require answers to "what is/are" questions. Underpinning these characteristics are "criteria" that define processes and metrics used to assess the presence of potential data quality issues. Thus, the level of error characteristic might be assessed by asking if the error falls into a predefined range and if the level of bias is significant. Criteria typically demand "yes" or "no" answers. In this chapter we are concerned mainly with data quality dimensions and criteria although we describe the hierarchical process for their selection.

Data Quality Evaluation Frameworks

At its most basic, a data quality evaluation framework (DQEF) is defined by Wang et al. (1996) as "a vehicle that an organisation can use to define a model of its data environment, identify relevant data quality attributes, analyse data quality attributes in their current

Copyright © 2007, Idea Group Inc. Copying or distributing in print or electronic forms without written permission of Idea Group Inc. is prohibited.

or future context, and provide guidance for data quality improvement."

In our terminology, a DQEF enshrines and enacts the processes and metrics (criteria) that assess whether the level of a dimension (e.g., accuracy) is acceptable or not. However, Eppler and Wittig (2000) describe a data quality framework as:

A point in time assessment and measurement tool, integrated into organisational processes, providing a benchmark for the effectiveness of any future data quality improvement initiatives and a standardised template for information on data quality both for internal and external users.

The same authors also add that a framework should not only evaluate but also provide a scheme to analyse and solve data quality problems by proactive management.

Ideally, therefore, a DQEF goes beyond straightforward quality assessment and becomes an integral component of the processes that an organisation puts in place to deliver its business goals (Willshire & Meyen, 1997). The framework then uses data quality to target poor quality processes or inefficiencies that may reduce profitability or lead to poor service (Wang et al., 1996). The implication of this extended framework is that the organisation will need to engage in a certain amount of business process reengineering. That is why the framework needs to be part of an organisational improvement programme and strongly tied to a data quality strategy.

Data Quality Strategies

Thus far, little has been published on what constitutes a data quality strategy, let alone an evaluation of a structured and tested improvement programme. Recently, however, this type of strategy has become increasingly important as a core requirement for many businesses. It is likely that some large organisations do have such strategies, improvement programmes, or components of them, but these are not currently documented and available in the literature. Davis (2003), publishing on the FirstLogic Web site, wrote several articles on his vision of a data quality strategy. According to Davis, a data quality strategy should include:

- A statement of the goals (what is driving the project)
- A description of the primary organisational processes impacted by the goals
- A high-level list of the major data groups and types that support the operations
- A description of the data systems where the data groups are stored
- A statement of the type of data and how they are used
- Discussion of cleansing solutions matching them to the types of data
- Inventory of the existing data touch points
- A plan for how, where, and when the data can be accessed for cleansing
- A plan for how often the cleansing activity will occur and on what systems
- A detailed list of the individual data elements

Whilst Davis' list is a useful starting point, it is based on an information providers' perspective. Other components should be added to incorporate the needs of consumers and to define and document these. This is still not easy to do given that customers often do not know what their needs are (Redman, 2001). A first step would be the identification of the

Copyright © 2007, Idea Group Inc. Copying or distributing in print or electronic forms without written permission of Idea Group Inc. is prohibited.

organisation's customers, or important customer groups, where there are too many individual customers for initial improvement programmes.

With this survey of the elements of data quality improvement programmes we can now look briefly at international attempts to apply the principles to health care.

International Health Data Quality Programmes

Health care delivery and planning rely heavily on data and information from clinical, administrative, and management sources, and quality data lead to quality and cost-effective care, improving patient outcomes and customer satisfaction. Data for health care delivery range from the clinical records of individual patients, detailing their interactions with medical services, to the administrative data required to manage the complex business of health care. When abstracted and aggregated in warehouses, and informed by other management and policy information, these "unit level data" produce knowledge bases for heath care planning and decision support. The totality of data from these various sources can then be used for further policy development (Al-Shorbaji, 2001). A prime example is the planning at government level to provide services that address the prevalence and distribution of diseases such as diabetes in a population. Clearly, any programme that improves the quality of data at all levels will improve the quality and cost-effectiveness of care and patient outcomes.

A review of international data quality improvement programmes in health care, including the National Health Service (NHS) (Department of Health, 2004) in the United Kingdom, the Canadian Institute for Health Information (CIHI) (2003b), HealthConnect Australia (Department of Health and Aging, 2003), and the United States Department of Health and Human Services (2002) identified similarities between the various programmes. All of the reviewed programmes note the multilevel, multidimensional complexity of data quality improvement initiatives. They seek to manage data proactively and ensure integrity by preventing data quality problems using a systematic total data quality management (TDQM) approach (Wang, 1998). There is also commonality of role expectations — the data suppliers are responsible for the quality of the data they provide to the central government, whilst central government is required to provide leadership and assistance to data suppliers by developing sectorwide standards and best practice guidelines.

The NHS in particular outlines clearly, and in detail, the substantial work that is required by any health care provider to ensure good data quality. The NHS developed an accreditation scheme that was initially thought to be all that would be needed to ensure the supply of good quality data. The scheme is extensive and was found to be very successful but did not sufficiently identify the responsibilities of the data supplier; central government was still monitoring more than it was leading. This discovery led to the more extensive guidelines developed around principles of data quality supported within the NHS. Several NHS Trusts have published data quality strategies on their Web sites that align to the NHS core strategy requirements. These efforts have been recognised in a recent review of the programme by the UK Audit Commission (2004), which found significant improvements to levels of data quality. However, similar issues to those initially found are still apparent after five years of targeted improvements and the report recommended:

Copyright © 2007, Idea Group Inc. Copying or distributing in print or electronic forms without written permission of Idea Group Inc. is prohibited.

- The development of a more coordinated and strategic approach to data quality
- Development of an NHS-wide strategy for specifying, obtaining, and using both national and local information
- Making more and better use of patient-based information
- Involving Trust board members
- Training and developing staff
- Keeping systems up to date

In Canada, the CIHI also briefly discusses accreditation for enhancing collaboration with data suppliers. They have undertaken extensive work on data quality through collaborative work with experienced statisticians from Statistics Canada and base their theories on research by the Massachusetts Institute of Technology in the U.S.

We now look at the relevance of this international experience in health data quality programmes to New Zealand health.

Towards a Health Data Quality Programme in New Zealand

The New Zealand Health Information Service (NZHIS) is a specialised group within the Ministry of Health responsible for the collection and dissemination of health-related data. NZHIS has as its foundation the goal of making "fit-for-purpose" information readily available and accessible in a timely manner throughout the health sector to support the sector's ongoing effort to improve the health status of New Zealanders. The vision of NZHIS is to be a leader in the provision of health information services in New Zealand, and to be recognised and respected as a leading organisation internationally. Effective and timely use of information is crucial to achieving this vision. NZHIS has responsibility for:

- The overall collection, processing, maintenance, and dissemination of health data, health statistics and health information
- The ongoing quality improvement of data entering the national data collections[1]
- The continuing maintenance and development of the national health and disability information systems
- The provision of appropriate databases, systems, and information products
- The development and provision of health and disability information standards and quality-audit programmes for data
- Coordination of ongoing national health and disability information collections and proposals for their development
- Analysis of health information, performance monitoring, benchmarking, and advice on the use of information obtained from NZHIS

Thus, while the NZHIS is responsible for the lead on data quality, this does not mean that it is solely accountable for solving data quality problems. The role of the NZHIS is rather to define data quality criteria and establish a framework in which health care organisations can assess the quality of their own data. This framework must also ensure that data quality

Copyright © 2007, Idea Group Inc. Copying or distributing in print or electronic forms without written permission of Idea Group Inc. is prohibited.

does not degrade when data are moved between organisations. These data move with the patients they refer to creating reciprocal dependence between the organisations so that poor data management in one organisation can adversely and incrementally affect other organisations and the care a patient receives. A national "systems" framework is therefore needed to certify that data used for decision making meet the same quality criteria and standards both within and between organisations.

Assessment of the national health collections at NZHIS (2003) showed that the required framework was unlikely to lead to sustainable improvements unless it was placed in the context of a national strategy that would reengineer data processes and embed the quality-centric revisions in normal, everyday practice. The resources to improve quality were already available, but they were being applied to the wrong processes and without consistency or direction. In addition, short-term priorities needed to focus on areas where benefits could be realised easily with long-term projects concentrating on implementing change.

Thus, as suggested by the previous discussion, the approach to the New Zealand Health Data Quality Improvement Programme is seen to consist of three stages.

1.   Determination of the criteria needed to judge health data quality in a New Zealand context
2.   Development of a practical framework to apply these criteria to existing and new database collection
3.   Development of a strategy to implement the framework and embed it in normal practice

The next sections describe the research methodology and the design and application of these three stages.

Research Methodology for the Programme Development

The research utilised several qualitative methodologies — action research, semi-structured interviews, focus groups, and a questionnaire to develop and formally assess a health data quality framework that could be tied to an implementation strategy and promulgated as a data quality programme. The two focus groups were derived from a Ministry Data Quality Team (MDQT) formed specifically to look at ways of improving quality in a consistent way across the organisation. Membership of the MDQT was selected from across the ministry to bring together business units that appeared to have similar issues with data quality but at that time had no formal infrastructure to coordinate quality initiatives. Members were mostly "information users" such as information analysts and business intelligence staff, but some were also members of the already existing operational Clinical Analysis Team. All regularly used data for a wide range of different purposes.

A grounded theory (Strauss & Corbin, 1998) approach was used to analyse the data for content themes that could reveal new concepts. The research concentrated on eliciting the opinions of the participants on areas such as:

Copyright © 2007, Idea Group Inc. Copying or distributing in print or electronic forms without written permission of Idea Group Inc. is prohibited.

- The applicability of the criteria, characteristics, and dimensions for the assessed collection
- Proposal of other dimensions that may be applicable
- The language used in the framework
- The language and examples provided in the user manual
- The length of time required to complete the assessment using the framework
- The value to users of the information provided from using the framework
- The table of contents for the data quality documentation folder

The DQEF then went through a pilot evaluation process using two health data collections. Initial assessment was made on the mortality data collection which is a national health collection considered to have good data quality in relation to other collections. The mortality collection has been established to provide data for public health research, policy formulation, development and monitoring, and cancer survival studies. A complete dataset of each year's mortality data is sent to the World Health Organization to be used in international comparisons of mortality statistics.

The second data collection consisted of clinical data held in a local hospital setting. These data are used to determine best health outcomes for clinical care pathways and they are consequently stored at a more granular level than the national health data.

Further details of methodology are given with the discussion of the research findings.

Research Findings

Selection of Health Data Quality Dimensions

The development of suitable dimensions for assessing health data quality in a New Zealand context was based as indicated on the Canadian Institute of Health Information (CIHI) data quality framework (Long, Richards, & Seko, 2002). This framework is itself based on Statistics Canada guidelines and methods, information quality literature, and the principle of continuous quality improvement (Deming, 1982). The CIHI is comparable in function to NZHIS and the health care systems of the two countries are also similar in many respects.

The CIHI data quality framework operationalises data quality as a four-level conceptual model (Long & Seko, 2002). At the foundation of the model are 86 criteria and these are aggregated using the framework algorithm into the second level of 24 characteristics that in turn define 5 dimensions of data quality: accuracy, timeliness, comparability, usability, and relevance. Finally, the five dimensions can be reduced using the algorithm into one overall database evaluation. Figure 1 provides a summary of the four-level conceptual CIHI model.[2]

The CIHI framework was first assessed for completeness, applicability, and ease of adaptation in New Zealand against current ministry information strategy documents. These include regional health care providers strategic plans and the WAVE report (working to add value through e-information) (WAVE Advisory Board, 2001), which is New Zealand's

Copyright © 2007, Idea Group Inc. Copying or distributing in print or electronic forms without written permission of Idea Group Inc. is prohibited.

Figure 1. The CIHI Data Quality Framework (Version 1) four-level model (Source: Long & Seko, 2002)

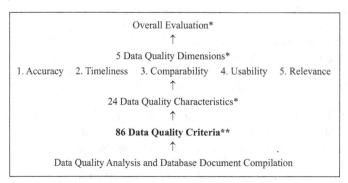

Note:
*0. not applicable, 1. unknown, 2. not acceptable, 3. marginal, and 4. appropriate
**0. not applicable, 1. unknown, 2. not met, and 3. met

national information management strategy for health. Compliance with New Zealand legislation was also considered.

The MDQT focus groups made minimal changes to the basic content of the CIHI framework retaining the hierarchical approach but removing some criteria that were thought inappropriate and adding others that were considered important in the New Zealand context, yielding a total of 69 from the original 86. The most significant change was the inclusion of an additional dimension, privacy and security, to satisfy New Zealand concerns. The CIHI states that privacy and security are implicit requirements that are embedded in all their data management processes. Whilst the same could also be said of the Ministry of Health, the pervading culture in New Zealand requires that privacy and security of information, in particular health information, are paramount. Therefore, the MDQT felt there was a requirement for explicit and transparent consideration of these quality dimensions. The underpinning characteristics for these new dimensions were developed by the senior advisors on health sector privacy and security to ensure alignment with the ongoing development of new privacy and security policies.

The six data quality dimensions chosen for the DQEF by analysis of the feedback from the focus groups are as follows with accuracy as the most important:

1. Accuracy is defined within the framework as how well data reflect the reality they are supposed to represent.
2. Relevancy reflects the degree to which a database meets the current and potential future needs of users.
3. Timeliness refers primarily to how current or up-to-date the data are at the time of use.
4. Comparability is defined as the extent to which databases are consistent over time and use standard conventions (such as data elements or reporting periods), making them similar to other databases.

Copyright © 2007, Idea Group Inc. Copying or distributing in print or electronic forms without written permission of Idea Group Inc. is prohibited.

5.   Usability reflects the ease with which data may be understood and accessed. If data are difficult to use, they can be rendered worthless no matter how accurate, timely, comparable, or relevant they may be.
6.   Security and privacy reflect the degree to which a database meets the current legislation, standards, policies, and processes.

Within the research participant group the understanding of the meaning of these dimensions varied. No one definition could be found for even the most commonly used data quality dimensions (Wand & Wang, 1996). For this reason it is important for the development of the DQEF to explicitly define each dimension. It was decided to utilise the definitions provided by the CIHI Framework where possible, as these aligned with the characteristics and criteria adopted throughout the framework. Importantly, the dimensions were found to be mutually exclusive and collectively exhaustive.

Definition of the Health Data Quality Evaluation Framework

The development of the health DQEF began with a current state analysis (New Zealand Health Information Service, 2003) through a preliminary survey of managers and users from across the ministry. This survey consisted of open questions requiring free-text answers to elicit information on a set of factors including historical and contextual information about the collection, the data collection processes, any changes made to data from within the ministry, what the data are used for, where they reside, and the nature and perceived effectiveness of existing data quality initiatives.

The gathering of this information proved difficult. The survey results showed there were currently no compiled and complete records of data quality for any of the national data collections administered or managed by the Ministry of Health and neither was there clear accountability for data quality in the health sector. The information is spread over a range of business units, people, and documents so that the Ministry cannot easily assess the scope or effectiveness of its data quality measures. Furthermore, the varying requirements for quality between centrally held and managed collections and those "at the coalface" led to considerable uncertainty as to what "quality" entailed. This situation and extensive discussions with data users involved in the development of the Ministry of Health Information Systems Strategic Plan served only to confirm the need for the DQEF and the availability of assessment tools that could provide information on the nature and levels of data quality and identify the sources of problems so as to allocate responsibilities.

For the New Zealand Ministry of Health, therefore, the DQEF takes the form of a tool that allows a consistent and accurate assessment of data quality in all national health data collections, enabling improved decision making and policy development in the health sector through better information. The DQEF standardises information on data quality for users, provides a common objective approach to assessing the data quality of all health information databases and registries, and enables the identification and measurement of major data quality issues.

The draft DQEF, consisting of the aligned set of quality criteria, characteristics, and dimensions, was sent to all group participants. A presentation to the MDQT was made prior to the focus groups to ensure all participants had a common understanding of the purpose of the DQEF and the desired outcome goals. The group participated in two focus groups of two

Copyright © 2007, Idea Group Inc. Copying or distributing in print or electronic forms without written permission of Idea Group Inc. is prohibited.

hours each. A member of the Ministry's Health Information Strategy and Policy Group (the researcher) led the focus groups and an administrator was present to make audio recordings and to later transcribe the recordings, noting also the interaction between group members on discussion points.

A template was developed to assist data managers and users to assess and document the effectiveness of the DQEF, its user manual, and the proposed data quality documentation folder for each data collection. The documentation folder houses all information pertaining to the quality of each data collection and makes it available in both paper and online format for access by all staff at the Ministry of Health. Following the focus group sessions, a second review of the DQEF, assessed using criteria developed by Eppler and Wittig (2000) ensured that the DQEF remained robust after localised changes.

The information provided by the DQEF evaluation highlighted data quality problems that were already known to the data custodians who had already initiated work to make improvements. However, several other deficiencies were highlighted, indicating where improvements in the current data quality work could be made, or in the case of timeliness, highlighting known issues that perhaps should be made a priority for improvement.

The issue of timeliness of the suicide in the mortality data collection data highlights a trade-off debate between dimensions. For example, data users are aware that some datasets are likely to be incomplete; then the data can be released without delay making them become usable at an earlier date. Eppler and Wittig (2000) note that trade-offs are not commonly addressed in frameworks. Research participants did not raise this issue and the DQEF does not explicitly address trade-offs between dimensions. However, an analysis of possible trade-offs and their implications could be included in the user manual. Different trade-offs would apply to different collections, and again may be different for specific uses of the data (Ballou & Pazer, 2003).

An issues register was kept to supply feedback to the researcher on the usability of the DQEF and user manual. Overall, the DQEF was found to provide useful data quality information by collection users and custodians and to provide sufficient information to make at least preliminary prioritised lists of essential data quality improvement projects. A detailed analysis of the feedback is provided.

Training

Further training was required to ensure that evaluators use the DQEF consistently and that it is a practical and easy tool to use. During training sessions it was found that many users of the DQEF initially made assumptions about the meaning of criteria and needed to refer to the metrics and definitions contained in the user manual. Consistency of meaning of criteria is important since many different users complete the evaluation both within an evaluation cycle and also from one evaluation to the next. For this reason a section was included under each criterion that asked the evaluator to describe in free text how they came to their decision, including references to any data quality information used to make their decision. This requirement also aids any subsequent evaluation of a collection.

Time Taken to Complete Evaluations

As noted in the findings of the Current State Analysis of Data Quality in the Ministry of Health, data quality information is held in many different locations and finding this in-

Copyright © 2007, Idea Group Inc. Copying or distributing in print or electronic forms without written permission of Idea Group Inc. is prohibited.

formation takes considerable time. The time taken to complete an evaluation of a data collection by already busy staff was estimated to be a minimum of four hours when all relevant documentation was available. In practice, the information was held in disparate locations by different staff and the initial evaluations took far longer. Repeated evaluations of the same collections would be completed much more efficiently, as much of the information could remain the same or merely need updating.

Intended Unit of Analysis

The researcher and participants also discussed the granularity of evaluation or intended unit of analysis. Participants asked, "was the DQEF able to evaluate a collection as a whole and also a column within a collection?" Price and Shanks (2005) found similar issues when implementing a data quality framework and noted the limitations of a framework on data that are not uniquely identifiable, such as those found in non-key columns. It was therefore decided to measure each collection as a whole. However, there are specific data elements that can be assessed individually and are extensively used for analysis and decision making. An example would be a registry, such as the National Health Index (NHI, a unique patient identifier), where each field of demographic information is the reference for other collections and provides information to prevent duplicate allocation. In this case, the DQEF can be used as a two-dimensional tool, assessing the registry as a whole and then each element.

User Manual

Extensive changes to the CIHI user manual were required to make it useful to the New Zealand health care environment. The findings show that the target audience for the accompanying DQEF user manual needed careful definition to ensure that the language was appropriate and the documents easy to use. In particular, the language used in the original CIHI version was found to be too simplistic for the intended audience. DQEF users are likely to be systems administrators, data quality advisors, and members of the Business Intelligence Team, but the language assumed little underlying knowledge of data and systems. The user manual could also be shortened by moving some of the underlying theory used to develop the Data Quality Improvement Programme to other documents intended for potential users taking part in education programmes.

Extent of Data Quality Information

Initial feedback from the data quality team at NZHIS showed that the DQEF did not provide sufficient information to make decisions on the quality of data. There appeared to be insufficient detail to manage data quality effectively. However, once the team became more familiar with the DQEF and began to understand the context of its use, the feedback became more positive. Users realised that the purpose of the DQEF was to provide guidance on the regular processes and measures needed to answer criteria questions. By presenting a more complete view of the data quality of a collection, these "answers" suggested new measures, not previously thought of by the data quality team. In effect, the DQEF is an invaluable guide or checklist that facilitates the consistent application of appropriate and wide ranging measures across all collections. It has the ability to raise the standard of work

Copyright © 2007, Idea Group Inc. Copying or distributing in print or electronic forms without written permission of Idea Group Inc. is prohibited.

expected in data quality by bringing about awareness of areas of deficiency in the current work programme.

Interestingly, findings from the mortality data collection evaluation show that the Business Intelligence Team (as data consumers) required the most detailed information on how the assessment was made for each criterion, whereas managers required only summary information. This variation reflects the different decisions made by the different groups and hence the distinctive uses and required granularity of data quality information. Clearly, reports on the outcomes of assessments should be tailored to provide this information specific to audience requirements. In support of this observation, Chengalur-Smith, Ballou, and Pazer (1999) noted the importance of information format in their research on the impact of data quality information on decision making. They found that users required complex data quality information to make simple decisions but that they did not make use of this information for complex decisions. We consider this reciprocity may be due to "information overload" where too much information can be counterproductive to decision making in more complex decision environments.

Although decisions made in the health care environment are often "complex," what a complex decision is to one user may not be to another. This implies that users need to have input into decisions on the granularity of the supplied data quality information. Chengalur-Smith et al. (1999) note that it may be most effective to provide users with data quality information that focuses on one or two key criteria that exhibit the greatest impact on the data.

A later study by the same group (Fisher, Chengalur-Smith, & Ballou, 2003) observes the impact of experience on the decision maker, whereby increasing use of data quality information is found as experience levels progress from novice to professional and suggests that data quality information should be incorporated into data warehouses used on an ad-hoc basis.

Metrics

The DQEF uses subjective metrics for data criteria that have been developed by the collections' data custodians. Whilst this is a valid form of measurement, the robustness of the DQEF requires additional objective metrics and these are derived from a structured system based on statistical process control (Carey & Lloyd, 2001). The metrics include measures that assess customer requirements for levels of data quality, trends in historical data within the national health collections, current key performance indicators for contracted data suppliers, and legislative requirements for the provision of data by health care providers and the Ministry of Health to international bodies such as the World Health Organisation. Further work is still required to develop applicable metrics.

In summary, the pilot of the DQEF in the NZHIS environment elicited these issues:

- Training was required before using the DQEF.
- Users felt considerable time was needed to complete the evaluations.
- The extent and detail of information (particularly about how evaluation decisions are made) provided by the DQEF assessment process must meet the needs of data users, such as the Business Intelligence Team.
- Granularity/units of analysis need to fit the type of collection; registries such as the NHI require more granular, element level analysis.

Copyright © 2007, Idea Group Inc. Copying or distributing in print or electronic forms without written permission of Idea Group Inc. is prohibited.

- Language in the user manual and DQEF is an important consideration.
- Further work is required on metrics development.

Overall, collection users and managers found the DQEF to offer sufficient information on data quality to make preliminary, prioritised lists of essential data quality improvement projects. Further training has been necessary to ensure assessors use the DQEF consistently and that it is a practical and easy tool to use. The CIHI also found considerable training and change management were necessary to implement the CIHI Framework due in part to already heavy workloads (Long & Seko, 2002).

Pilot of the Framework in a Hospital Environment

The purpose of this pilot was to assess the application of the DQEF to the clinical integrated system (CIS) model that is currently used in clinical practice at Auckland District Health Board (A+). The assessment would indicate the applicability of the DQEF and its chosen data quality dimensions in the wider health sector. The CIS Model is an interdisciplinary computerised model of patient care that replaces paper notes and requires all staff members to document care via the computer. The software programme was developed by the A+ Network Centre for Best Patient Outcomes. This model has been in clinical practice since 2000 and has been used for 6,000 patients (Fogarty, 2004). The main objectives were to review the DQEF criteria against the CIS model database to:

- determine the appropriateness of the criteria for a clinical database
- assess the documented data quality of the CIS model against the DQEF criteria
- assess the clarity of DQEF documentation

Positive feedback was given on the usefulness of the information provided by the assessment process and the applicability of the DQEF. The majority of the criteria could be applied to an external clinical database as shown in Table 1. This table highlights that 52 out of the possible 69 criteria used in the DQEF conform to the data quality requirements of the clinical database held at the local hospital level. The language used in the DQEF was further improved to ensure consistent understanding using the detailed feedback on each criterion provided by this assessment.

The DQEF evaluation process also proved valuable to the hospital submitting the clinical data set. It was suggested by the hospital data analyst who completed the evaluation that

Table 1. Applicability of the DQEF with a hospital clinical data collection

MOH framework criteria	Hospital collection compliance
Conformed	52 items
Not applicable	9 items
Did not conform	8 items

Copyright © 2007, Idea Group Inc. Copying or distributing in print or electronic forms without written permission of Idea Group Inc. is prohibited.

some formal, sectorwide criteria based on the DQEF, together with a certification process such as accreditation, would help to ensure that clinical databases are valid and reliable.

Evaluation of the Framework Against Eppler and Wittig Criteria

The resulting DQEF, with changes as recommended by focus group participants and the hospital environment, was assessed using Eppler and Wittig's (2000) criteria. The feedback can be found in Table 2. The recommendations centre on the development of business processes that support the effective use of the DQEF in the Ministry of Health environment and the content of the manual that instructs users on the implementation methodology. This supports Eppler and Wittig's (2000) theory that a framework requires tools, such as guidelines and manuals, to be effectively implemented. CIHI also found that a detailed step by step guiding process is required to implement a framework (Long & Seko, 2002).

The summary information gained from evaluations of all national health data collections was collated to form a prioritised list of data quality improvement initiatives across the ministry. Ongoing assessment using the DQEF will provide information on the success of such initiatives. The DQEF remains an iterative tool, whereby those that use the tool

Table 2. Assessment of the New Zealand Data Quality Evaluation Framework using criteria defined by Eppler and Wittig (2000)

Eppler and Wittig (2000) Criteria	NZDQEF Response	Findings	Recommendations
1.1 Definitions	Definitions of the dimensions and the characteristics exist and are provided.	References/index are not provided making it difficult to locate information quickly. Some definitions are unclear and simplistic and do not relate to the NZ health sector. For example, the use of nursing homes.	An index should be added to the manual. Content should be trimmed down and made more relevant to the audience (systems staff).
1.2 Positioning	Yes, meets the requirements.	The context of the framework is clear. The limits of the framework are not explicitly documented.	The limits of the framework should be explicitly documented.

Copyright © 2007, Idea Group Inc. Copying or distributing in print or electronic forms without written permission of Idea Group Inc. is prohibited.

Table 2. continued

Eppler and Wittig (2000) Criteria	NZDQEF Response	Findings	Recommendations
1.3 Consistency	Some confusion was experienced in understanding the differences in some framework criteria.	If the assessors have not had training in the use of the framework and are not familiar with the collection, this will have some impact. The criteria in some respects are still subjective and so comparing across data collections may be problematic.	Assessors need training on the use of the framework. Data should be assessed by staff who are familiar with the collection.
2.1 Conciseness	The framework is not overly large. It took over four hours to answer all criteria because the collection respondents were not familiar with it.	Once the assessor is familiar with the framework it should be easily remembered.	Training should be provided, and/or a trained assessor should assist the assessor. A preassessment checklist should be developed to assist assessors and to ensure conditions for an assessment and all required information are available.
2.2 Examples	The examples are not specific to NZ environment and did not seem relevant in some cases. For example: the use of nursing home, the use of Corporation instead of District Health Board.	Providing NZ specific examples helps to guide users with contextual information.	Develop NZ specific and illustrative examples to help explain the various criteria.

will improve its usefulness with growing knowledge of data quality theory, the level of data quality of the national health collections, and the priorities for improvement. In particular, the data quality improvement strategy described in the remainder of the chapter will support the ongoing refinements to the DQEF.

Copyright © 2007, Idea Group Inc. Copying or distributing in print or electronic forms without written permission of Idea Group Inc. is prohibited.

Table 2. continued

Eppler and Wittig (2000) Criteria	NZDQEF Response	Findings	Recommendations
2.3 Tools	Yes – a tool template and a guide exists.	The audience is not clear. The manual appears to target novices with little or some knowledge about data quality or data, but the instrument itself assumes a high level of knowledge of data collections and terminology. The guide is simplistic and does not explain succinctly what the criteria mean.	The audience needs to be defined (i.e., likely to be systems people) who already know about the collection). The manual needs to be culled of novice content. The manual needs to be extended to provide succinct definitions for criteria. The tool template could be further automated to make data entry easier.
Other	Use of colour coding in the manual is meaningless when printed	Unless the manual is printed in colour and distributed or read online, colour coding is of no value.	The manual needs to be coded in a way that does not depend on colour or only distributed electronically.

Development of the Health Data Quality Strategy

As mentioned earlier, little has been published on what constitutes a data quality strategy, let alone an evaluation of a structured and tested improvement programme. It is particularly important to note that a data quality improvement strategy is not an "information technology strategy," nor an "information systems strategy." Although such strategies may provide insight and tools to underpin a data quality improvement strategy, data quality improvements cannot be attained merely through information technology; the problem is one of processes and people. As noted in Ward and Peppard (2002), "clearly, technology on its own, no matter how leading edge is not enough."

Technology can support the achievement of an organisation's business goals at an operational level by increasing efficiency and at a strategic level by reengineering the business processes to be more effective. At both levels, however, the technology is merely an enabler and it is information and its management that makes the difference. Since the quality of the information rests on the quality of the raw data used to derive it, data quality is a critical issue. Technology can be used to improve data quality in some processes and also to exploit the superior quality for better business outcome in others.

Unfortunately, whilst the technical aspects of data quality assurance are usually well-documented, documentation of the business processes that support good data quality is often lacking. Information processes must be carefully documented to make the meaning

Copyright © 2007, Idea Group Inc. Copying or distributing in print or electronic forms without written permission of Idea Group Inc. is prohibited.

of data transparent to all users. For example, data sources should always be identified to provide the data user with context around the data collection process. Imposing standards and maintaining consistency across business units with data definitions, business rules, and even systems architecture can lead to greater data integration and utility and hence perceived quality. This is where a "whole of health sector" strategy begins to have a significant effect on the quality of data and where centralised leadership is required to ensure that the views of all those who manage and use data are taken into account. Thus, good documentation carries the two-fold importance of establishing standards and managing change.

Change management is the main driver of the health data quality strategy (DQS) that, together with the data quality dimensions and framework, comprise the overall Data Quality Improvement Programme at the New Zealand Ministry of Health.

The DQS uses the dimensions derived in the DQEF to set data quality standards for designing, developing, and maintaining the national health data collections and data management throughout New Zealand. A practical strategy has to consider the complexity of the health sector since the data, their structure and use, and the products, are potentially much more varied than are found in financial or manufacturing organisations.

The development of the strategy was informed throughout by several stakeholders. Ongoing communication with health sector groups, including the Ministry of Health staff was essential to ensure sector buy-in and to maintain input and interest in the strategy development and implementation. Full consultation with a wide range of data suppliers and users was also necessary. Finally, surveys and discussions with organisations outside of health, both within New Zealand and overseas, on the management of data quality and implementation of strategy help to inform the ongoing and iterative development of the strategy.

The standards established by the DQS aim to achieve the improved health outcomes by:

- Better decision making to target areas of improvement in national health data collections with a transparent prioritisation tool for data quality improvement projects
- Improved relationships with data suppliers, developing a whole-of-sector responsibility for data quality
- Improved awareness of a data quality culture throughout the sector
- Improved understanding of the processes involved in developing an information product
- The development of best practice guidelines leading to accreditation of data suppliers
- Education and support to data suppliers
- Minimum data quality requirements for existing and new national collections
- Minimum requirements for regular operational data quality initiatives across all national health collections and an approach to rooting out persistent quality errors

In particular, the last bullet point demands a systematic approach to data quality management such as total data quality management (TDQM) mentioned earlier in the chapter.

Some approaches to data quality management target specific errors within a collection or an entire collection but often do not devise solutions to prevent systemic problems. In contrast, TDQM focuses on two key aspects of data management: the data flow processes that constitute the organisation's business and the recognition that information is a product, rather than a by-product, of these processes (Wang, 1998). Regarding the processes

Copyright © 2007, Idea Group Inc. Copying or distributing in print or electronic forms without written permission of Idea Group Inc. is prohibited.

themselves, TDQM seeks to ensure that none of them changes the initial meaning of the data leading to systematic errors and repeated data quality problems. Systematic process errors can be prevented by several means, some of which will depend upon the nature of the business unit and its data. However, we can identify generic prevention mechanisms across business units to include:

- The systematic and ongoing education of data suppliers
- Education within the Ministry of Health
- Regular reviews of recurrent data quality problems from suppliers and information feedback to suppliers on issues with support provided for improvement
- Internally developed data quality applications to reduce time spent on assessment of data quality problems (limited in use for complex health data)
- A continuous cycle of define, measure, analyse, and improve using the framework to inform the assessment process

Concerning the role of information as a product of process, TDQM draws attention to the need to manage information so that organisations:

- Know their customers/consumers of the information and their information needs
- Understand the relationship between technology and organisational culture
- Manage the entire life cycle of their information products
- Make managers accountable for managing their information processes and resulting products

TDQM at the Ministry of Health

The foundation of the New Zealand data quality strategy is the institutionalisation of TDQM principles by which data quality management processes are embedded in normal business practice and accepted at all levels in the sector. This installation is achieved by the "define, measure, analyse, improve" sequence, as described in the next four sections.

Define

The definition of what data quality means to health sector professionals is clearly a fundamental requirement and this was done through the development of the data quality dimensions and the data quality framework. The dimensions define what health care data collectors, custodians, and consumers consider important to measure.

A cross-organisational data quality group is used to facilitate the discussion of data quality issues from an organisation-wide perspective. The group includes representatives of business units that collect, manage, or use data, as well as clinicians and clinical coders. The strategy then provides for whole of sector input into the data quality dimensions considered important, where data quality improvement should be targeted, and how and where accountability should lie. Continual assessment of the needs of data customers is required and will be managed through a yearly postal survey of customers and discussions at forums and training sessions.

Copyright © 2007, Idea Group Inc. Copying or distributing in print or electronic forms without written permission of Idea Group Inc. is prohibited.

Measure

Active and regular measurement of data quality avoids a passive reliance on untested assumptions as to the perceived quality of the data. Reporting on data quality levels becomes transparent and justifiable. The regular measurement programme involves:

- Regular use of the data quality dimensions and evaluation framework on national collections
- Developing appropriate statistical process control (SPC) measures
- Developing data production maps for all major information products outlining flow of data around the organisation and the health sector and possible areas of data quality issues
- Checking the availability of data quality assessment software or the potential for in-house development

Measuring the quality of data supplied by organisations to the national collections involves performance measurement based on key performance indicators (KPIs) developed through SPC (Carey & Lloyd, 2001). SPC uses historical information to define the ranges of acceptable data so that outliers or variations identify areas for improvement that can be negotiated with data suppliers.

Data production maps for all major information products are another active management tool for improving data quality. These maps model the flow of data around the organisation and highlight potential quality issues by detecting points where data quality may be compromised. When properly developed and supported by senior management, they can be effectively applied to solve complex, cross-functional area problems (Wang, Lee, Pipino, & Strong, 1998). Where data cross from one organisation to another, significant data quality issues can arise, and this is evident within the New Zealand health care system. Maps can also be used to summarise issues for managers and provide them with a tool to understand the implications of data quality.

Analyse

The complexity of health care requires an extensive range of decisions, both administrative and health-related, and a single data element can substantiate many decisions and carry impacts across the sector. But what level of data quality do we need to make good decisions? The importance of data quality analysis is that it allows us to determine the appropriate quality levels and identify areas for improvement where current processes do not support good data quality work. Analysis can draw upon:

- **Clinical analysis and data modelling:** what cannot be done due to data quality
- Surveys of customer needs
- Consideration of current and future uses of data
- Realistic expectations vs. expectations of stakeholders
- **Corporate knowledge:** what the organisation already knows is important and/or relatively easy to fix
- **International standards:** does the organisation compare well with appropriate standards and are our expectations realistic?
- Resources available to make improvements

Copyright © 2007, Idea Group Inc. Copying or distributing in print or electronic forms without written permission of Idea Group Inc. is prohibited.

Improve

Actively finding data quality issues before they cause problems is made easier by the regular assessment of collections using the data quality measurements outlined previously. Prevention, rather than cure, is now a large part of the ministry's work through the proactive approach outlined here:

- Regular minimum data quality initiatives for all collections with specific initiatives for single collections only
- Preventing poor data quality in new collections through a "data quality plan" developed in the early phases of projects with full involvement of the data quality team. Data quality is embedded in the system and processes of the new collection prior to going live
- Continuing "what works" as the data quality team have learnt a considerable amount about the operational requirements of maintaining data quality levels
- The endorsement of standards for the collection, management, storage, and use of specific data elements by the Health Information Standards Organisation; this way all stakeholders know and agree to all steps in the data flow process
- Stewardship and data access policies that provide clear ownership and access guidelines for the data
- The proposed development of a National Data Dictionary to address the standardisation of the major data elements found in the National Health Data Collections. This standardisation is likely to provide for considerable improvement to data quality through a nationally consistent understanding of data definitions

Through these initiatives it is expected that expensive, one-off projects can be avoided and money can be allocated for regular operational requirements that will enable an ongoing prevention programme. Projects may only improve processes and data in one collection, whereby regular prevention mechanisms help to ensure all data are of high quality.

TDQM in the Wider Health Sector

Some of the wider benefits of institutionalising TDQM through the strategy include:

- Getting everyone talking about data quality through the agreement of a strategic direction
- Raising the profile of data quality within health care organisations through organisation-wide data quality groups
- Getting the sector moving in the same direction through the development of organisation-wide data quality strategies that align with the national strategic direction
- Drawing on current practice/knowledge through best practice guidelines developed by the sector and widely disseminated
- Clear expectations of data suppliers through accreditation/KPIs/contracts
- Actively reviewing strategic direction regularly

A key issue raised by the data quality proposals described in this chapter is how to identify and disseminate best practice and embed it in normal day-to-day operation. The

Copyright © 2007, Idea Group Inc. Copying or distributing in print or electronic forms without written permission of Idea Group Inc. is prohibited.

approach favoured in New Zealand is accreditation rather than audit. Accreditation suggests devolvement, ownership, and a supporting role from the ministry. For example, the ministry requires District Health Boards to produce annual plans but the boards themselves will be responsible for addressing data quality issues within a national framework and getting them approved at the highest level of regional health care funding and provision.

The ministry, through the Quality Health New Zealand and/or the Royal Colleges health care provider's accreditation process, will provide sector organisations with clear guidelines on how to achieve accreditation as good data suppliers. The accreditation process will be developed in consultation with the sector following the development and testing of best practice guidelines. Those organisations that have been able to implement extensive data quality programmes, as outlined previously, will be accredited as good data suppliers. This should lead to a reduction in the need for peer review and audit.

The proposed sector work programme requires that health care organisations can achieve accreditation if they:

- Take part in a sector peer review/audit process
- Meet KPIs
- Implement an in-house data quality education programme
- Develop and implement a local data quality improvement strategy
- Organise regular meetings with a cross-organisational data quality group
- Align with best practice guidelines (when developed)

Conclusion

This chapter has described the development of a health data quality programme for the Ministry of Health in New Zealand. The ministry's purpose is to realise the full value and potential of the data that it collects, stores, and manages. Building "trust" in the data throughout the health sector will ensure that data are used frequently and to their greatest possible benefit. With the right framework and strategy, data that are highly utilised for a range of reasons will incrementally improve in quality. Extensive data mining, combining currently disparate collections, will also provide far more granular information and knowledge to improve these collections. A data quality strategy will provide coherent direction towards total data quality management through a continuous cycle of work. The improved data quality will then ensure that the health sector is better able to make informed and accurate decisions on health care policy and strategy.

These aims are relevant to national and regional health authorities and providers in many countries and the key principles, described here and developed from pioneering work by the Canadian Institute for Health information, can be deployed successfully in many health care and related scenarios.

In summary, for the development and application of the data quality evaluation framework, it is important to:

- Define the underpinning data quality criteria carefully involving all stakeholders to ensure common understanding and direction

Copyright © 2007, Idea Group Inc. Copying or distributing in print or electronic forms without written permission of Idea Group Inc. is prohibited.

- Consider the critical quality dimensions that reflect how the organisation uses data and how data flow throughout the business processes
- Document business processes identifying data sources and their reliability
- Appreciate that the framework requires practical supporting tools (e.g., documentation) to make it effective
- Customise the language of the data quality user manual with regard to the level and experience of the intended users
- Be aware of the importance of both education and training at all necessary stages and levels; training is essential to affect the culture change that must accompany the realisation of the importance of data quality
- Be aware that application of the framework is an iterative, ongoing process; the required outcomes cannot be achieved in a single pass

For the data quality improvement strategy, it is important to:

- Derive and impose standards that facilitate data and information transfer whilst preserving quality
- Reengineer the business processes to deliver the quality data needed for efficient service planning and the effective practice of integrated patient care
- Identify and disseminate best practice to reduce the development time needed to improve data quality
- Ensure data quality levels are not unnecessarily rigorous to maintain user ownership and workloads at reasonable levels
- Define user accountabilities for data quality and the mechanisms to enforce them
- Seek to embed the search for data quality in normal working practices and recognise its achievement in appropriate ways such as with accreditation

Work on extending and improving the health data quality programme continues, particularly with regard to the formulation of objective metrics for the underlying data quality criteria.

References

Al-Shorbaji, N. (2001). *Health and medical informatics*. Cairo: World Health Organisation.

Ballou, D. P., & Pazer, H. (2003). Modeling completeness versus consistency tradeoffs in information decision contexts. *Transactions on Knowledge and Data Engineering, 15*(1), 240-243.

Ballou, D. P., & Tayi, G. K. (1999). Enhancing data quality in data warehouse environments. *Communications of the AMC*. Retrieved April 9, 2006, from http://delivery.acm.org /10.1145/300000/291471/p73-ballou.pdf?key1=291471&key2=3297921511&coll=p orta&dl=ACM&CFID=11111111&CFTOKEN=2222222

Canadian Institute for Health Information. (2003a). *Data quality framework*. Ottawa, Ontario: Author.

Copyright © 2007, Idea Group Inc. Copying or distributing in print or electronic forms without written permission of Idea Group Inc. is prohibited.

Canadian Institute for Health Information. (2003b). *Earning trust. Key findings and proposed action plan from the Data Quality Strategies Study*. Ottawa, Ontario: Author.

Canadian Institute for Health Information. (2005). *Data quality framework June 2005 revision*. Ottawa, Ontario: Author.

Carey, R. G., & Lloyd, R. C. (2001). *Measuring quality improvement in healthcare. A guide to statistical process control applications*. Milwaukee, WI: Quality Press.

Chengalur-Smith, I., Ballou, D. P., & Pazer, H. (1999). The impact of data quality information on decision making: An exploratory analysis. *IEEE Transactions on Knowledge and Data Engineering, 11*(6), 853-864.

Davis, F. (2003). *Data quality strategy*. Retrieved April 9, 2006, from http://www.firstlogic.com/_gics10643/DQ/article.asp?articleID=32

Deming, W.E. (1982). *Out of the crisis*. Cambridge: Massachusetts Institute of Technology.

Department of Health. (2004). *A strategy for NHS information quality assurance*. Author.

Department of Health and Aging. (2003). *Health Connect*. Canberra: Author.

Department of Health and Human Services. (2002). *HHS guidelines for ensuring and maximising the quality, objectivity, utility, and integrity of information dissemination to the public*. Retrieved April 9, 2006, from http://www.hhs.gov/infoquality/part1.html

Eppler, M. J., & Wittig, D. (2000). *A review of information quality frameworks from the last ten years*. Retrieved April 9, 2006, from http://www.knowledgemedia.org/modules/pub/view.php?id=knowledgemedia-2&page=1

Fisher, C., Chengalur-Smith, I., & Ballou, D. P. (2003). The impact of experience and time on the use of data quality information in decision making. *Information Systems Research, 14*(2), 170-188.

Fogarty, A. (2004). *Review of the MOH data quality evaluation framework on a clinical database*. Auckland: Auckland District Health Board.

Gates, B. (1999). *Business @ the speed of thought: Using a digital nervous system*. London: Penguin Books.

Juran, J. M., & Godfrey, A. B. (1999). *Juran's quality handbook* (5th ed.). New York: McGraw-Hill.

Levitin, A. V., & Redman, T. C. (1993). A model of the data (life) cycles with application to quality. *Information and Software Technology, 35*(4), 217-223.

Long, J. A., Richards, J. A., & Seko, C. E. (2002). *The Canadian Institute for Health Information Data Quality Framework, Version 1: A meta-evaluation and future directions*. Retrieved April 9, 2006, from http://secure.cihi.ca/cihiweb/dispPage.jsp?cw_page=quality_e

Long, J. A., & Seko, C. E. (2002). *A new method for database data quality evaluation at the Canadian Institute for Health Information*. Paper presented at the 7th International Conference on Information Quality, Boston.

New Zealand Health Information Service. (2003). *Current state analysis of data in the national health collections*. Wellington: Ministry of Health.

Pautke, R. W., & Redman, T. C. (2002). The organisation's most important data issues. In G. M. Piattini C. Calero, & M. F. Genero, (Eds.), *Information and database quality*. Dordrecht: Kluwer.

Price, R. J., & Shanks, G. (2005). *Empirical refinements of a semiotic information quality framework*. Paper presented at the 38th International Conference on Systems Sciences, Hawaii.

Copyright © 2007, Idea Group Inc. Copying or distributing in print or electronic forms without written permission of Idea Group Inc. is prohibited.

Redman, T. C. (2001). *Data quality. The field guide.* Boston: Digital Press.

Strauss, A., & Corbin, J. (1998). *Basics of qualitative research.* Thousand Oaks, CA: Sage Publications.

Strong, D. M., Lee, Y. W., & Wang, R. Y. (1997). Data quality in context. *Communications of the ACM, 40*(5), 103-110.

UK Audit Commission. (2002). Data remember. Improving the quality of patient-based information in the NHS. In *Management Paper* (p. 42). London: Author.

UK Audit Commission. (2004). *Information and data quality in the NHS.* London: Author.

Wand, Y., & Wang, R. Y. (1996). Anchoring data quality dimensions in ontological foundations. *Communications of the ACM, 39*(11), 86-95.

Wang, R. Y. (1998). A product perspective on total data quality management. *Communications of the ACM, 41*(2), 58-63.

Wang, R. Y., Lee, Y. W., Pipino, L. L., & Strong, D. M. (1998, Summer). Manage your information as a product. *Sloan Management Review,* 95-105.

Wang, R. Y., Strong, D. M., & Guarascio, L. M. (1996). Beyond accuracy: What data quality means to data consumers. *Journal of Management Information Systems, 12*(4), 5-33.

Ward, J., & Peppard, J. (2002). *Strategic planning for information systems* (3rd ed.). Chichester, UK: John Wiley & Sons.

WAVE Advisory Board. (2001). *From strategy to reality. The WAVE (Working to Add Value through E-information) project. Health Information Management and Technology Plan* (Project Report). Wellington: Ministry of Health.

Willshire, M. J., & Meyen, D. (1997). A process for improving data quality. *Data Quality, 3*(1). Retrieved from http://www.dataquality.com/997meyen.htm

Endnotes

[1]   A national collection is either a long-term collection of nationwide data or a reference dataset, of which NZHIS is the custodian on behalf of the sector, and which is used for analysis and information provision to improve the services and capabilities of the publicly funded health and disability sector.

[2]   Version 1 of the CIHI Framework was superseded by a revised version 2 in June 2005 after this work was completed. The two versions (Canadian Institute for Health Information, 2003a, 2005) are essentially the same although the newer version has fewer criteria (58) but has added "documentation" as a sixth dimension.

Copyright © 2007, Idea Group Inc. Copying or distributing in print or electronic forms without written permission of Idea Group Inc. is prohibited.

Chapter VI

Assessment and Improvement of Data and Information Quality

Ismael Caballero, University of Castilla - La Mancha, Spain

Mario Piattini, University of Castilla - La Mancha, Spain

Abstract

This chapter introduces a way for assessing and improving information quality on organiza-tions. Information is one of the most important assets for today's enterprises since it is the basis for organizational decisions. However, as information is produced from data, both data and information quality must be managed. Although many researchers have proposed technical and managerial solutions to some specific information quality problems, an integrative framework which brings together these kinds of solutions is still lacking. Our proposal consists of a framework for assessing and improving information quality through the concept of information management process (IMP). An IMP is assessed according to an information quality maturity model by using an assessment and improvement methodol-ogy. The framework provides a consistent roadway for coordinating efforts and resources to manage information quality with a strategic perspective. As an application example, a study case has been included in the chapter.

Copyright © 2007, Idea Group Inc. Copying or distributing in print or electronic forms without written permission of Idea Group Inc. is prohibited.

Introduction: The Problem

It is a widely known fact that an organization depends on data and information quality for effective operations and decision making (Price & Shanks, 2005). These decisions directly affect both the success of the business (Eppler & Wittig, 2000; Gertz, Tamer, Saake, & Sattler, 2004; Pipino, Lee, & Wang, 2002) and the overall efficiency of organizations (Burgess, Gray, & Fiddian, 2003; Kim & Choi, 2003; Redman, 1996) since data and information are to be seen as among the most important assets for organizations (Huang, Lee, & Wang, 1999).

This situation leads organizations to take caution with their data and information to avoid problems due to poor quality. But dealing with information problems is not a trivial issue; it is not free and many resources are required (Xu, 2003) because quality assurance and management is a complex process, in which the difference between costs and required information quality is closely linked to the context of the application and organization requirements (Bringel, Caetano, & Tribolet, 2004). Most of the actual achieved pragmatic and theoretical efforts on information quality research are focused on solving specific and concrete objectives or subjective problems (Price & Shanks, 2005) regarding the technical or managerial information quality issues. These efforts often lack a strategic perspective that does not allow organizations to optimize the effectiveness of their information quality initiatives in an organizational scope because, among other important causes, there are no commitments from organization heads to improve the quality of existent data and information and new data (Motha & Viktor, 2001). All of these commitments must be oriented to avoid some kinds of potholes which can generate serious problems like data not used, barriers to data accessibility, or data utilization difficulty (Strong, Lee, & Wang, 1997). These problems may translate into important consequences at a technical level — as in data warehouse implementation (Celko, 1995) — at an organizational level — loss of customers (Redman, 1996), important financial losses (Loshin, 2001; Strong et al., 1997), or unsatisfied data workers (English, 1999) — or at the legal level because of privacy regulations. Many organizations, having identified their data and information quality problems, do not have the right techniques, tools, and practices to implement some of the proposed solutions from research (Kim & Choi, 2003). Information quality issues are not usually understood as a global problem for entire organizations, but punctual and isolated ones. It might be a matter of a quality management team, encouraged by organization heads, who must draw a clear understanding of the meaning of the term *information quality* (Price & Shanks, 2005) and information quality management. Then, they might implement several quality management concepts like information quality policy, information strategy, information quality planning, information quality control, and information quality assurance through organization (Helfert & von Maur, 2002; Hinrinchs, 2000) implying all workers by commitments and trying to coordinate efforts and resources in order to control and improve information quality issues with a strategic perspective (Motha & Viktor, 2001). Unfortunately, there is not yet an integrative framework that guides organizations to achieve information quality goals through management by implementing the previously mentioned concepts (Eppler, 2003; Pipino et al., 2002; Price & Shanks, 2005). The main aim of this chapter is to fulfill this lack by providing the necessary elements to improve not only quality of data and information, but also data and information management.

Copyright © 2007, Idea Group Inc. Copying or distributing in print or electronic forms without written permission of Idea Group Inc. is prohibited.

The remainder of this chapter is structured as follows: in the second section, the necessary background for understanding our proposal is exposed as the elements of the framework explained in the third and fourth sections. Finally, in the fifth section, a case study of applying the framework to a public enterprise can be found. Finally, in the sixth section, several conclusions are drawn.

Background

The problem is the need of organizations to have an integrative framework that allows for assessing and improving data and information quality to make decisions (Redman, 1996; Strong et al., 1997), which do not lead to certain errors affecting organization efficiency or business success, since they are not based on data and information quality with a poor quality.

Although much research covering different specific issues on data and information quality has been appearing over the last few years (Eppler & Wittig, 2000; Wang, Storey & Firth, 1995), there is still a lack of well-founded and practical approaches to assess or even guarantee, in an integrative way, a required degree of data and information quality (Gertz et al., 2004) because information quality goes beyond the definition of data and information quality dimensions and metrics (Xu, 2003) to manage it. Our idea of "integrative" includes not only technical data and information quality goals, but also managerial ones which can guide the organization towards the achievement of the best data and information quality management.

The starting point was to consider that an information system can be seen as a set of production processes, which are controlled by several quality management processes. These quality management processes can affect one or several production processes or even some of the elements that take part in the different processes. Moreover, these management processes could implement several quality and quality management policies. This initial consideration agrees with several lines of researching which propose the treatment of information as a product (Wang, 1998), where data is considered as the raw input material in the process of production (Ballou, Wang, Pazer, & Tayi, 1998; Dedeke, 2003; Huang et al., 1999; Lee, Strong, Kahn, & Wang, 2001), and information (data products) as the output of the production processes.

This analogy between information and typical products enables organizations to apply the classic principles and foundations of product quality management to quality management of data and information products (Firth & Wang, 1993) from an engineering point of view. This has been implicitly or explicitly suggested by several authors (such as Bobrowski, Marré, & Yankelevich, 1998). It is precisely this analogy that leads us to think about a production process as part of an information system. As said previously, this transformation/production process can be affected by one or several (quality) management processes.

For a data product to be able to become sound information, data (raw materials of this process) need to be gathered, stored, consulted, and presented/displayed according to certain rules of data and information quality, so that the production processes can generate data products that satisfy user requirements and needs. All these quality rules are part of the quality management processes. The quality management process could be defined as the set of activities and processes that an organization can develop in order to (1) design

Copyright © 2007, Idea Group Inc. Copying or distributing in print or electronic forms without written permission of Idea Group Inc. is prohibited.

and establish several quality policies and (2) identify techniques and procedures to assure the organizational resources for data and information are the right ones for the present and potential uses of the data (Ballou et al., 1998), that they fit the use of a product or service (Juran, 1988), or look for conformity with the requirements established previously (Crosby, 1979) so as to guarantee the customer requirements.

We need to draw up some reasoning to include and to connect this set of concepts and foundations. Fugata states, "A software process can be defined as the coherent set of policies, organizational structures, technologies, procedures, an artifacts that are needed to conceive, develop, deploy, and maintain a software product" (2000). If the set mentioned is compared to the definition of software process given by Fuggeta, (2000) and considering that the quality of any product cannot simply be assured by inspecting the product or by making mere statistical controls, it might make us think that a good approach to data and information management in organizations might be done taking into account the definition of the concept of the "information management software process (IMP)." IMP is intended to model how data and information and data and information quality is managed for a specific application. In this way, data and information quality is going to be managed by assessing and improving a specific IMP.

This hypothesis is supported by McLeod (1990) who explains that all software processes are formed by two subprocesses: production and management. The latter affects the production subprocess, controlling it so that the execution of some of the activities of the subprocess of management does not directly affect the quality of the developed data and information product.

With this reasoning and bearing in mind that there are several assessment and improvement frameworks for software processes like CMMI (SEI, 2002) or ISO 15504 (ISO, 1998), our aim was to develop a framework adapted to data and information quality issues.

Taking IMP into account as a software process allows us to consider an information system (IS) as a set of IMPs sharing several organizational resources. So, if an organization wants to improve its data and information quality level in an overall sense, an identification of IMPs and subsequent assessment and improvement must be done. To support this activity, two important elements should be provided:

- A data and information quality management model, known as CALDEA, similar to CMMI and SPICE, where the required and structured key processes areas (KPA) to satisfy each level are described. These KPAs focus on management and technical issues. For each KPA, some tools, techniques, standards, and practices and metrics as required are proposed, although each organization can use the ones that suit its needs best.
- An assessment and improvement methodology, known as EVAMECAL, similar to CBA-IPI (Dunaway, 1996), SCAMPI (SEI, 2001), or SPICE (ISO, 1998b), which consists of a set of steps that provide a basis for data/information quality measurement and that achieve improvement through proactive management.

Looking at the variety of lines of research on different data and information quality issues, our aim was to develop a framework as universal as possible, with the understanding that "universal" means that it is valid for any situation and any organization.

Copyright © 2007, Idea Group Inc. Copying or distributing in print or electronic forms without written permission of Idea Group Inc. is prohibited.

CALDEA: The Data and Information Quality Management Model

CALDEA defines five information quality management maturity levels for an IMP: initial, definition, integration, quantitative management, and optimizing. The levels are ordered by taking into account several information quality goals and their relative importance, providing a systematic and concise set of criteria according to which information can be assessed (Eppler & Wittig, 2000). Thus, at higher levels where more information quality issues are assured, it possible to state that more organizational requirements are satisfied. It is also possible to affirm that the higher the information quality maturity levels an organization has reached for its most important IMPs, the more competitive this organization can be due to the lack of information quality problems. The levels are established in the same way as the staged ones of CMMI, because it appears to be easier to work with a well-defined sequence of improvements (which cover basic management project fundamentals to complex data quality management issues). As previously mentioned, for each level, CALDEA addresses specific KPAs, which meet specific information quality goals. These KPAs are focused on not only technical but also managerial issues, providing the basis for information quality measurement and management and integrating both aspects in order to compensate for the lack of integrative frameworks mentioned in the introduction. Each KPA has been broken down into activities and tasks, which can be satisfied by using several techniques, practices, and tools. We should point out that the chosen KPAs, and their activities and tasks, are based on both CMMI's KPAs (SEI, 2002), and we learned a lesson as a result of our experiences in industrial and scientific initiatives regarding information quality.

Initial Level

An IMP is said to be at Initial Level when no efforts are made to achieve any information quality goals.

Definition Level

An IMP is said to be at definition level or defined when it has been defined and planned. This implies identifying all its components and their relationship. To achieve this goal, the following KPAs need to be satisfied:

- **Information quality management team management (IQMTM):** Data and information management quality initiatives required people having direct responsibility for them and for their integrity to support all of the activities that must be performed. These people must work in accordance with the organization's ideas and trends and must encourage the entire organization to show commitment to information quality policies (Ballou & Tayi, 1999), by making corresponding efforts in support of the activities of this maturity model. Among their abilities must be data and information quality and managerial abilities. Redman (2001) points out the need for upper managers to lead data and information quality initiatives. This implies selecting people to take care of data and information quality through IMP, and supporting activities related to

Copyright © 2007, Idea Group Inc. Copying or distributing in print or electronic forms without written permission of Idea Group Inc. is prohibited.

it, like standardization and measurements. Any techniques or tools related to human resources management may be used.

- **IMP project management (IPM):** The main goal of this KPA is to create a plan for coordinating efforts and draw up a document, which clearly describes an agenda of activities and a budget for optimizing the IMP. This document can be made by following IEEE 1058.1 (IEEE, 1987), for instance. Among other planned activities, the following must be carried out: a data and information requirements management, an analysis of these requirements, the design of a solution for satisfying them, the implementation of the process based on previous design, and testing of the implemented process. Any techniques or tools used on project development may be used here, for instance, PERT or CPM.

- **User requirements management (URM):** User requirements must be collected and documented. Three kinds of requirements might be identified (Wang, Kon, & Madnick, 1993): those related to the final product (URS), those related to IMP — which must be gathered in the User Requirement Specification for the IMP document (URS-IMP) — and those related to information quality — which must be gathered in the information quality user requirements specification (URS-IQ). These requirements are the starting point for modeling the IMP, the database or data warehouse, and other procedures. Some tools and techniques can help developers to get each document, like IEEE 830 (IEEE, 1998). There are some known graphical techniques for these issues, for example: for IMP, IP-MAP, given by Shankaranarayanan, Wang, and Ziad (2000); for database or data warehouse and data quality issues, the extended entity-relationship model proposed by Wang, Ziad, and Lee (2001).

- **Data sources and data targets management (DSTM):** Due to particular intrinsic characteristics of data, it is necessary to identify and to document data sources as well as data targets from URS-IMP in order to avoid problems like uncontrolled data redundancy or problems with data format interchange (Loshin, 2001). Ballou et al. (1998) and Hinrichs and Aden (2001) discuss these issues and suggest several ways of treating information from multiple sources. In a data warehouse environment, tools and techniques like ETLs must be used in order to unify the semantics and formats of incoming data (English, 1999).

- **Database or data qarehouse acquisition, development or maintenance project management (AIMPM):** Raw data must be collected and stored in an appropriate database or a data warehouse. In order to better assure information quality, it is highly recommended to draw up a project for acquisition, development, or maintenance of a database or a data warehouse management system, supporting both URS-IQ and URS-IMP. This KPA may also include other minor subactivities like data quality assurance (Jarke & Vassiliou, 1997), configuration management, maintenance management or commercial solution election management.

- **Information quality management in IMP components (DIQM):** The use of metrics for measuring IMP efficiency may help to improve it. It is therefore necessary to identify from the URS-IQ the dimensions of quality of information (in the same way as ISO 9126 (ISO, 2001) proposes for software) for each information quality component that must be controlled (Hoxmaier, 2001; Huang et al., 1999), as well as the metrics adapted for each one of those dimensions (Eppler, 2003; Kahn, Strong, & Wang, 2002; Pipino et al., 2002). A description of data quality dimension and a discussion about which are the most important can be found in the works of the major-

Copyright © 2007, Idea Group Inc. Copying or distributing in print or electronic forms without written permission of Idea Group Inc. is prohibited.

ity of the consulted authors. In order to make our proposal as universal as possible, no dimensions are mandatory, as this is not possible (Pipino et al., 2002) due to the fact that data and information quality depend directly on data/information problems. However, as guidance, the adopted standard data quality dimensions set, proposed by Strong et al. (1997), is recommended to information quality managers who are encouraged to find out the one best fits their problems. For helping them, generic methodologies might be used like IEEE 1061 (IEEE, 1992) or GQM, given by van Soligen and Berghout (1999). Even authors like Loshin (2001) have proposed a more specific data and information quality measurement framework with several and specific data quality issues to measure: data quality of data models, data quality of data values, data quality of data representation, or data quality of information policy. On the other hand, some authors like Ballou and Tayi (1999), Bouzeghoub and Kedad (2000), or Calero and Piattini (2002) have proposed metrics for measuring specific issues of specific components of IMP. An important aspect of measurements is the need to automate measurements, as required by Hinrichs (2000).

Integration Level

An IMP is said to be at integration level or Integrated when besides being defined (definition level has been achieved), many efforts are made to assure the IMP complies with organizational information quality requirements, standards, and policies. This implies standardizing different information quality learned lessons through information quality standards and policies to avoid previous errors and to allow better work in the future. The following KPAs must be satisfied:

- **Information products and IMP components validation and verification (VV):** Both information products and IMP components must be verified and validated to correct defects and discordances with the USR-IMP, USR-IQ, and the organizational information quality policies. A technique that can be used could be software inspections (Fagan, 1976; Gilb & Graham, 1993) but adapted to data/information quality issues. A more specific methodology, which can be used, is data testing proposed by Kiszkurno and Yankelevich (2001), expanded to IMP, because the data testing model is limited to data stored in an information system. In order to coordinate efforts, a plan for testing could be designed and drawn up by following, for instance, IEEE 1012 (IEEE, 1986).
- **Risk and poor information quality impact management (RM):** It is necessary to determine the impact of risks due to the poor quality of information in the IMP to limit them at the organizational level (English, 1999). Getto (2002) proposes a methodology that can be adapted to information quality issues to collect and document all risks.
- **Information quality standardization management (IQSM):** All lessons learned through specific experiences should be properly gathered, documented, and transmitted to the organizational knowledge base. An example of standardization could be the sixth process of TQdM (English, 2002, p. 86), which seeks to accomplish these issues "by integrating quality management beliefs, principles, and methods into the culture of the enterprise." Only by incorporating the latest data and information quality management experiences, the IMP performance will be higher than it would be otherwise.

Copyright © 2007, Idea Group Inc. Copying or distributing in print or electronic forms without written permission of Idea Group Inc. is prohibited.

- **Organizational information quality policies management (OIQPM):** A way to implement all the efforts previously mentioned consists of defining information quality policies based on the previously defined standards affecting not only single IMPs, but also the whole organization. The information quality management team must work on data and information quality policies, which reflect organizational culture. Loshin (2001) presents the elements that are the subject of data/information policy design. Organizations can be said to have an information quality culture when all their processes, related or not to information and information quality management, take into account data quality issues in order to improve it.

Quantitative Management

An IMP is said to be at a quantitative management level or quantitatively managed when integrated (itegration level has been achieved), several measurement plans have been developed and implemented, and measurement procedures have been automated. Therefore, the main information quality goal of this level is to obtain an automated quantitative compliance that IMP performance over a reasonable time period is as consistent as required in terms of variation and stability through a reliable set of measurements (Florac & Carlenton, 2002) information quality dimensions of IMP. This level is composed of the following KPA:

- **IMP measurement management (MM):** The aim of this KPA is to get some metrics that must be used to check conformity to specifications (Grimmer & Hinrichs, 2001; Loshin, 2001). As Meredith (2002) states, a plan for software quality measurements starts with the decision to take measures. This implies choosing "what," "when," and "how" to measure and how to represent these measures and to "whom" the measures will be presented. Since metrics about the IMP have been drawn up at definition level ("what" question), the plan must focus on the remaining questions. As regards the "when" question, the answer is when measurements do not alter the IMP results. As far as the "how" question is concerned, some algorithms might be outlined in order to make measurements repeatable. Finally, as important as the metrics is the way in which the results are represented and to "whom." Many authors, such as English (1999) or Loshin (2001), propose the use of several control diagrams as a way of representing data about IMP. Another complementary way of representing the results is proposed by Humphrey (2002), in which Kiviat's diagrams are used to relate several aspects of the IMP or the data/information quality components.
- **IMP measurement plan automation management (AMP):** In order to increase the reliability and repeatability of measures, measurement procedures and algorithms (defined at MM KPA) must be automated as required by Hinrichs (2000). This KPA aims to study all the issues in relation to the automation of these management procedures.

Copyright © 2007, Idea Group Inc. Copying or distributing in print or electronic forms without written permission of Idea Group Inc. is prohibited.

Table 1. KPAs, their acronyms, and their criticalness degree (CD) for each maturity level

Level	Acronym	Stands for	CD	Level	Acronym	Stands for	CD	Level	Acronym	Stands for	CD
Definition Level (2)	IQMTM	Information Quality Management Team Management	10%	Integration Level (3)	VV	Information Products and IMP Components Validation and Verification	25%	Quantitative Management Level (4)	MM	IMP Measurement Management	70%
	URM	User Requirements Management	15%		RM	Risk and Poor Information Quality Impact Management	25%		AMP	IMP Measurement Plan Automation Management	30%
	IPM	IMP Project Managment	25%		OIQPM	Organizational Information Quality Policies Management	25%	Optimizing Level (5)	CADPM	Causal Analysis for Defects Prevention Management	50%
	DIQM	Data and Information Quality Management in IMP Components	10%		IQSM	Information Quality Standardization Management	25%		IODM	Innovation and Organizational Development Management	50%
	DSTM	Data Sources and Data Targets Management	25%								
	AIMPM	Database or Data Warehouse Acquisition, Development and Maintenance Project	25%								

Optimizing Level

An IMP is said to be at optimizing level when, quantitatively managed, the obtained measurements are used to develop a continuous improvement process by eliminating defects or by proposing and implementing several improvements. The following two KPAs must be satisfied:

- **Causal analysis for defects prevention management (CADPM):** From the study of the measurements results, some typical quality techniques and tools like statistical control process (SPC) can be applied to detect defects of information quality and identify their root causes. The conclusions obtained must provide a basis for a corresponding maintenance process for removing detected defects in affected resources. Smith and Heights (2002) offers a framework for defect prevention.
- **Innovation and organizational development management (IODM):** This is the basis for the concept of continuous improvement. Similar to previous KPA, here, the results can be used to improve the IMP in terms of higher performance, more efficient planned time or lower budget. Learned lessons in IMP must provide a basis not only for defect prevention, but also for continuous improvements.

Table 1 summarizes all KPA and their corresponding acronyms.

Copyright © 2007, Idea Group Inc. Copying or distributing in print or electronic forms without written permission of Idea Group Inc. is prohibited.

Table 2. Possible states for each item

Items	Possible States
Maturity Level	{"Achieved", "Not Achieved"}
KPA	{"Fully Satisfied", "Satisfied", "Partially Satisfied", "Not Satisfied"}
Activity in each KPA	{"Fully Executed", "Executed", "Partially Executed", "Not Executed"}
Component	{"Fully Optimized", "Optimized", "Partially Optimized", "Not Optimized"}

Figure 1. Formula to calculate ML-IQV

$$ML - IQV = \sum_{i=1}^{n} KPA - IQV_i * CD_i$$

EVAMECAL: The Assessment and Improvement Methodology

As stated, the main aim of EVAMECAL is to assess and improve a specific IMP of a given organization. It was originally based on Deming's (1986) PDCA, but it has been restructured by following the define-measure-analyze-improve sequence. As well as this adaptation, a new step has been added. This is to standardize the lessons learned through the most recent experiences.

The definition of goals, the measurement processes, the analysis criteria, and the improvement plans are carried out in terms of information quality maturity levels given by CALDEA. As each maturity level groups several KPAs, each KPA groups several activities, and each activity takes into account several components (any of the hardware or software elements or even persons belonging or not to the information system which takes a place in the IMP), the assessment process has the task of generating a state for each one. Table 2 gathers the mentioned states.

These states for maturity levels are calculated by using several questionnaires and several information quality values (IQVs) for each item; the IQVs are calculated by making a weighted average of the values of several metrics or responses to questionnaires. The weight for each IQV depends on the relative importance of the studied item in relation to a major item. So, for a maturity level having several KPAs, each KPA has a relative importance (criticalness degree). Let us call *ML-IQV* the IQV for a maturity level, *KPA-IQV* the IQV for each KPA, and *CD* the criticalness degree for each KPA. To calculate the ML-IQV for a given maturity level, the formula in Figure 2 must be applied (it is similar to the activities for each KPA and for components in each activity).

Proposed values for the criticalness degree for each KPA are shown in Table 1, in the column tabulated "CD." There is equivalence between the values of IQV (which are compatible to ISO/IEC 15504) and the corresponding states defined for each item (see Table 2). This equivalence is summarized in Table 3.

Copyright © 2007, Idea Group Inc. Copying or distributing in print or electronic forms without written permission of Idea Group Inc. is prohibited.

Table 3. Equivalence of value range for IQVs and corresponding states

Value Range for IQV		ItemState
IQV for Components, Activities, and KPAs	$0 \leq IQV \leq 20$	*"Not Optimized/Executed/Satisfied"*
	$21 \leq IQV \leq 60$	*"Partially Optimized/Executed/Satisfied"*
	$61 \leq IQV \leq 85$	*"Optimized/Executed/Satisfied"*
	$86 \leq IQV \leq 100$	*"Fully Optimized/Executed/Satisfied"*
IQV for Maturity Levels	$0 \leq ML\text{-}IQV \leq 90$	*"Not Achieved"*
	$91 \leq ML\text{-}IQV \leq 100$	*"Achieved"* if all inferior levels are at *"Achieved"*

Combining the activities required for a methodology of assessment and improvement applied to data and information quality as proposed by Ballou and Tayi (1999) and with Deming's PDCA cycle in mind, we can give a brief summary of the definition of EVAME-CAL as follows:

EVAMECAL – PLAN (EMC-P):

- **EMC-P.1. Assessment of the current state of data and information quality of the IMP:** The main goal of this step is to determine what the current state of the IMP is, in terms of information quality maturity levels and IQVs. This implies the next substeps:
  - *EMC-P.1.1. Assessment of data and information management maturity level of the IMP*, using a set of questionnaires that has been developed.
  - *EMC-P.1.2. Calculation of IQV for IMP components*, by measuring the chosen information quality dimensions and metrics for each component, in order to calculate the corresponding A-IQV.
- **EMC-P.2. Definitions of improvement goals in terms of data and information quality maturity level:** Any information quality initiative must set out a plan covering the goals to be improved. For the purpose of defining a plan for improving the most critical items first, EVAMECAL proposes to use the IQV as guidance for the identification of items mentioned.

EVAMECAL-DO (EMC-D):

- **EMC-D.1. Analysis of potential causes and development of an improvement plan:** The main goal of this activity is to determine the reasons why an IMP is not working as expected. To achieve this goal, the two following substeps are proposed:
  - *EMC-D.1.1. Analysis and comprehension of the problem.* To check whether any of the analyzed components have registered any kind of problems, several tests that allow the identification of these troubles and their possible sources need to be designed and executed.
  - *EMC-D.1.2. Detailed analysis of real causes of problems.* The main aim of this activity is to discover the real causes of problems in data and information quality.

Copyright © 2007, Idea Group Inc. Copying or distributing in print or electronic forms without written permission of Idea Group Inc. is prohibited.

o   *EMC-D.1.3. Development of a plan for improvements*, taking into account the required goals. A plan establishing the actions that must be performed to obtain a set of improvements for the IMP, it also defines when and how these actions must be executed, by whom, and what resources are implied.

- **EMC-D.2. Execution of the improvement plan:** Once an improvement plan has been drawn up and its viability has been approved, all actions for correction described in the plan must be carried out if the resources necessary are available.

EVAMECAL – CHECK (EMC-C):
- **EMC-C.1. Check the efficiency of the improvement plan:** To validate the success of the plan empirically, once more a set of tests must be performed. This implies measuring the current state of the maturity level again and checking whether information quality goals have been achieved.

EVAMECAL-ACT (EMC-A):
- **EMC-A.1. Obtain conclusions:** After checking the efficiency of the improvement plan, some conclusions are drawn with respect to the problems identified and their origins. These conclusions may be the basis for avoiding future problems or for solving similar ones.
- **EMC-A.2. Standardize the learned lesson in order to avoid future problems:** The Information Management Team must standardize the knowledge acquired through experience, the aim being to avoid future problems and to get better results.

The Surveys

For the assessment process, a set of surveys has been drawn up, which uses four different classes of questionnaires with different goals. These are to:

- Specify the nature of the organization and set out its particular character (with a total of 15 questions).
- Give the particular specifications of the IMP which is to be assessed and define its character (six questions).
- Assess the degree of achievement of each maturity level: several questions organized in different selective blocks. The questions are focused on the KPAs, activities, tasks, proposed techniques, tools and practices, along with the required products to be developed. The idea of organizing the questionnaire in several levels of depth is so that questions will be asked from the top, going down to lower levels only if neces-

Table 4. Number of questions by maturity and depth levels

DEPTH LEVEL:	1	2	3
Level Maturity 2	12	18	82
Level Maturity 3	8	7	24
Level Maturity 4	3	2	11
Level Maturity 5	4	2	11
Total Questions per depth level:	28	31	131
Total Questions in Questionnaire:		190	

Copyright © 2007, Idea Group Inc. Copying or distributing in print or electronic forms without written permission of Idea Group Inc. is prohibited.

sary. Thus, the block of questions of the first depth level serves to evaluate if KPAs are satisfied or not, thus avoiding, at this depth level, further questions which are not important when establishing specific aspects about the accomplishment of the more specific issues. These latter issues are dealt with at lower levels of depth. Thus, if all the answers to the questions of the first depth level differ from "Not Satisfied," then questions in the level immediately below should be answered, and so on. Altogether, 190 questions would be answered in the case of all the replies to the questions of the first and the second depth level differing from "Not Satisfied." In order to calculate the corresponding IQV for each item, the answers to these questions must be subjectively ranked from 0 to 100, 0 the most negative response and 100 the most positive one. For instance, if an organization wants to evaluate if an activity is executed or not, the response might be 0 if it is not carried out, 50 if it is partially performed, or 100 if it is fully executed. In the appendix of this chapter, the survey for the first level can be found.

- Finally, in order to collate and compare the answers with previous questionnaires, there is a final block of questions with descriptive and textual language.

A Case Study

The framework was applied to different organizations. In the following subsection, the results of the application to an information system consulting company are summarized.

Description of the Organization

The organization in which the framework has been applied is the Centro Provincial de Informática (CENPRI) of the Excelentísima Diputación Provincial of Ciudad Real. The main aim of this organization is to give the necessary hardware and software support to the Diputación Provincial (Provincial Council) itself and to the town councils of the province of Ciudad Real. It also gives support to the training of nearly 50% of the 800 workers who use a computer in their daily job. For software support, the CENPRI develops its own applications using DBMS Ingress. They have wide and solid experience in the use of this DBMS, experience demonstrated at an international level. All applications have been developed under internal software quality rules, policies, and standards. These standards have been developed internally by adapting several other software engineering standards to the work carried out there everyday. The experience accumulated over many years in the data and information quality field is taken into account, along with that gained from solving issues arising in the area of the quality of data and information used. Work sessions were conducted from September 2004 to February 2005 with the Director of the CENPRI.

Description of the Studied IMP

Among all those IMPs managed by the CENPRI, "Tribute Management" was decided on as an object of study, since it was considered to be one of the most important IMPs of the organization. Basically, the phases of this process are:

Copyright © 2007, Idea Group Inc. Copying or distributing in print or electronic forms without written permission of Idea Group Inc. is prohibited.

- Collection of data from the different town councils of the province in any possible format (CD, diskette, electronic mail, etc.).
- Cleaning of the data before it is stored into the databases. Cleaning them consists, fundamentally, of assuring that the format is the right one and that data is sound. In order to achieve this goal, data is going to be compared to supposedly trustworthy stored data. With unsuccessful data, a report with errors must be generated. All of these errors must be solved by the administrative personnel using other traditional tools and techniques.
- Once data is clean, it must be stored in corresponding databases. If new errors arise, then they must be gathered in a report so as to be corrected as soon as possible.
- The processes of generation and receipt emission are executed. Then receipts are sent to the contributors.
- During the period of payment, several associate banks receive the money from the contributors and when this time is over, they send the corresponding data about what has been paid to CENPRI. This data is validated before being stored in the database.
- Once the data is validated, the information compiled is sent back to the different municipal governments (town councils).

All these steps are drawn using IP-MAP (Shankaranarayanan et al., 2000) in Figure 2.

In this process, information coming from municipal government (data sources and format in which incoming data is sent) and output information (emission and sending out of receipts to the contributors) are of great importance (data product targets) since they are the main goal of this process. The organization has invested a major part of its efforts since 1991 in improving data and information quality for these two elements. These efforts have been directed towards the improvement of data quality by the production of several filters that allow the identification and correction of data which have erroneous values and formats. During this time, these filters have allowed them to improve the proportion of taxes collected from 75% in 1992 to 95% at present. This has meant a greater amount of income for the Diputación Provincial of Ciudad Real (Provincial Government). Regarding data and information quality dimensions, it should be pointed out that they do not have an explicit definition. Suitable treatment of this aspect has been sought implicitly, in most cases. As regards the metrics related to the corresponding quality dimensions, some of these have been produced to measure the degree of efficiency of the software developed.

Description of the Application of the Framework

EVAMECAL was applied to the "Tribute Management" IMP to assess its maturity level and to make a list of all possible improvements that it could undergo. It was agreed that the focus would be on KPAs for the level of definition only. This study took place as a pilot scheme so as not to disturb the rest of the organization's work.

The application of the framework was planned for the period from September 2004 to February 2005. The assessment work (EMC-P.1) took about three and a half weeks. After the assessment period, a list of improvement proposals (EMC-P.2) was suggested to the organization. Once the root causes for disparities in relation to the reference model were identified, an improvement plan was drawn up (EMC-D.1.3): an Improvement Implementation Time (hereafter IIT) of five months for EMC-D.2 was agreed on, before beginning the

Copyright © 2007, Idea Group Inc. Copying or distributing in print or electronic forms without written permission of Idea Group Inc. is prohibited.

Figure 2. Modeling the "Tribute Management" IMP using IP-MAP

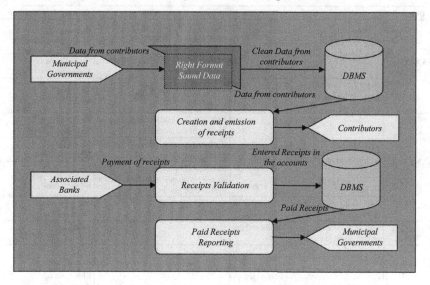

EMC-C.1 step. By the first of February 2005, the reassessment work (EMC-C.1) began again and this took about two weeks. Finally, and as a part of EVAMECAL-ACT phase, members of CENPRI were working hard on conclusions and the way to standardize it. Table 5 shows the agenda that is proposed for the application of the framework.

Conclusions about assessment and improvement are presented and corresponding graphs and diagrams about quantitative results in the evaluation are drawn in the following sections.

Execution of EVAMECAL-PLAN

The two main goals of EVAMECAL-PLAN are, on one hand, to determine the actual state of the IMP and, on the other hand, to define the improvement goals.

In order to determine the present state of the IMP, the questionnaires were sent to the Director of the CENPRI, and IQV were calculated when possible. The main conclusions of the assessment were:

- **Data and information quality management team (IQMT) management (IQMTM):** The organization does not yet possess any team specialized in managing data and information quality. It had no roles or responsibilities regarding this and no standards, techniques, and tools were observable. Nevertheless, all related tasks and activities are carried out by the director of the CENPRI, although there is no documented catalogue of activities and tasks. The KPA-IQV was calculated as 18 (from results of questionnaires); thus the KPA was in a "Not Satisfied" level. As a measure to improve this KPA, the creation of a data and information quality management team and the identification of roles and responsibilities were proposed.

Copyright © 2007, Idea Group Inc. Copying or distributing in print or electronic forms without written permission of Idea Group Inc. is prohibited.

Table 5. Agenda for application of the framework at CENPRI

Phase	Steps	Activities	Agreed Starting Date
EVAMECAL — PLAN.	EMC-P.1. Assessment of the current state of data and information quality of the IMP.	EMC-P.1.1. Assessment of Data and Information Management Maturity Level of the IMP.	First week of September 2004
		EMC-P.1.2. Calculation of IQV for IMP Components.	Second week of September 2004
	EMC-P.2. Definitions of improvement goals in terms of information quality maturity level.		Third week of September 2004
EVAMECAL — DO.	EMC-D.1. Analysis of potential causes and development of an improvement plan.	EMC-D.1.1. Analysis and Comprehension of the problem.	Fourth week of September 2004
		EMC-D.1.2. Detailed Analysis of real causes of problems.	Fourth week of September 2004
		EMC-D.1.3. Development of a plan for improvements taking into account the required goals.	First week of October 2004
	EMC-D.2. Execution of the improvement plan.		Second week of October 2004
EVAMECAL — CHECK.	EMC-C.1. Check the efficiency of the improvement plan.		First week of February 2005
EVAMECAL — ACT.	EMC-A.1. Obtain Conclusions.		First week of March 2005
	EMC-A.2. Standardize the learned lesson in order to avoid future problems.		First week of April 2005

- **IMP project management (IPM):** Something similar to the drawing up of a project for this IMP had already been achieved, since the organization had managed this process for years using its experience gained over that time. This has never been seen as a data transformation process, but in spite of this, much of the work required by CALDEA in relation to this issue had already been achieved. From the replies in the questionnaires, this KPA has obtained a value of 42 ("partially satisfied"). As an improvement proposal, the formalization of a project for the IMP that was assessed here was suggested. This suggestion involved making several estimations whose aims were to define a life cycle for data and a plan for its correct implantation.
- **User requirement management (URM):** User and user quality requirements for procedures were managed properly, but data and information quality requirements were dealt with in an implicit way, without any formalization or documentation. As the organization has enough infrastructure to support this KPA, and considering the answers of the interlocutor, this KPA was assessed with a value of 45 ("partially satisfied"). With the aim of improving the data and information quality requirement management, a formalization and documentation of this KPA was proposed.
- **Data sources and data target management (DSTM):** Data sources and targets were completely identified, and several filters and mechanisms have been developed to give uniformity in the formats of the data. This situation caused this KPA to fall within the level of "fully satisfied" (87). No improvement proposals were suggested at this KPA since there were other more important goals to achieve.
- **Database or data warehouse acquisition, development or maintenance project management (AIMPM):** The database, where data is stored, belongs to the organization and has been suitably designed and developed to support "tribute management," following internal standards and development methodologies. The procedure and data

Copyright © 2007, Idea Group Inc. Copying or distributing in print or electronic forms without written permission of Idea Group Inc. is prohibited.

models were designed and developed with the database. They used the DBMS Ingress; nevertheless, no part of the aspect of data and information quality had been monitored. The qualification obtained for this KPA-IQV was 59 ("partially satisfied") as recommended by the replies to questionnaires. Since data and information management quality user requirements have not been observed, and although several mechanisms to avoid respective data and information quality problems have been implemented, the main improvement proposal was to implement those kinds of requirements when possible. Another suggestion was to get proper documentation of the database linked to the IMP, and to put a configuration control for changes into operation.

- **Information quality management in IMP components (IQM):** Although many data and information quality initiatives have been implemented, the organization does not yet have a sense of the dimension of data and information quality or the metrics to deal with several data and information quality trouble points. All they have done is to identify several problems, and they have hardly worked at all towards solving these or have avoided them. For this reason, the qualification obtained in this KPA was only a 12 ("not satisfied"). So, as an improvement proposal, the choice of the most appropriate data and information quality dimensions and metrics for each one of the components of the IMP was forcefully suggested and encouraged.

Execution of EVAMECAL-DO and EVAMECAL-CHECK

Having carried out the assessment as well as proposing a plan for the implementation of the improvements and as the agenda agreed upon had been set, the work to achieve the improvements was carried out during the improvement implementation time (IIT). When this period ended, the reassessment work to check the efficiency of the plan began, obtaining the following results:

- **Data and information quality management team management (IQMTM):** To satisfy the improvement proposal for this KPA, the need to create an IQMT was demonstrated to the organization. Once this need was accepted, the organization set aside a series of human and material resources to have an IMQT which has put into operation all the activities and tasks related to data and information quality. After the reassessment work, the qualification for this KPA was a value of 62, thereby achieving a state of "satisfied."
- **IMP project management (IPM):** This KPA was not satisfied because the data and information management area had not been monitored and because several basic project rules had not been used. The IQMT worked on this KPA, trying to implement all suggested improvement proposals during the IIT. In the end, several goals were achieved and a qualification of 70 ("satisfied") for the KPA-IQV was obtained.
- **User requirement management (URM):** To satisfy the main goals of this KPA, all data and information quality user requirements must be gathered, documented, and observed in an appropriate way. As the organization has worked with other types of different user requirements, an observation of this kind of requirement can be done easily. After the IIT, all types of requirements were gathered and documented, but they were not completely implemented. The new evaluation of this KPA got a "satisfied" (75) qualification

Copyright © 2007, Idea Group Inc. Copying or distributing in print or electronic forms without written permission of Idea Group Inc. is prohibited.

Figure 3. States of the KPAs for level of definition before and after IIT

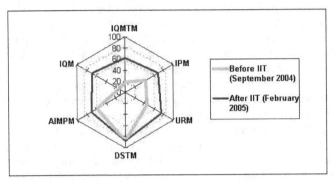

- **Data sources and data target management (DSTM):** As no improvement proposals were suggested, no activities were planned or executed. This KPA kept the same qualification of 87 ("fully satisfied").
- **Database or data warehouse acquisition, development or maintenance project management (AIMPM):** The main improvement proposal depended on the execution of an improvement plan for the URM KPA. As this plan was successfully implemented, the introduction of data and information management requirements would, logically, also be done. But after IIT, not all requirements were implemented, due to limits on time. For this reason, the reassessment work gave a qualification of 71 ("satisfied") for this KPA.
- **Information quality management in IMP components (IQM):** The problem when achieving this KPA was that the workers of the IQMT did not have a sense of data and information quality dimensions and metrics. So, in order to achieve the main goal of the improvement proposal, the concept itself and other foundations related to data and information quality dimensions and metrics were explained to the members of IQMT. After the IIT, some dimensions for data value quality and for the relational schema of the database were identified and some metrics from these dimensions were derived and applied. The qualification of this KPA after the improvements went up to "satisfied" (68).

Figure 3 shows the results of the application of the framework to the IMP. Making the corresponding calculations, the "tribute management" IMP has "not achieved" the level of maturity of "definition" either before (ML-IQV = 45,8) or after (ML-IQV = 78,4) the improvements.

Execution of EVAMECAL-ACT

After the experiences applying the framework, members of CENPRI were working on several conclusions (EMC-A.1) about the obtained results. The main one was that the intervention of the directives of the organization and their commitments with the data and information quality initiatives is necessary. Other conclusions related to technical and

Copyright © 2007, Idea Group Inc. Copying or distributing in print or electronic forms without written permission of Idea Group Inc. is prohibited.

managerial issues were formulated, and several data and information quality policies and rules were formulated in order to standardize the learned lesson to avoid future problems (EMC-A.2).

Conclusion

In this chapter, the concept of IMP and a framework to optimize information quality in organizations have been presented. It consists of two elements: an information quality management model (CALDEA) and an assessment and improvement methodology (EVAME-CAL). The way to use this framework may be stated as follows: first, identify the IMPs of the organization and choose the most critical ones; second, apply EVAMECAL for assessing and improving the chosen IMPs. Assessment and improvement sequences are going to be made having CALDEA as a reference.

These components satisfy the conditions proposed by Eppler and Wittig (2000) for a good information quality framework: CALDEA provide a systematic and concise set of criteria for information quality according to which information can be evaluated. EVAME-CAL provide a schema to analyze and solve information quality problems. Some KPAs in CALDEA provide the basis for information quality measurement and proactive management. CALDEA is by itself a conceptual map that can be used to structure a variety of approaches, theories, and information quality related phenomena since KPA does not propose a closed set of tools, techniques, and methodologies.

It is important to realize that the framework has only focused on KPAs of level of definition, and the application of the framework has been done in a limited time framework that had been agreed on beforehand. After the experience, several conclusions were reached related to the framework:

- CALDEA successfully supports all issues related to data and information quality management. Although one of the most important goals for the framework was to develop a universal and independent one, a set of tools and techniques might be gathered in order to give a complete catalogue to the organizations which are not yet familiar with any.
- EVAMECAL can be applied again and again until IMP gets the qualification of "Achieved" for this level. Since the reference model has KPAs in different maturity levels which can be interdependent, it would be not possible to apply EVAMECAL to the same IPM at the same time for the purpose of assessing and improving several KPAs addressed at different levels.

Acknowledgments

This research is part of both CALIPO supported by Dirección General de Investigación of the Ministerio de Ciencia y Tecnología (TIC2003-07804-C05-03) and DIMENSIONS project supported by FEDER y la Consejería de Educación y Ciencia de la Junta de Comunidades de Castilla-La Mancha (PBC-05-012-1).

Copyright © 2007, Idea Group Inc. Copying or distributing in print or electronic forms without written permission of Idea Group Inc. is prohibited.

References

Ballou D., Wang R., Pazer, H., & Tayi, G. K. (1998). Modeling information manufacturing systems to determine information product quality. *Management Science 44*(4), 462-484.

Ballou, D., & Tayi, G. K. (1999, January). Enhancing data quality in data warehouse environments. *Communications of the ACM, 42*(I), 73-78.

Bobrowski, M., Marré, M., & Yankelevich, D. (1998, November). A software engineering view of data quality. In *Proceedings of Second International Software Quality in Europe*, Belgium.

Bouzeghoub, M., & Kedad, Z. (2000, June 5-6). A quality-based framework for physical data warehouse design. In *Proceedings of the International Workshop on Design and Management of Data Warehouse (DMDW 2000)*, Stockholm, Sweden (pp. 9.1 to 9.12). Retrieved June, 2006, from http://sunsite.informatik.rwth-aachen.de/Publications/CEUR-WS//Vol-28/index.html

Bringel, H., Caetano, A., & Tribolet, J. (2004, April 14-17). Business process modeling towards data quality assurance. In *Proceeding of ICEIS'2004*, Porto, Portugal (pp. 565-568).

Burgess, M. S. E., Gray, W. A. & Fiddian, N. J. (2003, November 7-9). A flexible quality framework for use within information retrieval. In *Proceedings of the Eighth International Conference on Information Quality (ICIQ'2003)* (pp. 297-313). Cambridge; Boston: MIT.

Calero, C., & Piattini, M. (2002). Metrics for databases: a way to assure the quality. In *Information and database quality* (pp. 57-84). Norwell, MA: Kluwer Academic Publishers.

Celko, J. (1995, October 15). Don't warehouse dirty data. *Datamation,* 42-52.

Crosby, P. B. (1979). *Quality is free.* New York: McGraw Hill.

Dedeke, A. (2003, November 7-9). Managing processes for information quality: A framework for process metadata development. In *Proceedings of the Eigth International Conference on Information Quality (ICIQ'2003)* (pp. 224-233). Cambridge; Boston: MIT.

Deming, W. E. (1986). *Out of the crisis.* Cambridge, MA: MIT Center for Advanced Engineering Study.

Dunaway, D. K. (1996). *CMM SM-based appraisal for internal process improvement (CBA IPI) lead assessor's guide* (CMU/SEI-96-HB-003). Pittsburgh, PA: Software Engineering Institute, Carnegie Mellon University.

English, L. P. (1999). *Improving data warehouse and business information quality: Methods for reducing costs and increasing profits.* New York: Willey & Sons.

English, L. P. (2002). Total quality data management (TQdM), methodology for information quality improvement. In *Information and database quality* (pp. 85-110). Norwell, MA: Kluwer Academic Publishers.

Eppler, M. J. (2003). *Managing information quality.* New York; Secacus: Springer-Verlag.

Eppler, M. J., & Wittig, D. (2000). Conceptualizing information quality: A review of information quality frameworks from the last ten years. In *Proceedings of the 2000 Conference on Information Quality* (pp. 83-96). Cambridge; Boston: MIT.

Copyright © 2007, Idea Group Inc. Copying or distributing in print or electronic forms without written permission of Idea Group Inc. is prohibited.

Fagan, M. (1976). Design and code inspections to reduce errors in program development. *IBM Systems Journal, 15*(3), 182-211.

Firth, C., & Wang, R. (1993, November 7-9). *Closing the data quality gap: Using ISO 9000 to study data quality.* Cambridge; Boston: MIT. Retrieved June, 2006, from http://web.mit.edu/tdqm/papers/93/pass1/93-03.html

Florac, W. A., & Carleton, A. D. (2002). Using statistical process control to measure software process. In T. Daughtrey (Ed.), *Fundamental concepts for the software quality engineer* (pp. 133-144). Milwaukee, WI: American Society for Quality.

Fuggeta, A. (2000). Software process: A roadmap. In A. Finkelstein (Ed.), *The future of software engineering* (pp. 27-34). ACM Press.

Gertz, M., Tamer, M., Saake, G., & Sattler, K. (2004, March). Report on the Dagstuhl Seminar —"data quality on the Web". *Proceedings of SIGMOD Record, 33*(1), 127-132.

Getto G. (2002). Risk management supporting quality management of software acquisition projects. In T. Daughtrey (Ed.), *Fundamental concepts for the software quality engineer* (pp. 25-38). Milwaukee, WI: American Society for Quality.

Gilb, T., & Graham, D. (1993). *Software inspection.* London: Addison-Wesley Longman.

Grimmer, U., & Hinrichs, H. (2001). A methodological approach to data quality management supported by data mining. In *Proceedings of the Sixth International Conference on Information Quality* (pp. 217-232). Cambridge, Boston: MIT.

Helfert, M., & von Maur, E. (2002). A strategy for managing data quality in data warehouse systems. In *Proceedings of the Sixth International Conference on Information Quality* (pp. 62-76). Cambridge; Boston: MIT.

Hinrichs, H. (2000). CLIQ — inteligent data quality management. In *Proceedings of the Fourth IEEE International Baltic Workshop on Databases and Information System.*

Hinrichs, H., & Aden, T. (2001, June 4) An ISO 9001:2000 compliant quality management system for data integration in data warehouse system. In *Proceedings of the International Workshop on Design and Management of Data Warehouse (DMDW'2001),* Interlaken, Switzerland.

Hoxmeier, J. A. (2001). Dimensions of database quality. In S. Becker (Ed.), *Developing quality complex database systems: Practices, techniques, and technologies* (pp. 28-47). Hershey, PA: Idea Group Publishing.

Huang, K. T., Lee, Y., & Wang, R. (1999). *Quality information and knowledge.* Upper Saddle River, NJ: Prentice Hall.

Humprhey, W. (2002). The software standard profile. In T. Daughtrey (Ed.), *Fundamental concepts for the software quality engineer* (pp. 3-16). Milwaukee, WI: American Society for Quality.

IEEE. (1986). *IEEE STD 1012-1986 IEEE Standard for Software Verification and Validation Plans.* New York: IEEE Computer Society.

IEEE. (1987). *IEEE STD 1058.1-1987 IEEE Standard for Software Project Management Plans.* New York: IEEE Computer Society.

IEEE. (1992). *IEEE STD 1061-1992. IEEE Standard for a Software Quality Metrics Methodology.* New York: IEEE Computer Society.

IEEE. (1998). *IEEE STD 830-1998. IEEE Standard guide to Software Requirements Specification.* New York: IEEE Computer Society.

ISO. (1998). *ISO IEC 15504 TR2: 1998, part 2: A reference model for processes and process capability, ISO/IEC JTC1/SC7.* Geneva, Switzerland: International Organization for Standarization.

Copyright © 2007, Idea Group Inc. Copying or distributing in print or electronic forms without written permission of Idea Group Inc. is prohibited.

ISO. (1998). *ISO IEC 15504 TR2: Software Process Assessment — Part 7: Guide for use in process improvement, ISO/IEC JTC1/SC7.* Geneva, Switzerland: International Organization for Standarization.

ISO. (2001). *ISO/IEC 9126: Information technology — software product evaluation — quality characteristics and guidelines for their use.* Geneva, Switzerland: International Organization for Standarization.

Jarke, M., & Vassiliou, Y. (1997). Data warehouse quality: A review of the DWQ project. In *Proceedings of the Second Conference on Information Quality.* Cambridge, MA: MIT.

Juran, J. M. (1988). *Juran on planning for quality.* New York: McMillan.

Kahn, B., Strong, D., & Wang, R. (2002, April). Information quality benchmarks: Product and service performance. *Communications of the ACM, 45*(4), 184-192.

Kim, W., & Choi, B. (2003, July-August). Towards quantifying data quality costs. *Journal of Object Technology, 2*(4), 69-76.

Kiszkurno, E., & Yankelevich, D. (2001, September 10-12). Testing de Datos. In *Proceedings of the Second Argentine Symposium on Software Engineering ASSE 2001*, Buenos Aires, Argentina.

Lee, Y. W., Strong, D., Kahn, B., & Wang, R. (2001). AIMQ: A methodology for information quality assessment. *Information & Management 40*(2), 133-146.

Loshin D. (2001). *Enterprises knowledge management: The data quality approach.* San Francisco: Morgan Kauffman.

McLeod, R. (1990). *Management information systems.* New York: McMillan Publishing.

Meredith, D. C. (2002). Managing with metrics: Theory into practice. In T. Daughtrey (Ed.), Fundamental concepts for the software quality engineer (pp. 145-154). Milwaukee, WI: American Society for Quality.

Motha, W. M., & Viktor, H. L. (2001, July 22-25). *Expanding Organizational Excellence: The Interplay Between Data Quality and Organizational Performance, International Conference on Systems, Cybernetics and Informatics (SCI'2001),* Orlando, FL (Vol. XI, pp.60-65).

Pipino, L., Lee, Y., & Wang, R. (2002, April). Data quality assessment. *Communications of the ACM, 45*(4).

Price, R., & Shanks, G. (2005). A semiotic information quality framework: Development and comparative analysis. *Journal of Information Technology, 20*(2), 88-102.

Redman, T. C. (1996). *Data quality for the information age.* Boston: Artech House Publishers.

Redman, T. C. (2001). *Data quality: The field guide.* Newton, MA: Digital Press.

SEI. (2002). *SEI Capability Maturity Model® Integration (CMMI^{SM}), Version 1.1 CMMI^{SM} (CMMI-SE/SW/IPPD/SS, V1.1) Staged Representation (CMU/SEI-2002-TR-012 ESC-TR-2002-012).* Retrieved July, 2005, from http://www.sei.cmu.edu/publications/documents/02.reports/02tr002.html

Shankaranarayanan, G., Wang, R., & Ziad, M. (2000). IP-MAP: Representing the manufacture of an information product. In *Proceedings of the 2000 Conference on Information Quality* (pp. 1-16). Cambridge, MA: MIT.

Copyright © 2007, Idea Group Inc. Copying or distributing in print or electronic forms without written permission of Idea Group Inc. is prohibited.

Smith, C., & Heights, A. (2002). Defect prevention: The road less traveled. In T. Daughtrey (Ed.), *Fundamental concepts for the software quality engineer* (pp. 95-104). Milwaukee, WI: American Society for Quality.

SEI. (2001). *Standard CMMI SM Appraisal Method for Process Improvement (SCAMPI SM), Version1.1: Method Definition Document (CMU/SEI-2001-HB-001).*

Strong, D. M., Lee, Y. W., & Wang, R. Y. (1997). Data quality in context. *Communications of the ACM, 40*(5), 103-110.

Van Soligen, R., & Berghout, E. (1999). *The goal/question/metric metodology: A practical guide for quality improvement of software development.* London: McGraw-Hill.

Wang, R. (1998, February). A product perspective on data quality management. *Communications of the AM, 41*(2), 58-65.

Wang, R., Kon, H., & Madnick S. (1993). Data quality requirements analisys and modeling. In *Proceedings of the Ninth International Conference of Data Engineering,* Vienna, Austria (pp. 670 – 677).

Wang, R., Storey V. C., & Firth, C. F. (1995). A framework for analysis of data quality research. *IEEE Transactions on Knowledge and Data Engineering, 7*(4), 623-640.

Wang, R., Strong, D., & Guarascio, L. M. (1996, Spring). Beyond accuracy: What data quality means to data consumers. *Journal of Management Information Systems, 12*(4), 5-33.

Wang, R., Ziad, M., & Lee, Y. W. (2001) *Data quality.* Boston: Kluwer Academic Publishers.

Xu, H. (2003). Would organization size matter for data quality. In *Proceedings of the Eighth Conference on Information Quality ICIQ'2003* (pp. 365-379).

Appendix: Questionnaire of First Level

This is the block of questionnaires of the First Level for EVAMECAL. The idea is the following: once all the questions have been asked and depending on the values of the responses, the Information Quality Management Team must assess if it is worth it to keep on asking more specific questions about specific issues in which the organization does not have any of its energies deployed and where all the responses will probably be "No/Never."

To evaluate the degree of satisfaction of issues in each question subjectively, the responses could be "Yes/Always," "Sometimes/Partially," or "No/Never." As this assessment process is meant to be automated, for the corresponding calculations of the IQV, it is recommended that the responses be assigned a numerical value, with 100 or close to it being "Yes/Always," 50 or close to it for "Sometimes/Partially," and 0 or close to it for "No/Never." Threshold values for the IQVs of each block must be established, and these can be used by the IQMT as criteria in deciding whether there is any need to ask further questions or not.

Questions are grouped by level, and for each level they are grouped by KPAs. So questions are codified by adding a "Q" of "Question" to the abbreviations for the KPA names according to Table 1 of this chapter.

Copyright © 2007, Idea Group Inc. Copying or distributing in print or electronic forms without written permission of Idea Group Inc. is prohibited.

Grouped by levels, the questions are:

Level 2: Definition
- IQMTM-Q.a. Has the Information Quality Management Team (IQMT) Management been satisfied?
- IQMTM-Q.b. Have any standards, techniques, and/or tools been used in the management of the IQMT?
- IQMTM-Q.c. Has the IQMT's work satisfied the organization?

- IMP-Q.a. Has the management of a project for the IMP been carried out?
- IMP-Q.b. Have standards, techniques, and/or tools been used for the design of the IMP project?
- IMP-Q.c. Has this management of the IMP project satisfied the organization?

- URM-Q.a. Have the user requirements been managed appropriately?
- URM-Q.b. Have any standards, techniques, and/or tools been used for the identification and documentation of user requirements?
- URM-Q.c. Has this management of user requirements satisfied the organization?

- DSTM-Q.a. Have both data sources and data product targets been managed appropriately?
- DSTM-Q.b. Have any standards, techniques, or tools been used for the management of sources and drains of data?
- DSTM-Q.c. Has this management of both data sources and data product targets satisfied the organization?

- AIMPM-Q.a. Has any project for the acquisition, the development, or the maintenance of a database or data warehouse been outlined?
- AIMPM-Q.b. Have any standards, techniques, or tools been used for the acquisition, the development, or the maintenance of a database or data warehouse?
- AIMPM-Q.c. Has this management of projects for the acquisition, the development, or the maintenance of the database or data warehouse satisfied the organization?

- DIQM-Q.a. Has data and information quality for the components of the IMP been managed correctly?
- DIQM-Q.b. Have IQV for data and information quality been calculated?
- DIQM-Q.c. Has this management of IQVs satisfied the organization?

Level 3: Integration
- VV-Q.a. Has the validation and verification of the components of the IMP been carried out in an appropriate way?
- VV-Q.b. Have any standards, techniques, or tools been used for the validation and verification?
- VV-Q.c. Has the validation and verification of the IMP and their components satisfied the organization?

Copyright © 2007, Idea Group Inc. Copying or distributing in print or electronic forms without written permission of Idea Group Inc. is prohibited.

- RM-Q.a. Has the impact of the risks on the IMP derived from poor data and information quality been managed appropriately?
- RM-Q.b. Have any standards, techniques, or tools been used for the management of risks originating from poor data and information quality?

RM-Q.c. Has this management of the impact of risks satisfied the organization?

- IQSM-Q.a. Has the standardization of the quality of the data been managed in the right way?
- IQSM-Q.b. Have any standards, techniques, or tools been used for the management of data and information quality standardization?
- IQSM-Q.c. Has this management of data and information quality standardization satisfied the organization?

- OIQPM-Q.a. Have organizational data and information quality policies been managed appropriately?
- OIQPM-Q.b. Have any standards, techniques, or tools been used for the management of organizational data and information quality policies?
- OIQPM-Q.c. Has this management of organizational data and information quality policies satisfied the organization?

Level 4: Quantitative Management
- MM-Q.a. Have the IMP measurements been managed appropriately?
- MM-Q.b. Have any standards, techniques, or tools been used for the management of measurement of data and information quality?
- MM-Q.c. Has this management of measurement of data and information quality satisfied the organization?

- AMPM-Q.a. Have the automation of measurement processes been managed in the right way?
- AMPM-Q.b. Have any standards, techniques, or tools been used for the automation of measurement processes of data and information quality?
- AMPM-Q.c. Has this management of automation of measurement processes for data and information quality standardization satisfied the organization?

Level 5: Optimizing
- PACDP.a. Has a causal analysis for defect prevention been performed?
- PACDP.b. Have any standards, techniques, or tools been used for the causal analysis of defect prevention?
- PACDP.c. Has the way in which the causal analysis for defect prevention has been made satisfied the organization?

- IODM-Q.a. Has innovation and organizational development for the improvement of productivity in aspects related to data and information quality been carried out?
- IODM-Q.b. Have any standards, techniques, or tools been used for innovation and organizational development?
- IODM-Q.c. Has the way in which the innovation and organizational development has been done satisfied the organization?

Copyright © 2007, Idea Group Inc. Copying or distributing in print or electronic forms without written permission of Idea Group Inc. is prohibited.

Section III

IQ Process Mapping

Chapter VII

Integrating IP-Maps with Business Process Modeling

Elizabeth M. Pierce, Indiana University of Pennsylvania, USA

Abstract

This chapter takes the basic constructs of the IP-Map diagram and demonstrates how they can be combined with the event-driven process chain methodology's family of diagrams. This extended family of diagrams can be used to more fully describe the organizational, procedural, informational, and communication structure of a business process while at the same time highlighting the manufacture of the information products used by that business process. The chapter concludes with a review of requirements for a software package that will allow analysts to model and explore their business processes with an emphasis on improving the quality of the organization's information products.

Copyright © 2007, Idea Group Inc. Copying or distributing in print or electronic forms without written permission of Idea Group Inc. is prohibited.

Introduction

Traditionally information systems (IS) professionals have focused on the computer-based systems that produce the reports, charts, data extracts, invoices, and other data-based items that people use for conducting day-to-day activities or for making decisions. Within the last few years; however, there has been a growing movement among data quality researchers to view information as a product and to manage it in much the same way that a manufacturing company would manage the quality of its physical products (Wang, Lee, Pipino, & Strong, 1998). Under this view, the focus is on the information product rather than on the system that produced the product. Although the quality of the system is still important under the new paradigm, it is important for a different reason. A well designed, efficient, and effective information system is important insofar as it contributes to a higher quality information product being produced by that system.

Although there is much to be gained by using an analogy of a manufactured physical product, it should be noted that there are some notable differences between the characteristics of an information product and those of a physical product (Wang, 1998).

1. Unlike a physical product where the overall product and its quality are of interest to the consumer, for an information product it is the data items that comprise the information product and the quality of each that are of importance to the consumer. The information product must therefore be identified in terms of the data items used to manufacture it and must be specified by the final consumer of the information product. This breakdown drives the requirements of the raw information (raw data items) and the semiprocessed information (component data items) needed to manufacture the information product.
2. Raw data items and the component data items do not deplete when an information product is manufactured. While the raw data items may be stored for long periods of time, the component data items are stored temporarily until the final product is manufactured. The component items are regenerated each time an information product is needed. The same set of raw data and component data items may be used (sometimes simultaneously) in the manufacture of several different information products. The set of information products that use the same set of raw and component data items may be considered a group.
3. When describing the quality of raw data, component data, or information products, it should be noted that while some characteristics of quality apply to both physical and data-based products (e.g., completeness, availability, up-to-date, easy to use), other characteristics of information quality, such as believability, lack a counterpart in physical product manufacturing.

Another issue that adds to the complexity of managing information as a product is that information products can take several forms.

•   Information products like invoices, business reports, contracts, medical prescriptions, and paychecks have a prescribed format and are produced either on demand or on a scheduled basis for usually a large number of consumers. This type of information

Copyright © 2007, Idea Group Inc. Copying or distributing in print or electronic forms without written permission of Idea Group Inc. is prohibited.

product is similar in nature to a mass produced item. Although the data contained in the information product may vary among consumers, the format and rules for generating the information product remain the same. Improving the quality of this type of information product requires a thorough understanding of the information design needs of the consumer, how the raw data is collected and entered, and how the information product is created from the raw data.

- Other information products are more ad-hoc in nature. The results of queries or data analysis are typically of a flexible format, generated on demand and are used by only a few consumers. This type of information product is similar in nature to a one-of-a-kind or custom-made manufactured product. The consumers of these information products tend to be business analysts with a strong technical background. With the wide variety of data access tools available, the business analyst may act as both data consumer and producer. Cleaning up databases, improving the quality of metadata, or implementing a data warehouse often accomplishes improving the quality of this type of information product.

- Sometimes the information product is a collection of records such as a file, catalog, or database. Managing the quality of this information product is analogous to managing physical inventory. There are two aspects of quality to consider for this type of information product. One aspect is the quality of the individual records. The other aspect is the quality of the organization and management of the data collection. Quality of the individual records can be improved in the same way that a standardized information product can be improved. Quality of the organization and management of the data collection involves a review of the metadata, database/file design, and procedures used to manage the data store.

- The last type of information product includes such items as books, newspaper and magazine articles, and radio broadcasts. This type of information product is characterized by the complex way (text, pictures, sounds) its message is conveyed. In addition, this type of information product is often custom-made by a few people and then disseminated to a wide audience. These information products can suffer from quality problems such as disreputable sources, biasness, or poor presentation that prevent or distort the correct information from being communicated.

Regardless of the type of information product in question, quality is always an important consideration. Quality is a term that possesses many interpretations. Quality has been described in the literature as "a degree of excellence," "standards that have been met," "zero defects," "consistently meeting customers' expectations," and "fitness of use," to name just a few of the more common meanings. This chapter will consider any type of information products to be of high quality if they are fit for their intended use in conducting business operations, decision making, and planning as perceived by the customer (Redman, 2001).

To be able to effectively manage the quality of information products, IS professionals can employ several information management tools. Some of these tools are already in existence. For example, a good data dictionary containing data element definitions, table definitions, database schema, entity-relationship models, and access rights provides the IS professional with an excellent reference tool for understanding the structure of data stored within an organization. Data dictionaries are especially of value to the system development staff when they need to work on the applications that process the data within an organization.

Copyright © 2007, Idea Group Inc. Copying or distributing in print or electronic forms without written permission of Idea Group Inc. is prohibited.

Another example of a useful information tool is an electronic document management system (EDMS). EDMS tools aid people in the creation, management, control, and distribution of electronic documents such as legal papers for a major lawsuit or engineering plans for a major project. EDMS tools offer a variety of features such as catalog and search services, network support, document security, full text retrieval, document viewing, archiving, version control, document history, and group access control. EDMS tools are especially useful for people who want to effectively manage their documents once they have been created.

However, between the data dictionary that describes the structure of the data and the EDMS that manages the finished documents, there is a gap. There does not seem to be sufficient tools in place to assist the IS professional in understanding the production process, which transforms the raw data collected by the organization into the intermediate component data. These component data are then formed into the final information products distributed to the consumers in the organization. In terms of a manufacturing analogy, the data dictionary describes the raw data available to production while the EDMS manages the finished goods inventory. In between there should be tools to assist the IS professional in tracking the delivering, processing, and assembling of data into the finished information products. One of the emerging tools to address this gap is the IP-Map.

An information production map (IP-Map) is a graphical model designed to help people to comprehend, evaluate, and describe how an information product (e.g., an invoice, customer order, or prescription) is assembled (Shankaranarayanan, Wang, & Ziad, 2000). The IP-Map is aimed at creating a systematic representation for capturing the details associated with the manufacture of an information product. Although the IP-Map can be used to map the creation process of any type of information product, it is probably most suited for representing standardized information products that are mass produced in nature.

Ballou, Wang, Pazer, and Tayi (1998) first introduced the IP-Map approach to model the information production process using symbolic blocks similar to those used in data flow diagrams. To distinguish this model, which emphasizes terminology and parameters based on manufacturing concepts as well as introducing the data quality construct, Ballou et al. (1998) refers to these diagrams as information manufacturing models. Shankaranarayanan et al. (2000) later enhanced the work done by Ballou et al. (1998) by adding three new blocks to model decision points, IS boundary points, and organization boundary points. Shankaranarayanan et al. (2000) also added metadata describing the department/role, location, business process, data composition, and base system to each of the blocks so that the IP-Map would contain relevant descriptive information that would allow the data administrator to more easily retrieve details about each of the IP-Map constructs.

Shankaranarayanan et al. (2000) list several advantages of IP-Maps:

1.   The IP-Map representation allows a manager to visualize the most important phases in the manufacture of an information product and identify the critical phases that affect its quality.
2.   Using this representation, managers are able to pinpoint bottlenecks in the information manufacturing system and estimate the time to deliver the information product.
3.   Based on the principles of continuous improvement for the processes involved, the IP-Map representation helps identify ownership of the processes at each of these phases and helps in implementing quality-at-source.

Copyright © 2007, Idea Group Inc. Copying or distributing in print or electronic forms without written permission of Idea Group Inc. is prohibited.

4.   The representation helps managers to understand the organizational (business units) as well as information system boundaries spanned by the different processes/stages in the IP-Map.
5.   The representation permits the measurement of the quality of the information product at the different stages in the manufacturing process using appropriate quality dimensions. The IP-Map includes a repository for capturing the metadata associated with the IP-Map constructs. The metadata adds to the ability of the IP-MAP to comprehensively track and manage the information associated with the information product and serves to resolve issues concerning the quality of the information product.

Although IP-Maps are extremely useful for describing the manufacture of a given information product, it is difficult to capture within the IP-Map how various business processes may use the finished information product or contribute to its form and function. If one is to fully assess whether an information product is of sufficient quality, that is, meeting all criteria for fitness of use, it is important that one also understands the business processes that use and interface with this information product.

Thus, it would be helpful if IP-Maps could be extended to capture the answers to the following questions:

*   How does an information product fit into the business processes of an organization in terms of when and where it is used in the sequence of tasks that make up those business processes?
*   What is the communication structure between the data sources, data consumers, and various organizational groups involved in the manufacture and use of an information product?
*   What is the hierarchy or relationship between the different organizational groups involved in the manufacture and use of an information product?
*   What is the hierarchy or relationship between the different functions/tasks involved in the manufacture and use of an information product?
*   What is the relationship between the different information products, data storages, and other data components manufactured and used by an organization?

Therefore, the purpose of this chapter will be to demonstrate how the IP-Map's modeling of the manufacture of information products can be combined with the modeling of business processes that interface with these information products to create an integrated set of information product maps for quality improvement. The background section will illustrate the use of IP-Maps on a hypothetical example. The main thrust of the chapter will show how a business process modeling methodology like event-driven process chain diagrams can be combined with IP-Maps to give a complete picture of both the manufacture and utilization of an information product. The Future Trends and Conclusion section will summarize ongoing research in this area as well as review the main ideas presented in this chapter.

Copyright © 2007, Idea Group Inc. Copying or distributing in print or electronic forms without written permission of Idea Group Inc. is prohibited.

Background

To illustrate the use of IP-Maps, consider the case described earlier by Pierce (2001) of a fictitious school called Big State University (BSU). To improve the quality of its information products, BSU has embarked on a data quality campaign. BSU begins its campaign by asking each university department to identify the information products they use. One of these departments, the Office of Alumni Affairs, has identified mailing labels as an important information product. Incorrect or out-of-date mailing labels are a problem for alumni affairs. Undeliverable mail costs the school money in terms of unrecoverable printing and mailing costs, as well as potential lost donation revenue from missing or disgruntled alumni.

After the end of each semester, data about graduating seniors are taken from the Big State University's active student database by the registrar office and transferred to alumni affairs so they can add this information to their alumni database. Alumni are encouraged to send name/address corrections and other changes (marriages, divorces, births, phone number changes) to Alumni Affairs so that their information can be kept up to date. Alumni may choose to phone in the information, send e-mail via the Big State University's alumni Web site, stop by the alumni affairs office, or send updates via regular mail. The secretary at alumni affairs records this information into the alumni database on a weekly basis.

Unfortunately, only about 1 in 10 alumni remember to inform Big State University of their name and address changes. To track down moving alumni, every quarter alumni affairs sends a list of its mailing labels to a change of address service, which compares the address of alumni against its master list and identifies those addresses that have changed. This service has demonstrated it is able to detect and correct 95% of the changed addresses and can also identify misspelled addresses and names. In other words, 5% of the changed or incorrect addresses remain undetected by the change of address service. Besides the problem of incorrect or out-of-date addresses, there is also the problem of identifying deceased alumni. While relatives may contact Big State University about 20% of the time to stop the mailings to deceased alumni, in many cases, there is no notification. To help it identify deceased alumni, once a year, Big State University sends its active mailing list to an obituary service, which compares the list to its master list and can identify about 80% of the alumni who are now dead. When it is time for Big State University to send out an alumni publication, alumni affairs runs a program to create a list of mailing labels. The alumni affairs secretary checks the labels for format quality before pasting the labels onto the outgoing publication and sending them to the university post office for mailing. The alumni affairs group has determined that the criteria from Table 1 need to be met to be considered a list of mailing labels that are "fit for postal use."

To minimize the quantity of undeliverable mail going out to its alumni, BSU has decided to employ the IP-Map technique to model the manufacturing process of its alumni mailing labels.

There are eight types of construct blocks that form the IP-Map (Table 2). Each construct block is identified by a unique and non-null name and is further described by a set of attributes (metadata). The metadata identifies the following:

- The type of block and its identifier
- The business unit associated with this block

Copyright © 2007, Idea Group Inc. Copying or distributing in print or electronic forms without written permission of Idea Group Inc. is prohibited.

Table 1. List of quality issues identified for mailing label

Mailing Label		
Components	**Subcomponents**	**Potential Problems**
Recipient Line	Name treated as a whole	Typos — Mistakes in the spelling of the name occur infrequently and typically do not interfere with the publication's delivery. Changed (most often occurs in alumni data (STO_2) when female alumni marry or divorce). Alumni affairs estimates that about 6% of the alumni per year request a name change. Alumni Affairs also estimates that about 60% of the name changes also involve an address change as well.
Delivery Address Line	Address treated as a whole	Alumni affairs estimates that a small percentage of alumni have mistakes in their address. Typically typos include incorrect or missing direction suffix, wrong street name or number, wrong or missing route number, and wrong or missing apartment number. The address change service will generally catch and correct these mistakes. Changed (most often occurs in alumni data (STO_2) when alumni move). Alumni affairs estimates that 16% of their alumni change addresses each year.
Post Office, State, Zip Code + 4 Line	1. Post Office (City)	Alumni affairs estimates that a small percentage of alumni have mistakes in the city, state or zip fields. The address change service will generally catch and correct these mistakes. Changed (most often occurs in alumni data (STO_2) when alumni move to a new city). Alumni affairs estimate that 1/2 of the moves involve a change of city.
	2. State	Changed (most often occurs in Alumni Data (STO_2) when alumni move out of state). Alumni affairs estimates that one fourth of the moves involve a change of state.
	3. Zip Code + 4	Changed (most often occurs in alumni data (STO_2) when alumni move to a new zip code region). Alumni affairs estimates that three fourths of the moves involve a change in zip code.
Mailing Label as a Whole		Obsolete (occurs in alumni data (STO_2) when alumni die). Alumni affairs estimates that 8% of its alumni die each year. Duplicate labels — Duplicate labels rarely occur now that the program that loads new graduate data now checks for alumni with multiple degrees.

- The location of the business unit associate with the block
- A description of the business process associated with the block
- The data elements(s) that make up the data associated with the block
- The underlying IT system in which the data was stored and from which it originates
- Any quality issues identified with this block

Copyright © 2007, Idea Group Inc. Copying or distributing in print or electronic forms without written permission of Idea Group Inc. is prohibited.

Table 2. Constructs used in IP-Map diagrams (Source: Shankaranarayanan et al., 2000)

Construct Description	Construct Icon
Function or process block: Task that describes any transformations, manipulations, or calculations performed (i.e., What should be done? Example: Create purchase order, Update database.)	P_i
Source (raw input data) block: This block is used to represent the source of each raw (input) data that must be available in order to produce the information product expected by the consumer.	DS_i
Customer (output) block: This block is used to represent the consumer of the information product. The consumer specifies in this block the data elements that constitute the "finished" information product.	CB_i
Data quality block: This block is used to represent the checks for data quality on those data items that are essential in producing a "defect-free" information product. Therefore, associated with this block is a list of the data quality checks that are being performed on the specified component data items.	QB_i
Data storage block: This block is used to represent the capture of data items in storage files or databases so that they can be available for further processing.	STO_i
Decision block: In some complex information manufacturing systems, depending on the value of some particular data items(s), it may be necessary to direct the data items to a different set of blocks downstream for further processing. In such cases, a decision block is used to capture the different conditions to be evaluated and the corresponding procedures for handling the incoming data items based on the evaluation.	D_i
Business boundary block: The business boundary block is used to specify the movement of the information product (or raw/component data) across departmental or organizational boundaries. The role of the business boundary block in the IP-Map is to highlight the data quality problems that might arise when crossing business unit boundaries and therefore assign accountability to the appropriate business unit.	BB_i
Information system boundary block: This block is used to reflect the changes to the raw input data items or component data items as they move from one information system to another type of information system (Example: Paper to Electronic). These system changes could be intra or inter-business units.	SB_i
There are circumstances where the raw input data items or component data items go through both a business boundary and a system boundary change. The combined business-information system boundary block is defined for this purpose.	BSB_i

After thoroughly interviewing the alumni affairs' staff, BSU documents the process for the production of alumni mailing labels using an IP-Map and a set of metadata tables (Figure 1; Tables 3 and 4).

Main Thrust of the Chapter

In addition to the IP-Map, alumni affairs would also like to better document the business processes that use the information product. Event-driven process chains (EPCs) are an example of one technique used to model business processes (Curran & Ladd, 2000).

Copyright © 2007, Idea Group Inc. Copying or distributing in print or electronic forms without written permission of Idea Group Inc. is prohibited.

Figure 1. IP-MAP for production of alumni mailing labels

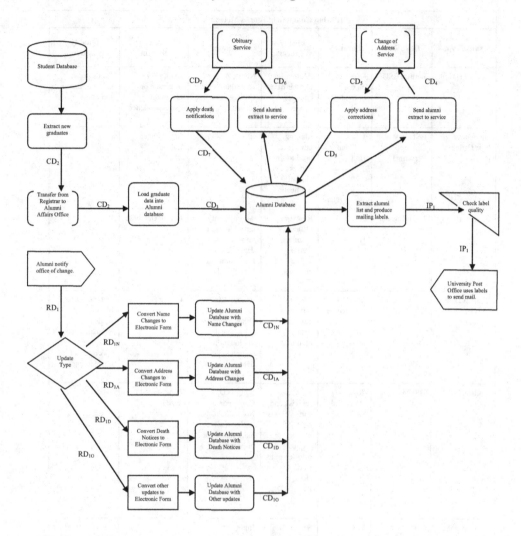

Note: *This map shows several source changes that alter the alumni data used to produce the mailing list; these sources include data for new graduates that are transferred from the registrar to alumni affairs, updates that are routinely received from alumni, and periodic mass clean-ups conducted by alumni affairs with the help of specialized vendors.*

Copyright © 2007, Idea Group Inc. Copying or distributing in print or electronic forms without written permission of Idea Group Inc. is prohibited.

Table 3. Metadata for BSU's mailing labels

IP-Map Component Blocks Metadata						
Name/Type	Dept/Role	Location	Business Process	Composed of	Base System	Quality Issues
Alumni (DS$_1$)	Former BSU students	Depends on the individual	Alumni send in their data changes	Name, Address, and other Status Changes in a free format	Mail, phone, in-person or electronic correspondence	Typos or misinformation sometimes occur
University Post Office (CB$_1$)	BSU Post Office Personnel	111 Sullivan Hall	Mailing labels are used to address alumni publications	IP$_1$	Set of Paper Labels	
Student (STO$_1$)	BSU Register Office	222 Carpenter Hall	Registrar Office maintains data on active students	All university data collected on students. See data dictionary for a complete list of fields	Oracle Database	
Alumni Data (STO$_2$)	BSU Alumni Affairs Staff	204 Breezedale Hall	Alumni Affairs maintains data on alumni	Alumni Mailing Information, Other Alumni Data. See data dictionary for a complete list of fields	Oracle Database	Data becomes obsolete as it sits in the database. See component description for obsolescence rates
Update Type (D$_1$)	BSU Alumni Affairs Secretary	204 Breezedale Hall	Secretary reviews and sorts various types of update requests into separate folders. (RD$_{1N}$, RD$_{1A}$, RD$_{1D}$, RD$_{1O}$)	Input: RD$_1$ - Correspondence from alumni (either mail, e-mail, phone, or in-person)	Paper-based system	
Convert name change to electronic form (SB$_1$)	BSU Alumni Affairs Secretary	204 Breezedale Hall	Secretary records update request into an online update file	Input: RD$_{1N}$	Visual Basic Application	Secretary may commit a typo when recording
Convert address change to electronic form (SB$_2$)	BSU Alumni Affairs Staff	204 Breezedale Hall	Secretary records update request into an online update file	Input: RD$_{1A}$	Visual Basic Application	Secretary may commit a typo when recording

Copyright © 2007, Idea Group Inc. Copying or distributing in print or electronic forms without written permission of Idea Group Inc. is prohibited.

Table 3. continued

Convert death notices to electronic form (SB$_3$)	BSU Alumni Affairs Staff	204 Breezedale Hall	Secretary records update request into an online update file	Input: RD$_{1D}$	Visual Basic Application	
Convert other changes to electronic form (SB$_4$)	BSU Alumni Affairs	204 Breezedale Hall	Secretary records update request into an online update file	Input: RD$_{1O}$	Visual Basic Application	
Extract new graduates (P$_1$)	Registrar Office Personnel	222 Carpenter Hall	Registrar Office with help from BSU IT Staff extracts list of graduates (CD$_2$) at the end of each semester	Input: Extract from Student Database (STO$_1$)	Cobol Program	Information is accurate at the time of update, but frequently changes soon after graduation
Load graduate data into Alumni Database (P$_2$) (This process also duplicate-checks for multi-degree alumni)	Registrar Office Personnel	222 Carpenter Hall	Alumni Affairs with help from the BSU IT Staff updates Alumni Database with list of new graduates (CD$_3$)	Input: CD$_2$	Cobol Program	
Update Alumni Database with Name Changes (P$_{3N}$)	BSU Alumni Affairs Staff	204 Breezedale Hall	Secretary loads CD$_{1N}$ (name updates) into Alumni Database	Input: CD$_{1N}$	Visual Basic Application.	Only 10% of alumni self-report name changes
Update Alumni Database with Address Changes (P$_{3A}$)	BSU Alumni Affairs Staff	204 Breezedale Hall	Secretary loads CD$_{1A}$ (address updates) into Alumni Database	Input: CD$_{1A}$	Visual Basic Application	Only 10% of alumni self-report address changes
Update Alumni Database with Death Notices (P$_{3D}$)	BSU Alumni Affairs Staff	204 Breezedale Hall	Secretary loads CD$_{1O}$ (death updates) into Alumni Database	Input: C$_{1D}$	Visual Basic Application	Only 20% of alumni deaths are reported to BSU by family & friends

Copyright © 2007, Idea Group Inc. Copying or distributing in print or electronic forms without written permission of Idea Group Inc. is prohibited.

Table 3. continued

Update Alumni Database with Other Changes (P_{30})	BSU Alumni Affairs Staff	204 Breezedale Hall	Secretary adds CD_{10} (other updates) to Alumni Database	Input: CD_{10}	Visual Basic Application	Only 10% of alumni self-report other types of changes
Send alumni extract to Address Service (P_4)	BSU Alumni Affairs Staff	204 Breezedale, Hall	Alumni Affairs prepares an extract file (CD_4) to send every quarter.	Input: Extract from Alumni Data (STO_2)	COBOL Extract program, transmit tape	
Apply address corrections (P_5)	BSU Alumni Affairs Staff	204 Breezedale Hall	Alumni Affairs receives address updates from NCOA and applies updates to Alumni database with help from BSU IT Staff	Input: CD_5	Tape received. COBOL program used to load updates into database	Change of Address service is 95% effective at catching wrong or out of date addresses
Send alumni extract to Obituary Service (P_6)	BSU Alumni Affairs Staff	204 Breezedale Hall	Alumni Affairs prepares extract file (CD_6) to send every year.	Input: Extract from Alumni Data (STO_2)	COBOL Extract program, transmit tape	
Apply death notifications (P_7)	BSU Alumni Affairs Staff	204 Breezedale Hall	Alumni Affairs receives obituary updates and applies updates to Alumni database with help from BSU IT Staff	Input: CD_7	Tape received. COBOL program used to load updates into database	Obituary Service is 80% effective at catching alumni who are deceased
Extract alumni list and produce mailing labels (P8)	BSU Alumni Affairs Staff	204 Breezedale Hall	Alumni Affairs runs a program to produce a set of mailing labels (IP1)	Input: Extract from Alumni Data (STO2)	COBOL program used to extract data, produce mailing labels	

Copyright © 2007, Idea Group Inc. Copying or distributing in print or electronic forms without written permission of Idea Group Inc. is prohibited.

Table 3. continued

Check label quality (QB1)	BSU Alumni Affairs Secretary	204 Breezedale Hall	Secretary performs final check of mailing labels for format quality.	Input: IP1	Hand Check	
Transfer from Registrar Office to Alumni Affairs Office (BB1)	BSU Registrar Office, BSU Alumni Affairs Staff	222 Carpenter Hall, 204 Breezedale Hall	Registrar office with help from BSU IT Staff sends extract to Alumni Affairs after each semester	Input: CD2	File is sent via FTP	
Address Service (BSB1)	NCOA, Inc, BSU Alumni Affairs	NCOA HQ, MD 45545 204 Breezedale Hall	Address Service performs match operation against their database	Input: CD4	Vendor System	
Obituary Service (BSB2)	Obituary, Inc., BSU Alumni Affairs	Obituary Service HQ, VA 53533 204 Breezedale Hall	Obituary Service performs match operation against their database	Input: CD6	Vendor System	

Table 4. Data element metadata

IP-Map Raw, Component, and Information Product Metadata		
Name/Type	**Data Elements**	**Quality Issues**
RD_1 (Raw)	Update information in free format (phone, mail, e-mail, in person visit)	A typo may infrequently occur.
RD_{1N} (Raw)	Name update information in free format (phone, mail, e-mail, in person visit)	
RD_{1A} (Raw)	Address update information in free format (phone, mail, e-mail, in person visit)	
RD_{1D} (Raw)	Death notice information in free format (phone, mail, e-mail, in person visit)	

Copyright © 2007, Idea Group Inc. Copying or distributing in print or electronic forms without written permission of Idea Group Inc. is prohibited.

Table 4. Data element metadata

RD_{10} (Raw)	Other update information (marriage, divorce, births) in free format (phone, mail, e-mail, in person visit)	
CD_{1N} (Component)	Social Security Number, Old Name, New Name, Effective Date, formatted for Alumni Database	1 in 10 alumni report name changes.
CD_{1A} (Component)	Social Security Number, Old Address, New Address, Effective Date formatted for Alumni Database	1 in 10 alumni report address changes.
CD_{1D} (Component)	Social Security Number, Status Change to Death, Effective Date formatted for Alumni Database	1 in 5 alumni have family members who report the death.
CD_{1O} (Component)	Social Security Number, Change Information, Effective Date formatted for Alumni Database	Approx. 1 in 10 of self-reporting alumni.
CD_2 (Component)	Social Security Number, Title (Ms., Mrs., Mr., Dr.) First Name, Middle Name, Last Name, Address, City, State, Zip Code, Degree, Department, College, Date Awarded, Birth date, Marital Status, Gender, Ethnic Code in Student Database Format	
CD_3 (Component)	Social Security Number, Title (Ms., Mrs., Mr., Dr.) First Name, Middle Name, Last Name, Address, City, State, Zip Code, Degree, Department, College, Date Awarded, Birth date, Marital Status, Gender, Ethnic Code in Alumni Database Format	
CD_4 (Component)	Social Security Number, First Name, Middle Name, Last Name, Address, City, State, Zip Code in prescribed Address Service Format.	
CD_5 (Component)	Update Code (Changed, Same), Social Security Number, First Name, Middle Name, Last Name, Address, City, State, Zip Code in prescribed Address Service Format.	5% of address changes remain undetected.
CD_6 (Component)	Social Security Number, First Name, Middle Name, Last Name, Address, City, State, Zip Code in prescribed Obituary Service Format.	
CD_7 (Component)	Status Code (Dead, Alive, Unknown), Social Security Number, First Name, Middle Name, Last Name, in prescribed Obituary Service Format.	20% of inactive alumni remain undetected.
IP_1 (Information Product)	Name, Address, City, State, Zip Code in U.S. Postal Service Standard Address Format.	

Copyright © 2007, Idea Group Inc. Copying or distributing in print or electronic forms without written permission of Idea Group Inc. is prohibited.

Figure 2. EPC - BSU magazine publication process

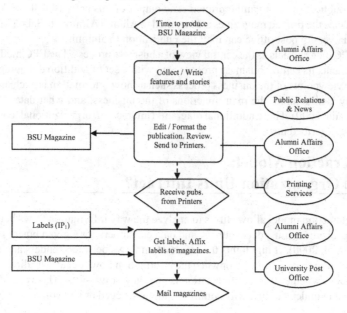

EPCs employ a set of geometric shapes to portray the interconnections between tasks, data, organization units, and the logical time sequence involved in completing a business process. It is important for each EPC to begin with at least one event (the start event) and to end with at least one final event (the finish event). An event in turn triggers one or more tasks. The organizational units (departments, people, etc.) responsible for doing the task and the resources (information, raw materials, etc.) needed to complete the task are added to the chain to show a complete picture of how tasks are performed for a given business process. Alumni affairs has documented their alumni magazine publication process in the EPC diagram in Figure 2. The diagram indicates that at periodic points in time, the Alumni Affairs Office in conjunction with public relations assembles the rough draft and layout for

Figure 3. Interaction model for maintaining alumni mailing data

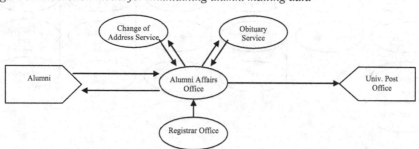

Copyright © 2007, Idea Group Inc. Copying or distributing in print or electronic forms without written permission of Idea Group Inc. is prohibited.

the next issue. The next activity involves both alumni affairs and printing services as they finalize the publication so it can be printed. The output of this activity is the *BSU Alumni Magazine*. Once the printed magazines are returned to Alumni Affairs, the labels are affixed so that the university post office can mail the publication to alumni.

The EPC diagram acts as the central view of a business process. The EPC methodology then supplements its central business process map with a set of additional diagrams which model other viewpoints of the business process such as how information is exchanged, how the company is structured, the main functions of the business, and what data are needed (Curran & Ladd, 2000). These additional diagrams (interaction, organizational, component, and data) are described next.

The Interaction Model: How Do Organization Units Interact?

The interaction model allows firms to analyze the way information flows between the different organization units, data sources, and data consumers for a given business process (Curran & Ladd, 2000). It highlights the information flows between senders and receivers without going into great detail why or when the information flows occur. The direction of the arrows indicates whether the communication is one-way or two-way. This type of diagram may be useful in understanding why communications succeed or sometimes fail during the

Figure 4. BSU organization diagram

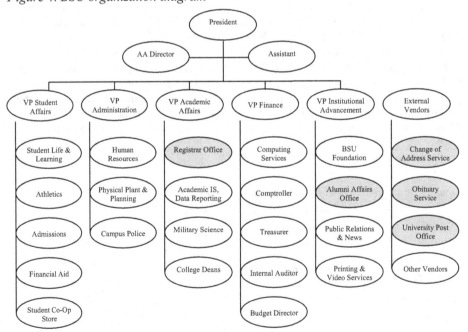

Copyright © 2007, Idea Group Inc. Copying or distributing in print or electronic forms without written permission of Idea Group Inc. is prohibited.

execution of a business process. For example, the diagram may reveal that a department does not have interaction with another group, which may explain why improper decisions are made during a business process. Figure 3 illustrates an Interaction Model for the production of alumni mailing labels.

The Organizational Model: Who Does What?

The organizational viewpoint is essentially a traditional organization chart that shows the hierarchy or relationship between the different organizational groups (Curran & Ladd,

Figure 5. Alumni affairs office represented as a component model

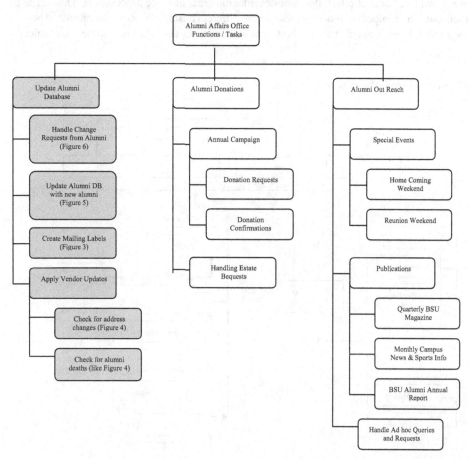

Note: Highlighted blocks represent tasks or functions associated with the production of alumni mailing labels; blocks such as the "Handle Change Requests from Alumni" could be expanded into greater detail to coincide with the tasks listed in the EPC diagrams; the remaining blocks represent other tasks or functions associated with the office of alumni affairs.

Copyright © 2007, Idea Group Inc. Copying or distributing in print or electronic forms without written permission of Idea Group Inc. is prohibited.

2000). This chart allows people to see the overall structure of the organization and to explore the relationships between the organization structure and the distribution of business processes, functions, and information products. This chart can be organized into several levels of detail depending on the complexity of the organization's structure. In addition, color can be used to highlight those units participating in a particular business process. For example, the organization units highlighted in Figure 4 represent those units directly involved in the production of alumni mailing labels. This type of diagram can be useful when analyzing a business process to determine how closely related the groups involved in the business process are in terms of their positions in the organization's overall structure.

The Component Model: What Happens?

The component model uses a function tree to show what the main business processes are (Curran & Ladd, 2000). It does not describe the order of those processes or who carries them out. The component model represents the different business process functions and how they relate to each other. It shows how functions or tasks activate one another and which

Figure 6. Alumni affairs represented as a data model

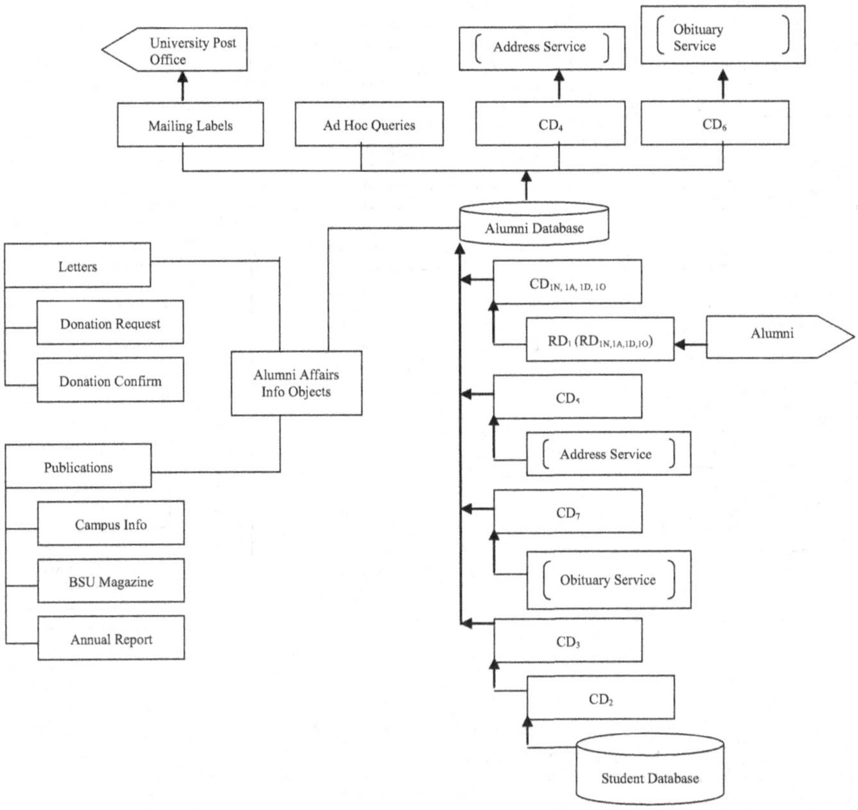

Copyright © 2007, Idea Group Inc. Copying or distributing in print or electronic forms without written permission of Idea Group Inc. is prohibited.

Table 5. Constructs used in IP-Map and EPC's diagrams (Source: Shankaranarayanan et al., 2000; Curran & Ladd, 2000)

Construct Description	Type of Construct	Construct Icon
Event: Events describe the occurrence of a status that in turns acts as a trigger for a business process (i.e., When should something be done? Example: Order is received).	EPC Construct	E_i
Organization: Organization units describe the outline structure of an enterprise (i.e., Who should do it? Example: Sales department, plant, secretary).	EPC Construct	O_i
Information, material, or resource object: Business object entities (i.e., What is needed to complete the task? Example: physical material, order inquiry, raw data, component data, information product).	EPC Construct	RD_i, CD_i, IP_i
Logical operators: Connectors that describe the logical relationship between events, functions, processes (i.e., And, Or, Exclusive Or).	EPC Construct	A O X
Control flow: Arrows that describe the chronological and logical interdependencies of events and functions or processes.	EPC Construct	- - - - - - - - - -▶
Resource/Organization unit assignment: Lines that describe which unit (employee) or resource is associated with a function or process.	EPC Construct	———————
Information/Material flow: Arrows that define whether a function reads or changes an information product.	EPC / IP-Map Construct	——————▶
Function or process block: Task that describes any transformations, manipulations, or calculations performed (i.e., What should be done? Example: Create purchase order, Update database).	EPC / IP-Map Construct	P_i
Source (raw input data) block: This block is used to represent the source of each raw (input) data that must be available in order to produce the information product expected by the consumer.	IP-Map Construct	DS_i
Customer (output) block: This block is used to represent the consumer of the information product. The consumer specifies in this block the data elements that constitute the "finished" information product.	IP-Map Construct	CB_i
Data quality block: This block is used to represent the checks for data quality on those data items that are essential in producing a "defect-free" information product. Therefore, associated with this block is a list of the data quality checks that are being performed on the specified component data items.	IP-Map Construct	QB_i
Data storage block: This block is used to represent the capture of data items in storage files or databases so that they can be available for further processing.	IP-Map Construct	STO_i

Copyright © 2007, Idea Group Inc. Copying or distributing in print or electronic forms without written permission of Idea Group Inc. is prohibited.

Table 5. continued

Decision block: In some complex information manufacturing systems, depending on the value of some particular data items(s), it may be necessary to direct the data items to a different set of blocks downstream for further processing. In such cases, a decision block is used to capture the different conditions to be evaluated and the corresponding procedures for handling the incoming data items based on the evaluation.	IP-Map Construct	D_i
Business boundary block: The business boundary block is used to specify the movement of the information product (or raw/component data) across departmental or organizational boundaries. The role of the business boundary block in the IP-Map is to highlight the data quality problems that might arise when crossing business unit boundaries and therefore assign accountability to the appropriate business unit.	IP-Map Construct	BB_i
Information system boundary block: This block is used to reflect the changes to the raw input data items or component data items as they move from one information system to another type of information system (Example: Paper to Electronic). These system changes could be intra or inter-business units.	IP-Map Construct	SB_i
There are circumstances where the raw input data items or component data items go through both a business boundary and a system boundary change. The combined business-information system boundary block is defined for this purpose.	IP-Map Construct	BSB_i

functions are subordinate to another. Functions can be broken down into several levels, each level representing units at varying degrees of detail and precision. In addition, for this family of diagrams, the component model can be augmented with some of the specialized task constructs from the IP-Map, namely the verification block, IS boundary block, and business boundary block. Figure 5 depicts a component diagram for the alumni affairs example.

The Data Model: What Is Needed?

The data model depicts the relationship between the different information objects used by an organization (Curran & Ladd, 2000). For Figure 6, the data model has been altered from its original EPC model conception to include the IP-Map constructs describing the data storages, data consumers and sources, information products, and raw and component data.

In summary, the EPC family of diagrams documents the interconnections between tasks, data, and organization units, and the logical time sequence involved. It helps to answer the question of how an information product fits into the business processes of an organization in terms of when and where it is used. The EPC family of diagrams is very flexible and can model any business process regardless of whether or not it interacts with information products.

Copyright © 2007, Idea Group Inc. Copying or distributing in print or electronic forms without written permission of Idea Group Inc. is prohibited.

It should be emphasized that the EPC diagrams depicted in this chapter have been augmented from the traditional EPC diagrams to include several constructs from IP-Maps. Data sources can be associated with a particular raw data component while customers can be associated with a particular information product. Data storages can be represented along with other information, material, or resource objects to highlight which databases are used in a business process. In addition, these EPC diagrams can incorporate the IP-Map constructs for representing data quality checks, system or organization boundary transfers in addition to the process/function construct to more aptly categorize the type of task taking place. Table 5 contains the list of combined EPC and IP-Map constructs. Together this extended collection of constructs allows organization to more fully visualize and model the events and processes that create information products with the business activities that interact with the information products.

Future Trends

Although EPC and IP-Map diagrams are useful for modeling and analyzing a business process and its information needs, the construction and manipulation of these models is a long and tedious process if done by hand. In order for analysts to take full advantage of their business process and information product models, they need a software product that will integrate a variety of important features.

1.   Organizations need the ability to generate, view, modify, delete, customize, save, and distribute their business process and information product diagrams. Individuals need to have the ability to zoom in and out of the diagrams as well as the ability to drill up or down in the diagram's hierarchy in order to see the business process at various levels of detail. Micrografx EnterpriseCharter (a plug-in module for Micrografx FlowCharter) and Microsoft's Visio 2000 are two examples of software products that provide this type of functionality for constructing diagrams.

2.   This tool should also incorporate a metadata repository so that every business object in a diagram links to a set of descriptive characteristics about that object. Many vendors offer database products either as stand-alone products or as part of another package such as a business process reengineering or case tool that could be used to organize a set of metadata tables.

3.   Organizations need to be able to interface their business process and information product diagrams with other types of software such as enterprise resource planning (ERP) systems or case tools for system development so that these diagrams can easily be translated into the code requirements for rapid system development. Groups like the workflow management coalition are working on standards they hope vendors will incorporate to permit "flow to code" capabilities or at least the ability to check that the code covers all aspects of the business process flow chart.

4.   Organizations need the ability to integrate their business process diagrams with a new class of generic software called workflow management systems (WFMS). WFMS has its roots in products like image processing, document management tools, groupware, and project support software. Today's WFMS software products offers organizations assistance in the following:

Copyright © 2007, Idea Group Inc. Copying or distributing in print or electronic forms without written permission of Idea Group Inc. is prohibited.

a.   Provide computer-based support for making the business process logic explicit so that a business can both enforce and document the business rules it uses.
b.   Provide organizations with a means to create, collect, and evaluate metrics relating to the time, cost, or quality of performing a process and its constituent tasks.
c.   Provide run time control functions for managing the process in an operational environment as well as assistance in sequencing the various activities to be handled as part of each process.
d.   Provide the capability to match the tasks that need to be done with the people needed to perform them and the information resources needed to perform them.

5.   Organizations need the ability to perform what-if analysis so that the impact of a proposed change to a business process can be evaluated. It would be very useful if an analyst could use software to change a business process diagram and then run a simulation feature to get an assessment of how that change would affect specified time, cost, or quality metrics for that business process. Several high-end business process reengineering packages exist today that allow people to perform modeling, analysis, simulation, and animation capabilities with their business process models.

6.   Organizations need the ability to mine their database of business objects to seek out patterns among business processes and to ask questions such as "How many business processes use a particular information product?" or "How many organizations are involved in the production of this information product?" The repository information system available in the SAP R/3 software package is a good example of a module that allows business and IS people to query a database of business objects to find out where they are used. In addition, link analysis and visualization tools may also provide a means to assist people in mining their business diagrams to uncover areas of redundancy or inefficiency.

Although a software package that incorporates all these features does not yet exist, there are vendor specific software products and analytical techniques that accomplish some of these features. The challenge will be to encourage vendors to incorporate an information product methodology as they expand the features and functionality of their software products to encompass advanced modeling and analytical capabilities so that business analysts can fully explore complex sets of business processes and information needs across an entire organization.

Conclusion

To be able to effectively manage the quality of information products, information system professionals need several information management tools. Some of these tools such as data dictionaries and electronic document management system already exist. However, between the data dictionary that describes the structure of the data and the EDMS that manages the finished documents, there is a gap. There needs to be a tool in place to assist IS professionals in understanding the production process that transforms the raw data collected by the organization into the intermediate component data that are then formed into the final information products that are distributed and used by the consumers in the organization.

Copyright © 2007, Idea Group Inc. Copying or distributing in print or electronic forms without written permission of Idea Group Inc. is prohibited.

The modeling capabilities of the IP-Map in combination with business process models like the event process-driven chain methodology is an example of techniques that helps to fill this gap. However, this new modeling methodology is still in its infancy. More work must be done to develop the supporting software and information product repositories so that these tools can be fully exploited for achieving better information quality to support an organization's business process needs.

References

Ballou, D. P., Wang R. Y., Pazer, H., & Tayi, G. K. (1998). Modeling information manufacturing systems to determine information product quality. *Management Science, 44*(4), 462-484.

Curran, T.A., & Ladd, A. (2000). *SAP R/3 Business Blueprint: Understanding enterprise supply chain management* (2nd ed.). Upper Saddle River, NJ: Prentice Hall PTR.

Pierce, E.M. (2001). Using control matrices to evaluate information product maps. In *Proceedings of the Conference on Information Quality* (pp. 412-423). Cambridge, MA: Massachusetts Institute of Technology.

Redman, T. (2001). *Data quality: The field guide* (p. 74). Boston: Butterworth-Heinemann.

Shankaranarayan, G., Wang, R. Y., & Ziad, M. (2000). Modeling the manufacture of an information product with IP- MAP. In *Proceedings of the Conference on Information Quality* (pp. 1-16). Cambridge: Massachusetts Institute of Technology.

Wang, R.Y. (1998). A product perspective on total data quality management. *Communications of the ACM, 41*(2), 58-65.

Wang, R. Y., Lee, Y. L., Pipino, L., & Strong, D. M. (1998). Manage your information as a product. *Sloan Management Review, 39*(4), 95-105.

Copyright © 2007, Idea Group Inc. Copying or distributing in print or electronic forms without written permission of Idea Group Inc. is prohibited.

Chapter VIII

Procedure for Mapping Information Flow:
A Case of Surgery Management Process

Latif Al-Hakim, University of Southern Queensland, Australia

Abstract

This chapter considers information flow an important dimension of information quality and proposes a procedure for mapping information flow. The surgery management process (SMP) of a public hospital is used as a case in which to illustrate the steps of the developed procedure. The chapter discusses the issues that make information mapping of SMP a challenging task and explains the difficulties associated with traditional process mapping techniques in determining the interdependencies and information flow within and between various elements of SMP activities. The proposed procedure integrates a structured process mapping technique known as IDEF0 with another structured technique referred to as dependency structured matrix (DSM) to map the information flow within SMP. The chapter indicates that it is possible to reduce feedback from other activities that affect the performance of SMP by administratively controlling the information flow through certain activities of SMP.

Copyright © 2007, Idea Group Inc. Copying or distributing in print or electronic forms without written permission of Idea Group Inc. is prohibited.

Introduction

Information has become a critical component of business operations (Sen, 2001). Today's technology allows businesses to collect and analyse "enormous volumes of information and manipulate it in different ways to bring out otherwise unforseen areas of knowledge" (Abbott, 2001). Managers make decisions based on information available to them, and misinformed people tend to make poor decisions (Fisher & Kingma, 2001). An information flow system providing quality information in terms of completeness, relevancy, timeliness, and accessibility of information plays a major role in supporting the decision-making process. Information mapping depicts information flow between various entities of a process. Several studies (Bosset, 1991; Evans & Lindsay, 2002; Fadlalla & Wickramasinghe, 2004) stress the importance of process mapping and emphasise the role information flow plays in improving the decision-making process. This chapter considers information mapping as a component of two dimensions of information quality. These are the contextual dimension and the accessibility dimension.

This chapter deals with information mapping of the surgery management process (SMP) in hospitals. Surgery is performed in operating theatres which are equipped for the performance of surgical operations (TheFreeDictionary, 2006). However, SMP is not limited to the activities taking place within an operating theatre. SMP begins when a general practitioner, physician, or specialist determines a patient's need for a surgical procedure and ends when the patient is discharged from hospital after surgery has been performed. Accordingly SMP is a hierarchical process comprising several stages. Each stage includes several operations and each operation can be divided into activities.

Several studies (District Commission, 2002; New Health, 2002; Schofield et al., 2005) stress the importance of process mapping and emphasise the role of information flow in improving or redesigning the surgery management process. This chapter deals with process mapping of SMP and provides a conceptual procedure for mapping the information flow throughout the stages of SMP. It divides SMP into seven stages: preadmission, admission, preassessment, perioperative, procedure (or the surgery), postoperative, and discharge.

Dimensions of Information Quality

Customers view quality in relation to differing criteria based on their individual roles in the production-marketing chain (Evans & Lindsay, 2002). Thus it is important to understand the various perspectives from which information quality (IQ) is viewed. Wang (1998) finds an analogy between quality issues in product manufacturing and those in information, and further asserts that information manufacturing can be viewed as a processing system acting on raw data to produce information products. Wang urges organisations to manage information as they manage products if they want to increase productivity. Based on the analogy of Wang, information quality can be viewed by information consumers from various perspectives as "fitness for intended use," or as "meeting or exceeding customer expectations."

Just like quality management of physical products, IQ has multiple dimensions. IQ dimensions refer to issues that are important to information consumers. However, there are no uniform lists of IQ dimensions as illustrated in Table 1. The choice of these dimensions is primarily based on intuitive understanding, industrial experience, or literature review

Copyright © 2007, Idea Group Inc. Copying or distributing in print or electronic forms without written permission of Idea Group Inc. is prohibited.

(Huang et al., 2001) and depends on the actual use of information. Good information for a specific user in one case may not be sufficient in another case. Strong, Lee, and Wang (1997) group the IQ dimensions into four categories. These categories are contextual, intrinsic, accessibility, and representation. These categories are widely acceptable in the literature (Li, Tan, & Xie, 2003) and can imply other dimensions as shown in Table 1.

An effective information flow allows users of an information system to receive the correct amount of information (completeness), only relevant information (relevancy), updated information (timeliness) at the required time (currency) and with adequate level of accessibility (accessibility). As can be seen from Table 1, completeness, relevancy, timeliness, and currency are dimensions within the IQ contextual category while easy access to information is within the IQ accessibility category. Accordingly, information flow is directly related to two categories of IQ dimensions: contextual and accessibility.

Surgery Management Process (SMP)

SMP is not limited to the operations and activities related to the surgical intervention in an operating theatre. It is a complicated health care delivery process starting from referral of a patient to a hospital and ending with the discharge of the patient from the hospital after performing the surgery. SMP is a process with hierarchical structure, which comprises the stages of SMP referred to previously. Each stage includes several operations and each operation has several activities. A brief description of the main stages of SMP is:

- **Preadmission:** This includes receiving the referral form from the general practitioner or specialist by the hospital admission registry and booking an appointment with a surgeon or specialist or surgeon. The patient at this stage is provided with consent and admission forms.
- **Booked admission:** This stage includes an appointment with a specialist to tentatively evaluate the patient's needs for surgery. The specialist determines the required clinical tests. This stage includes determining the date for the preassessment stage and entering the patient into the bed allocation list. Patients, at this stage, may be told the date they will be admitted to the hospital, possibly months in advance (Gallivan, Utley, Treasure, & Valencia, 2002).
- **Preassessment:** At this stage all the required clinical tests are performed. Based on the results, the surgeon and anaesthetists assess the surgery requirements.
- **Perioperative:** This stage may include all operations before admitting a patient to an operating theatre. For the purpose of this chapter, the perioperative stage starts after the admission of the patient to the hospital and includes all the activities required to be performed prior to surgery in preparation for surgery.
- **Procedure:** This includes activities to perform the surgery inside the operating theatre.
- **Postoperative:** This stage starts immediately after the surgery. The postoperative

Copyright © 2007, Idea Group Inc. Copying or distributing in print or electronic forms without written permission of Idea Group Inc. is prohibited.

*Table 1. Dimensions of IQ dimensions and categories (Adapted from Al-Hakim & Xu, 2004; * also mentioned in Turban, Aronson, and Liang, 2005; # adopted from Lee, Strong, Beverly, & Wang, 2002)*

Category	Implication/ Definition	IQ Dimension				
		Delone and McLean (1992)	Goodhue (1995)	Wang and Strong (1996)	Strong et al. (1997)*	Jarke and Vassiliou (1997)#
Intrinsic	Information has quality in its own right.	Accuracy, precision, reliability, freedom from bias.	Accuracy, reliability.	Accuracy, believability, reputation, objectivity.	Accuracy, objectivity, believability, reputation.	Believability, accuracy, credibility, consistency, completeness.
Contextual	DQ must be considered within the context of the task.	Importance, relevance, usefulness, content, completeness, currency, sufficiency.	Currency, level of detail.	Value-added, relevance, completeness, timeliness, appropriate amount.	Relevancy, value added, timeliness, completeness, and amount of data.	Relevance, usage, timeliness, source, currency, data warehouse currency, nonvolatility.
Accessibility	Information is interpretable, easy to understand and manipulate.	Useability, quantitativeness, convenience of access.	Accessibility, assistance, ease of use, location.	Accessibility, ease of operations, security.	Accuracy and access security.	Accessibility, system availability, transaction availability, privileges.
Representation	Information is represented concisely and consistently.	Understandability, readability, clarity, format, appearance, conciseness, uniqueness, comparability.	Compatibility, meaning, presentation, lack of confusion.	Understandability, interpretability, concise representation, consistent representation, arrangement, readable, reasonable.	Interpretability, ease of understanding, concise representation, consistent representation.	Interpretability, syntax, version control, semantics, aliases, origin.

Copyright © 2007, Idea Group Inc. Copying or distributing in print or electronic forms without written permission of Idea Group Inc. is prohibited.

stage starts in the recovery room or postanaesthesia care unit (PACU). This unit is dedicated to minimising postoperative complications. In the PACU the patient may wear certain devices to automatically monitor their vital signs (Radts & Spinasanta, 2004). The overall condition of the patient is assessed at this stage.

- **Discharge:** This stage includes activities related to transition of patients from the hospital to their place of residence.

Aims of SMP

Consulting surgeons historically determine the urgency of patients' conditions, the nature of the required surgery, and the timing of the operation. They make clinical decisions based on their opinions of the physical status and medical needs of their patients (McAleer, Turner, Lismore, & Naqvi, 1995). Decisions regarding the physical status of a patient include assigning the patient to a certain category of emergency and surgical requirements. Surgeons form their opinions based on the patient's health history, information received from various medical reports, results of various clinical tests, and so forth. Without proper, updated, and complete information related to a patient's health status, a surgeon may make a wrong assessment. Medical errors resulting from the surgery at a later stage may not merely be attributed to an error which occurred during the surgery itself.

The key targets of SMP are to improve patient flow throughout the surgery process and to eliminate medical errors. To achieve these targets, surgery management decisions should be based on relevant, timely, and updated information about a patient's health status. In addition information related to queues in the waiting lists, available resources, available beds, and process variations are critical factors affecting the SMP decision related to patient flow in a hospital. Accordingly, SMP aims to effectively manage four main functions: process complexity, medical errors, operating theatre waiting list (OTWL), and capacity management.

Process Complexity

Giddens (1984) in Biazzo (2002) describes a process as a series of interdependent actions or activities embedded in a structure. Giddens views a structure as a set of rules and resources which can both constrain and enable social actions. SMP process is a constructive example that fits Giddens' concept and, accordingly, the SMP can be considered as not just a group of activities. Rather, it is a "sociotechnical" system (Keating, Fernandez, Jacobs, & Kauffmann, 2001) in which each operation or activity has additional elements other than that activity's input and output. These additional elements are the resources including information necessary to perform the activities and the rules that govern the activity's implementation. The complexity of SMP arises from two aspects:

- The process mapping aspect which relates to the interdependencies between the elements of various activities of the process
- The sociotechnical aspect which requires designing work such that a balance can be struck between the technology and the people using the technology. This is known as joint optimisation

Copyright © 2007, Idea Group Inc. Copying or distributing in print or electronic forms without written permission of Idea Group Inc. is prohibited.

There are four variables that make both defining interdependencies between the elements of the various activities of the operation theatre management process and achieving joint optimisation extremely important:

- **Object behaviour:** The behaviour of the object (patient) is not predictable and could vary considerably. Significant disruption could result from patient behaviour, for example, cancellation of surgery by a patient. This makes every patient a unique object in the system.
- **Surgeon effectiveness:** Surgeons differ in skill and expertise. It is hard to measure the effectiveness of a surgeon in dealing with various complexities during surgery.
- **Surgery success:** Because of the level of complexity and variability, it is hard to predict the degree of success of a surgery.
- **Surgical time:** Though the time required for surgery can be partly predicted, complexities during surgery may considerably affect the surgery time. The high probability of the unpredictability of time required for surgery renders difficult any attempt to precisely schedule operating theatre waiting lists and the performance of SMP.

While some of these variables are uncontrollable, their impact on SMP can be considerably reduced and effectively managed with (a) correct and real-time flow of information and (b) coordination of the various interdependencies between elements of the activities involved in the SMP process. Realising the role of information flow and interdependencies as the main drivers of SMP highlights the need for effective information mapping.

Medical Errors

A simple Internet search reveals a tremendous number of medical errors as a result of judgement based on receiving incomplete or incorrect information. While medical errors are usually attributed to mistakes made by individuals, errors resulting from poor information flow (incomplete data and information, lack of communication, lack of timely data, lack of information accessibility, etc.) plays a major role in contributing to this error rate. Unfortunately, cause and effect resulting from poor information flow go unmonitored. Examples of medical errors that can result from the lack of performing adequately one or more dimensions of information quality that relate to information flow are listed next:

- A family received an undisclosed settlement after a 5-year-old girl died following a medical error. She had gone into the hospital to have surgery to correct a hole in the heart and leaky valves. A solution used to prepare the heart for surgery was administered but it was missing two ingredients. This caused her heart to stop beating irreversibly (WrongDiagnosis, 2004).
- A 67-year-old man went into surgery for bladder cancer; he came out of surgery missing more than he ever expected — his penis. In an interview, the man said "It was never even discussed. And I felt like he [the surgeon] ought to have at least told us that this might be a possibility so that we could have talked it over even before I was admitted to the hospital (ABC News, 2003; Urban Scrawl, 2003).

Copyright © 2007, Idea Group Inc. Copying or distributing in print or electronic forms without written permission of Idea Group Inc. is prohibited.

- Another cancer patient was actually admitted to the operating theatre, about to have his prostate removed, when a call came from the pathology department indicating there had been a mistake.
- In 1998 a lady had sought laser eye surgery to correct her astigmatism. But after surgery her vision fails to improve. It is found that wrong data were entered into the LASIK machine, causing the laser to operate on the wrong part of the lady's eye, which made the problem worse rather than better.
- Eighteen months after having a common bowel operation, an X-ray revealed a pair of 15-cm surgical scissors, slightly opened, lodged between a patient's lower bowel and her spine. The hospital explained it did not count scissors after the surgery because they were considered too large to lose (Pirani, 2004).

Table 2 provides two examples of the same medical error from different countries at different times. Both examples reflect an error in information flow.

The examples from Table 2 reflect the importance of information flow mapping within and between various sections of SMP.

Operating Theatre Waiting List

There are commonly two kinds of waiting lists in hospitals: outpatients and surgery (Gonzalez-Busto & Garcia, 1999). The first type of waiting list includes patients waiting for consultation in certain sections, including the Accident and Emergency Departments. Patients on the second type of waiting list are awaiting a surgical intervention to be conducted in an operating theatre of the hospital. The second type of waiting list is a reference to the operating theatre schedule. This research deals with the second type which is referred to as the operating theatre waiting list (OTWL).

OTWLs are critical for many reasons: their societal and political impact, their potential link to the patients' life; their relationship to the economic management of operating theatres and the allocation of scarce resources such as surgeons, specialists, nurses and equipment (Al-Hakim, 2006).

Once drawn up, the composition of a waiting list is unprotected in that it is subject to multiple alterations and modifications, without prior notice or agreement with patients

Table 2. Two examples of poor information flow

Example from USA	Example from Australia
In May 2002, two doctors switched the pathology slides of an American lady's breast biopsy with another woman's. After the surgery she was told that she actually had no sign of cancer (WrongDiagnosis, 2004).	Two women with the same first name attended an Australian hospital in the same day to have a breast biopsy. One had breast cancer. One did not. It was discovered that the biopsy results had been mixed up and the patient without breast cancer had endured months of chemotherapy and was minus a breast. The woman with the breast cancer died after nine months (Pirani, 2004).

Copyright © 2007, Idea Group Inc. Copying or distributing in print or electronic forms without written permission of Idea Group Inc. is prohibited.

already on the list. Unanticipated changes affect the quality of patient care and may escalate costs considerably. Patients who have their consultation or procedure time altered can suffer prolonged anxiety, pain and discomfort, frustration, anger, and stress (Buchanan & Wilson, 1996). For the organisation, delayed or cancelled procedures usually result in activity targets not being achieved.

The OTWL process has a multiple-criteria objective:

1.   Compliance with all due dates and times of the scheduled consultations and operations
2.   Ensuring a quick and convincing response to unanticipated changes to the waiting list

These criteria may conflict with each other in that the waiting list requires changes in response to unanticipated clinical needs rather than order of arrivals, as well as logistical factors, such as readily available resources (Al-Hakim, 2006). The difficulty of compromising the two conflicting criteria of OTWL objective arises mainly from the process complexity and improper flow of information.

Capacity Management

Capacity management is about admission of appropriate patients when necessary, providing the appropriate treatment in an appropriate environment, and discharging patients as soon as appropriate (Proudlove & Boaden, 2005). Capacity management includes bed management and resources management.

The ideal situation is where the demand of incoming patients is predictable and matches the capacity of the hospital in terms of available beds and resources. However, literature and common practices indicate that demand considerably exceeds hospital capacity (Buchanan & Wilson, 1996; District Commission, 2002; McAleer et al., 1995). SMP attempts to relieve the common mismatch between new incoming patients and outgoing discharge patients. The variability in the surgery's times and the length of stay of patients in recovery wards considerably disturb capacity management decisions and lengthen the OTWL. Time constraint and accessibility of information may prevent discovering medical errors even if the information entered in the system is accurate. There is a clear need to have an effective flow of information that allows revising decisions related to hospital capacity and then better determining the admission date for new patients during the booked admission stage of OTWL or allocating the scarce resources. One case reported by Davies and Walley (2000) was the lack of data from the computer system of a hospital, which either did not keep records of potentially relevant information, or was not kept up to date. As a consequence, many capacity decisions were based on subjective judgement or commonly held beliefs. Hospitals often overlook the opportunity to coordinate short-term demand with capacity.

Specialised beds usually represent the first bottleneck that block new patients from being admitting to the hospital (Hill, 2006). Because it is difficult to move patients out from PACU based only on predetermined assessment rather than actual patient's health status, PACU does not have the capacity to accept new patients, thus creating a bottleneck preventing admission of patients to the operating theatre.

Copyright © 2007, Idea Group Inc. Copying or distributing in print or electronic forms without written permission of Idea Group Inc. is prohibited.

The affect of lack of resources on capacity management is readily apparent. The key bottleneck resources are surgery specialists, such as surgeons, and specialised surgery equipment. However, cases are reported where delays in surgery have not resulted from a lack of resources but because of lack of coordination. Buchanan (1998) reports a hospital case in which there were a number of complaints from surgeons and anaesthetists about apparent delays in transporting patients to and from operating theatres.

Unpredictability of surgery cancellation by patients is another factor affecting capacity decisions. Surgery could be cancelled by a patient even after admission to the hospital. Cancellation can occur because of lack of resources, surgeons, or anaesthetists, and so forth. However, Davies and Walley (2000) stress that 2% of operations cancelled in one case hospital were due to the hospital's inability to actually find patients who had been admitted to the ward! This is an obvious example of lack of effective information flow. A study conducted at a major Australian hospital reveals that the percentage of cancellations on the day of intended surgery exceeds 11%. The main reasons recorded include overrun of previous surgery (18.7%), no postoperative bed (18.1%), change in patient clinical status (17.1%), procedural reasons (including unavailability of surgeon, list error, administrative cause, and communication failure totalled 21%), and finally cancellation by patient (17.5%). This reflects the fact that more that 83% of surgery cancellations on the day of intended surgery are related to flow of information and could be avoided or minimised with a good information flow system.

Case Study

The case study approach can be used to provide a detailed description of a phenomenon (Yin, 1994). The findings of this chapter are based on the operating theatre suite of a public hospital located in a remote area. The hospital employs 2,000 staff in 13 clinical sections, including surgical, anaesthetic, orthopaedic, obstetric and gynaecology, paediatrics, emergency, critical care, medical imaging, medical, renal, public health, oncology, and rehabilitation. It has a total of 261 beds, including 164 acute beds, 57 mental health beds, and 40 day beds. The operating theatre suite consists of six operating theatres. Four are used for elective surgery. The other two theatres are dedicated to 24-hour emergency and caesarean surgeries. The suite has eight recovery wards. There are six types of specialised waiting lists in this hospital: general surgery; ear, nose, and throat (ENT); gynaecology surgery; ophthalmology; urology, and orthopaedic.

The research methodology comprises semistructured, biweekly interviews with several senior managers and specialised staff for a period of three months during 2005. The interviews were arranged by the author and two of his postgraduate students. The research was conducted on the condition that there was no access to identifiable patient information and no direct contact with patients or staff other than those specified.

Process Mapping and Information Mapping

Process mapping is a technique used to detail business processes by focusing on the important elements that influence their behaviour (Soliman, 1998). It consists of constructing a model that shows the relationships between the activities, people, data, and objects involved in the production of a specified output (Biazzo, 2002). Lin, Yang, and Pai (2002) argue that

Copyright © 2007, Idea Group Inc. Copying or distributing in print or electronic forms without written permission of Idea Group Inc. is prohibited.

process mapping performs two important functions. The first function is to capture existing processes by structurally representing their activities and elements. The second function is to redesign the processes in order to evaluate their performance.

SMP cuts across several stages and functional boundaries that are managed by different staff. At each stage several activities are performed. The value of each activity is not only derived from its connection with the other SMP activities but derived also from the consistency of its rules with other activities' rules and the coordination between the resources, which perform the whole SMP. The effectiveness of activity coordination is directly related to process complexity. Browning (1998) stresses that process complexity is a function of at least four factors: (1) the number of activities, (2) the individual complexity of each activity, (3) the number of relationships (or interdependencies) between activities, and (4) the individual complexity of each interdependency. Giddens's (1984) seeks additional relationships and interdependencies between resources and rules governing the actions. This research adds four additional important factors: (5) the relationships or interdependencies between activities and the associated resources and rules, (6) the interdependencies between the resources, (7) the interdependencies between the resources and rules, and (8) the complexity of these interdependencies. Accordingly, to successfully map SMP, it is necessary to go beyond the detailing of each activity in a chart that only shows the flow of work from one activity to another.

An effective process mapping should therefore consider the interrelationships between activities as well as the objects (patients) involved, the resources needed to perform the process's activities, the rules and policies that govern the implementation of activities, and the flow of information between various elements of the activities.

Traditional process mapping, such as flow and Gantt charts, are not robust enough to handle the process complexity. Traditional process mapping techniques focus only on sequencing the activities or work flow. They do not take into consideration other activity's elements such as rules and resources including information flow. Accordingly these techniques cannot be used to map the interdependencies between the elements of the activities and hence cannot deal with the complexity factors mentioned above. One structured process mapping technique, referred to as IDEF0, can be used to map the various elements of activities.

IDEF0

The name IDEF originates from the United States Air Force program for Integrated Computer Manufacturing (Mayer et al., 1995). IDEF0 is one of the IDEF series of techniques that was originally developed in order to describe, specify, and model business processes in a structured graphical form (Fulscher & Powell, 1999; Lin et al., 2002). IDEF0 describes a business process as a series of linked *activities* in which each activity is specified by four elements: inputs, controls, outputs, and mechanisms. These elements are referred to as ICOMs (Lin et al., 2002). Figure 1 illustrates generically how IDEF0 is used to depict activities and their associated elements.

IDEF0 results in a model that consists of diagrams (boxes), text, and glossary, cross-referenced to each other. The box and arrow meanings are used to relate several subfunctions on a diagram comprising a more general function. Inputs are objects and data that are consumed or transformed by an activity, and they are represented by arrows entering the left side of the box. Outputs are objects and information that are the direct results of an activity,

Copyright © 2007, Idea Group Inc. Copying or distributing in print or electronic forms without written permission of Idea Group Inc. is prohibited.

Figure 1. IDEF0 elements: inputs, outputs, controls, and mechanisms

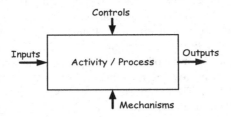

and they are shown as arrows leaving the right side of the box. Information outputs from an activity may form an input to other activities. Controls are information that specifies conditions which must exist for an activity to produce correct outputs and is represented by arrows entering the top of the box. External or internal factors may control an activity. Controls of an activity include actions, policies, or regulations that control the activity, while mechanisms refer to the resources required to achieve the activities. Information outputs from an activity may form a feedback to control other activities. Mechanisms refer to the resources (people) required to achieve the activities. We assume that each activity may have several inputs and outputs, may be embraced by a number of controls, and may require several resources. Input, output, and control elements of an activity can be used to map the flow of information between the activities. A box in an IDEF0 model may represent a stage, a process, or a certain course of action within the process. The IDEF0 representation fits with the Giddens concept of a business process as well as the sociotechnical system definition. IDEF0 has been commonly used in mapping processes of manufacturing systems (Bal, 1998). There have been a few attempts to use it in the hospital context (Wong & Busby, 2003).

IDEF0 allows a hierarchical or top-down decomposition approach to analyse processes at multiple levels of abstraction (Kappes, 1997). Figure 2 illustrates the hierarchical concept of IDEF0. The essence of hierarchical decomposition approaches to business process mapping, in which a basic, single-activity description of the process is decomposed step-by-step into its constituent activities to whatever level of detail appropriate for mapping purposes (Fulscher & Powell, 1999).

This hierarchical decomposition of activities helps to organise the development of IDEF0 models and proves critical in abstracting the essence of the process itself from the details of current practice. The top level activity which represents the subject of the model is always given the number A_0. The next level of activities are numbered A_1 to A_n where n indicates the number of "child" activities that A_0 was broken into. Figure 3 illustrates an overview or macrolevel view of A_0 details of SMP mapping for the case of a hospital using IDEF0.

Determining Interdependency

The elements of an activity do not exist in isolation from elements of other activities in the waiting list management process and the relationships between these elements form the interdependencies between the process's activities. There are six basic forms of inter-

Copyright © 2007, Idea Group Inc. Copying or distributing in print or electronic forms without written permission of Idea Group Inc. is prohibited.

Figure 2. Example of IDEF0 hierarchical top-down concept

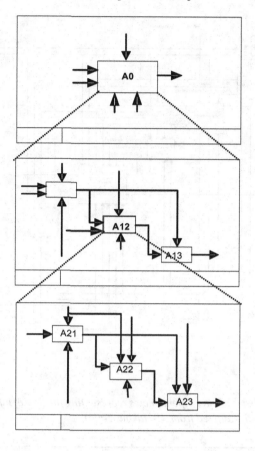

dependencies between elements of activities representing the flow of information mapping (Al-Hakim, 2006); (1) input/input dependency — as between activities A1 and A2, (2) input/output dependency, (3) output/control dependency, (4) input/control dependency, (5) control/control dependency, and (6) resource/resource dependency (Figure 4).

The Activity/Concept (A/C) matrix window of IDEF0 displays in matrix format which concepts (elements) are attached to which activities and how they are attached — as inputs, controls, outputs, or mechanisms (Figure 5). The A/C matrix can be used to depict the interdependencies within and between activities. For example, the A/C matrix of Figure 5 illustrates that the advice of an anaesthetist is needed during implementing activities: preassessment, perioperations, procedure, and discharge, and the anaesthetic output from preassessment controls the other three activities (perioperations, procedure, and discharge). However, IDEF0 is not designed precisely to map information feedback needed from other

Copyright © 2007, Idea Group Inc. Copying or distributing in print or electronic forms without written permission of Idea Group Inc. is prohibited.

Figure 3. Macro-map of SMP process using IDEF0

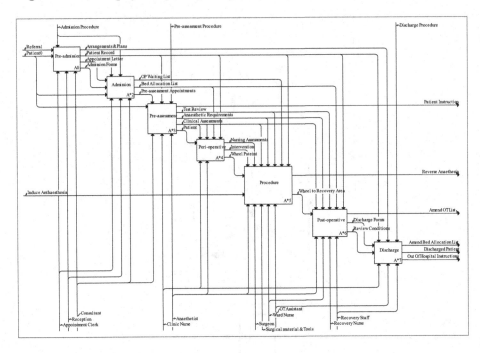

Figure 4. Six basic forms of interdependencies representing the flow of information mapping, numbered from 1 to 6 (Adapted from Al-Hakim, 2006)

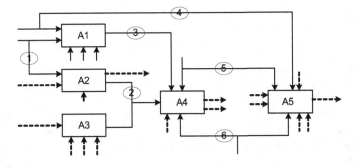

Copyright © 2007, Idea Group Inc. Copying or distributing in print or electronic forms without written permission of Idea Group Inc. is prohibited.

Figure 5. Part of A/C matrix

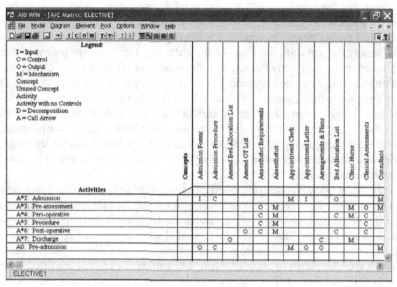

activities before the start of the current one. Accordingly, IDEF0 cannot be actively used to group activities for the purpose of information flow. This research integrates IDEF0 with another structured technique known as dependency structured matrix.

Dependency Structured Matrix

Steward (1981) described the concept of dependency structure matrix or design structure matrix (DSM) and its application to design process. The actual use of DSM in industry began around 1990 as part of a postgraduate study project conducted at MIT (Browning, 1998). Design process requires complex feedback. One or more prior design activities could be reworked or modified as a result of new information gained from performing another activity at a later stage of the design. Interdependent activities that benefit each other in this way are known as coupled activities (Eppinger, 2001). Coupled activities drive the iterations of the design process. DSM can successfully be used to reduce design project cycle time and control the iterations by grouping design activities into three types of sets: sequential activities, parallel activities, and coupled activities. The core concept of DSM is to rely on information flow between activities rather than on work flow. Relying on information flow is what distinguishes DSM from traditional mapping techniques. In traditional mapping techniques, such as flowcharts and Gantt charts, the start of an activity depends on the completion of certain other activities, and accordingly these techniques answer the question: "what other activities must be completed before the start of the current activity?" DSM answers a

Copyright © 2007, Idea Group Inc. Copying or distributing in print or electronic forms without written permission of Idea Group Inc. is prohibited.

very different question (Eppinger, 2001): "what information is needed from other activities before completing the existing one?" Analysing information flow allows resequencing of activities such that both cycle time and iterations are reduced.

DSM is a square matrix in which each activity is represented by one row and one column. Initially the activities are listed in the order in which they are presently carried out with upstream or early activities listed in the upper rows (Browning, 1998; Eppinger, 2001). Entries across a row corresponding to an activity represent the other activities that supply information to the current one. Entries below the matrix diagonal signify information received from activities carried before the current one. Entries above the matrix diagonal imply feedback from activities that will be implemented at later stages — the potential for iteration in the process. In regard to SMP, entries above the matrix diagonal determine the operations which have the potential to affect the performance of SMP, for example, affecting the operating theatre waiting list.

The entries of DSM represent the interdependencies between activities. There are four forms of information dependencies. Where the entries ij and ji are empty, this indicates that activities (i) and (j) have no direct interdependencies (dependent activities) and they can performed simultaneously. That is, they form parallel set of activities. Figure 6 represents DSM for a system of five activities from which activities B and C form a parallel set. Two activities are interdependent or coupled when both entries (ij) and (ji) are filled, such as activities D and E in Figure 6. The third form of information dependency is when one only entry (ij) or (ji) is filled. When (ij) is filled, activity (j) should follow activity (i); that is,

Figure 6. Sequential, parallel, and coupled set of activities

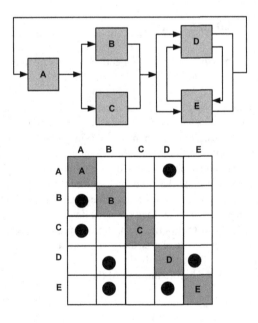

Copyright © 2007, Idea Group Inc. Copying or distributing in print or electronic forms without written permission of Idea Group Inc. is prohibited.

activities (i) and (j) are independent and form a sequential set of activities. Activity B of Figure 6 should follow activity A because the entry BA is filled. The third form of information dependency is created when any other entry below the diagonal is filled, such as entry

Figure 7. An overview mapping of SMP with DSM

Copyright © 2007, Idea Group Inc. Copying or distributing in print or electronic forms without written permission of Idea Group Inc. is prohibited.

(CA) of Figure 6. Any other filled entry above the diagonal creates feedback — the fourth form of information dependency. In Figure 6, activity A receives feedback from activity D. However, because activities D and E form a coupled set, feedback from any of them may change the situation of activity A.

There are three objectives of using DSM to map SMP. The first objective is to rearrange the sequence of activities such that the number of entries above the matrix diagonal is minimised. This will reduce the amount of feedback that affects SMP and then the number of times SMP is revised or amended. The second objective is to identify the parallel activities such that these activities can be implemented concurrently in order to reduce operation cycle time. The third objective is to recognise the coupled activities so that information can smoothly flow between them without any delay. This objective also helps the restructuring of the operating theatre process by ensuring that the activities of each set of coupled activities are managed by the same authority. This kind of reorganisation will reduce the number of decision-making authorities. Figure 7 depicts an initial DSM matrix for the macromap of SMP, in which stages of SMP form activities of DSM.

Integrating IDEF0 with DSM

Despite the strength of IDEF0 specifically in identifying various elements of activities in the form of output, input, control, and mechanism and additionally in its ability to graphically map interdependencies between these elements, it still does not expressly or effectively accommodate the full mapping of information. It also does not capture the specific sequencing logic between the process activities and explicitly consider time-order constraints between activities or the parallelism of activities (Plaia & Carrie, 1995). For instance, for a complex process like the operating theatre process it is difficult to determine activities or sets of activities that may be implemented concurrently or sequentially. DSM can be used to overcome the deficiencies of IDEF0. However, the inability of DSM to identify interdependencies apart from those related to flow of information makes the integration of DSM and IDEF0 very valuable.

All the dot points above the diagonal of the DSM matrix in Figure 7 provide feedback that may require changes in the capacity plans of SMP. For example, at the preadmission stage, the initial SMP capacity plans, such as waiting list and bed allocation plan, are formed or amended. The dot point in the cell of preadmission and postoperative illustrates that preadmission should receive feedback information from the postoperative section in order to perform duties related to SMP. This feedback cannot be easily detected during process mapping using IDEF0. Benefiting from DSM, IDEF0 mapping can be revised to accommodate these feedbacks.

Analysis of DSM reveals difficulty in rearranging the sequence of activities to reduce feedback. However, from the information flow perspective, some of these activities can be combined. The first two stages, preadmission and booked admission, can be administratively combined into one function referred to as "admission." The three activities (stages), perioperative, procedure, and postoperative, require information from each other and provide feedback to each other. These three activities form a "coupled" set of activities. From the information flow perspective, the information for these three activities should be between

Copyright © 2007, Idea Group Inc. Copying or distributing in print or electronic forms without written permission of Idea Group Inc. is prohibited.

Figure 8. IDEF0 chart for the modified SMP

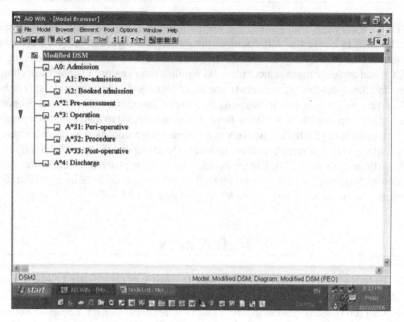

Figure 9. The modified DSM

Activity	Admission	Preassessment	Operation	Discharge
Admission			•	
Preassessment	•			
Operation		•		
Discharge			•	

them in real time and under one authority. The three activities can be administratively merged
into one function, say "operation." The preadmission and admission activities can also be
administratively combined. Figure 8 illustrates the IDEF0 chart for the modified organisational structure of SMP. The resulting DSM becomes as shown in Figure 9.

Based on the modified DSM, changes in SMP will be affected only as a result of a
single feedback from the operation stage.

Copyright © 2007, Idea Group Inc. Copying or distributing in print or electronic forms without written permission
of Idea Group Inc. is prohibited.

Conclusion

This chapter deals with information mapping and uses the operating theatre suite of a public hospital as a case study. It discusses the surgery management process (SMP) complexity, and factors affecting the main SMP functions; the operating theatre waiting lists (OTWL); and capacity management plan. It identifies the dynamic variables affecting the process and concludes that the impact of these variables on SMP can be considerably reduced by effectively mapping and then managing the flow of information. The chapter proposes a procedure for mapping the information flow. It employs IDEF0 to map the SMP operations and points to the lack of IDEF0 to actively map information feedback. The chapter integrates IDEF0 with another structured technique known as Dependency Structured Matrix (DSM) to overcome the pitfalls in IDEF0. The results indicate that it is possible to reduce the amount of feedbacks from SMP operations that affect the performance of SMP by administratively controlling the information flow through certain operations of SMP.

References

Abbott, J. (2001). Data data everywhere and not a byte of use? *Qualitative Market Research, 4*(3), 182-192.

ABC News. (2003). *Man experiences terrible shock after cancer surgery.* Retrieved November 11, 2005, from http://abclocal.go.com/wls/story?section=News&id=436965

Al-Hakim, L. (2006). Web-based hospital information system for managing operating theatre waiting list. *International Journal of Healthcare Technology and Management, 7*(3/4), 266-282.

Al-Hakim, L., & Xu, H. (2004). On work alignment: Do IT professionals think differently? In A. Sarmanto (Ed.), *Issues of human computer integration* (pp. 291-320). Hershey, PA: IRM Press.

Bal, J. (1998). Techniques: Process analysis tools for process improvement. *The TQM Magazine, 10*(5), 342-254.

Biazzo, S. (2002). Process mapping techniques and organisational analysis: Lessons from sociotechnical system theory. *Business Process Management Journal, 8*(1), 42-52.

Bosset, J. L. (1991). *Quality function deployment. A practitioner's approach.* Milwaukee, WI: ASQC Quality Press.

Browning, T. R. (1998, July 15-17). Use of dependency structure matrices for product development cycle time reduction. In *Proceedings of the Fifth ISPE International Conference on Concurrent Engineering: Research and Applications,* Tokyo, Japan.

Buchanan, D. (1998). Representing process: The contribution of re-engineering frame. *International Journal of Operations & Production Management, 18*(12), 1163-1188.

Buchanan, D., & Wilson, B. (1996). Re-engineering operating theatres: The perspective assessed. *Journal of Management in Medicine, 10*(4), 57-74.

Davies, C. L., & Walley, P. (2002). Quality of care: Replacing or removing ineffective services. *International Journal of Health Care Quality Assurance, 15*(2/3), 124-129.

Delone, W. H., & McLean, E. R. (1992). Information system success: The quest for the dependent variable. *Information Systems Research, 3*(1), 60-95.

Copyright © 2007, Idea Group Inc. Copying or distributing in print or electronic forms without written permission of Idea Group Inc. is prohibited.

District Commission. (2002). *Operating theatres: A bulletin for health bodies* (District Audit). Retrieved April 11, 2006, from http://www.district-audit.gov.uk

Eppinger, S. (2001, January). Innovation at the speed of information. *Harvard Business Review*, 149-158.

Evans, J. R., & Lindsay, W. M. (2002). *The management and control of quality* (5th ed.). Cincinnati, OH: South-Western, Thomson Learning.

Fadlalla, A., & Wickramasinghe, N. (2004). An integrative framework for HIPAA-compliant I*IQ healthcare information systems. *International Journal of Health Care Quality Assurance, 17*(2), 65-74.

Fisher, C. W., & Kingma, B. R. (2001). Criticality of data quality as exemplified in two disasters. *Information & Management, 39*, 109-116.

Fulscher, J., & Powell, S. G. (1999). Anatomy of a process mapping workshop. *Business Process Management Journal, 5*(3), 208-237.

Gallivan, S., Utley, M., Treasure, T., & Valencia, O. (2002). Booked inpatient admission and hospital capacity: Mathematical modelling study. *BMJ, 324*(7332), 280-282. Retrieved April 11, 2006, from http://pubmed-central.nih.gov/articlerender.fcgi?art id=65062&rendertype=abstract

Giddens, A. (1984). *The constitution of society*. Cambridge: Polity Press.

Gonzalez-Busto, B., & Garcia, R. (1999). Waiting lists in Spanish public hospitals: A system dynamics approach. *System Dynamics Review, 15*(3), 201-224.

Goodhue, D.L. (1995). Understanding user evaluations of information systems. *Management Science, 41*(12), 1827-1844.

Hill, M. (2006). Medical staff role in hospital capacity. *EMPATH*. Retrieved April 11, 2006, from http://www.empath.md/about_us/MD_Role_in_Capacity.pdf

Huang, K.-T., Lee, Y. W., & Wang, R. Y. (1999). *Quality information and knowledge*. Upper Saddle River, NJ: Prentice Hall PTR.

Jarke, M., & Vassiliou, Y. (1997). Data warehouse quality: A review of the DWQ project. In *Proceedings of Information Quality Conference* (pp. 299-313). Cambridge, MA: Massachusetts Institute of Technology.

Kappes, S. (1997). Putting your IDEF0 model to work. *Business Process Management Journal, 3*(2), 151-161.

Keating, C. B., Fernandez, A. A., Jacobs, D. A., & Kauffmann, P. (2001). A methodology for analysis of complex sociotechnical processes. *Business Process Management Journal, 7*(1), 33-49.

Lee, W. Y., Strong, D. M., Beverly, K., & Wang, R. Y. (2002). AIMQ: A methodology for information quality assessment. *Information & Management, 40*(2), 133-146.

Li, N. Y., Tan, K. C., & Xie, M. (2003). Factor analysis of service quality dimension shifts in the information age. *Managerial Auditing Journal, 18*(4), 297-302.

Lin, F., Yang, C., & Pai, Y. (2002). A generic structure for business process modelling. *Business Process Management Journal, 8*(1), 19-41.

Mayer, R. J., Menzel, C. P., Painter, M. K., DeWitte, P. S., Blinn, T., & Perakath, B. (1995). *Information integration for concurrent engineering (iice) IDEF3 process description capture method report*. Knowledge Based Systems.

McAleer, W. E., Turner, J. A., Lismore, D., & Naqvi, I. A. (1995). Simulation of a hospital theatre suite. *Journal of Management in Medicine, 9*(3), 14-26.

New Health. (2002). *Operating theatre management project: Supplementary report on process mapping*. NSW: NSW Health Department.

Copyright © 2007, Idea Group Inc. Copying or distributing in print or electronic forms without written permission of Idea Group Inc. is prohibited.

Pirani, C. (2004, January 24-25). How safe are our hospitals. *The Weekend Australian.*

Plaia, A., & Carrie, A. (1995). Application and assessment of IDEF3 — process flow description capture method. *International Journal of Operations & Production Management, 15*(1), 63-73.

Proudlove, N. C., & Boaden, R. (2005). Using operational information and information systems to improve in-patient flow in hospitals. *Journal of Health Organisation and Management, 19*(6), 466-477.

Radts, M., & Spinasanta, S. (2004). *What is post-operative care?* Retrieved April 11, 2006, from http://www.spineuniverse.com/displayarticle.php/article613.html

Schofield, W., Rubin, G., Piza, M., Lai, Y., Sindhusake, D., Fearnside, M., et al. (2005). Cancellation of operations on the day of intended surgery at a major Australian referral hospital. *Medical Journal of Australia, 182*(12), 612-615.

Sen, K. (2001) Does the measure of information quality influence survival bias? *International Journal of Quality and Reliability Management, 18*(9), 967-981.

Soliman, F. (1998). Optimum level of process mapping and least cost business process re-engineering. *International Journal of Operations & Production Management, 18*(9/10), 810-816.

Steward, D. (1981). The design structure system: A method for managing the design of complex systems. *IEEE Transaction on Engineering Management, 28*, 71-74.

Strong, D. M., Lee, Y. W., & Wang, R. Y. (1997). Data quality on context. *Communication of the ACM, 40*(5), 103-110.

TheFreeDictionary. (2006). *Operating theatre.* Retrieved April 11, 2006, from http://www.thefreedictionary.com/operating+theater

Turban, E., Aronson, J. E., & Liang, T. P. (2004). *Decision support systems and intelligent systems* (7rd ed.). Upper Saddle River, NJ: Prentice Hall.

Urban Scrawl. (2003). *Man loses penis* (Archived entry). Retrieved June 10, 2006, from http://demon.twinflame.org/archives/2003/08/man_loses_penis.php

Wang, R. Y. (1998). A product perspective on total data quality management. *Communications of the ACM, 41*(2), 58-65.

Wang, R. Y., & Strong, D. M. (1996). Beyond accuracy: What data quality means to data consumers. *Journal of Management Information Systems, 12*(4), 5-34.

Wong, C., & Busby, C. (2003). Redesigning the medication ordering, dispensing and administration process in an acute care academic health sciences centre. In S. Chick, P.J. Sanchez, D. Ferrin, & D. J. Morrice (Eds.), *Proceedings of the 2003 Winter Simulation Conference* (pp. 1894-1902). New Orleans, Louisiana.

WrongDiagnosis. (2004). *Medical new summary: Medical error causes girl's death following routine surgery.* Retrieved on February 10, 2006, from http://www.wrongdiagnosis.com/news/medical_error_causes_girls_death_following_routine_surgery.htm

Yin, R. (1994). *Case study research: Design and methods.* Thousand Oaks, CA: Sage.

Copyright © 2007, Idea Group Inc. Copying or distributing in print or electronic forms without written permission of Idea Group Inc. is prohibited.

Section IV

Applications in Manufacturing and Management

Chapter IX

A Methodology for Information Quality Assessment in the Designing and Manufacturing Process of Mechanical Products

Ying Su, Tsinghua University, China

Zhanming Jin, Tsinghua University, China

Abstract

Product information quality (PIQ) is critical in manufacturing enterprises. Yet, the field lacks comprehensive methodologies for its evaluation. In this chapter, the authors attempt to develop such a methodology, which is called activity-based measuring and evaluating of PIQ (AMEQ) to form a basis for PIQ measurement and evaluation. The methodology encompasses a roadmap to measure and improve PIQ, an indicator system based on characteristics and logic-temporal sequences of processes, and a set of models to quantificationally describe, operate, and measure the designing and manufacturing processes of mechanical product information. The methodology is illustrated through a business case. The results of the methodology are useful for determining and reviewing the best area for PIQ improvement activities.

Copyright © 2007, Idea Group Inc. Copying or distributing in print or electronic forms without written permission of Idea Group Inc. is prohibited.

Introduction

In this information age, there are two kinds of manifestations for products in manufacturing enterprises (MEs): one is physical form, which is called entity product; the other is information form, which is called information product. An entity product is the result of information product materialized, such as automobile, machine tool, pump, tool, and bearing; an information product usually comes from an entity product, such as data, message, information, knowledge, arithmetic, software, document, drawing, language, news, service, and consultation. The information gathered and processed in ever increasing quantities, if presented in a timely and accurate manner, can create a life-or-death situation within a company. Enterprise resource planning (ERP) developers and implementers have always considered the quality of information to be important. A survey of the reasons for ERP failures showed that information quality (IQ) is listed as one of the six categories in ERP design and implementations (Chatfield, Kim, Harrison, & Hayya, 2004; Chiu, Hsieh, & Kao, 2005; Graeme, Peter, & Leskie, 2003; Yang, Diane, Beverly, & Richard, 2002). Over the last decade, IQ research activities have increased significantly to meet the needs of organizations attempting to measure and improve the quality of information (Guy, 2001; Kuan, Yang, & Richard, 1999; Schwartz & Mayne, 2005; Zhang, 2002). In industry, IQ has been rated regularly as a top concern in computer-based management information systems (MIS) and data warehousing projects (English, 1999; Orr, 1998; Redman, 2001; Xu & Koronios, 2004).

Despite a decade of research and practice, hardly any techniques are available for measuring, analyzing, and improving product information quality (PIQ) in business processes of MEs (Nelson, Todd, & Wixom, 2005; Park & Barber, 2005; Price & Shanks, 2005). As a result, knowledge workers in MEs are unable to develop comprehensive measures of the quality of their information and to benchmark their efforts against that of other professionals (Johansson & Johansson, 2004; Parssian, Sarkar, & Jacob, 2004). Without the ability to assess the quality of their information, knowledge workers cannot assess the status of their PIQ and monitor its improvement. The challenge for this research is to develop an overall model with an accompanying assessment instrument for measuring PIQ. Furthermore, techniques must be developed to compare the assessment results against enterprise objectives and cross stakeholders. Such techniques are necessary for prioritizing PIQ improvement efforts.

This research was designed to meet these challenges. A methodology called activity-based measuring and evaluating of PIQ (AMEQ) has been developed to provide a rigorous and pragmatic basis for PIQ assessments and relationships with enterprise goals. It has four components. The first component is a framework of what IQ means to performance measurement (Su, Yu, & Zhang, 2002). This framework is process oriented and contains IQ metrics as one of the six internal measures.

Based on Su and Yu's dynamic integrated performance measurement system (DIPMS) (Su et al., 2002), in the second section, a roadmap for continuously improving PIQ is given to facilitate the processes of PIQ definition, measurement, assessment, and improvement. The roadmap consists of five processes of measuring and improving PIQ and provides a big-picture view of the AMEQ methodology. It will help the reader to understand the context for PIQ improvement, so that as the reader reads about a specific step, the reader has an understanding of how it fits into the overall methodology.

Copyright © 2007, Idea Group Inc. Copying or distributing in print or electronic forms without written permission of Idea Group Inc. is prohibited.

Figure 1. The roadmap for PIQ improvement

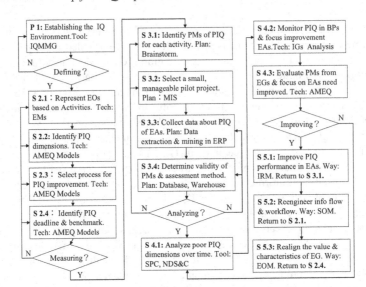

In the third section, an indicator system of PIQ dimensions grouped by characteristics and time-series of activities, is developed, which is the result of process 1 explained in the roadmap. This system has four specific cases and one generic case. Several IQ dimensions together measure PIQ for each activity depending upon upstream-downstream relationships of the activity. It can be applied to assessing the PIQ in the designing and manufacturing processes.

In the fourth section, three models for AMEQ, used to describe, operate, and measure the PIQ, are presented. They are used in processes 2 and 4 prescribed by the roadmap. In the fifth section, the application of AMEQ is illustrated by showing an example of a small manufacturing company. Finally, the last section offers the merits of AMEQ methodology and describes future work.

A Roadmap for Improvement

A solution should be found as to how to measure and improve PIQ in business processes. A roadmap is developed for DIPMS. PIQ improvement is not an end in itself; rather it is a means for improving business performance and customer satisfaction. The roadmap consists of the following five phases (see Figure 1):

Phase 1: Establish IQ Environment

Phase 1 is more than a single process. It represents the systemic, managing, and cultural requirements for a sustainable PIQ improvement environment. This phase is treated first because it is foundational to long-term IQ improvement. By managing IQ, an IQ team

Copyright © 2007, Idea Group Inc. Copying or distributing in print or electronic forms without written permission of Idea Group Inc. is prohibited.

is established to define what PIQ is, and how to manage the information or information flow over its life cycle. In reality, the reader will have to conduct activities from the other four phases.

This phase assesses the cultural readiness of organization, using the information quality management maturity grid (IQMMG). One of the most important outputs of phase 1 is the multiple dimensions of PIQ divided by characteristics and time-series of business activities (see the third section).

Phase 2: Define PIQ

The phase of PIQ definition is a precursor to measuring IQ. One cannot measure the quality of a product without knowing that the product specifications themselves are accurate and are what they should be. In order to measure PIQ out of a business process, it is necessary to establish the mapping from enterprise goals to activity PIQ measures first.

- **Step 2.1** represents the enterprise objects (EOs) based on activity.
- **Step 2.2** identifies the PIQ dimensions of enterprise activity using the results of phase 1.
- **Step 2.3** selects the process for PIQ improvement using the AMEQ models (see the fourth section).
- **Step 2.4** identifies benchmarks and deadlines of enterprise goals (EGs) about PIQ. These PIQ benchmarks constitute the EG objects.

Phase 3: Measure PIQ

To measure PIQ in business processes, MEs must develop a suitable set of metrics to perform the necessary measurements. The requirement for measuring is inextricably intertwined with the needs to analyze and improve PIQ. Based on the definition of PIQ dimensions, four steps are proposed that the IQ managers must recognize and use.

- **Step 3.1** identifies performance measures (PMs) of PIQ for each activity. The first step is the development of 6-12 items for PIQ dimensions. Then, IQ researchers make sure that they have covered the dimensions and have not included those that are overlapped. The items for each activity are also reviewed by users to ensure they are meaningful to information consumers who would be completing the survey. As a result of these reviews, items were added, deleted, and revised. This process of reviewing and editing was repeated until an agreement was reached on an initial set of the three items per PIQ dimension.
- **Step 3.2** selects a small, manageable pilot project. The purpose of the pilot project is to provide an initial assessment of the reliability of the items for each of the dimensions and to use this to reduce the number of items per dimension. To facilitate the comprehensive assessment, the scale used in assessing each item ranges from 0 to 1 where 0 is labeled "not at all" and 1 is labeled "completely."
- **Step 3.3** uses the complementary metrics and final questionnaire to collect data about PIQ of enterprise activities (EAs). Statistical analyses were made using some software tools that can integrate with the ERP system to facilitate the data extraction and data mining.

Copyright © 2007, Idea Group Inc. Copying or distributing in print or electronic forms without written permission of Idea Group Inc. is prohibited.

Step 3.4 determines the validities of measures about EA and the assessment method of business processes on the foundation of data analysis.

Phase 4: Analyze PIQ

From the measurement results, the IQ team investigates the root cause for potential PIQ problems. The methods and tools for performing this task can be simple or complex.

- **Step 4.1** analyzes the poor IQ dimensions over time by using statistical process control (SPC), nonlinear dynamic systems, and chaos (NDS&C).
- **Step 4.2** conducts information gap analysis to monitor the PIQ in business processes and to focus improvement activities. Two analysis techniques, semantic gaps and pragmatic gaps, are used to identify PIQ problem areas.
- **Step 4.3** adopts the AMEQ models (see fourth section) to synthetically evaluate the PMs of EAs from EGs and to focus on the EAs that most need to be improved.

Phase 5: Improve PIQ

Once the analysis phase is complete, the PIQ improvement phase can start. It is important that both technical solutions and business processes be introduced, disseminated, and institutionalized in the organization over time in order to sustain the long-term improvement of PIQ. The IQ team needs to identify key areas for improvement.

- **Step 5.1** carries out information resource management (IRM) to improve the PIQ performance in enterprise activities.
- **Step 5.2** conducts self-organization management (SOM) to reengineer information flow and workflow with infrastructure.
- **Step 5.3** develops enterprise objective management (EOM) to realign the value and characteristics of EG.

Activity-Based Defining to the Dimensions for PIQ

For a manufacturing firm, the concept of quality encompasses much more than material defects. David A. Garvin (1988) proposed an analytic framework encompassing eight dimensions of quality: performance, features, reliability, conformance, durability, serviceability, aesthetics, and perceived quality.

Product quality has been defined as fitness for use, or the extent to which a product successfully serves the purposes of consumers. While fitness for use captures the essence of quality, it is difficult to measure quality using this broad definition. Just as product quality has multiple dimensions, IQ also has multiple dimensions. The choice of these dimensions is primarily based on three approaches that have been used in the literature of IQ study: intuitive, systematic, and user-based.

An intuitive approach is taken when the selection of IQ attributes in a specific study is based on the individual's experience or intuitive understanding about what attributes are important. Many IQ studies fall into this category (Laudon, 1986; Morey, 1982).

Copyright © 2007, Idea Group Inc. Copying or distributing in print or electronic forms without written permission of Idea Group Inc. is prohibited.

A system approach to IQ focuses on how information may become deficient during the information manufacturing process. Wand and Wang (1996) use an ontological approach in which attributes of IQ are derived based on data deficiencies, defined as the inconsistencies between the view of a real-world system that can be inferred from a representing information system and the view that can be obtained by directly observing the real-world system.

The advantage of using an intuitive approach is that each study can select the attributes most relevant to the particular goals of that study. The advantage of a system approach has the potential to provide a comprehensive set of IQ attributes that are intrinsic to information. The problem with both of these approaches is that they focus on the information product in terms of development characteristics instead of application characteristics. They are not directed to capturing the voice of the consumer.

User-based approach analyzes information collected from information consumers to determine the characteristics they use to assess whether information is fit for use in their tasks. The advantage of the user-based is that it captures the voice of the customer. However, this is a highly subjective view of IQ which gives rise to two types of problems. First, there is the problem of aggregating widely different individual preferences which can lead to meaningful definitions of quality in terms of the design of information products and services. The second is how to distinguish between those information attributes that connote quality and those that simply maximize consumer satisfaction.

The coexistence of these different approaches to IQ in business processes may result in conflicting views of PIQ among information providers and business users. These differences can cause serious breakdowns in communications, among information suppliers and between information suppliers and users. But even with improved communication among them, each of the principal approaches to PIQ shares a common problem: each offers only a partial and sometimes vague view of the basic elements of PIQ.

In order to fully exploit favorable conditions of these approaches and avoid unfavorable ones, we present a definition approach of PIQ that is based on characteristics of enterprise activities (EAs) precedence relationship between them. EAs are processing steps within a process transforming objects and requiring resources for their execution. An activity can be classified as a structured activity if it is computable and controllable. Otherwise, it is categorized as a nonstructured activity. Manufacturing activities are typical examples of structured activities because they are defined by a process plan for a given part type, and many of them are executed by numerically controlled (NC) machines driven by a computer reading NC instructions. Accounting, planning, inventory control, and scheduling activities are other examples of structured activities. Typical examples of nonstructured activities are human-based activities such as design, reasoning, or thinking activities.

We assigned the four cases based on types of relationship of activities, as shown in the second and third columns of Table 1. When the type of upstream activity is nonstructured and downstream activity also is nonstructured, we chose the user-based definition approach of PIQ (shown in the first row of Table 1). When the type of upstream activity is nonstructured and downstream activity is structured, we chose the intuitive definition approach of IQ (shown in the second row of Table 1). When the type of upstream activity is structured and downstream activity is nonstructured, we chose the user-based definition approach of IQ (shown in the third row of Table 1). When the type of upstream activity is structured and downstream activity is also structured, we chose the system definition approach of IQ (shown in the fourth row of Table 1).

Copyright © 2007, Idea Group Inc. Copying or distributing in print or electronic forms without written permission of Idea Group Inc. is prohibited.

Table 1. Activity-based defining to the dimensions of PIQ

Activity Taxonomy	Upstream Activity	Downstream Activity	Definition Approach	Reference Dimensions of PIQ for Upstream Activity
CASE I	Nonstructured	Nonstructured	User-based	Consistent representation, Interpretability, Case of understanding, Concise representation, Timeliness, Completeness (Ballou & Pazer, 1985), Value-added, relevance, appropriate, Meaningfulness, Lack of confusion (Goodhue, 1995), Arrangement, Readable, Reasonable (Zmud, 1978).
CASE II	Nonstructured	Structured	Intuitive	Precision, Reliability, Freedom from bias (Delone & McLean, 1992).
CASE III	Structured	Nonstructured	User-based	See also **CASE I**
CASE IV	Structured	Structured	System	Data Deficiency, Design Deficiencies, Operation Deficiencies (Kuan et al., 1999; Yang et al., 2002).
Inherent PIQ	Accuracy, Cost, Objectivity, Believability, Reputation, Accessibility (Wang & Strong, 1996). Correctness, Unambiguous (Wand & Wang, 1996). Consistency (English, 1999).			

Before one can measure and improve information quality, one must be able to define it in ways that are both meaningful and measurable. In defining information quality, we differentiate between inherent and pragmatic information quality. Essentially, inherent quality is the correctness, unambiguous, consistency, accuracy, cost, objectivity, believability, reputation, and accessibility about facts. Inherent information quality is the degree to which data accurately reflects the real-world object that the data represents. The last row of Table 1 provides inherent indicators of information quality for all the cases mentioned previously. Pragmatic information quality is the degree of usefulness and value data has to support the business processes that enable accomplishing enterprise objectives. In essence, pragmatic information quality is the degree of customer satisfaction derived by the knowledge workers who use it to do their jobs. The reference dimensions of pragmatic information quality for upstream activity in the business processes are given in the fifth column of Table 1.

In our earlier research, we empirically derived the PIQ dimensions that are important to activity executors, using methods traditionally employed in market research. These formed a foundation for our current research. We also grouped the PIQ dimensions according to four cases (Table 1).

Our follow-up research has provided further evidence that these dimensions provide comprehensive coverage of the multidimensional PIQ construct. For example, a follow-up

Copyright © 2007, Idea Group Inc. Copying or distributing in print or electronic forms without written permission of Idea Group Inc. is prohibited.

qualitative study of PIQ improvement projects in enterprises used these dimensions as the codes in content analysis of the organizational attention to different aspects of PIQ during improvement projects. All PIQ aspects in the projects were covered by the IQ dimensions.

Academics' View of IQ Dimensions

The fifth column of Table 1 summarizes academic research on the multiple dimensions of IQ. The first row is Ballou and Pazer's (1985) study, which takes an empirical, market research approach of collecting data from information consumers to determine the dimensions of importance to them. Table 1 lists the dimensions uncovered in Zmud's (1978) pioneering IQ research study, which considers the dimensions of information important to users of hard-copy reports. Because of the focus on reports, information accessibility dimensions, which are critical with online information, were not relevant.

In contrast to these empirically developed dimensions, the next three studies developed their IQ dimensions from existing literature. The Jarke and Vassiliou (1997) study modified the Wang and Strong (1996) dimensions in their study of data warehouse quality. The first dimension in each of the four categories is their overall label for that category. Delone and McLean's (1992) review of the MIS literature, during the 1980s, reports 23 IQ measures from nine previous studies (Morey, 1982). Four of these studies include only one measure of IQ, either importance or usefulness. Two studies, one of which is the well-known user satisfaction study by Bailey and Pearson (1983), include nine measures. Goodhue's (1995) dimensions are developed from a literature review to find the characteristics of information that are important to managers who use quantitative data stored in computer systems (Goodhue, 1995). In Goodhue's (1995) study, the importance of the dimensions in the accessibility IQ category is apparent.

The last two rows present two studies that focus on a few dimensions that can be measured objectively, rather than a comprehensive list of dimensions important to information consumers. Ballou and Pazer's (1985) study focuses primarily on intrinsic dimensions that can be measured objectively. They use four dimensions that frequently appear in IQ studies: accuracy, consistency, completeness, and timeliness. While they acknowledge the gap between user expectations for IQ and performance of the information system (IS) group in delivering IQ, their research does not specifically address the contextual and more subjective IQ dimensions. The Wand and Wang (1996) study takes an ontological approach and formally defines four IQ dimensions: correctness, unambiguous, completeness, and meaningfulness. The quality along these four dimensions can be assessed by comparing values in a system to their true real-world values.

In comparing these studies, two differences are apparent. One is whether the viewpoint of activity executors is considered, which necessarily requires the inclusion of some subjective dimensions. The other is the difficulty in classifying dimensions, for example, completeness and timeliness. In some cases, such as in the Ballou and Pazer (1985) study, the completeness and timeliness dimensions fall into the intrinsic IQ category, whereas in the Wang and Strong (1996) study, these dimensions fall into the contextual IQ category. As an intrinsic dimension, completeness is defined in terms of any missing value. As a contextual dimension, completeness is also defined in terms of missing values, but only for those values used or needed by activity executors.

In summary, the academic research included several types of studies. One provided overall coverage for the IQ construct by empirically developing the dimensions from infor-

Copyright © 2007, Idea Group Inc. Copying or distributing in print or electronic forms without written permission of Idea Group Inc. is prohibited.

mation consumers, such as in the Wang and Strong (1996) study. Zmud's (1978) study was an early empirical effort based on hard-copy reports. Another type developed their dimensions from literature reviews, that is, the Delone and McLean (1992), Goodhue (1995), and Jarkeand Vassiliou (1997) studies. By grouping all measures from other authors together, they hoped to cover all aspects of the IQ construct. The third type of study focused on a few dimensions that can be objectively defined, for example, Ballou and Pazer (1985), and Wand and Wang (1996).

IQ Research Directions

Three different approaches were used to identify trends in IQ research. In the first two approaches, the attendees were the source of information. First, a brainstorming session was conducted to identify the interests and current research activities of the attendees. Second, attendees self-reported their research agendas. Last, there was an analysis of the session topics in the programs of the 1997 through 2004 International Conferences on Information Quality (Beverly, Elizabeth, Pierce, & Helinä, 2004; Pierce, 2004).

First, the research topics of the attendees were analyzed since they appeared to consist of the largest number of distinct topics. Only 24 attendees provided this information yielding 75 topics. These topics were aggregated into 22 distinct research streams as shown in the first column of Table 2. The first three rows are aggregations and were identified by the largest number of researchers, for example, several different topics related to the assessment and measurement of IQ. These were grouped into the research stream shown in the first row of Table 2. The several frameworks and taxonomies for IQ form the second row. The third row incorporates IQ and different types of systems such as data warehouses, financial systems, and other functional areas.

Table 2. IQ research topics

Aggregated Research Interests of Participants	Identified at Research Forum	Year as a Conference Sessions
Assessment, benchmarks, metrics, score cards, optimization, perceptions	Standards, Metrics, Tools, Benchmarking & Achievable Goals	1998, 1999, 2000, 2001, 2002, 2003, 2004
Methodologies, Frameworks, Tools, Paradigms	IQ Paradigms, Jargon/terminology, Standardization, Methodologies, Frameworks & Visualization	1998, 1999, 2000, 2001, 2002, 2003, 2004
Types of systems: financial, cooperative, accounting, health care (HIPPA), governmental, data warehouses, multimedia, scientific	Functional Areas Strategic vs. Operational Governmental (voting), data warehouses, mailing lists	1997. 1998, 2000, 2001, 2002, 2003, 2004
Application of data mining & Statistical Techniques to improve IQ		2004

Copyright © 2007, Idea Group Inc. Copying or distributing in print or electronic forms without written permission of Idea Group Inc. is prohibited.

Table 2. continued

Application of TDQM in different industries	Cross Industries	1997, 2001, 2003
Application: Six sigma and lean applied to IQ problems		2004
Case Studies: Successes & Failures	Best & Worse Practices Longitudinal vs. Snapshot	2002, 2003, 2004
Communication of DQ inside of organization	Visualization	2001
Cost of IQ IQ ROI	Cost/Benefit Analysis Cost Justification	2004
Cross country, cross culture DQ issues	Cross Disciplinary Focus Cultural Issues & IQ ROI	2003
Ecommerce: Web quality, XML	Web Quality	1999, 2000, 2001, 2002
Exchange of IQ information	Exchange of IQ Information, Use of IQ Information	2004
IQ considerations in systems and DB design	DQ of Software Design	1997, 2001, 2002
IQ education (self-contained courses, degree programs)	IQ Education	2001, 2002, 2003
IQ officer & specialists: role, responsibilities, skills needed, certification	Career Paths	2004
Knowledge management, Business Intelligence	Knowledge Management	2004
Managing IQ	IQ Governance	2000, 2001, 2003, 2004
National disasters Legislation: Sarbanes Oakley	National disasters/ "Big Splash," Homeland Security, Legal & Public Policy	2001, 2002 (Politics)
Tags for IQ: their use & impact		2001, 2002, 2003 (Organizational Impact)

Approximately 40 research topics of interests were identified in the brainstorming session. Some of these were virtually the same or were combined yielding 18 distinct research streams (shown in the second column of Table 2). Subsequently, these were mapped into the topics identified in the attendees' research interests (shown in the first column). The research streams from both sources are very similar as shown in the first two columns of Table 2. The application of TQM techniques (i.e., Six Sigma, Lean Manufacturing) and the

Copyright © 2007, Idea Group Inc. Copying or distributing in print or electronic forms without written permission of Idea Group Inc. is prohibited.

application of statistical and data mining techniques to IQ are current research interests but were not identified in the brainstorming session.

As the list of topics associated with information quality continues to grow, so do the techniques used by researchers and practitioners to study this growing MIS specialty area. A review of the literature indicates that individuals interested in studying the challenges associated with improving data and information quality have a variety of investigation techniques from which to choose.

The case study research methodology is one of the most common methods for analyzing data and information quality. The application of this method among practitioners and research-ers varies widely ranging from the recounting of simple anecdotal evidence or professional experiences to the more formal and rigorous applications of this methodology.

There are several good published examples of the case study approach for studying data quality issues. For example, Shankaranarayan, Wang, and Ziad (2000) used an in-depth hospital case study to illustrate the use of IP-Maps. Lee, Allen, and Wang (2001) used on-site observations, field interviews, and document examinations to study the manufacture of information products at an aircraft fuel pump supplier. Strong, Lee, and Wang (1997) studied 42 data quality projects from three data rich organizations (an airline, a hospital, and an HMO) to better understand data quality issues, while Funk, Lee, and Wang (1998) conducted an in-depth case study of information quality at the S.C. Johnson Wax Company.

A second technique that is often applied in data and information quality research is extending proven techniques in other fields so that they incorporate the tenets of data and information quality. For instance, Ballou and Pazer (1985) used a data flow diagram from structure analysis as the start of their model for assessing the impact of data and process quality upon the outputs of a multi-user information decision system. Pierce (2004) showed that control matrices, a proven technique from the IS audit literature, could be adapted to evaluating the overall quality of an information product.

Another method cited in the data and information quality literature is the use of surveys and statistical analysis. For example, Wang and Strong (1996) used a two-staged survey sampling approach to identify the data quality dimensions most important to data consumers. Lee, Allen, and Wang (2001) piloted their questionnaire and analysis techniques for assessing information quality in an empirical study involving personnel at six different companies.

Finally, researchers and practitioners continue to seek out and adopt approaches from other disciplines to develop their data and information quality concepts and methods. Whether using Wand and Wang's (1996) theoretic approach to define a set of data quality metrics or the use of the computer science approach to develop the concept and implications of corporate house holding for improving information quality or applying market research techniques to improving information product design, IQ researchers and practitioners are building a rich body of research based on a diverse set of tools and research methodologies.

Copyright © 2007, Idea Group Inc. Copying or distributing in print or electronic forms without written permission of Idea Group Inc. is prohibited.

Models of the Designing and Manufacturing Processes

The key techniques of the AMEQ are a set of models of enterprise object, coupling operation and IQ measure. These models are proposed based on the object-oriented approach (OOA).

The OOA makes the basic assumption that the world is made of an organized collection of objects. According to this hypothesis, anything within an enterprise is also considered an object characterized by its unique and invariant identifier, its object class, and its state defined by the values of its attributes (Vernadat, 1996). An enterprise object (EO) might be concrete things (e.g., an equipment, an employee, or a product), abstract things (e.g., an enterprise goal, a business process, an enterprise activity, a performance measure, or an operation), or relationships among things (e.g., a logical link between two objects).

Models of Enterprise Object

Models of enterprise object (EO) are the most important building blocks of our AMEQ methodology. From the OOA point of view, they are a description of a set of abstract EOs that share the same attributes. Our models of EO are made of eight kinds of objects:

- **Human resource (HR):** main body of cognition for information.
- **Information resource (IR):** direct or indirect formulization about states, processes, controls, forms, meanings, and effectiveness of things expressed by main body.
- **Enterprise activity (EA):** a set of elementary actions executed to realize some task with an enterprise, requiring time and resources for its execution, and transforming an input state into an output state.
- **Resource input (RI):** logical relation reflected by HR when receiving IR in an EA.
- **Resource process (RP):** transition among the IRs made by HR.
- **Resource output (RO):** logical relation reflected by HR when sending IR in an EA.
- **Performance measure (PM):** a metric used to quantify the dimensions of PIQ for an EA.
- **Enterprise goal (EG):** the measurable aspirations that managers set for a business. Goals are determined by reference to business strategy. Goals may be financial, for example, achieving 14% return on sales, or nonfinancial, for example, increasing market share from 6% to 9%.

In this chapter only the attributes of EOs closely related to PIQ research are given. The relationship among seven objects, their attributes, and domains can be represented graphically in a class diagram as shown in Figure 2. The formal expression of models follows.

Copyright © 2007, Idea Group Inc. Copying or distributing in print or electronic forms without written permission of Idea Group Inc. is prohibited.

Human Resource

Human resource (HR) can be defined as a 3-tuple:

$$HR = \{(\text{personID}, \text{roleName}, \text{prsType})\} \tag{1}$$

where *personID* is the identifier of a human resource; *roleName* is defined as the role of a person in the business process; *prsType* is the type of a person when it processes information resources, such as Listener, Processor, and Dispatcher.

Information Resource

An information resource (IR) can be defined as a 5-tuple:

$$IR\{(\text{inforResID}, \text{content}, \text{generationTime}, \text{periodOfValidaty}, \text{inforType})\} \tag{2}$$

where *inforResID* is the identifier of IR; *content* includes three components: clear definition or meaning of data, correct values, and understandable presentation (the format represented to HRs); *generationTime* refers to the time when the IR comes into being; *periodOfValidity* refers to the age of the IR remaining valid; *inforType* is the type of the IR which can be classified as environmental, inner, and efferent.

Figure 2. The relationship diagram of enterprise objects

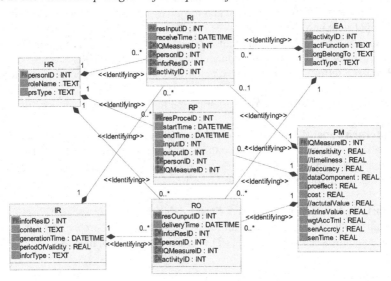

Copyright © 2007, Idea Group Inc. Copying or distributing in print or electronic forms without written permission of Idea Group Inc. is prohibited.

Enterprise Activity

An enterprise activity (EA) is defined as a 9-tuple:

$$EA=\{(activityID, actFunction, orgBelongTo, actType)\} \tag{3}$$

where *activityID* is the identifier of an EA; *actFunction* is defined as the function of EA; *orgBelongTo* defines the organization to which activity belongs; *actType* refers to the type of activity which can be catalogued as a structured activity and a nonstructured activity.

Resource Input

A resource input (RI) can be formalized as a 6-tuple:

$$RI=\{(resInputID, receiveTime, activityID, inforResID, personID, IQMeasureID)\} \tag{4}$$

where *resInputID* is the identifier of a RI; *receiveTime* refers to the time when an IR is obtained; *activityID* is the identifier of an EA; *inforResID* is the identifier of an IR; *personID* is the identifier of a listener; *IQMeasureID* is the identifier of a PM.

Resource Process

Resource process (RP) objects can be formalized as a 7-tuple:

$$RP=\{((resProceID, startTime, endTime, outputID, inputID, personID, IQmeasureID))$$
$$\tag{5}$$

where *resProceID* is the identifier of RP; *startTime* refers to the time when a HR starts to process an IR; *endTime* refers to the time when a HR finishes to process an IR; *outputID* is the identifier of an output EA; *inputID* is the identifier of an input EA; *personID* is the identifier of a processor; *IQMeasureID* is the identifier of a PM.

Resource Output

A resource output (RO) can be formalized as a 6-tuple:

$$RO=\{(resOunputID, deliveryTime, activityID, inforResID, personID, IQMeasureID))$$
$$\tag{6}$$

where *resOunputID* is the identifier of a RO; *deliveryTime* refers to the time when an IR is delivered to the customer; *activityID* is the identifier of an EA; *inforResID* is the identifier of an IR; *personID* is the identifier of a dispatcher; *IQMeasureID* is the identifier of a PM.

Copyright © 2007, Idea Group Inc. Copying or distributing in print or electronic forms without written permission of Idea Group Inc. is prohibited.

Performance Measure

The object of a performance measure (PM) is defined as a 12-tuple:

$$PM = \{(IQMeasureID, senCryVty, timeliness, accuracy, dataCmpAcy, proEffect,$$
$$cost, actutalValue, intrinsValue, wgtAccTml, senAccrcy, senTime)\}$$

(7)

where *IQMeasureID* is the identifier of PM; *timeliness, accuracy, cost,* and *actutalValue* are the targeted values of PIQ; *senCryVty, senAccrcy and senTime* are three parameters that allow us to control the sensitivity of ratios; *dataCmpAcy is* the accuracy of data component; *proEffect* is a measure of processing effectiveness; *intrinsvalue* is the intrinsic value of an IR; *wgtAccTml* is the weight that captures the relative importance to the customer of IR accuracy and IR timeliness.

Among these attributes, *timeliness, accuracy, cost,* and *actutalValue* are derived attributes of the PM which can be computed by other attributes through models of coupling operation and PIQ measure. In the third subsection of the fourth section, we will propose the various formulas to calculate these attributes. In the next section, we will present the models of coupling operation.

Enterprise Goal

An enterprise goal (EG) can be defined as a 7-tuple:

$$EG = \{(id, name, value, unit, startDate, finishDate, type)\}$$

(8)

where *id* is the identifier of EG; *name* is defined as the name of EG; *value* defines an assigned or calculated numerical quantity of EG; *unit* is the magnitude of the value; *startTime, finishTime* are start time and finish time of an EG; type is the dimension of PIQ to which an enterprise goal belongs (refer to Table 1).

Table 3 identifies the descriptive data for eight enterprise objects required to compute accuracy, timeliness, consistency, cost, and value of information to be delivered to an array of business activities.

Models of Coupling Operation

The coupling operation consists of a set of operations that take one or two sets as the input and produce a new set as their result. The fundamental operations in the coupling operation are S*elect, Project, Cartesian product,* and *Associative.*

The Select Operation

The *Select* operation selects tuples that satisfy a given predicate. We use the lower-case Greek letter sigma (σ) to denote selection. The predicate appears as a subscript to σ.

Copyright © 2007, Idea Group Inc. Copying or distributing in print or electronic forms without written permission of Idea Group Inc. is prohibited.

Table 3. Data for enterprise objects

Human resource (HR)		
personID	roleName	prsType
1	Plan Officer	Listener
2	Planner	Processor
...	...	...
26	Operator	Listener

Information Resource (IR)				
inforResID	inforType	generationTime	periodOfValidity	content
1	inner	2002-11-25	60	Master Production Plan
2	inner	2002-12-26	60	Manufacturing Plan
...	...	...	...	...
24	inner		1	Tools Information

Enterprise Activity (EA)			
activityID	actType	orgBelongTo	actFunction
1	structured	Planning Department	Plan & Control Production
2	non-structured	Shop Floor	Manufacturing
...	...	...	...
9	structured	Tool Library	Provide Tools

Resource Input (RI)					
resInputID	receiveTime	activityID	inforResID	personID	IQMeasureID
1	2002-12-13	1	1	1	1
2	2002-12-15	1	12	1	2
...	...	...	...	...	...
19	2003-5-30	2	24	26	58

Resource Process (RP)						
resProcID	startTime	endTime	outputID	inputID	personID	IQMeasureID
1	2002-12-24	2002-12-26	2	1	2	27
2	2002-12-01	2002-12-26	2	13	2	28
...	...	...	...	...	...	...
24	2003-3-18	2003-4-18	19	16	11	54

Resource Output (RO)					
resOunputID	deliveryTime	activityID	inforResID	personID	IQMeasureID
1	2002-12-27	1	2	3	13
2	2002-12-24	1	3	3	14
...	...	...	...	...	...
15	2003-4-20	4	19	12	55

Performance Measure (PM)							
IQMeasureID	cost	senCryVty	senTime	dataCmpAcy	proEffect	senAccrcy	wgtAccTml
1	1000	3	0.5	0.9	0.8	0.5	0.5
2	2500						
...	...	...	...	...	...	...	...
58	0.5	0.5	0.5	0.85	0.5	0.5	0.5

Enterprise Goal (EG)						
Id	type	Value	Unit	startDate	finishDate	Name
1	Accuracy	0.9	Null	2002-1-1	2004-1-1	Managing information
2	Timeliness	0.8	Null	2002-1-1	2004-1-1	Planning information
3	Consistency	0.9	Null	2002-1-1	2004-1-1	Order information
4	Cost	500	RMB	2002-1-1	2004-1-1	Processing information

The argument relation is in parentheses after the σ. Thus, to select those tuples of the IR in Equation 2 object where the *inforResID* is "1", we write: $\sigma_{inforResID = \text{"1"}}(IR)$

In general, we allow comparisons using $=, \neq, <, \leq, > \geq, \not\leq, \not\geq$ in the selection predicate. Furthermore, we can combine several predicates into a larger predicate by using the connectives and ($\wedge$), or ($\vee$), and not ($\neg$).

Copyright © 2007, Idea Group Inc. Copying or distributing in print or electronic forms without written permission of Idea Group Inc. is prohibited.

The Project Operation

Suppose we want to list all names and values of IR, but do not care about the identifier of IR. The *Project* operation allows us to produce this relation. The project operation is a unary operation that returns its argument relation, with certain attributes left out. Since a relation is a set, any duplicate rows are eliminated. Projection is denoted by the uppercase Greek letter pi (Π). We list those attributes that we wish to appear in the result as a subscript to Π. The argument relation follows in parentheses. Thus, we write the query to list all *periodOfValidity* of IR as: $\Pi_{periodOfValidity}$ (IR)

Composition of Coupling Operations

The fact that the result of a coupling operation a set is important. Consider the more complicated query "Find *periodOfValidity* of the IR which *inforResID* is 1." We write:

$$\Pi_{period\ of\ validity}(\mathsf{s}_{inf\ or\ Re\ sID\ =\ 1}(IR)) \tag{9}$$

The Cartesian-Product Operation

The *Cartesian-product* operation, denoted by a cross (×), allows us to combine information from any two objects. We write the Cartesian product of object o_1 and o_2 as $o_1 \times o_2$.

The Naming Operation

However, since the same attribute name may appear in both o_1 and o_2, we devise a naming operation to distinguish the object from which the attribute originally came. For example, the relation schema for R = IR × RI is:

IR × RI = {(IR.inforResID, IR.content, IR.generationTime, IR.periodOfValidity, IR.inforType
RI.resInputID, RI.receiveTime, RI.activityID, RI.inforResID, RI.personID, RI.IQMeasure)}

With this operation, we can distinguish IR.*inforResID* from RI.*inforResID*. For those attributes that appear in only one of the two objects, we shall usually drop the relation-name prefix. This simplification does not lead to any ambiguity. We can then write the relation schema for R as:

IR × RI = {(IR.inforResID, content, generationTime, periodOfValidity, inforType
resInputID, receiveTime, activityID, RI.inforResID, personID, IQMeasure)}

The Associative Operation

It is often desirable to simplify certain operations that require a Cartesian product. Usually, an operation that involves a Cartesian product includes a selection operation on the result of the Cartesian product. Consider the operation "Find the *contents* of all IRs which

Copyright © 2007, Idea Group Inc. Copying or distributing in print or electronic forms without written permission of Idea Group Inc. is prohibited.

come into the object of RI, along with the *peridodOfValidity* and *generationTime*." Then, we select those tuples that pertain to only the same *inforResID*, followed by the projection of the resulting *content, generationTime,* and *peridodOfValidity*:

$$\Pi_{content,\ generationTime,\ periodOfValidity}\ (s\ _{IR.inforResID=RI.inforResID}\ (IR \times RI))$$

The *Associative* operation is a binary operation that allows us to combine certain selections and a Cartesian product into one operation. It is denoted by the "join" symbol "". The *Associative* operation forms a Cartesian product of its two arguments, performs a selection forcing equality on those attributes that appear in both relation objects, and finally removes the duplicate attributes.

Although the definition of an associative operation is complicated, the operation is easy to apply. As an illustration, consider again the example "Find the *contents* of all IRs which come into the object of RI, along with the *peridodOfValidity* and *generationTime*." We express this operation by using the associative operation:

$$\Pi_{content,\ generationTime,\ periodOfValidity}\ (s\ (IR \boxtimes RI))$$

Models of PIQ Measure

Despite the availability of the various approaches to developing IQ measures, none of them attempted to quantify them. In this section we only consider four local measures and one global measure of PIQ: *timeliness, accuracy, cost,* and *value* are local attributes of PM; *profit* is a global attribute of information designing and manufacturing process. To evaluate the PIQ, these measures must be quantified and expressed using two kinds of models provided by preceding sections.

Timeliness of Information Resource

Our approach postulates that the timeliness of an information resource is dependent upon when the IR is received by the customer. Thus timeliness cannot be known until it is received. The purpose of producing a timeliness measure is to have a metric that can be used to gauge the effectiveness of improving the information manufacturing process.

The timeliness of an object of information resource (IR) is governed by two factors. The first, *currency*, refers to the age of the IR from generation to status change. The second, *period of validity*, refers to how long the item remains valid. The currency dimension is solely a characteristic of the capture of the IR; in no sense is it an intrinsic property. The validity of the IR is, however, an intrinsic property unrelated to the designing and manufacturing processes of product information, Equation 2. The currency of an IR is good or bad depending on the IR's period of validity. A large value of currency is unimportant if the useful-life is infinite. On the other hand, a small value of currency can be deleterious if the useful-life is very short. This suggests that timeliness is a function of the ratio of currency and a period of validity. This consideration in turn motivates the following timeliness measure for IRs.

Copyright © 2007, Idea Group Inc. Copying or distributing in print or electronic forms without written permission of Idea Group Inc. is prohibited.

$$Timeliness = \{\max[(1 - \frac{currency}{R.periodOfValidity}) \, 0\}^{\, M \, .senCryVty}$$

$$(10)$$

According to Equation 9, *periodOfValidity* of the IR whose identifier is 1 can be captured. The exponent *PM.senCryVty* is a parameter that allows us to control the sensitivity of timeliness to the currency validity ratio and can be obtained from Equation 7. We use three statuses to indicate when the IR was received, processed, and delivered (the lower right rectangle in Figure 3) in an activity. Therefore, three kinds of timeliness measure need to be presented.

1.   **Timeliness measure for information acquisition (T_A).** Suppose, for example, that the identifier of the IR received by EA is 1, and the identifier of input EA is 2. The currency measure can be obtained as follows:

$$currency = \prod\nolimits_{generationTime}(\textsf{S}_{\ \inf \ or \ Re \ sID \ = \ 1}(IR)) - \prod\nolimits_{recevieTime}(\textsf{S}_{\ \inf \ or \ Re \ sID \ = \ 1 \ \wedge \ activityID \ = \ 2}(RI))$$

$$(11)$$

T_A can be computed via Equation 10.

2.   **Timeliness measure for information processing (T_P).** Our goal is to attach a timeliness measure to each IR output. Each such output is the result of certain processing and various inputs. Each IR input, where we call inner IR, in turn can be the result of other processing and inputs. Each IR output is processed by the activity, both structured and nonstructured.

In a structured activity, output IR (y) can be expressed by function $y = f(x_1, x_2, \cdots, x_n)$. If $y.inforResID = 2$, the identifier of input IR (i) can be obtained $i \in \{\Pi_{inputID}(\textsf{s}_{\ outputID=2}(RP))\}$. The currency measure for x_i is computed as follows:

$$currency(x_i) = \prod\nolimits_{generationTime}(\textsf{S}_{\ \inf \ orSesID \ = \ i}(IR)) - \prod\nolimits_{startTime}(\textsf{S}_{\ inputID \ = \ i}(RP))$$

$$(12)$$

$T_P(x_i)$ denotes the timeliness measure for x_i and is calculated via Equation 10. Then we propose the following to represent or measure the timeliness of y.

$$T_P(y) = \sum_{i=1}^{n} w_i * T(x_i) \Big/ \sum_{i=1}^{n} w_i \quad \text{where } w_i = \left| \frac{\partial f}{\partial x_i} \right| * |x_i|.$$

$$(13)$$

In a nonstructured activity, input IR can undergo the processing that does not involve any arithmetical operation, then T(y) is the minimal value of $T(x_i)$.

$$T(y) = \min(T(x_1) \ T(x_2) \ \cdots, T(x_n))$$

$$(14)$$

Copyright © 2007, Idea Group Inc. Copying or distributing in print or electronic forms without written permission of Idea Group Inc. is prohibited.

3. **Timeliness measure for information transfer (T_{Tr}).** Suppose, for example, that the identifier of the IR disseminated by EA is 2, and the identifier of output EA is 1. Currency measure can be obtained as follows:

$$Currency = \prod_{generationTime}(\text{S}\ \inf_{orSesID\ =\ 2}(IR)) - \prod_{delievryTime}(\text{S}\ \inf_{orSesID\ =\ 2\ \wedge\ activityID\ =\ 1}(RO))$$

(15)

T_{Tr} can be computed via Equation 10.

Accuracy of Information Resource

Information resources (IRs) are manufacturing in the multiple stages of processing and are based on data that have various levels of accuracy. Let $DA(x_i)$ denote a measure of the data accuracy of data unit x_i. It can be determined by the number of error $N_{err}(x_i)$ and the total number of spot-check $N(x_i)$.

$$DA\ (x_i) = 1 - N_{err}(x_i) / N(x_i)$$

(16)

We use a scale from 0 to 1 as the domain for $DA(x_i)$ with 1 representing data without error and 0 representing those with intolerable error. If all data items should have a data accuracy measure equal to 1 and if all processing is correct, then the output accuracy measure should be 1 as well. Conversely, if the accuracy of all input IRs is 0, then the accuracy of the output IR should be 0 as well.

Given this reasoning, we form a weighted average of the $DA(x_i)$ value for the data accuracy of the output. Let y be determined by data items x_1, x_2, ..., x_n, that is, let $y = f(x_1, x_2, \cdots, x_n)$. Then accuracy of Data Component (*dataCmpAcy*), an estimate for the data accuracy of output y resulting solely from deficiencies in the input IR, can be obtained from:

$$dataCmpAcy = \sum_{i=1}^{n} w_i * DA(x) \bigg/ \sum_{i=1}^{n} w_i \quad \text{where } w_i = \left| \frac{\partial f}{\partial x_i} \right| * |x_i|.$$

(17)

Although it has been implicitly assumed that the processing activities are nonstructured, this is not necessarily the case. In most processes, some of the processing activities, such as product design, have manual components. Especially in this situation, the processing itself can introduce errors. Let proEffect be a measure of processing effectiveness; If proEffect = 1, then the processing never introduces errors. If proEffect = 0, then the processing corrupts the output to such a degree that the data accuracy measure for that output should be 0. Thus, the output accuracy of y is determined by both input data accuracy and processing effectiveness, that is:

$$Accuracy(y) = \sqrt{dataCmpAcy * proEffect}$$

(18)

Copyright © 2007, Idea Group Inc. Copying or distributing in print or electronic forms without written permission of Idea Group Inc. is prohibited.

Cost of Information Quality

The real cost of poor-quality information is most tangible, directly affecting the enterprise performance in two ways. The first is in the form of direct cost as a result of "information scrap and rework." The second is in the form of missed and lost opportunity. Missed and lost opportunity due to poor PIQ, while intangible, can be estimated fairly accurately given customer attrition patterns and complaint data.

Information production has both fixed and variable cost. Fixed costs are those required to begin producing information. They are the costs of developing applications and databases. Variable costs are those incurred in operating the applications in which information is created, updated, and used.

There are three categories of PIQ costs:

- **Nonquality information costs:** These are the costs incurred as a result of missing, inaccurate, untimely, imprecise, not well presented, or misleading or misunderstood information, which are avoidable. These costs include process failure costs, information scrap and rework costs, lost and missed opportunity costs.
- **IQ assessment or inspection costs:** These costs are to assure processes which are performing properly. Minimize these costs.
- **IQ process improvement and defect prevention costs:** The real business payoff is in improving processes that eliminate the costs of poor quality information.

In our methodology we adopt the activity-based costing (ABC), which facilitates the estimation of the product information's cost in a straightforward manner. Let $C(i, j)$ be the portion of the cost of IR j assigned to customer i. It can be obtained from:

$$C(i, j) = PM.\cos(i, j) \bigg/ \sum_{i=1}^{M} \sum_{j=1}^{N} PM.\cos t(i, j)$$

$$(19)$$

Value to the Knowledge Worker

Ultimately, the measure that counts is the value of the information resource (IR) to the knowledge worker in manufacturing enterprises. The intrinsic value of an IR includes two components: one is the actual value that a customer has applied; the other is the potential value that cannot be utilized by the customer. Any potential value can transform the actual value depending upon the quality of the IRs and the capabilities of the workers. Since our concern is with evaluating alternative business process so as to improve either timeliness or accuracy or both, it is natural in this context to limit consideration of the determinants of value to these dimensions. Thus for each knowledge worker C, the actual value V_A is a function of the intrinsic value V_I, the timeliness T, and accuracy A, and could be

$$V_A = V_I(\text{wgtAccTml}(A)^{\text{senAccrcy}} + (1 - \text{wgtAccTml})T^{\text{senTime}})$$

$$(20)$$

Copyright © 2007, Idea Group Inc. Copying or distributing in print or electronic forms without written permission of Idea Group Inc. is prohibited.

Figure 3. Activity model for the product information manufacturing system

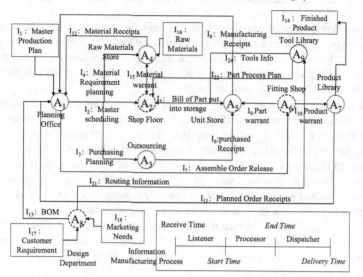

Here V_1, *wgtAccTml, senAccrcy,* and *senTime* are object dependent and have been defined in Equation 7 in previous research efforts.

Profit for the Whole Process

The principal purpose of improving PIQ is to maximize the profit P (total actual value V_A minus total cost $C(i, j)$) received by all customers for all information resource in the whole process. Suppose there are M customers and N information resources. Then for each customer I and IR j, the total profit can be expressed:

$$P = \sum_{i=1}^{M}\sum_{j=1}^{N}[V_A(i,j) - C(i,j)] \ \ subjct \ to: 0 \le V_A(i,j) \le 1, 1 \le i \le M, 0 \le C(i,j) \le 1, 1 \le j \le N.$$

(21)

Here, V_A can be captured in Equation 20, and $C(i, j)$ can be computed via Equation 19.

We have presented the core techniques of AMEQ for determining the local measures of each activity, such as timeliness, accuracy, cost, and value; and a global measure profit to the whole process. In the next section, an example is presented to illustrate some of the conceptual and computational issues that will be encountered when the process model is applied to real-world scenarios.

Copyright © 2007, Idea Group Inc. Copying or distributing in print or electronic forms without written permission of Idea Group Inc. is prohibited.

Illustrative Case

In this section we apply the model described in this chapter to a mission-critical product information system found in a manufacturing enterprise called QCJT. For expository purposes, we present the relevant portion of the case with a simplified system topology. Since the most difficult aspect of implementing the model is obtaining estimates for the various parameters needed by the model, we concentrate on this.

QCJT is a large manufacturing company with 1,000 factories throughout the country. It produces special paddle pumps of different sizes and complexity for automobile factories on demand. However, machining of the pump is carried out at eight manufacturing factories. Our analysis focuses on the new product development which is handled by the main factory. QCJT strives to differentiate itself in several ways, one of the most important, reducing time to market. This is a core competency in QCJT mission. However, at the present time, a problem with product information quality is not only costing the company over 3 million RMB on an annual basis but also are resulting in the loss of customers.

QCJT's product information manufacturing system is displayed in Figure 3. Several types of information, modeled as I_1, I_8, I_{11}, I_{12}, and I_{13}, are obtained and entered onto the planning office. They are Master Production Plan (I_1), Manufacturing Receipts (I_8) coming from Unit Store (A_5), Planned Order Receipts (I_{11}) coming from Product Library (A_7), Material Receipts (I_{12}) coming from Raw Materials Store (A_4), and Bill of Material (I_{13}) coming from Design Department (A_8). These types of information are batched and entered by the planner into the office's PC whenever the planner has free time, often at the end of day. Roughly 80% of the accuracy problems arise as a consequence of the this process.

Normally every month the planner forwards the Master scheduling (I_2) to shop floor (A_2). Every two months the planner releases the Purchasing planning to Outsourcing (A_3). Every three months the planner issues the Material requirement planning to Raw Materials Store (A_4). Twice a day the planner puts out Assemble Order Release (I_7) to Fitting Shop (A_6). Roughly 85% of the timeliness problems arise as a consequence of these processes.

In an activity represented by A_2, the shop floor queries the material warrant files (I_{15}) to determine if the raw material (I_{16}) is available. Bill of part (I_5) is then checked by the warehouseman (A_5) when semimanufactured goods are put into the storage for the completeness and correctness. In the activity A6, the fitting shop forwards part warrant (I_9) to determine if the part is available. Assuming no problem, it then forwards product warrant (I_{10}) to the Product Library (A_7) for finished product. Marketing needs (I_{18}) and customer requirement (I_{17}) are delivered to the design department (A_8) for BOM (I_{13}). In an activity represented by A_9, the tool library provides tools information (I_{24}) and part process plan (I_{22}) to the shop floor (A_2).

It is important to keep in mind that the every activity here includes an information manufacturing process which is supported by three kinds of people: listener, processor, and dispatcher. The product information, which is processed on an activity, has three phases denoted by receive time, start time, end time, and delivery time in turn (low-right portion of Figure 3).

The fraction of I_8, I_{12}, I_{21}, I_{22}, and I_{24} that exhibit some information quality problems at some stage is not excessive, as 85% of the product information is completely free of quality problems. Of those with deficiencies, two fifths relate to initial data gathering and entry, another two fifths to consistency errors, and one fifth due to inability to match the frame

Copyright © 2007, Idea Group Inc. Copying or distributing in print or electronic forms without written permission of Idea Group Inc. is prohibited.

chosen with the prescribed physical requirements for machining. Ten percent of all routing information (I_{21}) and (I_{22}) which are in error are never detected until the product checker receives the pumps. For the 5% of all finished product (I_{14}) where a problem is detected, the salesperson has to contact the customer, who usually has to come back into the store. As mentioned, this results in a nontrivial financial loss to the company. More importantly, it violates QCJT's desire to differentiate itself by reducing time to market and results in permanent loss of customers.

As indicated, the purpose of our model is to provide information regarding the impact of proposed changes to the product information system. The QCJT case illustrates substantial problems with all three dimensions tracked, that is, accuracy, timeliness, and cost. A management alternative is proposed and discussed. The processing steps for improving PIQ incorporate the roadmap (Figure 1) and are illustrated as follows:

Step 2.1: Enterprise objects, such as HR, IR, EA, are represented first by the IQ team.

HR={(1, Plan Officer, Listener), (2, Planner1, Processor), (3, Planner2, Dispatcher), (4, Shop Statistician, Listener)...(26, Operator3, Listener)};

IR={(1, Master Production Plan, 2002-11-25, 60, inner),(2, Manufacturing Plan, 2002-12-26, 60, inner),(3, Purchasing Planning, 2002-12-22, 120, inner),(4, Material Requirement planning, 2002-12-23, 180, inner), (5, Bill of Part Put into Storage, 2003-1-26, 30, inner), (6, Purchased Receipts, 2003-2-20, 30, inner), ..., (24, Tools Information, 2003-5-30, 1, inner)};

EA={(1, Plan & Control Production, Planning Department, structured), (2, Manufacturing, Shop Floor, non-structured), (3, Provide Purchasing Part, Outsourcing Enterprise, structured), (4, Storage & Retrieval Material, Materials Store, structured), (5, Storage & Retrieval Part, Unit Store, structured), (6, Assembling, Fitting Shop, nonstructured), (7, Storage & Retrieval Product, Product Library, structured), (8, Product Design, Designing Department, nonstructured), (9, Provide Tools, Tool Library, structured)};

RI={(1, 2002-12-13, 1, 1, 1, 1), (2, 2002-12-15, 1, 12, 1, 2), (3, 2002-12-3, 1, 8, 1, 3), (4, 2002-10-11, 1, 13, 1, 4), (5, 2003-1-2, 2, 2, 4, 5), (6, 2003-1-11, 3, 3, 7, 6), ..., (18, 2003-5-30, 2, 23, 26, 57), (19, 2003-5-30, 2, 24, 26, 58)};RO={(1, 2002-12-27, 1, 2, 3, 13), (2, 2002-12-24, 1, 3, 3, 14), (3, 2002-12-28, 1, 4, 3, 15), (4, 2003-1-24, 1, 7, 3, 16), ..., (14, 2003-5-11, 7, 11, 21, 26), (15, 2003-4-20, 4, 19, 12, 55)};

RP={(1, 2002-12-24, 2002-12-26, 2, 1, 2, 27), (2, 2002-12-1, 2002-12-26, 2, 13, 2, 28), (3, 2002-12-23, 2002-12-26, 2, 8, 2, 29), (4, 2002-12-16, 2002-12-22, 3, 1, 2, 30), (5, 2002-11-11, 2002-12-22, 3, 13, 2, 31), (6, 2002-12-18, 2002-12-22, 3, 8, 2, 32), (22, 2003-1-6, 2003-1-22, 15, 2, 6, 51), ..., (23, 2003-1-13, 2003-4-18, 19, 4, 11, 53), (24, 2003-3-18, 2003-4-18, 19, 16, 11, 54)}.

Here we only provide the identifiers of PMs, the values of which cannot be determined until Step 3.4.

In Step 2.2 we consider four dimensions of PIQ in this example: timeliness, accuracy, cost, and value-added.

In Step 2.3 we select a designing and manufacturing process of ZYB0809s01-001 pump for improvement.

Step 2.4: EG = {(1, Increase total net value of all the knowledge workers in the processes, 0.8,N, 2002–1-1,2003-1-1,PRF)}.

In phase 3, we can obtain PM = {(1, 3, .5, .5, .9, .8, 1000, .5, .96, .5, .5, .5), (2, 1.5, .6, .5, .9, .9, 2500, .5, .92, .5, .5, .5), (3, 1, .5, .5, .97, .95, 2500, .5, .9, .5, .5, .5),..., (5, 2, .5, .5,

Copyright © 2007, Idea Group Inc. Copying or distributing in print or electronic forms without written permission of Idea Group Inc. is prohibited.

Table 4. Evaluation of PIQ when information resources are received

EA	IR	Period of Validity	Generation Time	Receive Time	Cost	Timeliness	Accuracy	Actual Value	Cost	Profit
A_1	I_1	60	2002-11-25	2002-12-13	1000	.343	.849	.723	.015	.708
	I_{12}	5	2002-12-11	2002-12-15	2500	.089	.9	.574	.037	.537
	I_8	15	2002-12-1	2002-12-3	2500	.867	.96	.86	.037	.823
	I_{13}	200	2002-6-21	2002-10-11	2500	.663	.839	.831	.037	.794
	I_{11}	10	2002-12-9	2002-12-18	2500	.1	.96	.583	.037	.546
A_2	I_2	60	2002-12-26	2003-1-2	2000	.78	.5	.398	.029	.369
A_3	I_3	120	2002-12-22	2003-1-11	600	.913	.5	.582	.009	.573
A_4	I_4	180	2002-12-23	2003-1-3	800	.969	.524	.427	.012	.415
	I_{15}	5	2003-1-22	2003-1-23	450	.894	.5	.413	.007	.406
	I_{16}	180	2003-3-11	2003-3-12	450	.989	.5	.425	.007	.418
A_5	I_5	30	2003-1-26	2003-1-30	1569	.931	.5	.418	.023	.395
	I_6	30	2003-2-20	2003-2-25	789	.841	.5	.406	.012	.394
A_6	I_7	15	2003-1-22	2003-1-23	456	.966	.5	.296	.007	.289
A_7	I_{10}	10	2003-2-14	2003-5-11	987	0	.5	.177	.015	.162
A_8	I_{17}	150	2002-4-11	2002-5-14	4000	.78	.899	.87	.059	.811
	I_{18}	65	2002-4-15	2002-5-15	3000	.734	.798	.831	.044	.787

Table 5. Evaluation of PIQ when information resources are delivered

EA	IR	Period of Validity	Generation Time	Delivery Time	Cost	Timeliness	Accuracy	Actual Value	Cost	Profit
A_1	I_2	60	2002-12-26	2002-12-27	639	.975	.5	.424	.009	.415
	I_3	120	2002-12-22	2002-12-24	547	.987	.689	.593	.008	.585
	I_4	180	2002-12-23	2002-12-28	652	.982	.5	.637	.01	.627
	I_7	15	2003-1-22	2003-1-24	4782	.931	.5	.418	.07	.348
A_2	I_5	30	2003-1-26	2003-1-30	123	.807	.274	.355	.002	.353
	I_{15}	5	2003-1-22	2003-1-26	654	.447	.5	.344	.01	.334
A_3	I_6	30	2003-2-20	2003-2-24	951	.931	.5	.418	.014	.404
A_4	I_{12}	5	2002-12-11	2002-12-16	425	0	.474	.172	.006	.166
	I_{19}	5	2003-4-18	2003-4-20	680	.465	.798	.394	.01	.384
A_5	I_{20}	15	2003-2-28	2003-3-11	754	.516	.5	.356	.011	.345
A_6	I_9	10	2003-1-26	2003-1-27	456	.949	.5	.417	.007	.41
	I_{10}	10	2003-2-14	2003-2-16	754	.894	.5	.396	.011	.385
A_7	I_{14}	360	2003-5-11	2003-5-11	632	1	.5	.427	.009	.418
	I_{11}	10	2002-12-9	2003-5-11	852	0	.5	.177	.013	.164
A_8	I_{13}	200	2002-6-21	2002-12-3	487	.175	.899	.588	.007	.581

Copyright © 2007, Idea Group Inc. Copying or distributing in print or electronic forms without written permission of Idea Group Inc. is prohibited.

Table 6. Evaluation of PIQ when information resources are processed

I	O	Start Time	End Time	Intrins Value	Cost	Timeliness	Accuracy	Actual Value	Cost	Profit
I_1		2002-12-24	2002-12-26	.85	1547	.267	.75	.588	.023	.565
I_{13}	I_2	2002-12-1	2002-12-26	.95	1456	.185	.86	.645	.021	.624
I_8		2002-12-23	2002-12-26	.65	7541	0	.844	.299	.111	.188
I_1		2002-12-16	2002-12-22	.75	562	.524	.698	.585	.008	.577
I_{13}	I_3	2002-11-11	2002-12-22	.95	650	.049	.819	.535	.01	.525
I_8		2002-12-18	2002-12-22	.85	854	0	.798	.38	.013	.367
I_1		2002-12-20	2002-12-23	.5	147	.446	.771	.386	.002	.384
I_{13}	I_4	2002-12-15	2002-12-23	.5	1263	.339	.693	.354	.019	.335
I_{12}		2002-12-16	2002-12-23	.88	784	0	.698	.368	.012	.356
I_1	I_7	2003-5-11	2003-5-11	.5	417	0	.5	.177	.006	.171
I_2	I_5	2003-1-11	2003-1-31	.7	487	.856	.5	.571	.007	.564
	I_{15}	2003-1-6	2003-1-22	.5	430	.817	.5	.403	.006	.397
I_3	I_6	2003-1-15	2003-2-18	.5	201	.894	.524	.417	.003	.414
I_4	I_{19}	2003-1-13	2003-4-18	.6	1600	.883	.798	.55	.024	.526
I_{16}		2003-3-18	2003-4-18	.5	750	.98	.5	.424	.011	.413
I_5	I_{20}	2003-2-5	2003-2-28	.5	365	.816	.5	.403	.005	.398
I_6		2003-2-26	2003-2-28	.5	456	.809	.5	.402	.007	.395
I_9	I_7	2003-1-24	2003-1-26	.35	789	.931	.5	.293	.012	.281
I_{10}		2003-1-28	2003-2-8	.5	157	.775	.5	.397	.002	.395
I_{14}	I_{10}	2003-5-11	2003-5-11	.5	820	0	.5	.177	.012	.165
I_{11}		2003-5-11	2003-5-11	.5	985	0	.5	.177	.014	.163
I_{17}	I_{13}	2002-6-11	2002-11-21	.9	5600	.77	.748	.784	.082	.702
I_{18}		2002-5-17	2002-11-21	.8	690	.737	.784	.698	.01	.688

.5, .5, 2000, .9,.5, .5, .5, .5), (6, .5, .5, .5, .5, .5, 600, .5, .7, .5, .5, .5), (7, .5, .5, .5, .5, .55, 800, .5, .5, .5, .5, .5), (8, .5, .5, .5, .5, .5, 450, .5, .5, .5, .5, .5), (9, .5, .5, .85, .5, .5, 1569, .5, .5, .5, .5, .5), (10, .95, .5, .5, .5, .5, 789, .5, .5, .5, .5, .5), ..., (56, .5, .5, .5, .5, .5, .5, .5, .5, .5, .5, .5), (57, .5, .5, .5, .75, .5, .5, .5, .5, .5, .5, .5), (58, .5, .5, .5, .85, .5, .5, .5, .5, .5, .5, .5)}

In phase 4, we can use the data in IR, HR, RI, EA, and PM to compute the PIQ measures when information resources enter into all the activities. The parameters required to evaluate the PIQ can be obtained as follows:

$$\Pi_{\substack{IR.periodOfValidity,IR.generationTime,RI.receiveTime,PM.senCryVty,PM.dataCmpAcy,\\ PM.proEffect,PM.cost,PM.intrinsValue,PM.wgtAccTml,PM.senAccrcy,PM.senTime}}$$

$$(s_{RI.activityID)=i}(IR \boxtimes RI) \cup (HR \boxtimes RI) \cup (EA \boxtimes RI) \cup (PM \boxtimes RI)) \tag{22}$$

Copyright © 2007, Idea Group Inc. Copying or distributing in print or electronic forms without written permission of Idea Group Inc. is prohibited.

Table 4 provides *periodOfValidity, generationTime, receiveTime,* and *cost* required to evaluate the IRs received by the customers in activity *i*. The relevant *cost* is obtained from Equation 19. As discussed in the previous section, determining the timeliness value requires *currency* value which can be determined by Equation 11. Therefore, the *timeliness* value for information acquisition can be determined by Equation 10. By using the parameters coming from Formula 22, the *accuracy* value can be computed through Equation 18. Then the *actualValue* to the customers can be obtained from Equation 20. The profit for each activity can be computed through Equation 21.

In a similar manner, we can use the data in IR, HR, RO, EA, and PM to compute the PIQ measures when information resources are sent out from the activities. The parameters required to evaluate the PIQ can be obtained as follows:

$$\Pi_{\substack{\text{IR.periodOfValidity,IR.generationTime,RO.deliveryTime,PM.senCryVty,PM.dataCmpAcy,} \\ \text{PM.proEffect,PM.cost,PM.intrinsValue,PM.wgtAccTml,PM.senAccrcy,PM.senTime}}}$$

$$(S_{RO.activityID)=i}(IR \boxtimes RO) \cup (HR \boxtimes RO) \cup (EA \boxtimes RO) \cup (PM \boxtimes RO)) \qquad (23)$$

Table 5 provides part of the parameters required to evaluate the IRs sent by the dispatcher and results of PIQ measures. The currency value for information transfer can be determined by Equation 15; therefore the timeliness measure can be computed via Equation 10.

The parameters required to evaluate the PIQ for information processing can be obtained as follows:

$$\Pi_{\substack{\text{IR.periodOfValidity,IR.generationTime,RP.startTime,RP.endTime,PM.senCryVty,PM.dataCmpAcy,} \\ \text{PM.proEffect,PM.cost,PM.intrinsValue,PM.wgtAccTml,PM.senAccrcy,PM.senTime}}}$$

$$(S_{RO.activityID)=i}(S_{IR.inforResID =RP.inputID}IR \times RP) \cup (S_{IR.inforResID =RP.outputID}$$

$$IR \times RP) \cup (HR \boxtimes RP) \cup (EA \boxtimes RP) \cup (PM \boxtimes RP)) \qquad (24)$$

Table 6 presents part of the parameters and results. The Timeliness value can be determined by Equations 10, 12, 13, and 14.

By inspecting Table 6, it can be determined that the profit of four types of product information is under 0.2. Timeliness is rather poor for six kinds of product information, such as I_2, I_4, I_7, I_{14}, and I_{11}. This suggests a quality-timeliness trade-off which could be achieved by the elimination of time-consuming enterprise activities. Therefore, it involves a reengineering of the product information system, which substantially improves the timeliness and quality dimensions and hence the company's goal of superior customer service, but at an increased cost in terms of hardware and software.

The reengineering option is a decentralized version of the current system. In each function location the PC has been upgraded to include features such as a math coprocessor, and it now has the responsibility for most of the computations and processing. In the reengineered system a new enterprise activity, which can inspect timeliness of product information essentially incorporates the activities of A_1 and A_7 of the current system. If any problems are identified, they can be resolved immediately, as the computer would automatically remind the knowledge worker to process the information as soon as possible. An accuracy control activity would essentially combine the activity of A_5 and A_7. If there is no problem, the two

Copyright © 2007, Idea Group Inc. Copying or distributing in print or electronic forms without written permission of Idea Group Inc. is prohibited.

stores forward the I_9 and I_{10} to the server in the headquarters, which in turn forwards the I_{11} and I_{14} to the planning office and end user. This results in a major improvement in customer service and would serve to further differentiate QCJT on the service dimension.

In the reengineered system, the computer-based product information system performs the following functions: (1) maintains the most current version of I_2, I_3, and I_4. Periodically, it updates the data at the unit store and product library with the most current version. (2) Keeps track of the inventory level of raw material, part, component, and finish product (i.e., I_5, I_6, I_8, etc.) in the stores. Each store will periodically report its actual inventory level to the system for reconciliation purposes. (3) The system would compute, route, and report the PIQ measures to the appropriate person.

Conclusion and Future Work

We have developed the AMEQ methodology for assessing and benchmarking PIQ in business processes. This encompasses three major components except DIPMS research framework: the roadmap for PIQ improvement, the activity-based approach of defining PIQ, and the AMEQ techniques.

The roadmap for PIQ improvement describes the processes, steps, tools, and techniques to measure and assess PIQ of manufacturing enterprises. It provides a pragmatic basis for PIQ definition, measurement, assessment, and improvement as a management tool for business performance excellence.

The activity-based approach for defining the dimensions of PIQ lays a foundation for the whole roadmap. It can help manufacturing companies identify measures of activities more objectively and comprehensively. It is a prerequisite for the AMEQ techniques.

The AMEQ techniques provide the models by which organizations can represent their enterprise, set up the measures for basic activities, create a mapping between the goals and measures, and compute the performance of processes. Using these techniques, organizations can self-assess their PIQ based on benchmarks identified beforehand and determine appropriate areas on which to focus improvement efforts.

The key contribution of the overall research, however, stems from the integration and synthesis of these components. The AMEQ methodology as a whole provides a practical PIQ tool to business processes. It has been applied in various manufacturing industries and integrated with ERP systems, such as SAP, BAAN, and ORACLE. The methodology is useful in identifying PIQ problems, prioritizing areas for PIQ improvement, and monitoring PIQ improvements over time.

This research is particularly timely in light of the industrial trend toward total quality management and business process reengineering. At the intersection of these driving forces is information quality. Ultimately, we need to deliver high-quality product information to the customer in a timely and cost-effective manner.

Our experience suggests several possible future directions:

1.   The AMEQ approach and practice developed in this chapter can be most efficiently executed in an object-oriented database management system (ODBMS). Most OD-BMS support for the complex rules and mathematical expressions that can calculate

Copyright © 2007, Idea Group Inc. Copying or distributing in print or electronic forms without written permission of Idea Group Inc. is prohibited.

PIQ measures efficiently. Applying a large number of rules within the ODBMS would amount to better performance than our system.

2.   The enterprise objects explored in this chapter are designed to be applied to a simple database, but can be expanded to make PIQ assessments of multiple databases. Manufacturing enterprises often have redundant databases with no way to estimate which one is most valuable. Our approach may be useful in measuring the return on investment for each database by calculating the potential benefit of PIQ. This is most valuable in instances where value of information is unknown and there is no financial relationship with the entity associated with this information.

3.   In this chapter, we have not addressed the problem of choosing a reasonable weight or score for a PM, other than using intuition and personal experience. Instead of using intuition to ascertain the weight of a given PM, one can better estimate based on the historical or financial data of corporations.

4.   The process of identifying relationships between enterprise goals and enterprise activities is not only complex but also prone to human errors. The AMEQ approach discussed in this chapter suffers from the same problem as conventional validation, which failed to prevent the problem of PIQ in the first place. Relationships can easily get outdated and require continuous tuning to be effective. A possible solution can be to build a feedback mechanism from the consumer of the information to identify a problem. This information can be used to automatically identify another occurrence of the same problem in the future and also adjust the given weight of a PM.

5.   The QCJT case focused on a relatively small-scale product information system.

For large-scale systems, which may contain hundreds of processes, data units, and so forth, a hierarchical modeling approach is required. Under this approach an analyst would model, initially, at a higher (macro) level with each enterprise activity (EA) possibly representing a large number of related activities. That macromodel, which would contain a relatively small number of activities, is then analyzed. Those EAs that for whatever reason require more specific analysis are then replaced with a detailed micromodel.

Acknowledgments

We would like to thank NNSFC (National Natural Science Foundation of China) for supporting Ying Su and Zhanming Jin with a project (project number 70372004) for providing additional funding.

References

Bailey, J. E., & Pearson, S. W. (1983). Development of a tool for measuring and analyzing computer user satisfaction. *Management Science, 29*(5), 530-545.

Ballou, D. P., & Pazer, H. L. (1985). Modeling data and process quality multy-input, multi-output information systems. *Management Science, 31*(2), 150-162.

Copyright © 2007, Idea Group Inc. Copying or distributing in print or electronic forms without written permission of Idea Group Inc. is prohibited.

Beverly, K. K., Elizabeth, M., Pierce E. M., & Helinä, M. (2004, November 6). IQ research directions. In *Proceedings of the Ninth International Conference on Information Quality* (pp. 327-332). MIT.

Chatfield, D. C., Kim, J. G., Harrison, T. P., & Hayya, J. C. (2004). The bullwhip effect: Impact of stochastic lead time, information quality, and information sharing: A simulation study. *Production and Operations Management, 13*(4), 340-353.

Chiu, H. C., Hsieh, Y. C., & Kao, C. Y. (2005). Website quality and customer's behavioral intention: An exploratory study of the role of information asymmetry. *Total Quality Management & Business Excellence, 16*(2), 185-197.

Delone, W. H., & McLean, E. R. (1992). Information systems success: The quest for the dependent variable. *Information Systems Research, 3*(1), 60-95.

English, L. P. (1999). *Improving data warehouse and business information quality: Methods for reducing costs and increasing profits*. New York: Wiley.

Funk, J., Lee, Y. W., & Wang, R. Y. (1998, October 23). Institutionalizing information quality practice: The S. C. Johnson Wax case. In *Proceedings of the Third Conference on Information Quality* (pp. 1-17). MIT.

Garvin, D.A. (1988). *Managing quality: The strategic and competitive edge*. New York: Free Press; London: Collier Macmillan.

Goodhue, D. L. (1995). Understanding user evaluations of information systems. *Management Science, 41*(12), 1827-1844.

Graeme, S., Peter, B. S., & Leskie, P. W. (Ed.). (2003). *Second wave enterprise resource planning systems: Implementing for effectiveness*. New York: Cambridge University Press.

Guy, V. T. (2001). *Information quality management*. Cambridge, MA: NCC Blackwell.

Jarke, M., & Vassiliou, Y. (1997, October 24). Data warehouse quality: A review of the DWQ project. In *Proceedings of the Conference on Information Quality,* Cambridge, MA (pp. 299-313).

Johansson, E., & Johansson, M. I. (2004). The information gap between design engineering and materials supply systems design. *International Journal of Production Research, 42*(17), 3787-3801.

Kuan, T. H., Yang, W. L., & Richard, Y. W. (1999). *Quality information and knowledge*. Upper Saddle River, NJ: Prentice Hall PTR.

Laudon, K. C. (1986). Data quality and due process in large interorganizational record systems. *Communications of the ACM, 29*(1), 4-11.

Lee, Y., Allen, T., & Wang, R. Y. (2001, November 2). Information products for remanufacturing: Tracing the repair of an aircraft fuel-pump. In *Proceedings of the Sixth International Conference on Information Quality* (pp. 77-82). MIT.

Morey, R. C. (1982). Estimating and improving the quality of information in the MIS. *Communications of the ACM, 25*(5), 337-342.

Nelson, R. R., Todd, P. A., & Wixom, B. H. (2005). Antecedents of information and system quality: An empirical examination within the context of data warehousing. *Journal of Management Information Systems, 21*(4), 199-235.

Orr, K. (1998). Data quality and systems theory. *Communications of the ACM, 41*(2), 66-71.

Park, J., & Barber, K. S. (2005). Information quality assurance by lazy exploration of information source combinations space in open multi-agent systems. *Journal of Universal Computer Science, 11*(1), 193-209.

Copyright © 2007, Idea Group Inc. Copying or distributing in print or electronic forms without written permission of Idea Group Inc. is prohibited.

Parssian, A., Sarkar, S., & Jacob, V. S. (2004). Assessing data quality for information products: Impact of selection, projection, and Cartesian product. *Management Science, 50*(7), 967-982.

Pierce, E. M. (2004). Assessing data quality with control matrices. *Communications of the ACM, 47*(2), 82-84.

Price, R., & Shanks, G. (2005). A semiotic information quality framework: Development and comparative analysis. *Journal of Information Technology, 20*(2), 88-102.

Redman, T. C. (2001). *Data quality: The field guide.* Boston: Digital Press.

Schwartz, R., & Mayne, J. (2005). Assuring the quality of evaluative information: Theory and practice. *Evaluation and Program Planning, 28*(1), 1-14.

Shankaranarayan, G., Wang, R. Y., & Ziad, M. (2000, October 20). Modeling the manufacture of an information product with IP-MAP. In *Proceedings of the Fifth Conference on Information Quality* (pp. 1-16). MIT.

Strong, D. M., Lee, Y. W., & Wang, R. Y. (1997). Data quality in context. *Communications of the ACM, 40*(5), 103-110.

Su, Y., Yu, M., & Zhang, B. P. (2002, September 9). Performance measurement and application technologies in business process of manufacturing enterprise. In *Proceedings of the Industry Engineering & Enterprise Management 2002 Conference (IE&EM2002)* (pp. 19-21). Beijing, China, Tsinghua University.

Vernadat, F. (1996). *Enterprise modeling and integration: Principles and applications.* London; New York: Chapman & Hall.

Wand, Y., & Wang, R. Y. (1996). Anchoring data quality dimensions in ontological foundations. *Communications of the ACM, 39*(11), 86-95.

Wang, R. Y., & Strong, D. M. (1996). Beyond accuracy: What data quality means to data consumers. *Journal of Management Information Systems, 12*(4), 5-34.

Xu, H. J., & Koronios, A. (2004). Understanding information quality in e-business. *Journal of Computer Information Systems, 45*(2), 73-82.

Yang, L., Diane, S., Beverly, K., & Richard, W. (2002). AIMQ: A methodology for information quality assessment. *Information & Management, 40*(2), 133-146.

Zhang, B. P. (2002). Investigation on TQM for manufacturing information (part one). *Manufacturing Automation, 8*(24), 1-5.

Zmud, R. (1978). Concepts, theories and techniques: An empirical investigation of the dimensionality of the concept of information. *Decision Sciences, 9*(2), 187-195.

Copyright © 2007, Idea Group Inc. Copying or distributing in print or electronic forms without written permission of Idea Group Inc. is prohibited.

Chapter X

Information Quality in Engineering Asset Management

Andy Koronios, University of South Australia, Australia

Shien Lin, University of South Australia, Australia

Abstract

This chapter discusses the critical issues of information quality (IQ) associated with engineering asset management. It introduces an asset management (AM) specific IQ framework as a means of studying IQ in engineering asset management. It argues that it is essential to ensure the quality of data in monitoring systems, control systems, maintenance systems, procurement systems, logistics systems, and a range of mission support applications in order to facilitate effective AM. There is also a growing need to address the issue of IQ in enterprise asset management (EAM) systems, by analyzing existing practices and developing frameworks/models to assist engineering enterprises to capture, process, and deliver quality data and information. Furthermore, the authors hope that a better understanding of the current issues and emerging key factors for ensuring high quality AM data through the use of the AM IQ framework will not only raise the general IQ awareness in engineering asset management organisations, but also assist AM and IT professionals in obtaining an insightful and overall appreciation about what AM IQ problems are and why they have emerged.

Copyright © 2007, Idea Group Inc. Copying or distributing in print or electronic forms without written permission of Idea Group Inc. is prohibited.

Introduction

Industry has recently put a strong emphasis on the area of asset management. In order for organisations to generate revenue, they need to utilise assets in an effective and efficient way. Often the success of an enterprise depends largely on its ability to utilise assets efficiently. Therefore, AM has been regarded as an essential business process in many organisations. Furthermore, as companies today are running leaner than ever before, physical assets, such as equipment, plant, and facilities, are being pushed to their limits, as engineering enterprises attempt to continuously drive more productivity out of their equipment, in order to improve their bottom lines. Consequently, physical AM is moving to the forefront of contributing to an organisation's financial objectives. Effective physical AM optimises utilisation, increases output, maximises availability, and lengthens asset lifespan, while simultaneously minimising costs.

As today's companies are operating and competing on the ability to absorb and respond to information, not just manufacture and distribute products, data has become the lifeblood of most organisations. There is strong evidence that most organisations have far more data than they possibly use; yet, at the same time, they do not have the data they really need (Levitin & Redman, 1998); many say we are drowning in data and are starved of information. Modern organisations, both public and private, are continually insatiably generating more and larger volumes of data. On a personal level, according to Steenstrup (2005) of Gartner Research, each person on the planet generates an average of 250 Mb of data per annum, with this volume doubling each year while at the organisational level, there are incredibly large amounts of data, including structured and unstructured, enduring and temporal, content data, and an increasing amount of structural and discovery metadata. According to Hall (2005) of Computerworld, the situation will only get worse with radio frequency identification (RFID), which will balloon the amount of data that has generated and make indexing the information in a relational database prohibitively expensive and all but impossible. Outside the business environment, there is an increasing number of embedded systems such as condition monitoring systems in ships, aircraft, process plants, and other engineering assets, all producing gargantuan amounts of data.

Despite this apparent explosion in the generation of data it appears that, at the management level, executives are not confident that they have enough correct, reliable, consistent, and timely data upon which to make decisions. This lack of data visibility and control often leads to decisions being made more on the basis of judgment rather than being data driven (Koronios, Lin, & Gao 2005). Without good data, organisations are running blind and make any decision a gamble (ARC, 2004). They cannot make good decisions because they have no accurate understanding of what is happening within their company or the marketplace. They rely on intuition, which is dangerous in a fast-moving market with nimble competitors and finicky customers.

Poor IQ is pervasive and costly (Orr, 1998; Redman, 1998). There is strong evidence that data stored in organisational database are neither entirely accurate nor complete (Klein, 1999). In industry, error rates up to 75% are often reported, while error rates up to 30% are typical (Redman, 1996). Problems with IQ may lead to real losses, both economic and social. Davenport (1997) states that no one can deny that decisions made based on useless information have cost companies billions of dollars. The Data Warehouse Institute Data Quality Survey (Eckerson, 2002) reveals that problems due to poor IQ can lead to less

Copyright © 2007, Idea Group Inc. Copying or distributing in print or electronic forms without written permission of Idea Group Inc. is prohibited.

effective strategic business decisions, an inability to reengineer, mistrust between internal organisational units, increased costs, customer dissatisfaction, and loss of revenue. In some cases, it could also lead to catastrophic consequences such as massive power failures and industrial or aviation disasters.

It is clear that wrong data is likely to result in wrong decisions (Kingma, 1996). Although more and more organisations are realising that quality information is critical to their success, most are oblivious to the true business impact of defective data, and not many organisations have taken effective actions to ensure the quality of their data. English (1999) states that the business costs of non-quality data, including irrecoverable costs, rework of products and services, workarounds, and lost and missed revenue may be as high as 10 to 25 percent of revenue or total budget of an organisation.

As asset management is a broad area, this chapter places a special focus on IQ issues. In order to address the various aspects of IQ issues in enterprise asset management, the generic IQ concepts need to be summarised. Similarly, an overview of generic AM processes is provided. Within these understandings, a close examination is conducted to search for AM related IQ issues. A research framework is developed as a means of conducting IQ research in EAM. Based on the research findings, an insightful understanding of various AM related IQ issues are extracted. These findings will be useful to determine the problem areas that policy implementers need to focus on. Data and information are often used synonymously. In practice, managers differentiate information from data intuitively, and describe information as data that has been processed. Unless specified otherwise, this chapter will use data interchangeably with information, as well as use data quality (DQ) interchangeably with information quality (IQ).

Information Quality

IQ is one of the critical problems facing organisations today. As management becomes more dependent on information systems to fulfill their missions, IQ becomes a larger issue in their organisations (Fisher & Kingma, 2001).

IQ Dimensions

Numerous researchers have attempted to define IQ and to identify its dimensions (Fox, Levitin, & Redman, 1994; Hassan, 2003; Ives, Olson, & Baroudi, 1983; Kahn, Strong, & Wang, 2002; Levitin & Redman, 1998; Lillrank, 2003; Shanks & Darke, 1998; Strong, 1997; Wang & Kon, 1993). Traditionally, IQ has been described from the perspective of accuracy. Many researches have indicated that IQ should be defined as beyond accuracy and is identified as encompassing multiple dimensions. Through literature, many authors have tried to explain the meaning of all relevant dimensions from several points of view (Ballou, Wang, Pazer, & Tayi, 1998; English, 1999; Hoxmaier, 2001; Huang, Lee, & Wang, 1999; Kahn et al., 2002; Loshin, 2001; Redman, 1996; Wand & Wang, 1996). Even, any of them have tried to identify a standard set of IQ dimensions valid for any data product; but as Huang et al. (1999) state, it is nearly impossible due to the different nature of different data environments. Dimensions of IQ typically include accuracy, reliability, importance, consistency, precision, timeliness, fineness, understandability, conciseness, and usefulness

Copyright © 2007, Idea Group Inc. Copying or distributing in print or electronic forms without written permission of Idea Group Inc. is prohibited.

(Ballou & Pazer, 1995; Wand & Wang, 1996). Wand and Wang (1996) used ontological concepts to define IQ dimensions: completeness, unambiguous, meaningfulness, and correctness. Wang and Strong (1996) categorised IQ into four dimensions: intrinsic, contextual, representation, and accessibility. Shanks and Darke (1998) used semiotic theory to divide IQ into four levels: syntactic, semantic, pragmatic, and social. Recently, Kahn et al. (2002) used product and service quality theory to categorise IQ into four categories: sound, useful, dependable, and usable.

Although the many dimensions associated with IQ have now been identified, one still faces the difficulty of obtaining rigorous definitions for each dimension so that measurements may be taken and compared over time. Through literature, it is found that there is no general agreement as to the most suitable definition of IQ or to a parsimonious set of its dimensions. Some researches have special focus on criteria specified by the users as the basis for high quality information (English, 1999; Salaun & Flores, 2001; Strong, 1997). Orr (1998) suggests that the issue of IQ is intertwined with how users actually use the data in the system, since the users are the ultimate judges of the quality of the data produced for them.

The four most obvious IQ dimensions are accuracy, relevance, fineness, and timeliness (Ballou & Pazer, 1995; Huh, Keller, Redman, & Watkins, 1990; Wang, Storey, & Firth, 1995). Unfortunately, a set of data may be completely satisfactory on most dimensions but inadequate on a critical few. Furthermore, improving on one IQ dimension can impair another dimension. For example, it may be possible to improve the timeliness of data at the expense of accuracy (Ballou & Pazer, 1995). Moreover, different stakeholders in an organisation may have different IQ requirements and concerns (Giannoccaro, Shanks, & Darke, 1999). The IQ dimensions considered appropriate for one decision may not be sufficient for other types of decisions. As a result, Wang and Strong's (1996) widely-accepted definition of IQ, quality data are data that are fit for use by the data consumer, is adopted in this research.

Total Data Quality Management (TDQM)

To achieve a state of high IQ, an organisation needs to implement total data quality management (TDQM). Wang (1998) adapted Deming's method of defining, measuring, analysing, and improving products to the information manufacturing environment, and proposed TDQM, which emphasises the importance of continuous improvement and delivery of high-quality information products. The defining component of the TDQM cycle identifies important IQ dimensions (Wang & Strong, 1996) and corresponding IQ requirements. The measurement component produces IQ metrics. The analysis component identifies the root causes for IQ problems and calculates the impact of poor-quality information. Finally, the improvement component provides techniques for improving IQ.

Different industries with different goals and environments can develop more specific and customised programs for IQ management to suit their own needs. Kovac, Lee, and Pipino (1997) argue that regardless of differences, organisations must develop a set of measures for their important IQ dimensions that can be linked to the organisational general goals and objectives.

Copyright © 2007, Idea Group Inc. Copying or distributing in print or electronic forms without written permission of Idea Group Inc. is prohibited.

IQ Research Framework

Maintaining the quality of AM data is often acknowledged as problematic, but critical to effective enterprise management. Examples of the many factors that can impede IQ are identified within various elements of the IQ literature. These include inadequate management structures for ensuring complete, timely and accurate reporting of data; inadequate rules, training, and procedural guidelines for those involved in data collection; fragmentation and inconsistencies among the services associated with data collection; and the requirement for new management methods which utilise accurate and relevant data to support the dynamic management environment.

Clearly, personnel management and organisational factors, as well as effective technological mechanisms, affect the ability to maintain IQ. Wang, Storey, and Firth (1995) clarify this relationship by drawing an analogy between manufacturing and the production of data. In this way they derive a hierarchy of responsibilities for IQ, ranging from management down to the individual procedures and mechanisms. Their framework specifies a top management role for IQ policy, that is, overall intention and direction relating to IQ, and an IQ management function to determine how that policy is to be implemented. This, in turn, should result in an IQ system for implementing IQ management, within which IQ control is enforced through operational techniques and activities. IQ assurance then comprises all of the planned and systematic actions required to provide confidence that data meet the quality requirements.

A number of IQ frameworks (e.g., Caballero & Piattini, 2003; Eppler, 2001; Firth, 1996; Giannoccaro, Shanks & Darke, 1999; Jarke, Jeusfeld, Quix, & Vassiliadis, 1998; Kahn et al., 2002; Nauman & Roth, 2004; Price & Shanks, 2004; Shanks & Darke, 1998; Wand & Wang, 1996; Wang & Strong, 1996; Wang, 1998) have also been proposed to organise and structure important concepts in IQ and to provide a more complete perspective on IQ. The frameworks shown in Figure 1 represent some existing IQ research efforts. Most of these frameworks focus on the processes that produce high-quality data. Organisations can use these frameworks to assist them to better understand IQ, identify desirable IQ dimensions, and provide guidelines on how to design IQ policies to improve the IQ in their organisations.

Figure 1. Representative IQ frameworks

Authors	Representative IQ Frameworks
Shanks & Darke, 1998; Price & Shanks, 2004	A Framework of Understanding Data Quality Based in Semiotics
Giannoccaro, Shanks, & Darke, 1999	A Framework of Stakeholder Perceptions of Data Quality in Data Warehouse Environment
Kahn, Strong, & Wang, 2002	The Product and Service Performance Information Quality Model
Eppler, 2001	An Interdisciplinary Evaluation Framework for Information Quality Frameworks
Caballero & Piattini, 2003	A Data Quality Model for Data Quality Management Improvement

Copyright © 2007, Idea Group Inc. Copying or distributing in print or electronic forms without written permission of Idea Group Inc. is prohibited.

Figure 2. Summary of factors influencing IQ

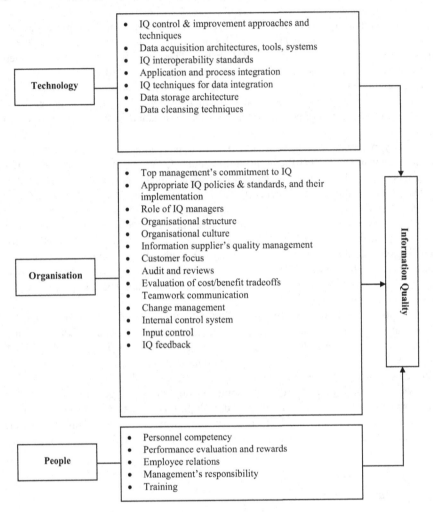

The IQ factors in Figure 2 are summarised from the literature review of IQ related research efforts (e.g., English, 1999; Firth, 1996; Gelle & Karhu, 2003; Kumar & Palvia, 2001; Saraph, Benson, & Schroeder, 1989; Segev, 1996; Vosburg & Kumar, 2001; Wang, 1998; Wang et al., 1995; Xu, Nord, Brown, & Nord, 2002) in order to understand the emerging IQ issues.

Asset Management

Asset management is a broad term and has many different definitions. The nature of the definition is largely dependent on what an organisation considers to be an asset. However,

Copyright © 2007, Idea Group Inc. Copying or distributing in print or electronic forms without written permission of Idea Group Inc. is prohibited.

according to the new British Standard (PAS 55), a common definition of asset management is that systematic and coordinated activities and practices through which an organisation optimally manages its physical assets and their associated performance, risks and expenditures over their lifecycles for the purpose of achieving its organisational strategic plan (Woodhouse, 2003). This discussion restricts the use of *asset* to physical engineering assets and excludes other assets such as digital assets or financial assets.

An asset life cycle starts at the time of designing the manufacturing system, and involves such activities as asset acquisition, operation, maintenance, decommissioning, and replacement (Bever, 2000). Asset management means the management of the plant and equipment during its whole life, that is, from specification through manufacturing, commissioning, useful life, maintenance, and then managing the consequences from the decision to refurbish or replace the item before final decommissioning and recycling any components. Asset management is a structured program to optimise the life-cycle value of the physical assets by reducing the cost of ownership, while providing the required level of service.

The objective of an AM system is to minimise the long-term cost of owning, operating, maintaining, and replacing the asset, while ensuring reliable and uninterrupted delivery of quality service (Eerens, 2003; Spires, 1996). At its core, AM seeks to manage the facility's asset from before it is operationally activated until long after it has been deactivated. This is because, in addition to managing the present and active asset, AM also addresses planning and historical requirements (Steed, 1988).

The process of AM is sophisticated. The processes are data centric--relying heavily on input data from many different parts of the organisation, as well as simultaneously producing substantial amount of data (IPWEA, 2002). This information must be maintained for many years in order to identify long-term trends. The AM engineering and planning process uses this information to plan and schedule asset maintenance, rehabilitation, and replacement activities. The information management system that captures, maintains, and provides the needed asset information is critical in providing effective asset management (Sokianos, Druke, & Toutatoui, 1998).

Steed (1988) indicates that, during its lifetime, the asset is subjected to a host of external factors: environmental conditions, system events, normal and abnormal loads, even changes brought about (for whatever reason) to the dielectric balance. At several critical stages, information is required on the condition of the assets. Knowing what to measure, how to measure it, and then what to do with the information becomes very important. Sandberg (1994) and Paiva, Roth, and Fensterseifer (2002) argue that contemporary AM demands an elevated ability and knowledge to continually support the AM process, in terms of data acquisition, real-time monitoring, and computer supported categorisation and recording of divergences from standard operations.

Figure 3 illustrates an overview of the integrated engineering AM framework and indicates the need to establish enterprisewide AM information systems. It is thought that these information systems will ease the processes of capturing, storing, processing, and maintaining large volumes of asset-related data for effective asset management (Badri, Davis, & Davis, 1995; Knox, 2004).

Copyright © 2007, Idea Group Inc. Copying or distributing in print or electronic forms without written permission of Idea Group Inc. is prohibited.

Asset Information Management

Engineering assets are complex and expensive with multistage life cycles. In order to provide a further in-depth description of the complex life cycle AM processes, the collaborative asset life cycle management model (ARC, 2004) is adopted. This model captures the complexity of life cycle asset management. There are three domains focused on the creation, use, and management of the manufacturing assets in the model. The *asset lifecycle domain* captures the processes related to asset creation, improvement, and retirement. It includes key processes like design, manufacture, installation, and decommissioning of complex facilities. The primary stakeholders in this domain are the asset owner and their engineer, procure, and construct (EPC) contractor. Once assets have been installed, they are operated and maintained by the respective groups in the owner/operator's organisation. The *asset operation domain* recognises that operations consume an asset's capabilities and these are restored periodically with parts and services acquired from the original equipment manufacturers (OEM). The *asset performance management domain* includes those processes that occur during operation to monitor an asset's condition and manage the performance of the asset and the maintenance processes. Key players in this domain are the condition monitoring systems, supervisory control and data acquisition (SCADA) systems, the maintenance and technical staff, and management. Asset management is at the heart of this model. This is a collaborative activity which includes the maintenance technicians, engineers, and operators charged with the care and improvement of the manufacturing assets. And these stakeholders depend upon a reliable service network of service and parts providers.

Asset information management underlies all the AM processes in each domain (ARC, 2004). As asset information is created and consumed by every process in the model, management of this information is vital to efficient and effective asset management and thus

Figure 3. CIEAM integrated asset management framework (Source: CIEAM, 2005)

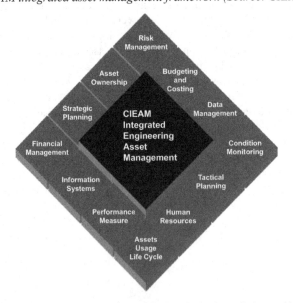

Copyright © 2007, Idea Group Inc. Copying or distributing in print or electronic forms without written permission of Idea Group Inc. is prohibited.

to the eventual return-on-assets of the investment. A variety of stakeholders are involved in creating asset information throughout an asset's life cycle. Other stakeholders use that information to perform their activities in the same or subsequent life cycle stages. Best practice solutions have been developed for various combinations of stakeholders and life cycle stages. The ARC (2004) model also defines the roles of these individual solutions in achieving a complete, integrated solution.

Information Quality in Asset Management

Asset-intensive companies in the process and manufacturing industries are dependent on complete information support. The system that provides this must be capable of collecting and managing all information throughout the entire life cycle of the facility. Previous studies in asset management (Eerens, 2003; IFS, 2004; IPWEA, 2002; Woodhouse, 2001, 2003) suggest that a common, critical concern with EAM is the lack of quality data. Asset IQ issues have become increasingly prevalent in practice, and the evidence indicates that most organisations, particularly engineering enterprises, have experienced some level of IQ problems (Eerens, 2003; Hipkin, 2001; Huang et al., 1999; Klein, 1999).

Despite its unique nature and role, asset management is not considered a core business activity by many businesses and therefore they depend on the traditional organisational information sources to manage assets. These traditional sources represent the tacit, implicit knowledge of engineers, operators, and information contained in information systems, which have been primarily designed to increase productivity rather than improve the efficiency of the processes involved in production. At the same time, a variety of operational and administrative systems exist in asset management, which not only manage the operation of asset equipment but also provide maintenance support throughout the entire asset life cycle. In practice, data are collected both electronically and manually, in a variety of formats, processed in isolation, stored in a variety of legacy systems, shared among various operational and administrative systems, and communicated through a range of sources to assorted business stakeholders. Data captured and processed by these systems is not comprehensive; it is process dependent, making it difficult to be reused for any other processes or process innovation (Koronios & Haider, 2003).

The effective process of AM has to utilise a large number of data for maintenance requirements. There has always been a limited degree to which data have been obtainable, sometimes due to the lack of data acquisition standards, sometimes due to company culture, and often due to the inability of a business to discern operational from strategic data and information. Furthermore, due to the multiplicity of systems and stakeholders, as well as the level of unpredictability in asset operation within asset management, it is impossible to tap user requirements, which consequently contribute to the "dirtiness" of asset data. In managing physical assets through the entire asset life cycle, large amounts of data are needed for long-term performance and reliability prediction, as well as for informing the decision making process on when to retire an asset. Although very large amounts of data are being generated from asset-condition monitoring-systems, little thought has been given to the quality of such generated data. Thus the quality of data from such systems may suffer from severe limitations (Saunders, 2004).

Copyright © 2007, Idea Group Inc. Copying or distributing in print or electronic forms without written permission of Idea Group Inc. is prohibited.

Figure 4. Engineering asset characteristics and management requirements

Engineering Asset Characteristics	Asset Management Requirements
Expensive	• Constant Accountability – location, status, who uses, who controls, etc. • Appropriate care of asset needed to get the most effective lifetime
Complex	• Process management across all significant lifecycle stages • Use of advanced physical asset management methodologies & technologies
Broad Impact On Enterprise	• Comprehensive view of asset information • Effective visibility of asset information by multiple stakeholders • Synchronization of asset lifecycle management with other enterprise processes
Extended Lifetime	• Asset performance and asset lifecycle performance management • Continuous improvement process

There is a growing need to address the IQ issues in engineering AM systems, by analysing existing practices and developing models to assist engineering enterprises to capture, process, and deliver quality information (Steenstrup, 2005). It is essential to ensure the quality of data captured from the monitoring systems, used for control systems, maintenance systems, procurement systems, logistics systems, and a range of mission support applications for facilitating asset availability, readiness, reliability, effectiveness, and management (McAndrew, Anumba, Hassan, & Duke, 2005).

The Need for a Specific IQ Framework for AM

It appears there has been little discussion in the literature on addressing IQ for AM. To address this problem, an IQ framework can be useful to first identify relevant IQ issues. However, due to the significant differences between engineering asset management and typical business environment, an AM specific IQ framework is required to identify the unique AM IQ issues.

The Unique Asset Characteristics and Management Requirements

Engineering enterprises have a broad range of physical assets and each type deserves attention. Engineering assets like machine, production equipment, and fleets have a unique set of characteristics that dictate the need for a separate strategy (Snitkin, 2003). Figure 4 summarises the unique nature of engineering asset management.

Copyright © 2007, Idea Group Inc. Copying or distributing in print or electronic forms without written permission of Idea Group Inc. is prohibited.

Figure 5. Asset life cycle stages and collaborative asset management (Source: Snitkin ARC CALM model, 2003)

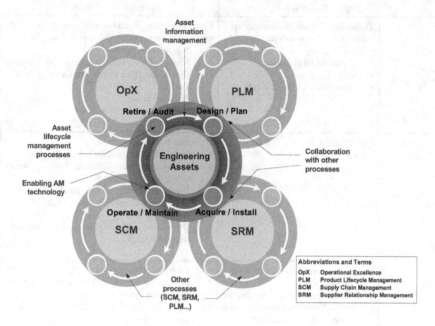

Sophisticated and Long Process

The AM process is thus sophisticated and involves the whole asset life cycle that can span a long period of time. The life cycle for a typical asset involves several interdependent stages. Coordinating these processes as well as collaborating among other organisational processes affected by asset performance is vital to the effective management of engineering assets (Figure 5).

Specialised Technology and Information Systems

A variety of specialised technical, operational, and administrative systems exist in asset management, which not only manage the operation of asset equipment but also provide maintenance support throughout the entire asset life cycle. Most companies today purchase specialised systems from many suppliers. Some of these technical systems include reliability assessment systems, machine vibration condition monitoring systems, and SCADA systems. Normally these systems are bought from multiple vendors and each is specialised to accomplish its task. Unfortunately, this leads to an extremely difficult integration job for the end user. The differences between engineering asset data and the data in typical business environment are summarised in Figure 6.

Copyright © 2007, Idea Group Inc. Copying or distributing in print or electronic forms without written permission of Idea Group Inc. is prohibited.

Figure 6. Difference between engineering asset data and typical business data

	Typical Business Environment	Engineering Asset Management
Data Characteristics	Transaction-Driven, product-centric business data environments: • Self-descriptive • Fewer or no constraints • Discrete value • Not difficult to be audited	Continuous data, process-centric open control system and manufacturing data environments: • Non self-descriptive • Need professional knowledge to interpret data • Continuous value with constraints (e.g., within a range) • Precision value • Difficult to be audited
Data Sources	Mainly transaction-based textual records	Disparate data sources: • Spatial data: plans/maps, drawings, photo • Textual records: inspection sheets, payment schedules • Attribute records: separate databases, maintenance/renewal records, fault/failure records, field books • Other sources: existing/previous staff and contractors, photos
Data Capture	• Often manually by data providers in fixed format • Data often entered by reasonably trained, dedicated personnel with proper relevant knowledge • Data entry environment is stable, well pre-organized • Data entry point is within the business	• Electronically, involving sensors, technical systems such as SCADA systems, condition monitoring systems • Manually, involving field devices, field people, contractors, business rules • Data collected in a variety of formats • Requires to collect substantial data from many different parts of the organization • Data often entered by less trained, less dedicated personnel without proper relevant knowledge • Data entry environment can be unstable, harsh, less pre-organized • Data entry point can be far from the organization site
Data Storage	• Data to be kept in accordance with appropriate compliance requirements • Data stored on functional information systems	• Very large amount of data to be maintained for extended time for AM engineering and planning process • Data stored on various operational and administrative systems

IQ Framework for Asset Management

Mitroff and Linstone (1993) argue that any phenomenon, subsystem, or system needs to be analysed from what they call a multiple perspective method — employing different ways of seeing, to seek perspectives on the problem. These different ways of seeing are demonstrated in the TOP model of Linstone (1999) and Mitroff and Linstone (1993). The TOP model allows analysts to look at the problem context from either technical, organisational, or personal points of view:

Copyright © 2007, Idea Group Inc. Copying or distributing in print or electronic forms without written permission of Idea Group Inc. is prohibited.

- The technical perspective (T) sees organisations as hierarchical structures or networks of interrelationships between individuals, groups, organisations, and systems.
- The organisational perspective (O) considers an organisation's performance in terms of effectiveness and efficiencies. For example, leadership is one of the concerns.
- The personal perspective (P) focuses on the individual's concerns. For example, the issues of job description and job security are main concerns in this perspective.

Mitroff and Linstone (1993) suggest that these three perspectives can be applied as three ways of seeing any problems arising for or within a given phenomenon or system. Werhane (2002) further notes that the dynamic exchanges of ideas which emerge from using the TOP perspectives are essential, because they take into account the fact that each of us individually, or as groups, organisations, or systems, creates and frames the world through a series of mental models, each of which, by itself, is incomplete. In other words, a single perspective on the problem context is not sufficient to elicit an insightful appreciation of it.

It is found that the IQ requirements can be best described by using the TOP multiple-perspectives approach. Moreover, having chosen a particular way of seeing, Linstone's TOP perspectives are still useful in practice. First, by employing TOP, the problem solvers can put stakeholders' perspectives into categories. This process may help problem solvers understand the interconnections between different emerging perspectives, in order to develop a "big picture." For example, the "T" perspective is a synthesis of concerns from all technical people (e.g., system administrators, machine operators, etc.); the "O" perspective gathers all managers' and leaders' thoughts; and the "P" perspective considers all other stakeholders' concerns. In addition, TOP could also be used to explore an individual's perspectives of the problem contexts. For example, "Do I have sufficient skills to complete the task?" is a technical concern. "Will my task contribute to the organisation's success?" is an organisational issue. "If I complete the task, will I get a promotion?" is certainly a personal motivation.

Generic IQ Research Framework

Drawing on both the processes of asset management (as illustrated previously), and the TOP perspectives, an IQ research framework is required, in order to guide the process of exploring the IQ issues emerged from the modern (EAM information systems facilitated) approach to asset management.

In addition to the TOP approach, this study also takes Wang's (1998) TDQM framework into consideration; however, the framework has not explicitly suggested an approach for defining/identifying specific IQ problems emerging from the business domain. Based on the previous discussion, it is felt that the process of modern asset management consists of the adoption of enterprisewide information systems, various business processes, participants (e.g., maintenance people, managers, etc.), and organisational policies (and business goals, structures, etc.). It is thought that Linstone's TOP approach can be used to establish a preliminary research model for this study (as a means of identifying emerging IQ issues from EAM). Based on the discussion on various IQ issues from the available literature (Gelle & Karhu, 2003; Kumar & Palvia, 2001; Wang et al., 1995; Xu, 2000; Xu, Nord, Nord, & Lin, 2003) and the AM unique requirements, the IQ research framework for AM was developed as shown in Figure 7, using the TOP perspectives theory.

There is strong evidence that most organisations have far more data than they possibly use; yet, at the same time, they do not have the data they really need (Levitin & Redman,

Copyright © 2007, Idea Group Inc. Copying or distributing in print or electronic forms without written permission of Idea Group Inc. is prohibited.

Figure 7. Generic IQ research framework (developed by the authors)

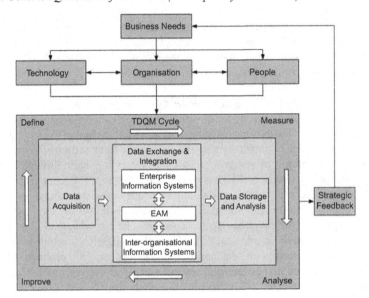

1998). Therefore, identification of business needs is essential. The TDQM methodology (Kahn et al., 2002; Wang, 1998) emphasised the importance of continuous improvement and delivery of high-quality information products. It demonstrated that defining requirements, measuring, analysing, and monitoring improvement are important processes within the information manufacturing system.

As data are not static, they are a dynamic, fluid resource. They flow in a data collection and usage process. The IQ problems that may arise at each stage are different, and require different metrics as well as solutions (Dasu & Johnson, 2003). Because of the continuum nature of data, IQ is not a one-time, fix-it-and-forget-it practice (Fisher, 2005). Building and keeping good quality corporate data takes constant vigilance and feedbacks in the context of the entire data life cycle. Feedback loop is an important IQ monitoring tool. The application of strategic feedback loop can serve to ensure business needs are up-to-date. This *framework* is useful to guide the research into AM IQ issues, because it highlights the three root perspectives (TOP) on IQ problems, illustrates how they emerge during the process of asset management, and in particular, outlines the four basic IQ measurement criteria.

Figure 7 has identified three possible angles of view — the technology, organisation, and people (TOP) perspectives to exploring IQ issues in various AM stages. However, AM is a broad concept, which is difficult to apply as an overall analysis. Thus, in order to explore the IQ issues, the individual AM process should be considered because data will be captured, created, and stored from these processes. Therefore, the collective understanding of various IQ problems emerging from individual AM processes allows researchers to obtain an insightful and overall understanding about what IQ problems are in AM and why they have emerged. Thus the IQ research framework for AM (Figure 8) is created, to illustrate this approach.

Copyright © 2007, Idea Group Inc. Copying or distributing in print or electronic forms without written permission of Idea Group Inc. is prohibited.

Figure 8. IQ research framework for life cycle asset management (the life cycle AM processes listed by IPWEA [2002] are adopted as the basis of this framework)

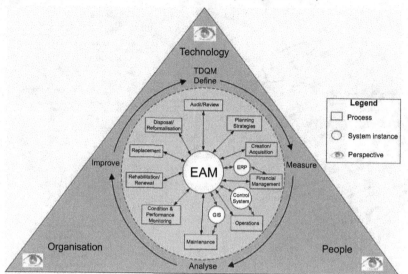

The AM Specific IQ Framework

Based on the discussions on various IQ issues (Gelle & Karhu, 2003; Wang et al., 1995; Xu, 2000; Xu et al., 2003), the unique asset characteristics, the specific requirements for specialised AM systems and sophisticated AM processes, together with the findings from a pilot case study of two large Australian utility organisations, the AM specific IQ framework was developed as shown in Figure 9. This model is useful to guide the research into IQ issues in AM, because it highlights the three root perspectives (TOP) on IQ problems, illustrates how they emerge during the process of AM, and outlines the basic IQ management criteria.

Asset information is a key enabler in gaining control of assets. Asset information is created, stored, processed, analysed, and used throughout an asset's life cycle by a variety of stakeholders together with an assortment of technical and business systems during the whole AM process. Asset information management underlies all the asset-based management processes, and ensured IQ for asset information management assists the optimisation of AM decision making.

The objective of constructing an asset hierarchy is to provide a suitable structure framework for assets, which segments an asset base into appropriate classifications. The intent of the asset structure/organisation is to provide the business with the framework in which data are collected, information is reported, and decisions are made. In most cases, organisations work with an informal asset hierarchy. This often leads to data being collected to inappropriate levels, either creating situations where costs escalate with minimal increases in benefits, or insufficient information is available to make informed decisions (IPWEA, 2002). The information needs of an organisation vary throughout the management

Copyright © 2007, Idea Group Inc. Copying or distributing in print or electronic forms without written permission of Idea Group Inc. is prohibited.

Figure 9. The AM specific IQ framework (developed by the authors)

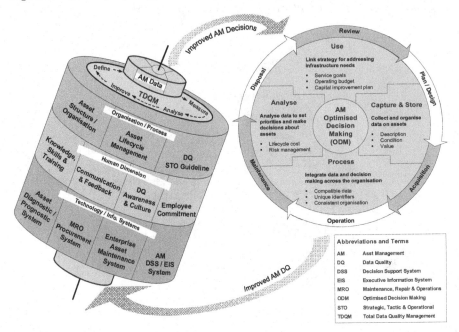

structure. At the operational workforce the key elements are operations, maintenance, and resource management, at a component level. At tactical and strategic management levels this information needs to be aggregated to provide details on assets, facilities, and systems as a whole in terms of finance, strategy, and policy. The development of the asset identification needs to be appropriate for the asset hierarchy and complement the data/information needs of the organisation (IPWEA, 2002).

The asset-based management process is sophisticated. It is an engineering and planning process and covers the whole asset life cycle. The process is associated with capital planning, asset acquisition, condition and performance assessment, and asset-related data strategy and guideline. A variety of specialised technical and business systems exist in asset management including SCADA, CMMS, EAM, GIS, ERP, and so forth, which not only manage the operation of asset equipment but also provide maintenance support throughout the entire asset life cycle (Koronios & Haider, 2003). AM requires linking those systems that are currently unrelated. In addition to the requirements for specialised IS/IT supporting systems and system integration and collaboration, the process of AM also require the participation of assorted engineering and business stakeholders, internally and externally. Because of the diversity and high turnover of AM stakeholders, AM outcome is greatly associated with organisational culture, management commitment, staff competency, communication and feedback, and training.

Copyright © 2007, Idea Group Inc. Copying or distributing in print or electronic forms without written permission of Idea Group Inc. is prohibited.

Figure 10. Summary of IQ issues in asset management (developed by the authors)

Perspective	IQ Issues in Asset Management
Technology	• Integration of AM-related technical systems as well as the integration between business systems and technical systems • Asset hierarchy • Data access • Database synchronization • Data exchange • Data standards for condition monitoring systems • Sensor calibration and integrity check for condition monitoring access
Organization	• Organisational readiness • Business process reengineering • Management commitment • Lack of codified business standard • Disconnect between business and IT while creating metrics for monitoring
People	• Training • Data recording • Communication and management feedback

Information Quality Issues in Asset Management

The IQ issues in AM (summarised in Figure 10) represent some of the empirical findings based on using the TOP model. The integration of AM-related technical systems, as well as the integration between business systems and technical systems, is particularly important (Lin, Gao, & Koronios, 2005).

Technology Perspective

Integration of AM-Related Technical Systems and Integration Between Business Systems and Technical Systems

A variety of specialised AM-related technical systems exist and include reliability assessment systems, asset capacity forecasting systems, enterprise asset maintenance systems, electrical motor testing systems, turbo-machinery safety systems, rotating machine vibration condition monitoring systems, operational data historians, root cause analysis systems, and physical asset data warehouse systems. Such specialised systems are acquired from multiple vendors and, as they are quite disparate, they often lead to significant integration problems.

There appears to be little cognizance when adopting business systems such as financial, human resource, and inventory information systems of the need to ensure compatibility with technical systems such as asset register systems, work order management systems, and condition monitoring systems. Most users are unable to translate the vast amounts of available

Copyright © 2007, Idea Group Inc. Copying or distributing in print or electronic forms without written permission of Idea Group Inc. is prohibited.

asset data into meaningful management information to optimise their operation and control the total asset base. This has led to the notion of "islands of information."

Such disconnects make it extremely difficult to bring real-time information from the plant into business systems. There are disconnects between the transaction-driven, product-centric business data environment and the continuous data, process-centric open control system and manufacturing data environments. The lack of process-to-product data transformation capabilities in linking business systems and plant floor EAM applications have significant IQ consequences and thus negatively affect data-driven decision making.

Asset Hierarchy

The objective of developing an asset hierarchy is to provide a suitable framework for assets, which segments an asset base into appropriate classifications. The asset hierarchy can be based on asset function, asset type, or a combination.

The intent of the asset hierarchy is to provide the business with the framework in which data are collected, information is reported, and decisions are made. In most cases (as found in one organisation) organisations work with an informal asset hierarchy. This often leads to data being collected to inappropriate levels, either creating situations where costs escalate with minimal increases in benefits, or insufficient information is available to make informed decisions.

Infrastructure assets generally have a clear hierarchical relationship that breaks down from the asset type as a whole to large units (facilities), then to assets and their components. The information needs of the organisation vary throughout the management structure. At the workface the key elements are operations, maintenance, and resource management, at a component level. At higher management levels this information needs to be aggregated to provide details on assets, facilities, and (infrastructure) systems as a whole in terms of finance, strategy, and policy.

Data Access

Designers and asset manufacturers represent the external source of asset data. As part of the asset acquisition process, all asset information required to own and operate the asset should be handed over to the user organisation at the commissioning of the asset, in a form that can be assimilated readily into the user organisation's asset information systems. These asset data may include a fully-fledged technical information database with GIS maps, technical specifications, and even video clips of the equipment and its operation.

The research has found that a data gap may exist between the maker and the user of asset equipment. The user organisation needs to populate the EAM with data from the manufacturer — particularly the component structure and spare parts. These capabilities exist in manufacturers' product data management (PDM) and product life cycle management (PLM) systems. Unless arrangements or contract conditions are made, in many cases, the data are not passed on to the buyer in a usable electronic format. In some cases, the asset data handed over to the user organisation does not conform to the physical assets delivered. In other cases, updated asset data, particularly the component structure, may not always

Copyright © 2007, Idea Group Inc. Copying or distributing in print or electronic forms without written permission of Idea Group Inc. is prohibited.

be passed on to the user organisation. Information such as job instructions, maintenance cycles, and advisory notices is also available. However, without standards and interfaces to share this information across systems, it is often held off-line either as paper documents or poorly linked electronic copies of instructions.

Database Synchronisation

The capability of EAM systems can be enhanced through a link with GIS to provide the ability to access, use, display, and manage spatial data. The ability to effectively use spatial asset data is important for utilities with geographically dispersed utility networks. However, it was found that one of the most critical activities is to establish synchronisation between the two database environments. One asset manager indicated that there has been an issue existed for overcoming the synchronisation of asset register in a very common work management system with GIS in the company. Both automated and manual processes needed to be defined and implemented to maintain synchronisation between the GIS and EAM databases. Database triggers and stored procedures need to be defined to automate the attribute update process maintaining synchronisation between the GIS and EAM databases. Workflows and business rules must be developed for GIS and EAM data editing, to ensure synchronisation from both applications.

Data Exchange

Both of the organisations indicated that there is a need for data exchange between AM applications for seamless access to information across heterogeneous systems and different departments within an engineering enterprise. The life cycle performance data of the various assets are kept in individual uncoordinated databases, which make interprocess, interfunctional analysis very difficult. Moreover, the various computer software programs designed for condition monitoring and diagnostics of machines, that are currently in use within the two organisations, cannot easily exchange data or operate in plug-and-play fashion without an extensive integration effort. For example, the maintenance work event forms, which contain the hours that a contractor has worked, cannot be directly input to the payroll system as an alternative to the traditional time sheets. This makes it difficult to integrate systems and provide a unified view of the condition of assets to users.

Data Standards for Condition Monitoring Systems

Although it appears that condition monitoring equipment and systems are proliferating, an apparent lack of dialogue among vendors (as found in one organisation) has led to incompatibilities among hardware, software, and instrumentation. Data collected by current outdated equipment could become obsolete and inaccessible to new, upgraded systems. To fully realise the integration of systems over the various levels of asset maintenance and management, new standards and protocols are needed. A focus on the standardisation of condition monitoring data modeling and exchange tools and methodologies, such as standard for the exchange of product model data (STEP), is critical.

Moreover, facility managers in one organisation indicate a need to be able to accurately assess asset condition with the capacity to comprehensively record key asset condition data,

Copyright © 2007, Idea Group Inc. Copying or distributing in print or electronic forms without written permission of Idea Group Inc. is prohibited.

as a fundamental objective of the inspection and maintenance policy. While comprehensive asset databases generally exist, not all of them have been designed to accurately record asset condition data. For example, one plant records system holds data on all items of operational plant in terms of age, location, and date last inspected/maintained, but it does not provide the means to hold data on the condition of the plant. Where a comprehensive asset database exists containing both asset details and recorded defects, the database, however, does not permit the recording of successive inspection data (any new record overwriting the current record) and so the important function of developing generic aging curves is not supported.

Sensor Calibration and Integrity Check for Condition Monitoring Access

Interviews with asset maintenance field workers indicate that data captured by intelligent sensors may not always be accurate. Data capturing devices typically used in condition monitoring are electronic sensors or transducers, which convert numerous types of mechanical behavior into proportional electronic signals, usually voltage-sensitive signals, producing analogue signals which in turn are processed in a number of ways using various electronic instruments. As signals are generally very weak, a charge amplifier is connected to the sensor or transducer to minimise noise interference and prevent signal loss. The amplified analogue signal can then be sent via coaxial cables to filtering devices to remove or reduce noise, before being routed to a signal conditioner and/or analogue-to-digital converters for digital storage and analysis. As SCADA systems are often used in industrial and engineering applications to control distributed systems from a master location, in order to ensure the data received by SCADA systems conforms to the original signal data captured by sensors, integrity checks for signal transmission process, and sensor calibration need to be performed and maintained. However, as the sensor calibration and integrity checks are often neglected in asset maintenance in most industries, the extent to which acquired data are correct and reliable was shown to be of concern with respondents.

Organisation Perspective

Organisational Readiness

Many companies that attempt to implement EAM systems run into difficulty because they are not ready for integration, and the various departments within it have their own agendas and objectives that conflict with each other. Organisational readiness can be described as having the right people, focused on the right things, at the right time, with the right tools, performing the right work, with the right attitude, creating the right results. It is a reflection of the organisation's culture. EAM implementations involve broad organisational transformation processes, with significant implications to the organisation's asset management model, organisation structure, management style and culture, and particularly, to its people.

An EAM implementation project within the engineering organisations is expected to have a high acceptance of the system in areas that provide just as good or better functionality than the old system. However some functions and processes did not get the full appreciation the legacy systems once had. It was found that field workers are frustrated with the need to use a new asset

Copyright © 2007, Idea Group Inc. Copying or distributing in print or electronic forms without written permission of Idea Group Inc. is prohibited.

maintenance work order management system and are losing confidence in it. Some staff member said that "with the new (EAM) system there are so many problems, people are not interested." Another interviewee said that "The new system hasn't solved the speed problem which you would have thought it would have. ...From day 1, workers were starting to acknowledge the good points of old systems compared to the new (asset management) system."

Business Process Reengineering

Organisational fit and adaptation are important to the implementation of modern large-scale enterprise systems. Like enterprise resource planning systems, EAM systems are also built with a predetermined business process methodology that requires a fairly rigid business structure for it in order to work successfully. They are only as effective as the processes in which they operate. Companies that place faith in EAM systems often do so without re-engineering their processes to fit the system requirements. Consequently, this often results in negative impacts on the effectiveness of both the EAM system and AM practices. It is concluded that the business process for AM in the organisation was not modified to fit the EAM system.

Management Commitment

Numerous interviews with AM stakeholders in the engineering organisations (including asset planning managers, GIS manager, field supervisors, senior managers, maintenance technicians, data entry staff, maintenance contractors, and subcontractors) indicate that management commitment and supports are critical to the success of IQ improvement programs. It appears to be that, at strategic level, managers know IQ problems, but it seems they do not treat the problems with high priority. Therefore, only limited resources were allocated to address the IQ problems. It was also found that, at tactical level, managers were frustrated by the poor quality information stored in the company's AM systems. It seems that they cannot do too much about it. They tend to rely on other information sources such as GIS for AM practice. They even suggested IQ should be linked with a reward system in order to make staff responsible for the IQ problems they caused. At operational level, staff were aware that the data collected and entered were not right, but it seems that they do not care. The operational supervisors know IQ problems existed in the AM systems, so they do not trust its data. Instead, they create their own islands of information (e.g., in Excel spreadsheets) for their own AM practice.

Lack of Codified Business Standard

To enforce business rules through monitoring, an organisation must have a set of data standards for corporate information. Having a codified set of rules makes data monitoring possible because users know what to enforce when establishing data-quality controls. But these rules must be consistent and agreed upon across lines of business and among business and technical users.

Copyright © 2007, Idea Group Inc. Copying or distributing in print or electronic forms without written permission of Idea Group Inc. is prohibited.

Disconnect Between Business and IT while Creating Metrics for Monitoring

While IT departments know how the data are stored and linked, the consumers of data (i.e., line-of-business employees who rely on data to make decisions) know what the data should look like. The two sides must work together to create a meaningful set of control metrics within the existing IT environment. Without collaboration, any data monitoring project will fail to yield measurable results because the metrics will not reflect the needs or "pains" of the business users.

People Perspective

Training

From an IQ perspective, training has not been sufficiently addressed. Thus, there was a lack of a general awareness of IQ. For example, staff often made mistakes in entries because they did not feel it was important to ensure a high level of IQ. In particular, they were not aware of the severe consequence caused by these mistakes. In the organisation, when the new statewide AM system was first introduced, several ordinary staff members were chosen to take a brief, 3-day training workshop and then were assigned to be trainers for the rest of the organisation. Due to the insufficient knowledge and skills of these trainers, the system implementation experienced tremendous problems. One manager mentioned that "training has been provided, but a lot of attendants are old and hence can't be bothered." However, through the interviews with field workers, one said that "training is the same for everyone" and "most of us have very little training, we're mostly self-taught." It was found that the gap between current practices and capabilities, and those required to harness everybody's best efforts, are wide in the organisation. On the education front alone, simple things like "awareness of the cost of downtime" and "how the data being collected are going to be used" can transform the motivation, performance, and creativity of the asset operators/technicians.

Managing assets requires all aspects of training as well as appropriate documentation of the system. It was found that organisations tended to focus more on the "hardware" part of the systems' development process, putting less effort on the "soft" part, that is, the training of how to operate and manage the system. People's skills and abilities to use the system efficiently are very critical to ensure IQ in AM systems. If people do not have the skills and knowledge to control the system, then even a perfect system would not be able to produce high quality information. Lack of training can cause serious damage and have an adverse impact on IQ. Unfortunately, it is easy for organisations to find reasons/excuses for avoiding adequate training for the staff and management.

Data Recording

In asset management, all of the analytical methods, prediction techniques, models, and so on, have little meaning without the proper input data. The ability to evaluate alternatives and predict the future depends on the availability of good historical data, and the source of such stems from the type of data information feedback system. The feedback system must not only incorporate the forms for recording the right type of data, but must consider the

Copyright © 2007, Idea Group Inc. Copying or distributing in print or electronic forms without written permission of Idea Group Inc. is prohibited.

personnel factors (skill levels, motivation, etc.) involved in the data recording process. The person who must complete the appropriate forms must understand the system and the purposes for which the data are being collected. If this person is not properly motivated to do a good, thorough job in recording events, the resulting data will of course be highly suspect.

Research into data collection has found that IQ and validation effectiveness improve, the sooner the collected data are entered, and the nearer the data entry is to the asset and its work. If the data entry point is remote from the asset, then the capability for accurately confirming the data is considerably reduced and the temptation to enter something — anything that the system will accept — is great. One manager said in the interview that "I feel that most of the (data) errors over time have been because of the lag between the field data and being contained in the computer somewhere. ...They (field people) might wait a week before they complete their work order (entry)." It was found that the longer the time lag between using the entered data and the time it was initially created, the less chance of cleaning up the data to make them useful.

Communication and Management Feedback

Competitive asset intensive companies have reported that most of their asset improvements come from their workforce. Despite the fact that "people are our greatest asset," evidence of the opposite was often found. People's problems, people's relationships, people's aspirations, and people's personal agendas are seldom given the consideration appropriate to their importance in the successful implementation of an EAM system. In fact, the problem needs to be stated more emphatically. Most system implementations neglect the people factor and, as a result, most systems ultimately fail to achieve the objectives upon which their original funding was justified. It appears to be that organisations continue to see the operators and technicians as skilled hands, rather than also having brains and being very sophisticated sensors. It was also found that field people within the organisation often generate the view that "year after year they filled out field data without feedback and a lot of them worked out that if they did nothing, nothing happens so why bother?"

Data Cleansing and Tools for IQ Improvement

During the last few years there has been an increase activity in the field of data cleansing. Research also emphasised different data cleansing methodologies. Each of the data cleansing methodologies, however, targets a different area of the bigger problem of data cleansing. Data cleansing requires cleansing of all the organisational data, which originates from within the organisation as well as from its business partners. Furthermore, there are numerous systems, data formats, metadata, and schemas involved in the business execution of any business. Therefore, data cleansing methodologies have targeted different areas within the bigger issue of data cleansing. The most popular data cleansing methodologies include AJAX, FreQL, Potter's Wheel, ARKTOS, and IntelliClean (Muller & Freytag, 2003). The evaluation of these methodologies reveal that data cleansing methodologies are aimed at static data only and do not provide data cleansing ability in real time. Consequently, the efforts are primarily aimed at instance levels or data warehouses, without making requisite progress towards data cleansing during data processing in real time, data exchange within

Copyright © 2007, Idea Group Inc. Copying or distributing in print or electronic forms without written permission of Idea Group Inc. is prohibited.

the organisational information systems as well as with business partners. Furthermore, there is no methodology that aims to embed data cleansing techniques in data exchange and transfer applications.

IQ tools include tools that are used to detect problems with input data at the time of the data capturing process and those which are dedicated to identifying problems by inspecting, discovering, and correcting the problems in existing data stores. The tools used at the data capture stage are often referred to as auditing tools. They are designed to intercept the data entered and test it in real time for errors and inconsistencies through comparison to business rules as well as wherever possible even enrich the data through access to internal/external databases. This approach is indeed the most effective, although not always possible, as the data can be inspected, corrected, and enriched before they are stored in some repository. Other tools focus on discovering and cleansing data in existing databases. These tools focus on identification of missing values, inconsistent values, duplicate records, errors, and integrity violations in order to clean, correct, and enrich the data in the database. In general, there are four main functions — data parsing/profiling function, data cleansing and verification/ matching function, data enrichment/enhancement function, and data monitoring function — incorporated in a typical IQ solution suite, which form the IQ improvement cycle.

Figure 11. A quantitative comparison of main features of IQ tools (Source: Howard, 2004; CIEAM SI-101Team, 2005)

Product Name	Data Discovery Features						Data Cleansing Features					
	Source Support	Structural Profiling	Content Profiling	Visualisation	QA Support	Integration	Analysis & Dictionary Support	Matching	Consolidation, Linking & Enrichment	Visualisation	Internationalisation	QA Support
Ascential Enterprise Integration Suite	6	6.5	7	5	8	7.5	7	5	7	6	7	5
Avellino Discovery 3.2	8	9	8	6	5	5.5						
Datanomic	5.5	6.5	7	5	8	9	8	7	6	6	8	7
Evoke Axio	7	8	8	6	5	5.5						
Firstlogic Information Quality Suite	5	6	6	5	5	7	7	8	7	6	7	5
Informatica PowerCenter 7	7	6	6	8	6	6						
Innovative Systems i/Lytics							8	7	8	5	6.5	5
KDI Data Investigator	5	2	5	4	4	7	3			5	5	5
SAS ETL	6	6	8	7.5	5	7	7	6	7	7.5	7	6
Similarity Systems ATHANOR Suite	5	4	8	7	6	7	6	6	7	7	7	7
The Trillium Software System							7	7	7	8	8	5

Copyright © 2007, Idea Group Inc. Copying or distributing in print or electronic forms without written permission of Idea Group Inc. is prohibited.

A quantitative comparison of the main features of these IQ solutions adopted from Howard (2004) and CIEAM SI-101 Team (2005) is shown in Figure 11. A comprehensive analysis of the major vendors and their IQ related products further attests that the issues posed to IQ for AM are quite unique in nature and cannot be resolved through the existing commercial off the shelf products. The immaturity of IQ research in AM and the formative nature of IQ present significant research opportunities in this field.

Conclusion

There are some implications for real-world engineering organisations and practitioners, which emerged from this research. The following conclusions and recommendations were drawn from the research findings.

Understand IQ Issues in Asset Management

IQ issues are critical to the success of asset management. The framework proposed in this chapter provides a useful tool for planning the establishment of an awareness of IQ issues in managing assets. In particular, it indicates the key areas where the policy implementers need to focus and to monitor. IQ issues need to be widely understood and managed in order to ensure effective AM. When analysis is required for making decisions, to establish an IQ project regarding the management of engineering assets, issues discussed in this chapter can help practitioners to perform a cost/benefit analysis in relation to IQ issues. The identification of IQ issues within the area of AM will also serve to provide additional research opportunities for the development of tangible solutions to IQ problems in AM.

Understand the Key Factors that Impact on IQ While Managing Assets

There are certain factors that influence IQ when managing assets. Organisations should focus on those key factors as defined by the framework in this chapter, which include asset structure/organisation, AM technology and information systems, training, communication and feedback, employee commitment, IQ awareness, and organisational culture. Understanding the key factors should lead to high-level IQ management practices for asset life cycle management, which is a key to the successful implementation of effective AM. The knowledge of specifications of the key factors of IQ management in engineering AM permits organisations to obtain a better understanding of IQ management practices, and perform better IQ controls in managing engineering assets. A particularly important factor for IQ projects is adequate training. Implementing an IQ project requires an effective IQ project team that holds essential knowledge, skills, and works together. Both engineering and IT personnel perform very important roles in the implementation process to ensure that the project is on the right track. Quality communication among engineering, business, and IT people will significantly reduce IQ problems.

Copyright © 2007, Idea Group Inc. Copying or distributing in print or electronic forms without written permission of Idea Group Inc. is prohibited.

Adequate Training Is Essential

Adequate training on IQ for all personnel involved in managing engineering assets is important for ensuring and improving IQ. People's ability to use the system is equally important to ensure a relatively high level of IQ in AM. Sufficient training should be provided to all employees to obtain a broad understanding of the system as a whole, as well as providing particular personnel with adequate documentation and specific training to deliver the critical mode of knowledge (know-what, know-how, know-why) for their specific data roles (data collector, data custodian, data customer, data manager) in their relevant functional areas in relation to the system.

Future Research

This chapter provided a better understanding of IQ issues for AM as well as useful practitioner findings from real-world practice. Key IQ issues discussed and the use of the identified framework should help organisations obtain a better understanding of IQ issues throughout the process, leading to activities which will help ensure IQ. Although the organisations may not have controls on those factors, organisations can actively manage those changes. Organisations could use external pressures to accelerate the quality management of internal information. Moreover, this chapter has provided some recommendations, with implications for practitioners. Thus, the prevention and correction techniques can be applied according to the issues found in order to ensure a high level of IQ. In addition, it has provided guidance to further explore how to implement IQ policies successfully in the future research study.

Acknowledgments

This research is conducted through the Centre for Integrated Engineering Assets Management (CIEAM). The support of CIEAM partners is gratefully acknowledged.

References

ARC Advisory Group. (2004). *Asset information management — a CALM Prerequisite.* White Paper. Dedham, USA: ARC Advisory Group.

Badri, M. A., Davis, D., & Davis, D. (1995). A study of measuring the critical factors of quality management. *International Journal of Quality and Reliability Management, 12*(2), 36-53.

Ballou, D. P., & Pazer, H. L. (1995). Designing information systems to optimize the accuracy-timeliness tradeoff. *Information Systems Research, 6*(1), 51-72.

Ballou, D. P., Wang, R. Y., Pazer, H. L., & Tayi, K. G. (1998). Modeling information manufacturing systems to determine information product quality. *Management Science, 44*(4), 463-485.

Copyright © 2007, Idea Group Inc. Copying or distributing in print or electronic forms without written permission of Idea Group Inc. is prohibited.

Bever, K. (2000, July/August). Understanding plant asset management systems. *Maintenance Technology,* 20-25. Retrieved May 12, 2004, from http://www.mt-online.com/articles/07-00mm2.cfm

Caballero, I., & Piattini, M. (2003, July 14-18). Data quality management improvement. In *Proceedings of the ACS/IEEE International Conference on Computer Systems and Applications (AICCSA'03),* Tunisia (pp. 56-65).

CIEAM. (2005). *CIEAM information brochure.* Brisbane, Australia: Centre for Integrated Engineering Asset Management. Retrieved April 15, 2006, from http://www.cieam.com/aboutus/

CIEAM SI-101 Team. (2005). *Data quality in asset management* (Project Report No.1). University of South Australia , School of Computer and Information Science.

Dasu, T., & Johnson T. (2003). *Exploratory data mining and data cleaning.* New York: John Wiley.

Davenport, T. H. (1997). *Information ecology.* New York: Oxford University Press.

Eckerson, W. W. (2002). *Data quality and bottom line: Achieving business success through a commitment to high quality data* (TDWI Report Series). Seattle, WA: The Data Warehousing Institute.

Eerens, E. (2003). *Business driven asset management for industrial & infrastructure assets.* Australia: Le Clochard.

English, L. P. (1999). *Improving data warehouse and business information quality: Methods for reducing costs and increasing profits.* New York: Willey & Sons.

Eppler, M. J. (2001). The concept of information quality: An interdisciplinary evaluation of recent information quality frameworks. *Studies in Communication Sciences, 1,* 167-182.

Firth, C. (1996, October 25-26). Data quality in practice: Experience from the frontline. In *Proceedings of 1996 Conference of Information Quality,* Cambridge, MA.

Fisher, C. W., & Kingma, B. R. (2001). Criticality of data quality as exemplified in two disasters. *Information & Management, 39,* 109-116.

Fisher, T. (2005, April 13). Meeting the data-quality challenge. *Computerworld.* Retrieved May 20, 2005, from http://www.computerworld.com/databasetopics/businessintelligence/story/0,10801,101040,00.html

Fox, C., Levitin, A. V., & Redman, T. C. (1994). The notion of data and its quality dimensions. *Information Processing & Management, 30*(1), 9-19.

Gelle, E., & Karhu, K. (2003). Information quality for strategic technology planning. *Industrial Management & Data Systems, 103*(8), 633-643.

Giannoccaro, A., Shanks, G., & Darke, P. (1999). Stakeholder perceptions of data quality in a data warehouse environment. *Australian Computer Journal, 31*(4), 110-117.

Hall, M. (2005, February 7). Databases can't handle RFID. *Computerworld.* Retrieved March 7, 2005, from http://www.computerworld.com/action/article.do?command=viewArticleBasic&articleId=99589

Hassan, B. (2003). Examining data accuracy and authenticity with leading digit frequency analysis. *Industrial Management & Data Systems, 103*(2), 121-125.

Hipkin, I. (2001). Knowledge and IS implementation: case studies in physical asset management. *International Journal of Operations & Production Management, 21*(10), 1358-1380.

Howard, P. (2004). *Data quality products: An evaluation and comparison* (Bloor Research Report). Bletchley; Milton Keynes, UK: Bloor Research.

Copyright © 2007, Idea Group Inc. Copying or distributing in print or electronic forms without written permission of Idea Group Inc. is prohibited.

Hoxmaier, J. A. (2001). Dimensions of database quality. In S. Becker (Ed.), *Developing quality complex database systems: Practices, techniques, and technologies* (pp. 28-47). Hershey, PA: Idea Group Publishing.

Huang, K., Lee, Y. W., & Wang, R. Y. (1999). *Quality information and knowledge*. Upper Saddle River, NJ: Prentice Hall.

Huh, Y. U., Keller, F. R., Redman, T. C., & Watkins, A. R. (1990). Data quality. *Information & Software Technology, 32*(8), 559-565.

IFS. (2004). *Enterprise asset management* (White paper). Stockholm, Sweden: IFS Applications.

IPWEA. (2002). *International infrastructure management manual* (Australia/New Zealand edition). Sydney, Australia: The Institute of Public Works Engineering Australia.

Ives, B., Olson, M., & Baroudi, J. J. (1983). The measurement of user information satisfaction. *Communications of the ACM, 26*(10), 785-793.

Jarke, M., Jeusfeld, M. A., Quix, C., & Vassiliadis, P. (1998, June 8-9). Architecture and quality in data warehouses. In *Proceedings of the Tenth International Conference (CAiSE'98)*, Pisa, Italy (pp. 93-113). Springer-Verlag.

Kahn, B. K., Strong, D. M., & Wang, R. Y. (2002). Information quality benchmarks: Product and services performance. *Communications of the ACM, 45*(4), 184-192.

Kingma, B. R. (1996). *The economics of information: A guide to economic and cost-benefit analysis for information professionals*. Englewood, CO: Libraries Unlimited.

Klein, B. D. (1999). Detection of data errors in the practice of inventory management. *Journal of Computer Information Systems, 40*(2), 34-40.

Knox, M. (2004). *Asset managers move to centralized data and data management* (Research note). Stamford, CT: Gartner Research.

Koronios, A., & Haider, A. (2003). Managing engineering assets: A knowledge based asset management methodology through information quality. *E-Business and Organisations in the 21th Century*, 443-452.

Koronios, A., Lin, S., & Gao, J. (2005, November 4-6). A data quality model for asset management in engineering organisations. In *Proceedings of the 10th International Conference on Information Quality (ICIQ 2005)*, Cambridge, MA (pp. 27-51).

Kovac, R., Lee, Y. W., & Pipino, L. L. (1997, October 24-26). Total data quality management: The case of IRI. In *Proceedings of the 1997 International Conference on Information Quality*, Cambridge, MA (pp. 63-79).

Kumar, A., & Palvia, P. (2001). Key data management issues in a global executive information system. *Industrial Management & Data Systems, 101*(4), 153-164.

Levitin, A. V., & Redman, T. C. (1998). Data as a resource: Properties, implications and prescriptions. *Sloan Management Review, 40*(1), 89-101.

Lillrank, P. (2003). The quality of information. *International Journal of Quality & Reliability Management, 20*(6), 691-703.

Lin, S., Gao, J., & Koronios, A. (2006). Key data quality issues for enterprise asset management in engineering organisations. *International Journal of Electronic Business Management, 4*(1), 96-110.

Linstone, H. A. (1999). *Decision making for technology executives: Using multiple perspectives to improve performance*. Norwood, MA: Artech House Publisher.

Loshin, D. (2001). *Enterprise knowledge management: The data quality approach*. London: Morgan Kaufmann, Academic Press.

Copyright © 2007, Idea Group Inc. Copying or distributing in print or electronic forms without written permission of Idea Group Inc. is prohibited.

McAndrew, S., Anumba, C., Hassan. T., & Duke, A. (2005). Potential use of real-time data capture and job-tracking technology in the field. *Facilities, 23*(1/2), 31-46.

Mitroff, I. I., & Linstone, H. A. (1993). *The unbounded mind: Breaking the chains of traditional business thinking*. New York: Oxford University Press.

Muller, H., & Freytag, J. (2003). *Problems, methods, and challenges in comprehensive data cleansing* (Tech. Rep. No. HUB-IB-164). Berlin: Humboldt University.

Nauman, F., & Roth, M. (2004, November 5-7). Information quality: How good are off-the-shelf DBMS? In *Proceedings of the 9th International Conference on Information Quality (ICIQ-04)*, Cambridge, MA (pp. 260-274).

Orr, K. (1998). Data quality and system theory. *Communications of the ACM, 41*(2), 66-71.

Paiva, E. L., Roth, A. V., & Fensterseifer, J. E. (2002). Focusing information in manufacturing: A knowledge management perspective. *Industrial Management & Data Systems, 102*(7), 381-389.

Price, R. J., & Shanks, G. (2004, July 1-3). A semiotic information quality framework. In *Proceedings of the Decision Support in an Uncertain and Complex World: The IFIP TC8/WG8.3 International Conference 2004*, Prato, Italy (pp. 658-672).

Redman, T. C. (1996). *Data quality for the information age*. Norwood, MA: Artech House.

Redman, T. C. (1998). The impact of poor data quality on the typical enterprise. *Communications of the ACM, 41*(2), 79-82.

Salaun, Y., & Flores, K. (2001). Information quality: Meeting the needs of the consumer. *International Journal of Information Management, 21*(1), 21-37.

Sandberg, U. (1994). *The coupling between process and product quality — the interplay between maintenance and quality in manufacturing*. Amsterdam, The Netherlands: Euromaintenance.

Saraph, J. V., Benson, P. G., & Schroeder, R. G. (1989). An instrument for measuring the critical factors of quality management. *Decision Sciences, 20*(4), 810-829.

Saunders, D. (2004, October 19-21). Innovation in asset management — achieving a nexus of cost and capability. In *Proceeding of the Undersea Defense Technology Conference & Exhibition (UDT Pacific 2004)*, Oahu, HI.

Segev, A. (1996, October 25-26). On information quality and the WWW impact a position paper. In *Proceedings of the 1996 Conference of Information Quality*, Cambridge, MA.

Shanks, G., & Darke, P. (1998). Understanding data quality in a data warehouse. *Australian Computer Journal, 30*(4), 122-128.

Snitkin, S. (2003). *Collaborative asset lifecycle management vision and strategies* (Research report). Dedham, MA: ARC Advisory Group.

Sokianos, N., Druke, H., & Toutatoui, C. (1998). *Lexikon Produktions Management*. Landsberg, Germany.

Spires, C. (1996). Asset and maintenance management — becoming a boardroom issue. *Managing Service Quality, 6*(3), 13-15.

Steed, J. C. (1988). *Aspects of how asset management can be influenced by modern condition monitoring and information management systems* (IEE Research Article). London: The Institution of Electrical Engineers.

Copyright © 2007, Idea Group Inc. Copying or distributing in print or electronic forms without written permission of Idea Group Inc. is prohibited.

Steenstrup, K. (2005). *Enterprise asset management thrives on data consistency* (Research article). Stamford, CT: Gartner Research.

Strong, D. M. (1997). IT process designs for improving information quality and reducing exception handling: A simulation experiment. *Information and Management, 31*, 251-263.

Vosburg, J., & Kumar, A. (2001). Managing dirty data in organisations using ERP: Lessons from a case study. *Industrial Management & Data Systems, 101*(1), 21-31.

Wand, Y., & Wang, R. Y. (1996). Anchoring data quality dimensions in ontological foundations. *Communications of the ACM, 39*(11), 86-95.

Wang, R. Y. (1998). A product perspective on total data quality management. *Communications of the ACM, 41*(2), 58-65.

Wang, R. Y., & Strong, D. M. (1996). Beyond accuracy: What data quality means to data consumers. *Journal of Management Information Systems, 12*(4), 5-33.

Wang, R. Y., Storey, V. C., & Firth, C. P. (1995). A framework for analysis of quality research. *IEEE Transactions On Knowledge and Data Engineering, 7*(4), 623-640.

Werhane, P. H. (2002). Moral imagination and systems thinking. *Journal of Business Ethics, 38*, 33-42.

Woodhouse, J. (2001). *Asset management.* The Woodhouse Partnership Ltd (2001) online. Retrieved April 10, 2004, from http://www.plant-maintenance.com/articles/AMbasicintro.pdf

Woodhouse, J. (2003). *Asset management: Concepts & practices* (Research article). Kingsclere, UK: The Woodhouse Partnership.

Xu, H. (2000, December 10-13). Managing accounting information quality: An Australian study. *In Proceedings of the International Conference on Information Systems (ICIS 2000)*, Brisbane. Australia.

Xu, H., Nord, J. H., Brown, N., & Nord, G. D. (2002). Data quality issues in implementing an ERP. *Industrial Management & Data Systems, 102*(1), 47-58.

Xu, H., Nord, J. H., Nord, G. D., & Lin, B. (2003). Key issues of accounting information quality management: Australian case studies. *Industrial Management & Data Systems, 103*(7), 461-470.

Copyright © 2007, Idea Group Inc. Copying or distributing in print or electronic forms without written permission of Idea Group Inc. is prohibited.

Section V

Applications in Developing Countries

Chapter XI

Quality Management Practices Regarding Statistical and Financial Data in China

Zhenguo Yu, Zhejiang University City College, China

Ying Wang, Zhejiang University City College, China

Abstract

This chapter presents a survey into quality management practice regarding statistics and financial data in China. As a fast-developing country, China is experiencing a significant reform in the decision mechanism, and it causes the changing of quality requirement for information and the necessities of total quality management for information. In this chapter we first talk about the understanding progress of the information quality in China, point out that the veracity of information is more sensitive in China, then we present the practice of China's quality management in social, organizational, and technological arenas.

Introduction

In the market economy information is used to monitor and support many fields in corporations, such as marketing, accounting, manufacturing, CRM, and so forth. It is the key factor that helps firms make decisions. Incorrect or incomplete information may cause

Copyright © 2007, Idea Group Inc. Copying or distributing in print or electronic forms without written permission of Idea Group Inc. is prohibited.

mistakes and failure. So, the quality of information is significant for corporations. Most corporations, large or small, have initiated total quality management (TQM) programs aiming at reaching 100% satisfaction for customers and no product defects. In the same way, corporations should not only regard information as a product, but they should always manage and control their quality. At the same time, the research in information quality management also becomes necessary and significant.

In China, the notion of the information quality was narrow in the past, which only paid attention to the veracity. But now it has been transformed into a multidimensional connotation, which includes timeliness, applicability, veracity, completeness, and so on. Gradually, meeting customers' demands is regarded as the criterion to evaluate information's quality. Now, we take examples from statistical data and financial data to introduce the development of information quality management practice in China.

In a developing and transition economy, challenges arise. The rapid growth in productive units outside the traditional reporting system, the adoption of novel statistical concepts and variables, the redefinition of economic variables by other government departments, data falsification at lower level tiers, political considerations, and shifting interests of reporting units, and changes in local government administration impact the quality of official Chinese data. The resulting data complications can be summarized as follows: definitions of variables and coverage of productive units for a particular variable; errors; data falsification; and mistakes in data presentation. Therein, the falsification of statistical data and accounting data is more prevalent compared to other countries. It is because of China's special situation and institution that the interests of data providers are related to the result of data. Thus, data providers deliberately submit incorrect data; local leaders are evaluated (promoted and remunerated), at least in part, according to the economic performance of the locality. Leaders by nature want to only hear good news. Once data in one year have been falsified, going back to accurate data in the following years is almost impossible; some enterprises make a false report to obtain illegal benefits. For example, small enterprises are likely to underreport their output when their sales revenue approach 5 million RMB annually in order to avoid having to fill in cumbersome monthly report forms for the statistical authority. Profit is likely to be underreported when managers wish to avoid high corporate income taxes. These are why the veracity of data is more sensible in China compared to other countries.

All of the materials in this presentation are based on published research. The authors explained the special understanding of notion of information quality in China, and special priority in China's IQ management regarding statistical and financial data.

Statistical Data's Quality in China

The National Bureau of Statistics (NBS) has constituted a periodical evaluating system for the primary statistical data. In 1999, NBS publicized the executive measure to evaluate the quality of 12 kinds of primary statistical data including gross domestic product (GDP), population, and so on, for the first time. The purpose was to obtain these statistical data's credibility. It can ensure using these data accurately, improving their quality to satisfy the needs of all circles.

In addition, China incarnates the tenet of guaranteeing information's quality in legislation. For example, statistic law is a fundamental law, which is used to guarantee and control the quality of statistical data. There are also a lot of supplementary statutes and detailed rules for further guarantee, just like detailed rules of statistic law, and so forth.

Copyright © 2007, Idea Group Inc. Copying or distributing in print or electronic forms without written permission of Idea Group Inc. is prohibited.

In recent years, NBS has taken several new measures against the challenges. Improving national economy calculation system enhanced the quality of national and regional data. To meet the needs of society, NBS established a scientific investigation system and perfected the statistical criteria.

Financial Data's Quality in China

Financial affairs are the foundation of economy and management. In the market economy system, the users of financial data are not only the company insiders anymore. Many other people need these data, too. They scream for financial data's veracity and comparability.

China enacted Accounting Law in 1985. It accelerated Chinese accounting modernization. Along with the development of the market economy, accounting affairs face more and more problems. On October 31, 1999, the republishing of China's Accounting Law was enacted, which is aimed to ensure the quality of accounting data ulteriorly.

At all times, China makes great efforts to enhance the quality of data. However, there is no systematic and integrated research in information quality management in China yet. Information quality management has not developed into a discipline either. As compared with many other developed countries, China still has much leeway in catching up.

As a developing country, China plays an important role in the world. After joining the World Trade Organization (WTO), China is facing more and more challenges from the whole world and also puts great impact on its trading partners. As information quality is one of the important factors to accelerate economic development, China should share the experience with other nations.

In this chapter, the main objectives are to demonstrate:

- Understanding of information quality in China
- Social issues and practice in China's IQ management
- Organizational issues and practice in China's IQ management
- Technological issues and practice in China's IQ management

Understanding of Information Quality in China

Veracity of Data

For a long time, when Chinese people talk about information quality, they focused on the veracity of the data. They believe that incorrect information stems mainly from incorrect original data. The scandals of accounting information fraud in China's stock market revealed in recent years are the major cause of accounting information fraud that widely exists in the economy, and the use of fake original documents to record fake transactions is one of the most popular criminals in accounting. When the value of data is involved in the interests of the stakeholders, that is, data providers, data collectors or data processors, the interests tend to actuate the stakeholders to illegally interfere with the data collection and let them lose the veracity. However, the fraud is not the only cause that will lead the data to lose their veracity. Honest mistakes, such as count error, writing mistakes in recording, and misunderstanding of the data collection standard, can also make source data incorrect. China is undergoing insti-

Copyright © 2007, Idea Group Inc. Copying or distributing in print or electronic forms without written permission of Idea Group Inc. is prohibited.

tutional changes — from a centrally planned economy to a market economy, plus has gone through many other political upheavals in the past half century. In the transit period, relatively less stricter regulation and audit let the criminal data fraud become the main concern of the public in mass media.

Recognizing veracity of data as the only indicator of the quality of data is a bias that not only exists in China, but also outside of the country. Let us take the following statistical data as an example.

Over the past 26 years, the average annual growth of the Chinese economy reached 9.4%. Such a high growth rate has indeed attracted the attention of the world. With common professional rules and practices, the experts in the international statistical community never made comments on Chinese official statistics. The World Bank has accepted the official GDP figures of China as an accurate indicator of the economy since 1999. The United Nations and the International Monetary Fund have also recognized China's official statistics. However, there were some other people who seemed to make stories from Chinese official statistics. For instance, at one moment, they cooked up the theory of "China threat." On another occasion, they advocated "the collapse of the Chinese economy" by claiming that Chinese statistics were not true. Some even laid ungrounded censure on Chinese official statistical agencies (Li, 2005).

China's veracity issue of statistical data stems mainly from the radical change of the environment where the statistics system works. China is experiencing fundamental economic and social changes. There are more stakeholders in the market and the way people invest, get employed, earn money, and consume become diversified; economic structures and economic relations become more complicated; and disparities between regions, urban and rural areas, and between social clusters are more prominent. As a result, respondents of statistical surveys increased in folds, and changed frequently. They are more concerned with the protection of privacy and commercial confidentiality, and are less supportive and cooperative in surveys. Another unique issue in China is that subnational or local statistics are used as yardsticks to measure the performance of local governments in promoting economic and social development of regions. Statistics are at the risk of manipulation by local authorities. All these make it more and more difficult to organize statistical surveys.

The quality of Chinese official data has been frequently questioned, on the belief that there exists data falsification at the national level in order to meet ambitious economic growth targets set by the leadership. Some of such criticism of Chinese statistics appears in Rawski and Mead (1998), Cai (2000), and Meng and Wang (2000, 2001). However, a most recent research report by Holz (2002) examines this criticism, and shows it "to be unfounded as it is based on misunderstandings about the meaning and coverage of particular data." The report conducts a detailed analysis to question the evidence on the falsification of aggregate nationwide output and economic growth data and finds no evidence of data falsification at the national level. In another article by Xu (1999), it is disclosed that a delegation led by the World Bank's Chief Statistician, Robin Lynch, visited China in 1999 and made a thorough and comprehensive investigation of China's statistical systems, methods, departments, and personnel as well as data sources, collections, calculations, and so on. After the investigation, the World Bank recognized that China's official data on the national economy are of quality up to the international standard, and there is no ground on which the World Bank could readjust the data before publishing and using them. One relevant message from these two articles is that the quality of China's national statistics is at least not too poor to be used for serious research.

Copyright © 2007, Idea Group Inc. Copying or distributing in print or electronic forms without written permission of Idea Group Inc. is prohibited.

Timeliness of Data

Besides the veracity of data, Chinese people have understood that the timeliness of data is an important dimension of the quality of data since the end of the 1970s. In the central decision planning system, the quality or feasibility of the annual national economic planning was based not only on the veracity of statistics, but also on the timeliness of the data. In the later time of the Great Cultural Revolution, after Mr. Deng Xiao-Ping came back to lead the team of the central government, the releasing of the national statistical report became an important requirement to the National Bureau of Statistics. Since 1974, all large- or middle-sized enterprises, employing more than 1,000 people, were instructed to send their monthly statistical report directly to the NBS and to their superior authorities in five days after due date of the statistics. This measure was significant to NBS to predict the value of the statistical indicators before all the local reporting of the period completed. At that time, the NBS could issue the predictive value of the main national economic indicators in 10 working days after the due date of a statistical period to top leaders of the government. The official statistical data would be published in one month after a statistical period for the monthly reporting and in three or four months for the yearly reporting. Making the best use of the Chinese official statistical system and modern communication means, nowadays the NBS can publish the latest statistical data timely. General monthly statistics, for instance, can be published about 15 days after the end of the reference month, with more detailed data on financial aspect published 25 days after the end of the month.

For the decision makers and planners, the timeliness of statistical data is as important as the veracity. The more timely data are, the more complete the information the decision maker has. For the researchers of economic theory, the timeliness of statistical data is less important than the veracity, in most cases. In central decision planning systems, the population of the decision maker is much smaller than that in the market economy today in China, and change rate of the patterns of public thinking is slower than that of economic structure. Therefore, in the majority of Chinese public opinion, timeliness of statistical data is less important than veracity. However, as the population of the investor in the stock market in China is getting larger, the importance of the timeliness of data is significantly increasing today for the public.

Applicability of Data

The requirements for data are different for different people; for example, the consistency of data collection standards is very important for the researchers of economic theory, and less important to the decision makers. In China's statistics system today, some surveys and indicators that were developed during the central planning economy are still needed for the time being. On the other hand, there is an explosive demand for statistics from the new market-oriented economic system that requires statistical information to actually reflect the national conditions and strength, to record and describe the process of economic and social transitions, to report and monitor the performance of the economy, to collect and analyze public opinions and views, and to depict problems in the course of economic and social development. The demand for statistical data is increasing from the public in general, who are more closely watching and using statistical information released by government statistical agencies. Timeliness of statistics becomes more important in addition to accuracy

Copyright © 2007, Idea Group Inc. Copying or distributing in print or electronic forms without written permission of Idea Group Inc. is prohibited.

and comprehensiveness. In recent years, an increasing concern and demand comes from the international community for Chinese statistical data, as the Chinese economy is closely integrated with the world economy.

Nowadays, China has the following official statistic data:

1. **Accounting of real sectors:** China carries out both annual and quarterly accounting with the new SNA method recommended by the United Nations, and compiles monthly statistics of industrial added values, imports and exports via customs, consumption prices of residents, incomes and expenditures of residents, and the turnover of retail sales.

2. **Banking and monetary statistics:** The monthly statistics we produce at present include the main indicators such as money supply, credits of commercial banks, and so forth. As for quarterly statistics, we can basically meet the demand of the International Financial Statistics published by the International Monetary Fund and produce simple monetary essentials. For the annual statistics, China can produce the detailed monetary essentials.

3. **Financial statistics:** Relatively speaking, China is weak in the publication of these statistics and in the expansion of their coverage. Our monthly financial statistics cover now, however, some of the most important indicators of revenue and expenditure in financial statistics, while annual statistics are even more detailed in this regard.

4. **Statistics of balance of international payments:** Apart from compiling annual statistics of balance of international payments according to international standards, we are now trying to compile comparatively rough statistics of balance of international payments on a 6-month basis.

5. **Population, social, and science statistics:** As a country with such a large population, our data of population statistics is comparatively complete and systematic. Moreover, statistics of education, public health, culture, sports, science and technology, enforcement of law, and other social and scientific and technical developments are also carried out on a normal basis.

To meet the requirement of data from the users, the NBS should design some new surveys and indicators, as well as keep the definition and the manipulation standard of the surveys and indicators stable. If it is necessary to modify the definition of some statistical indicator, the quantity relationship between the statistical results should be clear. The data user can use other statistical data to adjust the statistical results, so that the items in the time series of the statistical indicator are comparable. A recoverable definition change will destroy the consistency of a time series of data, and let it lose the value for researchers.

Social Issues in China's IQ Management

As discussed in the last section, the veracity of China's statistical and accounting is affected by the following human factors:

1. Legal person or natural person deliberately submit or declare incorrect data to obtain some illegal benefits or avoid legal obligation

Copyright © 2007, Idea Group Inc. Copying or distributing in print or electronic forms without written permission of Idea Group Inc. is prohibited.

2.   Concern of the public about the protection of privacy or of firms about the protection of commercial confidentiality causes the response rate of some surveys to be lower

3.   The local governments illegally interfere substatistics to obtain political interests, or some of the officers illegally interfere with substatistics for their career

4.   Honest human mistakes, such as misunderstandings of the definition or meaning of statistical indicators, count error, and writing mistakes in recording, lead the information to lose veracity

Fraud and Crime in the Information Disclosure in China's Securities Market

Similar to the Enron case in the U.S., China revealed dozens of fraud and crime cases in its securities market.

Incomplete statistics show that during July of 2000 and 2001, 11 listed companies have been investigated and prosecuted by the China Securities Regulatory Commission (CSRC) for improper listing operation against regulations. Nearly 30 companies have been condemned by the stock exchanges. Among these are some companies that disclose falsified performance, such as Guangxia (Yinchuan) Industry Co. Ltd., Zhengzhou Baiwen Co. Ltd., Macat, and so forth, and hide important information on guarantee and associated transaction, such as Huafang Company/Mailyard and MACRO. Some broke the regulations on trust investment, such as Liaohe Oilfield, Unicom Guomai Communications, and so forth. Twenty-three companies failed to release medium-term record alarm bulletins in time (Du, 2001).

Guangxia (Yinchuan) Industry Co. Ltd. (Yinguangxia) was set up in January 1994 and originally engaged in computer software. Prior to seeking a listing on the Shenzhen stock exchange, it redirected its activities into wine growing and subsequently diversified into real estate, hotels, and car dealerships. In 2001 it made plans for listing on the Hong Kong main board, but these plans were undermined when *Caijing* published allegations of serious fraudulent misrepresentation. At the core of the allegation was misrepresentation of the company's export activities, in particular, the wrongful claim that the company had close ties to an old well-established German company. In addition, the company had misstated the financial accounts of its subsidiaries. Only after the press had revealed this fraudulent scheme did the Shenzhen stock exchange and China's financial market regulator, the CSRC, become active and launched an investigation. During 1998-2001, its falsified revenue accumulated to 1049.6 million yuan, and hidden costs to 49.45 million yuan; as a result, the falsified profit is 771.57 million yuan.

Moreover, some agency institutions, including lawyers' offices, accountants' offices, and stockbrokers' offices, gang up with the listed companies practicing fraud. This is an extremely serious problem plaguing China's stock market. Just over one year after Sanjiu Medicine got listed, its large shareholders and related institutions have taken up over 2.5 billion yuan, accounting for 96% of its whole net assets. This has badly violated the benefits of middle and small investors and directly threatened the security of assets of the listed companies. MACRO made a guarantee for its former large shareholders for a loan of 75.048 million yuan in June 1999. Until 2001, it still shoulders the guarantee for 40.820 million yuan remaining from its former large shareholders. With such a huge amount of guarantee on hand, MACRO absolutely presents great risks. However, it even failed to fulfill

Copyright © 2007, Idea Group Inc. Copying or distributing in print or electronic forms without written permission of Idea Group Inc. is prohibited.

the obligation to release related information in time. In this way, MACRO has seriously violated the "Regulation of Listing." In addition, in the first two days after Huafang Company got listed, the 85.7421 million shares of the company held by Huacheng Investment, the company's largest shareholder, were seized. All of these problems reflect the severely improper operation by listed companies. Yet before the problems were exposed, some listed companies just regarded the information-releasing regulations as a trifling matter and did everything they could to conceal and deceive the public. Directors of the companies even banished their responsibility and credit from their minds (Du, 2001).

Law Enforcement Against the Fraud in the Information Disclosure

The law enforcements against the fraud in the information disclosure are a main weapon to protect the minority shareholders from the fraudulent misrepresentation of the CEOs and board of directors. Here we distinguish between private and public law enforcement. Private enforcement refers to civil litigation, whereas public enforcement assesses regulatory enforcement activities taken by the state regulator, the CSRC, and the stock exchanges. If the law enforcement is effective, the cost of fraudulent misrepresentation will be high and the fraud in the information disclosure will be diminished.

Private Enforcement

Private enforcement of investor rights have virtually been absent in China so far, not because of a lack of demand for them, but because courts have restricted investor law suits (Chen, 2003). Private litigation began to take off only in 2001 in response to a fraud at Guangxia Corporation, which was exposed by the financial journal *Caijing* (Magida, 2003). Disgruntled investors sought to take the matter into their own hands and brought civil action; 1,000 cases were filed in Wuxi, Jiangsu Province against Guangxia alone. A trial date for the Guangxia case was set for October 15, 2001, but prior to that date, the Chinese Supreme Peoples' Court (SPC) intervened with a "notice" that temporarily banned all investor lawsuits in China. The notice stated, "our country's capital markets are in a pe-

Table 1. Private enforcement in Chinese courts (Source: Compilation by authors from press reports; no claim is made that they fully reflect all pending cases)

Date	Defendant	Litigants	Court	Status
09/2001	Yorkpoint	Science and Technology	Beijing #1 Intermediate People's Court, Guangzhou Intermediate People's Court	Pending
06/2002	ST Jiuzhou	3 investors	Xiamen Intermediate People's Court	Rejected on procedural grounds
11/2002	Jiabao Industrial	1 investor	Shanghai #2 Intermediate People's Court	Investor receives compensation in settlement

Copyright © 2007, Idea Group Inc. Copying or distributing in print or electronic forms without written permission of Idea Group Inc. is prohibited.

Table 1. continued

11/2002	Hongguang	11 investors	Chengdu Intermediate People's Court	Investors settle with individual underwriter through mediation; cases against company still pending
12/2002	Jiabao Industrial	24 investors	Shanghai #2 Intermediate People's Court	Pending
09/2003	Daqing Lianyi	381 investors	Harbin Intermediate Court (Heilongjiang Province)	Current Status
2003	Bohai Group	1 investor	Jinan Intermediate People's Court	
02/2003	Jinzhou Gang	1 investor	Shenyang Intermediate People's Court	Pending
02/2003	ST Tongda	5 investors	Shanghai #1 Intermediate People's Court	Pending
03/2003	Shengwan Keji	72 investors	Harbin Intermediate People's Court	Pending
03/2003	Sanjiu Yiyao	3 investors	Shenzhen Intermediate People's Court	Pending
03/2003	ST Tianyi	1 investor	Wuhan Intermediate People's Court	Pending
04/2004	Yinguangxia	Several investors	Yinchuan Intermediate People's Court	Pending

riod of continuous standardization and development and a number of problems have arisen including insider trading, cheating, market manipulation and other behaviors." The court acknowledged that these behaviors "infringe upon investor's legal rights," but pointed out that "under current legislative and judicial limits [courts] still don't have the conditions to accept and hear this type of cases." The notice was opposed by investors as well as law firms representing them and was also criticized by the CSRC, which had supported investor litigation. In January 2002, the SPC modified the notice of September 2001. The court stated that investors might bring civil action for misrepresentation of information, however, not for insider trading or market manipulation. Lower level courts were directed to hear cases, but only after the CSRC had investigated them and had found wrongdoing. A lawsuit had to be filed within two years after the CSRC's rulings. Individual, or independent, actions as well as group, or joint, actions (*Gongtong*) were permitted, but class actions were explicitly ruled out. In January 2003 the SPC issued more extensive rules governing investor lawsuits, the Private Securities Litigation Rules (hereinafter, PSLRs). The 13 PSLRs relax the rules on joint litigation. Litigants are allowed to file jointly and to elect between two and five representatives. The PSLRs also require lawsuits filed in the jurisdiction where the defendant company is registered. This rule is likely to reinforce the well-known "home-bias" of China's courts (Lubman, 1995). It also implies that expertise in securities matters will take

Copyright © 2007, Idea Group Inc. Copying or distributing in print or electronic forms without written permission of Idea Group Inc. is prohibited.

a long time to build, as these cases will not be pooled in courts with the greatest expertise. Since the PSLRs were issued, many investor lawsuits have been refiled to comply with these rulings. Table 1 summarizes lawsuits filed after the September 2002 SPC ruling that have been widely reported in the Chinese press and their current state of resolution. So far not a single civil law case has resulted in liability imposed by a court, although some cases have been settled after court mediation. We interpret this evidence to suggest that so far civil liability has little deterrence effect.

Public Enforcement

Public law enforcement in the form of fines or other sanctions imposed by a regulator has been equally weak. Today the major regulatory agency of China's financial markets is China's Securities Regulatory Commission (CSRC). In the early days regulatory law enforcement powers were scattered among various state agents, including the state owned stock exchanges, the People's Bank of China (PBC), the CSRC, and the State Council Securities Commission (SCSC). The centralization of regulatory functions was a response to failures of this governance structure. Investor riots broke out in 1992 after it was discovered that the shares of a company to be floated to the public had been almost fully subscribed by government insiders, including agents of the PBC (Walter & Fraster, 2003). This event prompted the State Council to establish the State Council Securities Commission (SCSC) as well as the CSRC. In 1998, the two agencies were merged into a single agency, the CSRC. In 1998 the CSRC assumed ministerial status and in 1999 China's first comprehensive Securities Law was enacted. The law vests the CSRC with the primary power to regulate markets, yet allows it to delegate decisions to the stock exchanges. Under the law, the CSRC may issue implementing regulations. In fact, the CSRC has made extensive use of this authority by enacting a host of rules and regulations for issuing companies and intermediaries. One of the most important changes for the CSRC's role as regulator of financial markets came in 2000 with the expansion of its enforcement units in the central office in Beijing, as well

Table 2. Public enforcement by Chinese regulators 1998-2004 (Source: Enforcement data made available by CSRC; number of listed companies from http://www.csrc.gov.cn/en/stat-info/index.en)

Year	Enforcement Actions Taken by Regulatory Agencies*	Which Punishment	Number of Companies Listed on 2 Major Exchanges
1998	3	3	853
1999	12	9	950
2000	16	7	1088
2001	71	9	1160
2002	62	8	1235
2003	51	11	1287
Totals	215	47	N/A

*Note: *enforcement activities include actions taken by the CSRC, the Shanghai, and Shenzhen Stock Exchanges and other enforcement agencies, N/A = not applicable*

Copyright © 2007, Idea Group Inc. Copying or distributing in print or electronic forms without written permission of Idea Group Inc. is prohibited.

as in its local branch offices (Walter & Fraster, 2003). Still, available data on enforcement activities reflect a declining trend. Table 2 summarizes enforcement activities by the CSRC from 1998 until the end of March 2004. The numbers stand for enforcement events, not companies against which enforcement actions were taken, suggesting that the total number of companies that were subject to enforcement proceedings may be even lower.

Laws and the Effort to Improve Veracity of Statistics

The Statistics Law of the People's Republic of China was adopted at the Third Session of the Standing Committee of the Sixth National People's Congress, on December 8, 1983, and was revised in accordance with the Decision of the Standing Committee of the National People's Congress on Revising the Statistics Law of the People's Republic of China, adopted on May 15, 1996. Chapter 5 of the statistics law regulated the legal responsibility of the relevant people:

> *Article 26 Leading members of local authorities, departments or units who alter statistical data without authorization, or fabricate statistical data, or compel or prompt statistics institutions or statisticians to tamper with or fabricate statistical data shall be given administrative sanctions according to law and criticized in a circulated notice by the statistics institutions of the people's governments at or above the county level.*
>
> *Any leading member of local authorities, departments or units who retaliates against the statisticians who refuses to fabricate statistical data or opposes doing so shall be given administrative sanctions according to law; if the case constitutes a crime, he shall be investigated for criminal responsibility according to law.*
>
> *Statisticians who participate in tampering with or fabricating statistical data shall be criticized in a circulated notice and given administrative sanctions in accordance with law by the statistics institutions of the people's governments at or above the county level; or the said institutions may suggest that the departments concerned give them administrative sanctions in accordance with law.*
>
> *Article 27 Any unit or individual under statistical investigation that commits one of the following violations shall be ordered to put it right and criticized in a circulated notice by the statistics institutions of the people's governments at or above the county level; if the violation is relatively serious, administrative sanctions shall be given to the persons who are directly in charge and other persons who are directly responsible for it:*
>
> *1.   Making false entries in statistical data or concealing statistical data;*
> *2.   Falsifying or tampering with statistical data; or*
> *3.   Refusing to submit statistical reports or repeatedly delaying their submission.*
>
> *Any enterprise, institution and self-employed industrialist or businessman that commits any of the violations mentioned in the preceding paragraph shall be given a disciplinary warning by the statistics institution of the people's govern-*

Copyright © 2007, Idea Group Inc. Copying or distributing in print or electronic forms without written permission of Idea Group Inc. is prohibited.

ment at or above the county level, and may also be fined. However, if the same party has been fined for the same violation according to other laws, it shall not be fined a second time.

Article 28 If a person, in violation of the provisions of this Law, tampers with or fabricates statistical data and thus gains titles of honor, material rewards or promotion, the institution that made such decision or the institution at a higher level, or a supervisory institution shall have the titles of honor annulled, the material rewards recovered and the promotion canceled.

Article 29 Whoever makes use of statistical investigation to steal State secrets or violates the provisions of this Law regarding the maintenance of secrets shall be punished according to provisions of relevant laws.

Whoever makes use of statistical investigation to jeopardize public interests or engage in fraud shall be ordered by the statistics institution of the people's government at or above the county level to set it right and his illegal gains shall be confiscated, and he may also be fined; if the case constitutes a crime, he shall be investigated for criminal responsibility according to law.

Article 30 Statistics institutions or statisticians that, in violation of the provisions of this Law, disclose single-item personal or family investigation data or commercial secrets of an investigated unit or individual and thus cause losses shall bear civil liability, and the persons who are directly in charge and other persons who are directly responsible for the case shall be given administrative sanctions according to law.

Article 31 Any State organ that, in violation of the provision of this Law, draws up and issues statistical investigation forms without submitting the matter for examination or for the record shall be ordered by the statistics institution of the people's government at or above the county level to set it right and criticized in a circulated notice.[1]

In order to diminish the illegal conduct of obtaining political status, honor, and economic returns by providing misleading statistics, China amended the Detailed Regulation for the Implementation of the Statistics Law in 1999, stipulating that government officials involved in the production of misleading statistics will be punished. China waged a nationwide inspection in 2001 against fraud by local officials who distort statistics for political gain. In this year, the NBS discovered more than 62,000 cases of violating the Statistics Law. Among the cases, more than 19,000 have been put under investigation. By the end of October, more than 13,000 of the investigated cases had been concluded, with a number of offenders punished.

Organizations in China's IQ Management

China's Official Statistics Organizations

China's government sets up statistical agencies from the top to the bottom, which constitute the system of government comprehensive statistics. The National Bureau of Statistics

Copyright © 2007, Idea Group Inc. Copying or distributing in print or electronic forms without written permission of Idea Group Inc. is prohibited.

(NBS) is an agency directly under the State Council and has direct responsibility to the State Council. It takes charge of the organization, leadership, and integration of nationwide statistical work and national accounts work. The governmental departments (ministers and commissions, including the People's Bank of China) have their own statistical system.

System of Government Statistics Bureaus

Statistics bureaus are set up in central, provincial, municipal, and county governments in China. At the township level, full-time or part-time statisticians have been stationed to coordinate and manage statistical work. In addition, the National Bureau of Statistics (NBS) exercises direct control over the Rural Social and Economic Survey Organization, the Urban Social and Economic Survey Organization, and the Enterprise Survey Organization. The Statistics Law has regulated the functions and responsibilities of various statistical organizations.

The National Bureau of Statistics exercises the following functions and responsibilities:

1.   Formulating regulations concerning statistical work and programs to modernize statistical work and state statistical investigation plans, leading and coordinating national statistical work, and checking and supervising the implementation of statistical laws, regulations, and systems according to the relevant laws, administrative regulations, state policies, and plans.
2.   Improving the national economic accounting system and the system of statistical indicators, formulating the system of nationally unified forms for basic data reporting, formulating, solely or jointly with relevant departments, the national statistical standards and examining and approving departmental statistical standards.
3.   Under leadership of the State Council, organizing jointly with relevant departments major general survey of the national conditions and national strength, organizing and coordinating sample investigations of national social and economic conditions in urban and rural areas.
4.   In accordance with the needs of the state in deciding policies, formulating plans and carrying out administration, to collect, sort out, and provide basic statistical data of the nation and conduct statistical analysis, forecast and supervision of the conditions of national economy and social development.
5.   Examining the statistical investigation plans and the investigation programs of the various departments under the State Council and exercising control over the investigation forms issued by the various departments under the State Council.
6.   Checking, examining and approving, controlling, announcing, and publishing national basic statistical data and regularly issuing statistical bulletins concerning the conditions of national economy and social development.
7.   Leading and managing the investigation teams responsible for sample investigations of the national social and economic conditions in the urban and rural areas.
8.   Organizing and guiding national studies of statistical science, statistical education, training of statistical personnel, and publication of statistical books and periodicals.
9.   Conducting international exchanges in statistical work and statistical science.

Copyright © 2007, Idea Group Inc. Copying or distributing in print or electronic forms without written permission of Idea Group Inc. is prohibited.

The functions and responsibilities of the statistical agencies under the local people's governments at and above county level are:

1. Accomplishing tasks of national statistical investigations, implementing state statistical standards, and implementing the systems of nationally unified forms for basic statistical reporting.
2. Drafting plans to modernize local statistical work in their respective administrative areas, working out statistical investigation plans and programs, leading and coordinating the statistical work in their respective administrative areas including the work arranged by the central and local authorities, checking and supervising the implementation of statistical laws, regulations, and systems.
3. Collecting, sorting out, and providing basic statistical data and conducting statistical analysis, forecast, and supervision of the conditions of economic and social development in their respective administrative areas in accordance with local needs for planning and management.
4. Examining the statistical investigation plans and programs of the various departments in their respective administrative areas and exercising control over the investigation forms devised and issued by the various departments in their respective administrative areas.
5. Checking, examining and approving, managing, announcing, and publishing the basic statistical data of their respective administrative areas according to relevant state stipulations. The statistical agencies under the people's governments of the provinces, autonomous regions, and municipalities shall regularly publish statistical bulletins on the conditions of the economic and social development in their respective administrative areas. The statistical agencies under the people's governments of autonomous prefectures, counties, and autonomous counties, cities, and districts under jurisdiction of cities shall publish local statistical bulletins according to the decisions of the local people's governments at the same level.
6. Exercising unified administration over the teams responsible for sample investigation of the social and economic conditions in the urban and rural areas in their respective administrative areas.
7. Organizing and guiding the various departments and units in their administrative areas to strengthen their basic statistical work, statistical education, training of statistical personnel, and studies of statistical science, assessing the performance of the personnel of statistical agencies of the people's governments in their respective administrative areas.
8. The statistical agencies under the local people's governments at and above county level shall be under the dual leadership of the people's governments at the same level and the statistical agencies of the people's governments at higher level. In the statistical work, they shall be mainly subject to the leadership of the statistical agencies of the people's governments at higher level.

The statisticians in townships and towns shall be responsible for local comprehensive statistics. Their functions and responsibilities are:

1. Accomplishing tasks of the state and local statistical investigations, implementing the system of national statistical standards and the system of nationally unified statistical

Copyright © 2007, Idea Group Inc. Copying or distributing in print or electronic forms without written permission of Idea Group Inc. is prohibited.

standards of basic forms for statistical reporting, and checking and supervising the implementation of statistical laws, regulations, and systems.

2.   Collecting, sorting out, analyzing, providing, and managing the basic statistical data of the townships and towns in accordance with the state relevant stipulations.

3.   Organizing and guiding relevant departments and individuals of townships and towns in strengthening rural basic statistical work, improving systems of statistical accounting and statistical files in the townships and towns, and organizing the statistical work in places within their jurisdiction.

4.   The people's governments in the townships and towns shall post full-time or part-time statisticians in accordance with the relevant stipulations of the Statistics Law and the needs of the local statistical work and shall set up and improve a network of statistical information among townships and towns. In statistical work, statisticians shall be under the leadership of the statistical agencies under the people's government at the county level.

5.   The statistical work in villages shall be performed by persons specially appointed by the villagers' committees. In statistical work, these persons shall be under the leadership of township and town statisticians.

Statistical System of Governmental Departments Other Than NBS

The statistical system of governmental departments is composed of statistical agencies or offices of ministries and commissions (such as the Statistical Department of the People's Bank of China) and the corresponding offices of the local branches of these ministries and commissions (such as the statistical offices at the prefecture-level branches of the People's Bank of China). Major responsibilities of these departments and offices include:

1.   Organizing and coordinating statistical work of the functional departments of ministries and commissions, fulfillment of national and/or local statistical surveys and statistical programs, and collection, processing, and supply of statistical data about relevant departments.

2.   Conducting statistical analysis of relevant economic activities related to the specialized functions of the ministries concerned.

3.   Organizing and coordinating the statistical work of the enterprises and institutions affiliated to the ministries, including production and report of specialized statements of the ministries concerned.

Statistical Agencies in Enterprises

The statistical agencies in enterprises or institutions and persons in charge of comprehensive statistics in the units shall perform the following functions and responsibilities:

1.   Organizing, guiding, and coordinating in a comprehensive way the statistical work of the various functional organs and subordinate organs in the units, accomplishing jointly with them the tasks of the state, departmental, and local statistical investigations, formulating and implementing the statistical plans and systems of the units, implementing, checking, and supervising the implementation of statistical laws, regulations, and systems.

Copyright © 2007, Idea Group Inc. Copying or distributing in print or electronic forms without written permission of Idea Group Inc. is prohibited.

2.   In accordance with relevant state stipulations, reporting and providing statistical data to the competent departments, the statistical agencies under the local people's governments and statisticians in townships and towns and conducting statistical analysis and supervision of the implementation of the plans and the results of management and administration in the units.

3.   Administering the statistical investigation forms and basic statistical data of the units.

4.   In conjunction with relevant functional organs, strengthening systems of measurement and testing systems, improving systems of original records, statistical files of bookkeeping, and accounting systems.

5.   The statistical agencies or persons in charge of statistics in enterprises and institutions shall be under the guidance of the statistical agencies under the local people's governments or township and town statisticians in statistical work.

6.   In small- and medium-sized enterprises and institutions where there are no full-time statisticians, some persons can be appointed to be especially responsible for statistical work.

Because the current situation of China's statistics organization, over a long period of time, the tasks of China's government statistics have been mainly to serve for the economic management by the State Council and governments at provincial and local levels. In the design of statistical survey schemes and the arrangement and dissemination of statistical information, consideration is more taken into the needs of governments at various levels than those of enterprises, institutions for teaching and scientific research, and the public so as to reduce the benefits of government statistics to the society objectively. To change this situation, recently NBS set up a statistics library that is open to the public and will publish and provide more statistics, including the form of magnet medium, and launch a variety of service activities such as telephone consultation in order to improve the functions of statistics serving for the society.

Better Job Information Quality Assessment (GDP, in Particular)

Assessment and monitoring of information quality of major statistical indicators is one of the important ways to improve statistical data's quality. Assessment on statistical data's quality is to make scientific, realistic, and practical assessment of the statistical data obtained from survey and processing, and to make comments on data's accuracy. The purpose is to have a good understanding of the reliability and discrepancy of statistical data, to make good use of them, and to take effective and on-target measures of improving information quality, so as to meet the needs of governments in macroeconomic management.

The key statistical indicators of gross output that can mirror development of economy are logically interrelated. These indicators could be direct reflections of China's economic activities in their totality and the interrelationships among indicators themselves. Assessment on the information quality of such indicators could improve the quality of statistical data in general. It is therefore a regular assessment on the quality of integrated gross-output statistical data indicators, which reflect national economic activities, that should be made. For this purpose NBS has laid down rules for the information quality assessment and

Copyright © 2007, Idea Group Inc. Copying or distributing in print or electronic forms without written permission of Idea Group Inc. is prohibited.

asked departments in NBS and Provincial Bureaus of Statistics to make assessments on the following 13 indicators: GDP, gross production value of agriculture, grain output, per capita net income for peasants, added value of industry, growth rate of industry, output of major industrial products, investments in fixed assets, total retail sales of consumer goods, total population, price indices, per capita disposable income of urban residents, and living expenditure. A self-check and assessment on statistical data's quality of major indicators are made by sector at the frequency of a month, a quarter, half year, and a year. A check at random and reassessment are made on a number of selected units at different levels. The outcome of such check and reassessment is used in comparisons and analysis with aggregate data. Further, a systematic analysis using incorporated methods of assessment and detailed explanation and reasoning on the quality and accuracy of major statistical indicators are made. It is also required that the fundamental work of statistics should be enhanced and the rules of keeping statistical accounting book and primary records should be found and perfected, so that the channels of statistics could keep open, data processing is complete, and data are accurate.

NBS is responsible for assessment on quality of statistical data from each province and for assessment on link-up of principal national statistical data. The Provincial Bureaus of Statistics are responsible for assessment on quality of statistical data and link-up of principal statistical data of their own region. The departments in charge of national accounts are responsible for calling pertinent units in their respective bureaus into regular meetings of assessment, to make analysis and deliberations on quality of major statistical data, and put forward comments and measures for improvement.

GDP is a key indicator of economic scale and growth rate. NBS has laid down separate and strict requirements on GDP data's quality assessment:

1.   The basic data by industries for GDP calculation in each province must be approved by NBS before using such data in calculation;
2.   NBS has the right to demand that Provincial Bureaus of Statistics make adjustment on those GDP data that lack fidelity.

Furthermore, all the Departments of NBS dispatch, each year, officials and specialists to visit Provincial Bureaus of Statistics and grassroots reporting units to verify statistical data's quality.

The Organizations for Supervision of the Statistical Activities

The statistics law regulated the function of the NBS and its branches, as well as obligations of the statisticians in various government departments at different levels. Statistics supervision over the government performance is an important function of the government statistics. The behavior of the statisticians should also be under supervision.

According to Section 2 of Article 6 of the Statistics Law of the People's Republic of China, "Statistical work shall be subject to public supervision. Any unit or individual shall have the right to expose or report unlawful activities in statistical work, such as fraud and deception, and any unit or individual that has rendered meritorious service by exposing or reporting shall be rewarded."

Copyright © 2007, Idea Group Inc. Copying or distributing in print or electronic forms without written permission of Idea Group Inc. is prohibited.

The Organizational Efforts for Improving the Information Disclosure of Listed Corporations

The corporate scandals and capital flight cases that emerged in mid-2001 prompted officials at CSRC and other state regulatory bodies to put corporate governance at the top of their list of priorities for 2002. Reflecting this commitment, in January 2002 CSRC issued the Code of Corporate Governance of Listed Companies in China.

The new code aims to introduce solid corporate governance in listed companies by elevating requirements on accounting procedures and information disclosure, introducing independent directors' systems, and tightening the supervision of corporate management. CSRC officials, who drafted the code, and other similar legislation in the past, used the U.S. legal and regulatory systems as models. Though the code directly addresses many of the existing problems in China's financial sector, it will only prove effective if company managers honestly implement — and CSRC strictly enforces — its provisions.

Yet these provisions are promising. For example, the code expands the rights of shareholders. Article 2 states that minority shareholders should have equal status with other shareholders, and Article 4 gives shareholders the right to protect their interests through civil litigation and other legal approaches. Article 8 requires that listed companies make a genuine effort to use modern telecommunications technologies in shareholders' general meetings to improve shareholder participation. And Article 11 gives institutional investors more weight in the decision-making process, including in the nomination of directors.

The code attempts to strengthen the roles of the boards of directors and supervisors. According to Articles 29 and 31, a listed company must establish transparent procedures to select the board of directors, and a listed company in which the controlling shareholder owns a stake in excess of 30% should adopt a cumulative voting mechanism to ensure the voting interests of minority shareholders. Article 49 requires listed companies to introduce independent directors who do not hold any other positions within the company. Articles 60 and 61 state that members of the board of supervisors must be permitted access to information related to operational status and be allowed to hire independent intermediary agencies for professional consultation, without interference from other company employees.

Finally, the code includes specific provisions on information disclosure. Articles 88 and 89 require the listed company to disclose promptly any information that may have a substantial impact on the decision making of shareholders or associated parties. Articles 13 and 14 require the listed companies to fully disclose prices of related party transactions and prohibit them from providing financial collateral to related entities. Article 92 requires the listed companies to promptly release detailed information on controlling shareholders. And Articles 25 and 27 require controlling shareholders to honor the independence of the listed companies and to avoid interfering or directly competing with the listed entities (Shi & Weisert, 2002).

Improving the quality of information disclosure is much more difficult than in the statistics arena. There is no empirical investigation that can prove the measures of China's government on corporate governance are effective.

Copyright © 2007, Idea Group Inc. Copying or distributing in print or electronic forms without written permission of Idea Group Inc. is prohibited.

Technological Issues in China's IQ Management

Lack of technological support is an important problem that let China lag behind the developed countries in IQ management. The technology gap is on two aspects: knowledge of standards and the IT applications. In this section we take statistics and taxation as examples to introduce China's practice.

Reforming the National Account System and Improving the Quality of National and Regional Account Data

China adopted the general data distribution system that is recommended by the International Monetary Foundation (IMF) to release official statistics. The move is part of the Chinese government's drive to improve the quality of statistics and services in response to transparency requirements after the country's entry into the World Trade Organization. The statisticians are asked to establish a set of statistic rules, a system and methods according to the practical conditions of China, in line with international practice. China is continuing to reform its statistics system by adopting a new and precise method of calculating agricultural and industrial growth.

At present, we are implementing the National Economic Accounting System of China 2002, which is based on the 1993 SNA of the United Nations and is integrated with the internationally accepted standards and rules. We have revised the procedures and publications of GDP data, which now involve three steps of preliminary estimates, verified estimates, and final figures. We have established a system for the joint evaluation of provincial and local GDP data, under which provincial GDP figures are to be authorized by the National Bureau of Statistics for release as official data after joint evaluation. To increase the transparency of compilation, an advisory group has been established that consists of external experts on national accounts, who will provide their views on the GDP data on a quarterly basis. The national accounts data released by the National Bureau of Statistics of China are reliable, and they reflect the general level and trend of development of the Chinese economy.

Establishing a Scientific System of Statistical Surveys to Meet the Needs of Economic and Social Development

In order to ensure the accuracy of official statistics, the NBS had begun to adopt sampling methods in 1999, instead of relying on reports by local governments. The NBS collected data directly from the 5,000 biggest industrial enterprises and 3,000 real estate companies in the country this year so as to avoid intervention of local governments. The NBS will continue to spread the use of sampling and establish a new set of calculation methods for industrial and agricultural growth next year.

China modified the conduct of censuses by introducing a new Economic Census, which merged the census of manufacturing industries, the census of service industries, and the census of establishments, and included the construction sector in the new census. Two economic censuses are to be conducted in a span of 10 years. The first economic census of China, which is currently in full operation successfully despite its huge size, has mobilized over 10 million enumerators and supervisors with an estimated budget of over 3 billion RMB

Copyright © 2007, Idea Group Inc. Copying or distributing in print or electronic forms without written permission of Idea Group Inc. is prohibited.

yuan. In the first economic census the NBS invited the experts of the UNSD and shared their views and experiences in economic census. Sample surveys are widely used in the collection of statistics on population, households, farm production, prices, and small business. The NBS abolished the approach of constant prices that have been in use for over 50 years by adopting the production indexes using price deflators. Over 5,000 large manufacturing enterprises and 3,000 construction companies are reporting their data through an Internet system, further improving the timeliness of statistics.

Development of Statistical Informatics System

At the same time, China will use information technology and the Internet to collect data. The work will be done next year through a national survey of basic units.

- **Expansion of statistical informatics system:** Expanding the network of national statistics to strengthen capability of data collection transmission, processing, management and dissemination capability, and to promote data sharing among government agencies.
- **Development of national macroeconomic data bank:** The country set up a renewable data bank about all basic units of social and economic activities in China, updating it with the launch or closure of every company with legal person status.
- **Enhancing the quality of source data through electronic data recording and transmission from enterprise and promoting use of new technology in statistics:** Use of optical/electronic technology, remote sensing, geographic information system (GIS), and hand-held data collection devices.

Antifraud with Computer-Based Information Systems

The asymmetry of information is the foundation of fraud. Take the fraud with fraudulent original transaction document as an example. According to the principle of accounting, a legal original transaction document should include the information for auditing; that is, the auditor should be able to use the information for verifying the veracity of the data in the document. However, when some fraudulent original documents are mixed in the ocean of the original documents, the auditors will have a very difficult time finding them in a short period with manual verification. China has a successful case of antifraud in the value added taxation by using the information technology based on a nationwide computer network.

In 1994, China's taxation system in industry and commercial activities reformed into the value added tax (VAT) system. Because of the weakness of the monitoring system of taxation authorities at that time, the fraud with fraudulent tax receipts was a widespread crime in the economic domain. In some areas it was very severe, so that the government had to stop paying the VAT rebate for export. In an attempt to crackdown on tax fraud and evasion, China's central government announced plans to launch a nationwide computerized monitoring system, called the Golden Tax Project in 1995. The project, concentrated on keeping track of value-added tax payments in addition to supervising taxpayers' business activities and standardizing the behavior of tax collectors.

In an important step towards full implementation of the Golden Tax Project, taxation authorities first introduced certification monitoring and information management systems in

Copyright © 2007, Idea Group Inc. Copying or distributing in print or electronic forms without written permission of Idea Group Inc. is prohibited.

Beijing, Shanghai, Tianjin, and Chongqing municipalities and Jiangsu, Shandong, Liaoning, Zhejiang, and Guangdong provinces; then systems were put in place across the country in July 2001.

In December 2000, taxation authorities required a select group of companies, including industrial enterprises with annual sales of more than 1 million yuan (US$120,000) and commercial enterprises with annual sales of more than 1.8 million yuan (US$216,900), to use an antifraud monitoring system for business transactions.

These companies printed invoices using a computerized system that is connected to the State Administration of Taxation computers. By the end of 2002, all companies were required to install and use the monitoring system, a spokesman said, adding that China banned the use of hand-written invoices by January 1, 2003.

The Computerized VAT Monitoring System is a four-level computer network. It collects the data in the VAT invoices and VAT reports delivered by taxpayers, and stores them in a database. By periodic statistics analysis and sophisticated verifying of the system, they can find the clues of various kinds of fraud related to the VAT invoices, and send them to the relevant tax administration departments through a network to further verify. In addition to the cross verification of the data of VAT invoices, the system has a function to directly differentiate the fake invoices from the genuine invoices. The data on the VAT invoice printed by the specific printer of the system has an encrypted version on the same invoice. The key and algorithm of the encryption is confidential. When the taxation department verifies a VAT invoice, the system shall decrypt the encrypted data on the invoice and verify them with the plain data on it. If the plain data is not same as the decrypted data, the VAT invoice must be phony.

Since 2001, after the computerized VAT monitoring system went online, the number of cases related to fraudulent VAT invoicing has been decreasing; according to the National Administration of Taxation, in 2002, there were 28 cases of fraudulent VAT invoicing at the national level; of the 88 firms involved, 46 of them made fraudulent VAT invoices before 2001, 34 of them did in 2001, and only 8 of them did in 2002.[2]

Future Trends

The goal of Chinese information quality management is to enhance the quality of data and to guarantee data's veracity, timeliness, and applicability. With regard to statistical data, China will refer to international advanced statistical experience and establish a scientific, credible, and effective statistical system. In fact, China is taking the opportunity of GDP statistics reform to launch an overall reform of its statistical systems. Chinese Vice Premier, Zeng Peiyan, recently suggested that China establish a statistical regulation and method system that is integrated with international practices and the Chinese situation. The system proposed by Zeng consists of five parts: The first is a national economic accounting system, basically integrated with the SNA (system of national accounts), which is commonly used worldwide; the second is the statistical standard, which should be integrated with international practices; the third is a survey system; the fourth is a statistical indicator system, which is also basically integrated with international practices; and the fifth is a statistics system. NBS established three directly affiliated survey groups to obtain important statistical data.

Copyright © 2007, Idea Group Inc. Copying or distributing in print or electronic forms without written permission of Idea Group Inc. is prohibited.

In addition, China is going to establish a modern statistical survey system and national account system that is suitable to China's specific situation and is consistent with international statistical standards and practices, thus facilitating international comparison of statistical data. Furthermore, China is making full use of modern IT, such as computer systems, network communications, and databases to transform statistical operation to achieve high efficiency in survey design, data collection, transmission, processing, management, and dissemination. Finally, China is improving statistical legislation and supervision mechanisms and building up a large contingent of statisticians with profound knowledge on statistics with professional ethics and innovation through education and training programs.

With regard to financial data, first, China will deepen accounting reformation and carry out Accounting Law continuously. Then, electronic data processing accounting, which can markedly improve the quality of accounting data, will be strengthened. As a weapon, relative law should be perfected and carried out sternly. Finally, accountants' quality is very important, too. Establishing accounting ethics will also be given more attention.

These measures can improve the information quality and reduce data fraud to a certain extent. Nevertheless, big amelioration in institutions can improve the information quality radically. For instance, data providers should be impersonal and candid; their interests have no correlation with the statistical results. In the local leaders' evaluation arenas, their promotion and remuneration should be regardless of the economic performance. Compared to statistical data, improving the quality of information disclosure in accounting data is much more difficult. There is no empirical investigation that can prove the measures of China's government on the corporate governance are effective. However, protecting the benefits of minority stakeholders through policy and law is also a feasible measure to control the quality of information disclosure.

Conclusion

Nowadays Chinese people understand the quality of the information based on a multidimensional metrics. The veracity, timeliness, and applicability are the main dimensions. Because the veracity of the statistic data is closely connected with the credits of the government and the fraud in data disclosure directly affects the interests of millions of small investors, people pay more attention to be veracity of data.

Comparing the honest mistakes, deliberately falsify data is more severe. China's government put a lot of effort into registration on the statistical and accounting arena to crack down on fraud.

Through supervision across organizations and the different channels of statistics and surveys, China now can verify the main statistical indicator and ensure the veracity of the main statistical information.

With application of IT and adoption of the world standards, China made significant progress in all three main dimensions of information quality: the data fraud diminished; timeliness and applicability improved.

As in the transition period of social and economic structure reforming, China still has a lot of IQ problems at the macrolevel to solve. Without solutions to these problems, it is difficult for the public to pay attention to diminishing the honest mistakes in IQ management.

Copyright © 2007, Idea Group Inc. Copying or distributing in print or electronic forms without written permission of Idea Group Inc. is prohibited.

References

Cai, Y. (2000). Between state and peasant. Local cadres and statistical reporting in rural China. *The China Quarterly, 163*, 783-805.

Du, M. (2001). China stock market culling out "rotten apples." *Peoples' Daily*. Retrieved April 16, 2006, from http://english.people.com.cn/english/200110/11/eng20011011_82028.html

Holz, C. A. (2003). Fast, clear and accurate. How reliable are Chinese output and economic growth statistics? *The China Quarterly, 173*, 122-163.

Holz, C. A. (2004). China's statistical system in transition. Challenges, data problem, and institutional innovation. *Review of Income and Wealth, 50*(3), 381-409

La Porta, et al. (2004). *What works in securities laws?* Unpublished mimeograph, Harvard University.

Li, D. (2005). *China's official statistics. Challenges, measures and future development.* Retrieved April 16, 2006, from http://www.china-un.org/eng/smhwj/2005/t185674.htm

Lubman, S. (1995). The future of Chinese law. *The China Quarterly, 141*, 1-21.

Meng, L., & Wang, X. (2000). Dui Zhongguo jingji zengzhang tongji shuju kexindu de guji [An evaluation of the reliability of China's statistics on economic growth]. *Jingji Yanjiu [Economic Research Journal], 10*, 3-13.

Meng, L., & Wang, X. (2001). A reevaluation of China's economic growth. *China Economic Review, 12*(4), 338-406.

Rawski, T. G., & Mead, R. W. (1998). On the trail of China's phantom farmers. *World Development, 26*(5), 767-81.

Shi, S., & Weisert, D. (2002). Corporate governance with Chinese characteristics. *China Business Review, 29*(5).

Walter, C. E., & Fraster, J. T. H. (2003). *Privatizing China. The stock markets and their role in corporate reform*. Hoboken, NJ: John Wiley & Sons (Asia).

Xu, X. (1999). Shijie yinghang dui Zhongguo guanfang GDP shuju de tiaozheng he chongxin renke [Adjustment and reconfirmation of Chinese official data by the World Bank]. *Jingji Yanjiu [Economic Research Journal], 6*, 52-8.

Zhiwu, C. (2003). Capital markets and legal development. The China case. *China Economic Review, 14*, 451-484.

Endnote

[1]   The National Bureau of Statistics. Statistics Law of the People's Republic of China. http://www.stats.gov.cn/english/lawsandregulations/statisticallaws/t20020329_15257.htm, 2002-3-31/2005-8-15.

Copyright © 2007, Idea Group Inc. Copying or distributing in print or electronic forms without written permission of Idea Group Inc. is prohibited.

Chapter XII

The Effects of Information Quality on Supply Chain Performance:

New Evidence from Malaysia

Suhaiza Zailani, Universiti Sains Malaysia, Malayasia

Premkumar Rajagopal, Universiti Sains Malyasia, Malaysia

Abstract

This chapter introduces how information quality plays an important role in supply chain performance. In order to make smarter use of global resources, the companies should pay attention to the quality of information to provide better services to their customers. This chapter examines the factors influencing information quality and investigates the influences of information quality on supply chain performance. The information quality is classified into four types: accuracy, completeness, consistency, and timeliness. The influencing factors include technological, organizational, and environmental characteristics. Supply chain performance is measured based on financial and nonfinancial indices. It can be found that the extent of information quality will increase supply chain performance and the extent of information quality is influenced by technological, organizational, and environmental characteristics. The authors hope to understand the factors that influence information quality towards better supply chain performance and hope this will not only inform researchers of a better design for studying information quality but also assist in the understanding of intricate relationships between different factors.

Copyright © 2007, Idea Group Inc. Copying or distributing in print or electronic forms without written permission of Idea Group Inc. is prohibited.

Introduction

We are living in a technological age with knowledge workers and information factories, which receive input from external information sources, analyze and manage information, and create new knowledge. They give out information as output to the external world, producing information products. Hence, the quality of information is critical for the success of firms and managing information is their core competence. Pugsley et al. (2000) supported this in their study showing that an economy-based knowledge emerging with information is essential for any ongoing organization. The globalization of products, services, markets, and competition has increased the need for flexibility, quality, cost effectiveness, and timeliness (Hunter et al., 2002). A key resource for attaining these requirements is information quality and it has revolutionized business practices and now plays a more central part of business strategies (Pollard & Hayne, 1998).

In addition, growth in global business and technologies led to a dramatic rise in global supply chain. One key to effective supply chain is to make the materials function more efficiently (Bowersox, Closs, & Cooper, 2002). Supply chain has become an important source of competitive advantage. However, in order to deliver products quickly to customers, many companies seek to improve the information. Sauvage (2003) claimed that to fully satisfy the diversifying requirements of customers, many companies had improved their service efficiency by improving the quality of information. Chapman, Soosay, and Kandampully (2003) suggested that companies should pay more attention to information quality and the quality of information can only be implemented through technology, knowledge, and relationship networks.

Fuld (1998) warned companies of the dangers of old data and irrelevant information and noted that poor information quality on the chain can create impact to firms' business performance. Continuous technological advancement can assist companies to revolutionize the way they operate and conduct their business and the quality of information might enable companies to enhance their service abilities. Therefore the research questions of this study are: "What are the factors affecting the extent of information quality for companies?" and "Can information quality improve supply chain performance?" The study is conducted in Malaysia. Due to the trend of globalization, the Malaysian government has delivered several policies to make Malaysia a global supply chain center. Many companies in Malaysia have begun to pay more attention to information quality due to global supply chain policies. The next section illustrates a summary in information quality and supply chain performance, while the third section introduces the antecedents of information quality. A description of the research design and data collection in the fourth section leads us to an analysis of the results and a discussion of the findings are presented in the fifth section. This is followed by the conclusion and research implications.

Copyright © 2007, Idea Group Inc. Copying or distributing in print or electronic forms without written permission of Idea Group Inc. is prohibited.

Information Quality and
Supply Chain Performance

Information Quality

According to quality management literature, good product quality means the product fulfills its requirements. In the beginning of the quality management discipline, the concept of quality was only applicable to products. However present discussions include quality of services and information. Different strategies and tools, for example, quality control, quality awards, and statistical methods like six Sigma and ISO 9000 standards, can be used for implementing TQM ideas. Both TQM philosophy and TQM tools have a positive impact on business performance (Huang & Chen, 2002). However, the success factor is to recognize and develop core competencies of a business. Core competence is the capability to produce added value to the customer by combining existing resources and knowledge that has been growing in the company (Hammer, 2001). This capability to produce added value makes product or service imitations difficult to competitors. Since modern companies are information factories, their key competence is information management. Therefore developing information management skills and information quality is essential to their business.

According to Gelle and Karhu (2003), providing better tools to manage information in organizations is an essential part of quality management in information factories. Based on their study, to provide good quality information for business strategy in a company, they need to:

1.   Define the users' needs (their current problems)
2.   Plan and specify how information technology helps to fulfill customers' needs
3.   Implement methods and tools that conform to specifications
4.   Check how implementation fulfills customers' needs
5.   Plan how data quality can continuously be improved
6.   Implement small improvements

The modern view of quality consists of conformance to requirements (free of error) and the fulfillment of customer needs (quality of requirements and design). Information quality has been defined similarly as freedom of defects, such as inaccessibility, inaccuracy, out-of-date information, inconsistencies, incomplete and incomprehensive information, and possessing desirable characteristics, for example, timeliness, truthfulness, intelligibility, and significance (Gelle & Karhu, 2003). Information quality is typically conceptualized as a multidimensional concept. For example, in an early discussion of the quality of information systems, Davis and Olson (1985) identified three aspects of data quality: accuracy, precision, and completeness. Huh, Keller, Redman, and Watkins (1990) defined four dimensions of information quality: accuracy, completeness, consistency, and currency. They further defined accuracy as an agreement with either an attribute about a real world entity, a value stored in another database, or the result of an arithmetic computation. Completeness is defined with respect to some specific application and refers to whether all the data relevant to that application are present. Consistency refers to the absence of conflict between two datasets. Currency refers to whether the data are up to date.

Copyright © 2007, Idea Group Inc. Copying or distributing in print or electronic forms without written permission of Idea Group Inc. is prohibited.

Fox, Levitin, and Redman (1993) also identified these four dimensions of information quality (accuracy, completeness, consistency, and currency). Accuracy refers to whether information value matches some value considered to be correct. Completeness means that a collection of information contains values for all fields that should have values and that no records are missing. Consistency refers to whether information values conform to constraints that have been specified for that information. Currency refers to whether the information value is up to date. In contrast to these conceptual frameworks, Zmud (1978) and Madnick and Wang (1992) presented definitions of information quality derived from empirical obser-vation. Zmud (1978) used factor analysis to examine the dimensionality of the construct of information. Four dimensions were derived: quality of information, relevancy of information, quality of format, and quality of meaning. Madnick and Wang (1992) used observations of defective information in organizational databases to derive four components of information quality: completeness, accuracy, appropriateness, and consistency. Wand and Wang (1996) argued for a definition of information quality that is task-independent and identified four dimensions of intrinsic information quality: completeness, lack of ambiguity, meaningfulness,

Table 1. Information quality criteria

Class	Information Quality Criteria
Subject Criteria	Believability
	Concise representation
	Interpretability
	Relevancy
	Reputation
	Understandability
	Value-Added
Object Criteria	Completeness
	Customer Support
	Documentation
	Objectivity
	Price
	Reliability
	Security
	Timeliness
	Verifiability
Process Criteria	Accuracy
	Amount of data
	Availability
	Consistent representation
	Latency
	Response time

Copyright © 2007, Idea Group Inc. Copying or distributing in print or electronic forms without written permission of Idea Group Inc. is prohibited.

and correctness. These dimensions are said to be applicable across different applications applied to different tasks. On the other hand, increased speed and accuracy of information should strengthen relationships. Carter and Narasinhan (1996) highlighted accuracy and timeliness as important elements of information quality. Table 1 lists a comprehensive set of information quality criteria. These information quality criteria are taken from Naumann and Rolker (2000).

Definitions of Information Quality Criteria

1. **Availability:** percentage of time an information source is "up." Also: accessibility, reliability, irretrievability, performance.
2. **Accuracy:** quotient of the number of correct values in the source and the overall number of values in the source. Also: error rate, correctness, integrity, precision.
3. **Amount of data:** size of result. Also: essentialness.
4. **Believability:** degree to which the information is accepted as correct. Also: error rate, credibility, trustworthiness.
5. **Completeness:** quotient of the number of response items and the number of real world items. Also: coverage, scope, granularity, comprehensiveness, density, extent.
6. **Concise representation:** degree to which the structure of the information matches the information itself. Also: attribute granularity, occurrence identifiably, structural consistency, appropriateness, format precision.
7. **Consistent representation:** degree to which the structure of the information conforms to that of other sources. Also: integrity, homogeneity, semantic consistency, value consistency, portability, compatibility.
8. **Customer support:** amount and usefulness of online support through text, e-mail, phone, and so forth.
9. **Documentation:** amount and usefulness of documents with metainformation. Also: traceability.
10. **Interpretability:** Degree to which the information conforms to the technical ability of the consumer. Also: clarity of definition, simplicity.
11. **Latency:** amount of time until first information reaches user. Also: response time.
12. **Objectivity:** degree to which information is unbiased and impartial.
13. **Price:** monetary charge per query. Also: query value-to-cost ratio, cost-effective.
14. **Relevancy:** degree to which information satisfies the user's need. Also: domain precision, minimum redundancy, applicability, helpfulness.
15. **Reliability:** degree to which the user can trust the information. Note: *technical* reliability is synonymous to *availability*.
16. **Reputation:** degree to which the information or its source is in high standing. Also: credibility.
17. **Response time:** amount of time until complete response reaches the user. Also: performance, turnaround time.
18. **Security:** degree to which information is passed privately from user to information source and back. Also: privacy, access security.
19. **Timeliness:** age of information. Also: up-to-date, freshness, currentness.
20. **Understandability:** degree to which the information can be comprehended by the user. Also: ease of understanding.

Copyright © 2007, Idea Group Inc. Copying or distributing in print or electronic forms without written permission of Idea Group Inc. is prohibited.

21. **Value-added:** amount of benefit the use of the information provides.
22. **Verifiability:** degree and ease with which the information can be checked for correctness. Also: naturalness, traceability, provability.

Although there are no uniform lists for the information quality dimensions, the researchers adopt one of the commonly identified information quality dimensions for the purpose of this research:

1. Accuracy, which occurs when the recorded value is in conformity with the actual value;
2. Timeliness, which occurs when the recorded value is not out of date;
3. Completeness, which occurs when all values for a certain variable are recorded; and
4. Consistency, which occurs when the representation of the data values is the same in all cases (Ballou & Pazer, 1987).

Supply Chain Performance

Many models, stemming from conventional business and engineering principles, have been proposed to handle supply chain operational and design issues (Chopra & Meindl, 2001). However, models for the overall supply chain performance, which ought to consider the entire channel performances are scarce. Based on the existing literature on supply chain performance, the most promising model for supply chain performance is the supply chain operations reference (SCOR) model developed by the supply chain council (SCC). The SCOR model focuses on both the financial and nonfinancial metrics. The previous measurement was partially supported again by Ernst (2000) who offered an in-depth look at four key supply chain elements (demand planning and forecast, procurement, inventory, and outsourcing). He examined their role in effective supply chain practices, their direct link to maximizing profits, and how to avoid common pitfalls. In contrast, Yu, Yan, and Edwin (2002) in their research highlighted the benefits of the information quality sharing-based partnership, which will bring about reduction in inventory level and reduction of expected cost, which will reflect better performance of the chain. This again is a nonfinancial measurement.

Information quality processes are conceptualized in this research as the required bilateral information flow between supply chain members. For instance, a supplier may inform its customers of its manufacturing capacity constraints, just as a buying firm will inform its suppliers of its purchase requirements. Quality information is expected to improve supply chain performance by facilitating decisions that reflect a broad view of the supply chain and take into account interactions among the firms in the supply chain (Cachon & Fisher, 2000). The supply chain performance improvement in a firm might be expected in the form of increased inventory turns, better on-time delivery, improved responsiveness, better quality, reduced purchase prices, or reduced total cost which are very much related to nonfinancial measurement. Several other measures in the evaluation of supply chain performance have been identified (Beamon, 1999; Brewer & Speh, 2000; Gunasekaran, Patel & McGaughey, 2004; Rafele, 2004). Neely, Gregory, and Platts (1995) defined quality, time, flexibility, and cost as primary categories of performance measurements. Based on the available literature, supply chain performance measurements in this study consist of financial indices including profit margin, revenue growth, cost per order, cost per unit, and return on assets, and

Copyright © 2007, Idea Group Inc. Copying or distributing in print or electronic forms without written permission of Idea Group Inc. is prohibited.

nonfinancial indices including order fill rates, order cycle time, delivery time, customer requirements, number of faults, and flexibility.

Information Quality Dimension and Its Practical Application

Some researchers (Baglin, Bruel, Garreau, Greif, & van Delft, 1996; Christopher, 1997; Cooper, 1994) have explained the close links between information quality and the management of supply chain. Activities such as stocks that need replenishing, deliveries that need routing, and orders that need coordination require intensive quality of information flow. Accuracy, timeliness, completeness, and consistency in the information that flows along the channel in a supply chain can position a firm well especially when faced with world-class competitors. Information monitoring, control, and reporting systems are therefore essential for any management system, as firms drive the decisions based on the data collected through this system. These include the designing and planning of information systems at the initial stage, control and coordination, and cross-organizational coordination to ensure that the dimension of information quality (accuracy, timeliness, completeness, and consistency) are given due attention at the design stage on the information system. Information technology such as the intranet, extranet, Internet, WWW, and EDI facilitate the real-time or timeliness of information in a chain.

The Web platform has several advantages, which will allow a firm to overcome some traditional supply chain problems. These include real-time information on inventories, single data entry to minimize human errors as inputting of the data is handled by customers themselves, and there is no need to reenter the information, a real-time online ordering function for the build-to-order and build to backlog business model, and multilevel password control so that different functions can have different access levels which are again controlled by the respective authorized people. Migrating to a Web-based information system with a common platform for all of the channel partners will help in the standardization that can be accomplished only with the relationship and cooperation of all the channel partners in a chain.

The legacy systems that serve different needs, such as for shop floor manufacturing system, order recording, order delivery, and so on, are important for accurate and completeness of information flow in a supply chain. Migrating to a more advanced and integrated IT system will allow firms to expand their operations and enable their client, who has a separate database that is operated independently, to interface with the host database. Also firms need to reengineer the architecture of the IT system for their company regarding the type of information that should be made available, when and to whom. The IT system must be attempted to bring in the concept of two way and real-time information flow in a supply chain.

Information quality deals with the managing of information systems on the previously mentioned dimension with the objective of providing accurate information on the performance of different channel of the supply chain too. The information quality systems that flow are used for measuring the performance of, and controlling the operations in, a chain. Activities such as the collecting, processing, retrieving, reporting, and storing of data are part of information quality management. Techniques, such as groupware, IT/IS, shareware, data mining, and data warehousing, can be used for the purpose of managing quality information. The technologies of information should include EDI, e-commerce, ERP, Internet,

Copyright © 2007, Idea Group Inc. Copying or distributing in print or electronic forms without written permission of Idea Group Inc. is prohibited.

WWW, artificial intelligence (AI), and expert systems. This quality information will help to integrate various process/links along the supply chain.

The Relationship Between Information Quality and Supply Chain Performance

Many organizations are attempting to gain competitive advantage by integrating their suppliers more thoroughly into key supply chain processes. This calls for greater strategic and operational cooperation between buyer and supplier firms, often involving some degree of information flow. Advances in information technology are making it possible for firms to share planning information more quickly and easily. The notion that better information quality has had a positive effect on joint business outcomes has been previously studied in relation to supplier alliances (Mohr & Spekman, 1994; Monczka, Petersen, Handfield, & Ragatz, 1998), supplier integration into new product development (Ragatz, Handfield, & Scannell, 1997), supplier development (Krause, 1995, 1997), collaborative planning, forecasting, and replenishment (Barratt & Oliveira, 2001), and a host of other supply chain-related areas.

Simatupang, Wright, and Sridharan (2002) investigated collaborative efforts among supply chain members and found that the quality of information flows forward and backward among partners in the chain that provides adequate visibility across both internal functional and organization. Other writers (Anderson et al., 1998; Carbo, 2002; Muzumdar & Balachandran, 2001; Prasad & Tata, 2000; Spekman, Kamauff, & Myhr, 1998) noted information flow as a superseding element for effective supply chain performance. Lee (2002a) claimed that the network complexity, communication between entities, and accurate and timely transfer of information can be extremely difficult, distort demand information which can lead to excessive inventory, idle capacity, high manufacturing and transportation costs, and increasingly dissatisfied customers. Here again Lee discussed the importance of information with emphasis on quality. Even though ample information has been shared across the chain, again the question of quality comes into the picture. How much quality imbedded in the information that has been shared will determine the performance of the chain?

Lack of information with regard to demand visibility has been identified as an important challenge for supply chain management (Chen, 1988; Lee, 2002b). These were again stressed by Cachon and Fisher (2000), who claimed that information on demand is absolutely important for firms to make decisions on the building plan, the right number of units to be produced. The more accurate the information the better the avoidance of bullwhip effect along the chain. On the other hand if information on inventory level and velocity are not easily available, it will lead to inefficient capacity utilization, poor product availability, and high stock levels (Burbidge, 1989; Forrester, 1961; Houlihan, 1987; Lee, Padmanabhan & Whang, 1997; Towill, Niam & Wikner, 1992).

To fully satisfy the increasing requirements of customers, many companies have taken initiatives to broaden the scope of their services (Murphy & Daley, 2001). Recently, many companies tried to improve their operation efficiency by continuous information quality (Sauvage, 2003). Many firms are relying on technology in the form of linked information systems to supplement traditional modes of communication and information sharing with suppliers. These systems should facilitate the flow of information across organizational boundaries and improve the quality of the information shared. An example of a typical problem is where a small supplier may have a small amount of stock, which is held at a

Copyright © 2007, Idea Group Inc. Copying or distributing in print or electronic forms without written permission of Idea Group Inc. is prohibited.

cost to it. It is only prepared to hold greater amounts of stock against firm orders. If one large order is received, the company may well not be able to meet the demand through a lack of production capacity. Therefore, through poor timeliness and quality information, this company would be in a vulnerable position and is always likely to suffer from fluctuating demand. This company will be changing its output rates continually via overtime/short-time working or trying to cover demand fluctuations with high stock levels which may themselves lead to poor business performance. If the buyer moves to another similar supplier in an attempt to improve the situation, it is unlikely its position will get better unless information quality improves.

Information quality can reinforce competitive advantage for companies in markets where customer preferences change rapidly, where differentiation is limited, and where competition is intense (McAfee, 2002). A substantial body of research links information and performance for service industries (Gray, Matear, & Matheson, 2000; Li & Atuahene-Gima, 2001). In the supply chain literature, it has been shown that company's capabilities, such as information, are drivers for superior performance (Murphy & Poist, 2000). Customer-focused capabilities, including responsiveness and flexibility, can enhance performance (Zhao, Droge, & Stank, 2001). Lai (2004) suggested that a company with better service capability can attain a higher service performance. With the relationship among supply chain performance and information quality, there is little research that draws linkages between these constructs. Based on the previous discussions, the following hypothesis is proposed:

H1:   Companies with a more favorable attitude towards information quality will attain better supply chain performance.

Antecedents of Information Quality

Many researchers study information quality. Kwon and Zmud (1987) classified variables affecting information quality into individual, task-related, innovation-related, organizational, and environmental characteristics. Tornatzky and Fleischer (1990) suggested that the extent of information quality is affected by technological, organizational, and environmental context. Patterson, Grimm, and Corsi (2003) indicated that information quality affected by organizational size, structure, and performance, supply chain strategy, transaction climate, supply chain member pressure, and environmental uncertainty. Scupola (2003) used technological, organizational, and environmental characteristics to explain the information quality of Internet commerce. We will investigate the influence of technological, organizational, and environmental characteristics on information quality. The individual characteristic is not considered in this chapter.

Technological Characteristics

The speed of which technology and science constantly develop increases exponentially, producing more and more information everyday, for example; 90% of researchers who had ever existed are still living now (Basu, Poindexter, Drosen, & Addo, 2000). Since markets and technologies change fast, information that is relevant and recent today becomes obsolete fast. Tsai and Ghoshal (1998) indicated that an organization will have better information

Copyright © 2007, Idea Group Inc. Copying or distributing in print or electronic forms without written permission of Idea Group Inc. is prohibited.

when knowledge is shared more easily within the organization. Information quality can be achieved when the technology has higher transferability. The transferability of technology is determined by the explicitness of technology. It is more easy to transfer or share technological knowledge with higher explicitness (Grant, 1996; Teece, 1996). In addition to the explicitness of the technology, how the technology fits into information that a firm already possesses will also be another important technological characteristic (Chau & Tam, 1997; Tornatzky & Fleischer, 1990). Teece (1996) found that the cumulative nature of technologies will influence the information quality. Grant (1996) and Simonin (1999) also concluded that an organization with rich experience in the application or adoption of related technologies will have higher ability in information quality.

Therefore the following hypothesis is proposed:

H2a: The more explicit the technology, the more likely it is for the company to have information quality.

H2b: The more the accumulation of technology, the more likely it is for the company to have information quality.

Organizational Characteristics

Davenport and Beck (2001) presented the symptoms on an organizational level as an increased likelihood of having bad information when making decisions. They are diminished time for reflection, difficulty in holding others' attention, and a decreased ability to focus. Certain features of organizations themselves, including structures, climates, and cultures of organizations, will influence information quality (Kimberly & Evanisko, 1981; Russell & Hoag, 2004). Amabile (1988) indicated that management skills, organizational encouragement for information, and support of information resources would help the improvement of organizational information. Tornatzky and Fleischer (1990) suggested that informal linkages among employees, human resource quality, top manager's leadership behavior, and the amount of internal slack resources would significantly influence information quality. A firm with higher quality human resources, such as better education or training, will have higher ability in technological information.

Therefore the following hypothesis is proposed:

H3a: The more the organizational encouragement, the more likely it is for the company to have information quality.

H3b: The higher the human resource quality, the more likely it is for the company to have information quality.

Environmental Characteristics

Miles and Snow (1978) indicated that organizations will pay more attention to information when they face environments with higher instability and chaos. If the information we receive is lacking in social context, it is difficult to trust the information (Brown & Duguid, 2000; Davenport & Beck, 2001). Kimberly and Evanisko (1981) concluded that environmental complexity and uncertainty will influence organizational information quality. Damanpour (1991) indicated that an environment with high uncertainties will have a

Copyright © 2007, Idea Group Inc. Copying or distributing in print or electronic forms without written permission of Idea Group Inc. is prohibited.

positive influence on the organizational information. Zhu and Weyant (2003) suggested that demand uncertainty tends to increase a firm's incentive to have information quality. Governmental support is another important factor for information quality. Government's stringent regulation can both encourage and discourage information quality (Scupola, 2003; Tornatzky & Fleischer, 1990).

Therefore the following hypothesis is proposed:

H4a: The more the environmental uncertainty, the more likely it is for the company to have information quality.

H4b: The more the governmental support, the more likely it is for the company to have information quality.

Research Methodology

Based on the previous discussions, the research framework is shown in Figure 1. The data to test our hypotheses come from a mail survey of companies in Malaysia. The sample frame was drawn from members of the Federations of Malaysian Manufacturers. 400 questionnaires were mailed to the sampled companies in 2004. Questionnaires were mailed to general managers, as these target respondents were assumed to have a good knowledge of the information quality and performance of their companies. In total, 122 completed questionnaires were returned. Of these respondents, eight uncompleted or unconfident questionnaires were excluded. The overall response rate is 28.5%.

The measured scales were submitted to factor analysis and technological characteristics are factored by "explicitness of technology" and "accumulation of technology"; organizational characteristics are factored by "organizational encouragement" and "human resource quality"; environmental characteristics are factored by "environmental uncertainty" and "governmental support"; supply chain performance is factored by "financial" and "nonfinancial." The reliability analysis was also conducted and the smallest value of Cronbach's α for this study is 0.6742. This implies that the sampling results are reliable.

Results and Discussion

A large majority (37.8%) of the respondents are involved in the manufacturing of semiconductors and electrical goods. Of the 122 companies that participated, 30 (24.6%) are

Figure 1. Research framework

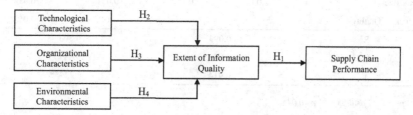

Copyright © 2007, Idea Group Inc. Copying or distributing in print or electronic forms without written permission of Idea Group Inc. is prohibited.

wholly owned by foreign companies. Out of those, the majority are affiliated with Japanese companies. Only 6 sites belong to wholly locally owned companies. The low percentage of wholly locally owned companies interested to participate in this research may be an interesting issue to explore but that is not pursued here. Another interesting trend is that the longer the firms operate in Malaysia, the tendency for them to have better supply chain performance is higher. Those that have been operating for more than 20 years represent 35.6% of companies who have responded.

The method of regression analysis was used to examine the influence of information quality on supply chain performance. Company history, number of employee and capital size are taken as control variables in the regression analysis. Based on the results shown in Table 2, it can be found that control variables do not affect the performance; however, the information quality exhibits significantly positive influences on supply chain performance. This means that the hypothesis H1 is not rejected. Companies with a more favorable attitude toward information quality will attain better supply chain performance.

In order to find the influence of technological, organizational, and environmental characteristics on the adoption of new logistics technologies, the method of regression analysis was also used. Company history, number of employees, and capital size were also taken as the control variables in the regression analysis. Based on the results shown in Table 3, it can be found that control variables do not have significant influences on the technology adoption; however, explicitness of technology, accumulation of technology, organizational encouragement, human resource quality, and governmental support exhibit significant influence on the technology adoption. This means that hypotheses H2a, H2b, H3a, H3b, and H4b are not rejected, but hypothesis H4a is rejected because most companies in Malaysia are small and medium sized, providing flexible logistics service to satisfy customers' varying requirements; this is their major competence and environmental uncertainty is also common to them. Therefore environmental uncertainty does not significantly influence the quality of information for companies in Malaysia.

It can be concluded that higher explicitness and accumulation of technology can help the transfer of technological knowledge within the organization and raise the level of infor-

Table 2. Standardized regression results for the supply chain performance

| Predictors | Dependent variables: Supply Chain Performance | | | |
| | Model 1 | | Model 2 | |
	Coefficient β	t	Coefficient β	t
Company history	0.027	0.901	0.017	0.898
Number of employee	0.021	0.628	0.025	0.706
Capital size	0.039	0.857	0.031	0.634
Information Quality			0.192	4.052**
R^2	0.093		0.503	
adj R^2	0.089		0.447	
F	0.914		6.279**	

Note: $^+ p<0.1$ $* p<0.05$ $** p<0.01$

Copyright © 2007, Idea Group Inc. Copying or distributing in print or electronic forms without written permission of Idea Group Inc. is prohibited.

Table 3. Standardized regression results for the antecedents of information quality

| | Dependent variables: The Extent of Information Quality | | | |
| | Model 1 | | Model 2 | |
Predictors	Coefficient β	t	Coefficient β	t
Company history	0.021	0.992	0.014	0.813
Number of employee	0.039	1.015	0.033	0.922
Capital size	0.044	1.371	0.039	1.325
Explicitness of technology			0.178	3.685**
Accumulation of technology			0.152	1.687+
Organizational encouragement			0.193	2.409*
Human resource quality			0.171	2.214*
Environmental uncertainty			0.127	1.017
Governmental support			0.186	2.512*
R^2	0.103		0.615	
adj R^2	0.098		0.524	
F	1.048		8.438**	

Note: $^+ p<0.1$ $* p<0.05$ $** p<0.01$

mation quality. Organizational encouragement can give employees motivation and support to better information. High quality of human resources means that employees are capable of delivering good information. Governmental support can encourage and guide companies to innovate in information technologies. The government can draw up public policies to encourage private sector performance improvements through trade and intermodal policies, infrastructure investment and development, creative financing arrangements, tax incentives, safety regulation, public/private partnerships, and special programs and projects (Morash & Lynch, 2002).

Conclusion

This study has investigated the extent of information quality for companies in Malaysia. Many companies in Malaysia begin to place emphasis on information quality. It is found that companies with a more favorable attitude toward information quality will attain better supply chain performance. The factors affecting information quality can be divided into technological, organizational, and environmental characteristics and they have positive influences on the quality of information. Moreover, it is found that higher explicitness and accumulation of technology can help the transfer of technological knowledge within the organization and can raise the capability of information quality. Companies can increase their level of information quality by encouraging or supporting their employees to have quality in information as well as by training and educating their employees to become intelligent workers.

Copyright © 2007, Idea Group Inc. Copying or distributing in print or electronic forms without written permission of Idea Group Inc. is prohibited.

References

Amabile, T. M. (1988). A model of creativity and innovation in organizations. In B. M. Staw & L. L. Cummings (Eds.), *Research in organizational behavior* (Vol. 10, pp. 123-167). Chicago: Aldine Publishing Company.

Andersen, B., Fagerhaug, T., Randmoel, S., Schuldmaier, J., & Prenninger, J. (1999). Benchmarking supply chain management: Finding the best practices. *Journal of Business & Industrial Marketing, 14*(5/6), 378-389.

Anderson, T. L., & Leal, D. R. (1998, April 26). Going with the flow: Expanding the markets. *Policy Analysis: A Cato Institute Publication,* 104.

Andersen, T., & Von Hellens, L. A. (1997). Information system work quality. *Information and Software Technology, 39*(12), 837-844.

Baglin, G., Bruel, O., Garreau, A., Greif, M., & van Delft, C. (1996). *Management industriel et logistique* (2nd ed.). Paris: Economica.

Ballou, D. P., & Pazer, H. L. (1987). Cost/quality tradeoffs of control procedures in information systems. *OMEGA: International Journal of Management Science, 15,* 509-521.

Barratt, M., & Oliveira, A. (2001). Exploring the experiences of collaborative planning initiatives. *International Journal of Physical Distribution & Logistics Management, 31*(4), 266-289.

Basu, C., Poindexter, S., Drosen, J., & Addo, T. (2000). Diffusion of executive information systems in organizations and the shift to the Web technologies. *Industrial Management & Data Systems, 100*(4), 271-276.

Beamon, B. (1999). Measuring supply chain performance. *International Journal of Operations & Production Management, 19*(3), 275-292.

Berglund, M., Van Laarhoven, P., Sharman, G., & Wandel, S. (1999). Third-party logistics: Is there a future? *International Journal of Logistics Management, 10*(1), 59-70.

Bitner, M. J., Brown, S. W., & Meuter, M. L. (2000). Technology infusion in service encounters. *Journal of the Academy of Marketing Science, 28*(1), 138-149.

Bowersox, D. J., Closs, D. J., & Cooper, M. B. (2002). *Supply chain logistical management.* New York: McGraw-Hill.

Brewer, P., & Speh, T. W. (2000). Using the balanced scorecard to measure supply chain performance. *Journal of Business Logistics, 21*(1), 75-93.

Brown, J. S., & Duguid, P. (2000). *The social life of information.* Boston: Harvard Business School Press.

Burbidge, J. L. (1989). *Production flow analysis for planning group technology.* Oxford: Clarendon Press.

Cachon, G., & Fisher, M. (2000). Supply chain inventory management and the value of shared information. *Management Science, 46*(8), 1032-1048.

Carbo, B. (2002). Align the organization for improved supply chain performance. *ASCET,* 44.

Carter, J. R., & Narasimhan, R. (1996). Purchasing and supply management: Future directions and trends. *International Journal of Purchasing and Materials Management, 32*(4), 3-11.

Chapman, R. L., Soosay, C., & Kandampully, J. (2003). Innovation in services and the new business model: A conceptual framework. *International Journal of Physical Distribution & Logistics Management, 33*(7), 630-650.

Copyright © 2007, Idea Group Inc. Copying or distributing in print or electronic forms without written permission of Idea Group Inc. is prohibited.

Chau, P. Y. K., & Tam, K. Y. (1997). Factors affecting the information of open systems: An exploratory study. *MIS Quarterly, 21*(1), 1-24.

Chen, F. (1998). Echelon reorder points, and the value of centralized demand inforation. *Management Science, 44*(12), 221-234.

Chopra, S., Meindl, P. (2001). *Supply chain management: Strategy, planning, and operation.* Upper Saddle River, NJ: Prentice Hall.

Christopher, M. (1993). Information and competitive strategy. *European Management Journal, 11*(2), 258-261.

Christopher, M. (1997). *Marketing logistics.* Oxford: Butterworth-Heineman.

Cooper, J. (1994). *Logistics & distribution planning: Strategies for management* (2nd ed.). London: Kogan Page.

Damanpour, F. (1991). Organizational innovation: A meta-analysis of effects of determinants and moderators. *Academy of Management Journal, 34*(3), 555-590.

Davenport, T. H., & Beck, J. C. (2001). *The attention economy.* Boston: Harvard Business School Press.

Davis, G. B., & Olson, M. H. (1985). *Management information systems: Conceptual foundations, structure, and development.* New York: McGraw-Hill.

De Brentani, U., & Cooper, R. G. (1993). Developing successful new financial services for businesses. *Industrial Marketing Management, 21*, 231-241.

Ernst, D. (2000, August). Inter-organizational knowledge outsourcing: What permits small Taiwanese firms to compete in the computer industry? *Asia Pacific Journal of Management* [special issue on 'Knowledge Management in Asia'].

Forrester, J. (1961). *Industrial dynamics.* Cambridge, MA: MIT Press.

Fox, C., Levitin, A., & Redman, T. (1993). The notion of data and its quality dimensions. *Information Processing & Management, 30*, 9-19.

Fuld, L. M. (1998, September 15). The danger of data slam. *CIO Enterprise Magazine*, 28-33. Retrieved April 16, 2006, from http://www.cio.com/archive/enterprise/091598_ic.html

Gelle, E. & Karhu, K. (2003). Industrial management+datasystems. *Wembley, 103*(8/9), 633-644.

Germain, R., Dröge, C., & Daugherty, P.J. (1994). A cost and impact typology of logistics technology and the effect of its adoption on organizational practice. *Journal of Business Logistics, 15*(2), 227-248.

Grant, R. M. (1996). Prospering in dynamically-competitive environments: Organizational capability as knowledge integration. *Organization Science, 7*(4), 375-387.

Gray, B. J., Matear, S. M., & Matheson, P. K. (2000). Improving the performance of hospitality firms. *International Journal of Contemporary Hospitality Management, 12*(3), 149-155.

Gunasekaran, A., Patel, C., & McGaughey, R. E. (2004). A framework for supply chain performance measurement. *International Journal of Production Economics, 87*, 333-347.

Hammer, M. (2001). *Agenda: What every business must do to dominate the decade.* New York: Crown Publishing.

Houlihan, J. B. (1987). International supply chain management. *International Journal of Physical Distribution & Materials Management, 17* (2), 51-66.

Huang, F., & Chen, Y. (2002). Relationships of TQM philosophy, methods and performance: A survey in Taiwan. *Industrial Management & Data Systems, 102*(4), 226-234.

Copyright © 2007, Idea Group Inc. Copying or distributing in print or electronic forms without written permission of Idea Group Inc. is prohibited.

Huh, Y. U., Keller, F. R., Redman, T. C., & Watkins, A. R. (1990). Data quality. *Information and Software Technology, 32*, 559-565.

Hunter, L., Beaumont, P., & Lee, M. 2002. Knowledge management practice in Scottish law firms. *Human Resource Management Journal, 12*(2), 4-21.

Irwin, J. G., Hoffman, J. J., & Geiger, S. W. (1998). The effect of technological adoption on organizational performance: Organizational size and environmental munificence as moderators. *The International Journal of Organizational Analysis, 6*(1), 50-64.

Johne, A., & Storey, C. (1998). New service development: A review of the literature and annotated bibliography. *European Journal of Marketing, 32*(3/4), 184-251.

Kanter, R. M. (1988). When a thousand flowers bloom: Structural, collective, and social conditions for innovation in organization. In B. M. Staw & L. L. Cummings (Eds.), *Research in organizational behavior* (Vol. 10, pp. 169-211). Chicago: Aldine Publishing Company.

Kimberly, J. R., & Evanisko, M. J. (1981). Organizational innovation: The influence of individual, organizational, and contextual factors on hospital adoption of technological and administrative innovations. *Academy of Management Journal, 24*(4), 689-713.

Klein, B. D. (2001). User perceptions of data quality: Internet and traditional text sources. *Journal of Computer Information Systems, 41*(4), 9-15.

Krause, D. (1997) Supplier development: current practices and outcomes. International *Journal of Purchasing and Materials Management, 33*(2), 12-19.

Kwon, T. H., & Zmud, R. W. (1987). Unifying the fragmented models of information systemsimplementation. In R. J. Boland & R. A. Hirschheim (Eds.), *Critical issues in information systems research.* New York: John Wiley & Sons Ltd.

Lai, K. H. (2004). Service capability and performance of logistics service providers. *Transportation Research Part E, 40*, 385-399.

Lee, H. L. (2002a). Aligning supply chain strategies with product uncertainties. *California Management Review, 44*(3), 105-110.

Lee, H. L. (2002b). Unleashing the power of intelligence. *ECR Journal, 2*(1), 61-73.

Lee, H. L. Padmanabhan, V., & Whang, S. (1997). Information distortion in a supply chain: The bullwhip effect. *Management Science, 43*(4), 546-58.

Li, H., & Atuahene-Gima, K. (2001). Product innovation strategy and the performance of new technology ventures in China. *Academy of Management Journal, 44*(6), 1123-1134.

Lynn, G. S., Maltz, A. C., Jurkat, P. M., & Hammer, M. D. (1999). New media in marketing redefine competitive advantage: a comparison of small and large firms. *Journal of Services Marketing, 13*(1), 9-20.

Madnick, S. E., & Wang, R. Y. (1992). *Introduction to the TDQM research program* (Working Paper No. 92-01). Total Data Quality Management Research Program.

Mason-Jones, R., & Towill, D. R. (1999). Using the information decoupling point to improve supply chain performance. *The International Journal of Logistics Management, 10*(2), 13-26.

McAfee, A. (2002). The impact of enterprise information technology adoption on operational performance: An empirical investigation. *Production and Operations Management, 11*(1), 33-53.

McGinnis, M. A., & Kohn, J. W. (2002). Logistics strategy-revised. *Journal of Business Logistics, 23*(2), 1-17.

Copyright © 2007, Idea Group Inc. Copying or distributing in print or electronic forms without written permission of Idea Group Inc. is prohibited.

Miles, R. E., & Snow, C. C. (1978). *Organizational strategy, structure, and process*. New York: McGraw-Hill.

Mohr, J., & Spekman R. (1994). Characteristics of partnership success: Partnership attributes, communication behavior and conflict resolution techniques. *Strategic Management Journal, 15*(2), 135-152.

Monczka, R. M., Peterson, R. C., Handfield, R. B., & Ragatz, G. L. (1998, January). Supplier integration into new product development. In *Proceedings of the 1996 NSF Design and Manufacturing Grantees Conference*.

Monczka, R. M., Trent, R. J., & Callahan, T. J. (1993) *Purchasing and supply chain management*. Cincinnati, OH: South-Western Publishing.

Morash, E. A., & Lynch, D. F. (2002). Public policy and global supply chain capabilities and performance: A resource-based view. *Journal of International Marketing, 10*(1), 25-51.

Murphy, P. R., & Daley, J. M. (2001). Profiling international freight forwarders: An update. *International Journal of Physical Distribution & Logistics Management, 31*(3), 152-168.

Murphy, P. R., & Poist, R. F. (2000). Third-party logistics: Some user versus provider perspective. *Journal of Business Logistics, 21*(1), 121-131.

Muzumdar, M., & Balachandran, N. (2001, October). The supply chain evolution, roles responsibilities and implications for management. *APICS Magazine*.

Naumann, F., & Rolker, C. (2000). Assessment methods for information quality criteria. In *Proceedings of the 2000 Conference on Information Quality* (pp. 148-162).

Neely, A., Gregory, M., & Platts, K. (1995). Performance measurement system design. *International Journal of Operations and Production Management, 15*(4), 80-116.

Olavarrieta, S., & Ellinger, A. E. (1997). Resource-based theory and strategic logistics research. *International Journal of Physical Distribution and Logistics Management, 27*(9/10), 559-587.

Patterson, K. A., Grimm, C. M., & Corsi, T. M. (2003). Adopting new technologies for supply chain management. *Transportation Research Part E, 39*, 95-121.

Petersen, K. J., Ragatz, G. L., & Monczka, R. M. (2005, Spring). An examination of collaborative planning effectiveness and supply chain performance. *Journal of Supply Chain Management, 41*(2), 14-27.

Pollard, L. T., & Hayne, A. S. A. (1998). Establishing an information quality programme for competitive advantage. *International Journal Information Management, 21*,151-165.

Prasad, S., & Tata, J. (2000). Information investment in supply chain management. *Logistics Information Management, 13*(1), 33-38.

Pugsley, H. J., Muttler, J. J., & McDermott, R. (2000).Why information technology inspired but cannot deliver knowledge management. *Management Review, 44*, 103-117.

Rafele, C. (2004). Logistic service measurement: A reference framework. *Journal of Manufacturing Technology Management, 15*(3), 280-290.

Ragatz, G. L., Handfield, R. B., & Scannell, T. V. (1997). Success factors for integrating suppliers into new product development. *Journal of Product Innovation management, 14*, 190-202.

Rieh, S. Y., & Belkin, N. J. (1998). Understanding judgment of information quality and cognitive authority in the WWW. *Journal of the American Society for Information Science, 35*, 279-289.

Copyright © 2007, Idea Group Inc. Copying or distributing in print or electronic forms without written permission of Idea Group Inc. is prohibited.

Russell, D. M., & Hoag, A. M. (2004). People and information technology in the supply chain: Social and organizational influences on adoption. *International Journal of Physical Distribution & Logistics Management, 34*(1/2), 102-122.

Sauvage, T. (2003). The relationship between technology and logistics third-party providers. *International Journal of Physical Distribution & Logistics Management, 33*(3), 236-253.

Scupola, A. (2003). The adoption of Internet commerce by SMEs in the south of Italy: An environmental, technological and organizational perspective. *Journal of Global Information Technology Management, 6*(1), 52-71.

Shan, K.C., & Marlow, P.B. (2005). Logistics capability and performance in Taiwan's major manufacturing firms. *Transportation Research Part E, 41*, 217-234.

Simatupang, T.M., Wright, A.C., & Sridharan, R. (2002). The knowledge of coordination for supply chain integration. *Business Process Management Journal, 8*(3), 289-308.

Simonin, B.L. (1999). Transfer of marketing know-how in international strategic alliances: An empirical investigation of the role and antecedents of knowledge ambiguity. *Journal of International Business Studies, 30*(3), 463-490.

Spekman, R.E., Kamauff, J.W., & Myhr, N. (1998). An empirical investigation into supply chain management: A perspective on partnerships. *International Journal of Physical Distribution and Logistics Management, 28*(8), 630-650.

Strong, D.M., Lee, Y.W., & Wang, R.Y. (1997). Data quality in context. *Communications of the ACM, 40*(5), 103-110.

Supply-Chain Council. (2002). An introduction to the supply chain operations reference model version 6.0. Retrieved April 16, 2006, from http://www.supply-chain.org

Teece, D.J. (1996). Firm organization, industrial structure, and technological innovation. *Journal of Economic Behavior and Organization, 31*(2), 193-224.

Tornatzky, L.G., & Fleischer, M. (1990). *The process of technological innovation.* Lexington, MA: Lexington Books.

Towill, D.R., Naim, M.M., & Wikner, J. (1992). Industrial dynamics simulation models in the design of supply chains. *Internatioanl Journal of Physical Distribution & Logistics Managemnt, 22*(5), 3-14.

Tsai, W., & Ghoshal, S. (1998). Social capital and value creation: The role of intra-firm networks. *Academy of Management Journal, 41*(4), 464-476.

Wand, Y., & Wang, R.Y. (1996). Anchoring data quality dimensions in ontological foundations. *Communications of the ACM, 39*(11), 86-95.

Wang, R.Y., & Strong, D.M. (1996). Beyond accuracy: What data quality means to data consumers. *Journal of Management Information Systems, 12*(4), 5-34.

Yu, Z., Yan, H., & Edwin, T.C. (2001). Benefits of information sharing with supply chain partnerships. *Industrial Management, 101*(3/4), 114-121.

Zhao, M., Droge, C., & Stank, T.P. (2001). The effects of logistics capabilities on firm performance: Customer-focused versus information-focused capabilities. *Journal of Business Logistics, 22*(2), 91-107.

Zhu, K., & Weyant, J.P. (2003). Strategic decisions of new technology adoption under asymmetric information: A game-theoretic model. *Decision Sciences, 34*(4), 643-675.

Zmud, R. W. (1978). An empirical investigation of the dimensionality of the concept of information. *Decision Sciences, 9*, 187-195.

Copyright © 2007, Idea Group Inc. Copying or distributing in print or electronic forms without written permission of Idea Group Inc. is prohibited.

About the Authors

Latif Al-Hakim is a senior lecturer of supply chain management in the Department of Economics and Resources Management, Faculty of Business at the University of Southern Queensland. His experience spans 35 years in industry, research, and development in organizations and universities. Dr. Al-Hakim received his first degree in mechanical engineering in 1968. His MSc (1977) in industrial engineering and PhD (1983) in management science were awarded from the University of Wales, UK. Dr. Al-Hakim has held various academic appointments and lectured on a wide variety of interdisciplinary management and industrial engineering topics. He has published extensively in facilities planning, information management, and systems modeling. Research papers have appeared in various international journals and have been cited in other research and postgraduate work. Dr. Al-Hakim is the editor of *International Journal of Information Quality* and associate editor of *International Journal of Networking and Virtual Organisation.*

* * *

Laure Berti-Équille is currently an associate professor with the Computer Science Department (IFSIC), University of Rennes, France. Her research interests at IRISA lab (INRIA-Rennes, France) are multisource data quality, quality-aware data integration, and data cleaning techniques, recommender system, and multimedia data mining. She is author of more than 20 papers mainly on data quality, published among others in the International Conference on Information Quality (IQ) at the Massachusetts Institute of Technology, Cambridge. She has cochaired with Divesh Srivastava (AT&T Research Lab) and Carlo Batini (University di Milano) the second edition of the International Workshop on Information Quality in Information Systems (IQIS) held in conjunction with the ACM 2005 PODS/SIGMOD Conference. She has been involved in several French and European projects on quality and metadata.

Copyright © 2007, Idea Group Inc. Copying or distributing in print or electronic forms without written permission of Idea Group Inc. is prohibited.

Ismael Caballero has an MSc and PhD in computer science from the Escuela Superior de Informática of Ciudad Real (UCLM). An assistant professor in the Department of Computer Science at the University of Castilla - La Mancha, in Ciudad Real, Spain, he has been researching in the data and information quality field for more than six years. Caballero is a member of the Alarcos Research Group and his research interests are data and information quality, data and information quality management, data and information quality of Web sites.

Zbigniew J. Gackowski has extensive experience in industry, public administration, and universities. His teaching and research bridge the gap between Central European and U.S. experience in computer information systems: Warsaw Polytechnic; University of Michigan (*Fulbright Research Scholarship*); Purdue University; Baruch College; CSU, Stanislaus; and University of Melbourne (Visiting). While in Poland, he published more than 120 items, among them four books. He presented many papers across Europe, the U.S., the Middle East, and South America. He is a member of ACM and DSI, and a charter member of the Association for Information Systems and the Institute of Informing Science.

Kimberly Hess is a product manager for Acxiom Corporation supporting Acxiom's core linking product AbiliTec. Since 1999 she has worked at Acxiom in various capacities from the initial rollout of AbiliTec to implementing corporate quality initiatives including participating in a joint venture with Acxiom and MIT and the MIT ICIQ conference. Her current focus is around the internal and external support of data integration initiatives including new products.

Zhanming Jin is a professor of strategic management in the Department of Business Strategy and Policy at Tsinghua University, China. Zhanming received his BS from Jilin University in 1980, his MS from the Chinese Institute of Agriculture and Mechanic in 1986, and a PhD from Chinese University of Mining and Technology in 1989. He achieved a postdoctoral degree from Tsinghua University in 1991. Dr. Jin's research interests include strategic management, strategic selection under e-business environment, strategic alliance, military strategy, and enterprise competition.

Karolyn Kerr is currently a health consultant working for the IT consultancy firm Simpl in New Zealand and studying toward a PhD in health informatics. Karolyn has a background as a cardiac care nurse with over 15 years experience in the health sector in New Zealand and the UK. Following the completion of a Masters in Health Informatics (Telehealth) in 2002, Kerr began working at the Ministry of Health advising on health information strategy and policy, bringing together the two disciplines of nursing and IT. Kerr has presented widely and internationally on the development of a data quality framework and improvement strategy for health care.

Andy Koronios received his PhD from the University of Queensland. He has extensive teaching experience both in the tertiary sector at undergraduate and postgraduate, MBA, DBA, and PhD levels as well as in the provision of executive industry seminars. He has numerous research publications in a diverse area such as multimedia and online learning systems, information security and data quality, electronic commerce, and Web requirements

Copyright © 2007, Idea Group Inc. Copying or distributing in print or electronic forms without written permission of Idea Group Inc. is prohibited.

engineering. His current research interests focus on data quality and the use of information in strategic decision making. He is currently a professor and the head of the School of Computer and Information Science at the University of South Australia.

Emily Kuo earned her MS in statistics from Stanford University in 2003. Her primary professional interests are statistical modeling and data mining, regression models, analysis of variance, and biostatistics.

Shien Lin is a researcher in the Strategic Information Management Laboratory for CIEAM at the University of South Australia. He has extensive experience working on various positions in the information system and finance sectors. He holds a master's degree in electronic commerce and is currently working toward the completion of a PhD in data quality for engineering asset management. His research interests cover many aspects of the data quality domain, particularly in developing data quality model to enhance the quality of data associated with the management of engineering asset.

Tony Norris is a professor of information systems at Massey University, Auckland, New Zealand. His research interests are in the strategic role of information technology and information management in the health sector and include the cultural and business issues associated with the application of IT, data quality, knowledge management, and telehealth. Dr. Norris is the author of the book, Essentials of Telemedicine and Telecare (Wiley, 2002). He is also the author of over 45 research papers in the field of health informatics as well as numerous papers in his first research areas of chemistry and mathematics.

M. Mehdi Owrang O. is currently a professor of computer science in the Department of Computer Science, Audio Technology, and Physics at American University in Washington, DC. Dr. Owrang authored or coauthored 55 papers in computer journals and conferences. His current research interest includes knowledge discovery in databases. He is a member of the ACM, IEEE, and the associate editor of software and information engineering of the *ISCA Journal*.

Mario Piattini has an MSc and PhD in computer science from the Polytechnic University of Madrid and is a certified information system auditor and certified information security manager from the ISACA (Information System Audit and Control Association). He is a full professor in the Department of Computer Science at the University of Castilla-La Mancha, in Ciudad Real, Spain. The author of several books and papers on databases, software engineering, and information systems, he leads the ALARCOS research group of the Department of Computer Science at the University of Castilla-La Mancha. His research interests are advanced database design, database quality, software metrics, software maintenance, and security in information systems.

Elizabeth M. Pierce is a professor in the MIS and Decision Sciences Department at the Eberly College of Business and Information Technology, Indiana University of Pennsylvania, USA. Since 1997, she has been actively involved with the Conference on Information Quality sponsored by MIT. Her research focuses on data, information, and knowledge quality. Pierce received her PhD from the University of Michigan.

Copyright © 2007, Idea Group Inc. Copying or distributing in print or electronic forms without written permission of Idea Group Inc. is prohibited.

Premkumar Rajagopal is currently pursuing a PhD in supply chain management under USM, and a full-time managerial staff in a MNC. Since year 2000 I have played an active role in part-time lecturing for distance learning MBA students, subjects on human resource management, logistics management, supply chain management, and strategic management. The universities engaged for this program are University of Hawaii, Fedrick Taylor University, Berne University, Metropolitan Business School, Nottingham Trent University, University of East London, University of Southern Queensland, and University of Sunshine Coast. In 2002, Rajagopal was invited to present a critical paper on supply chain management at ICORD, which is an international conference held in Chennai, India.

Ying Su received a BS in mechanical engineering in 1992 from Hohai University, Nanjing, Jiangsu Province, China. In 1999, he received an MS in mechanical engineering from Southeast University. During 2000, he completed his doctoral studies from the Department of Precision Instruments and Mechanology at the Tsinghua University, Beijing, China. From 1992 to 1996, he was an engineer and technologist at an iron and steel plant. He is an author of many scientific and research papers. His current research interests include information quality, business process modeling (BPM), enterprise resource planning (ERP), supply chain management (SCM), performance measurement and control, agile manufacturing, simulation, advanced planning and scheduling, quality function deployment (QFD), and computer aided process planning (CAPP).

John Talburt is the leader for new products and solutions for Acxiom Corporation and director of the Acxiom Laboratory for Applied Research. He led the team that developed the Acxiom Data Toolkit and the Acxiom Data Quality Scorecard Solution. Before going to Acxiom, Talburt was a professor and chair of the Computer and Information Science Department at the University of Arkansas at Little Rock, USA. He has authored numerous publications in areas of information quality, data management, knowledge representation, and intelligent systems.

Richard Wang is director of the MIT Information Quality Program, USA. Before heading the MITIQ program, Wang served as a professor at MIT for a decade. He was also on the faculty of the University of Arizona and Boston University. In 1996, Wang organized the premier International Conference on Information Quality, for which he has served as the general conference chair. Wang's books on information quality include *Quality Information and Knowledge* (Prentice Hall, 1999), *Data Quality* (Kluwer Academic, 2001), and *Journey to Data Quality* (MIT Press). Wang is the recipient of the 2005 DAMA International Academic Achievement Award.

Ying Wang is a postgraduate student of Zhejiang University China, majoring in management science and engineering. Her research field is mainly data quality management. One of her papers, titled "The Present State Analysis of the Supply Chain Management in Small and Medium Enterprises of Zhejiang Province" was presented in the international academic conference of enterprises network and economic growth and collected in proceedings of the symposium on *Enterprises Network and Economic Growth*.

Copyright © 2007, Idea Group Inc. Copying or distributing in print or electronic forms without written permission of Idea Group Inc. is prohibited.

Zhenguo Yu is a professor at Zhejiang University China and a certified consultant of the SAP R/3 application. He has extensive experience in industry, public administration, and universities. As a visiting scholar, he has visited the Technical University of Berlin, Sussex University, Grenoble University, National University of Singapore, Rensselier Polytechnic Institute, and University of South Queensland. In China, he has published more than 40 items, one of which is the textbook on manufacturing operations management. His research on quality management was supported by the Natural Science Foundation of China.

Suhaiza Zailani graduated from Lancaster University, UK for MSc in operational research and PhD in management science and is currently a senior lecturer attached to the School of Management, Universiti Sains Malaysia, Penang. Teaching areas are operations management, productivity and quality control, and management science. Current areas of interest are supply chain management, benchmarking, new product development, and quality and productivity in organizations in general. Zailani has also jointly produced five articles that published in a local journal and international journal such as *International Journal of Information Management, Supply Chain Management: An International Journal, Sasin Journal of Management,* and so forth.

Copyright © 2007, Idea Group Inc. Copying or distributing in print or electronic forms without written permission of Idea Group Inc. is prohibited.

Index

Copyright © 2007, Idea Group Inc. Copying or distributing in print or electronic forms without written permission of Idea Group Inc. is prohibited.

Copyright © 2007, Idea Group Inc. Copying or distributing in print or electronic forms without written permission of Idea Group Inc. is prohibited.

M

market 67, 197, 254, 261
media 82
mediation system 23
medical error 172, 175
Ministry Data Quality Team (MDQT) 100

N

national account system 270
national and regional account data 270
National Bureau of Statistics (NBS) 253
National Health Service (NHS) 98
national macroeconomic data bank 271
New Zealand Health Data Quality Im-
    provement Programme 100
New Zealand Health Information Service
    (NZHIS) 99

O

object-oriented approach 201
operating theatre waiting list 174
organizational effort 269
organization unit 159, 160, 164
outpatient 174

P

partition similarity 7
People's Bank of China (PBC) 261
performance measure (PM) 201
population statistics 257
private enforcement 259
private securities litigation rule (PSLR)
    260
process mapping 172, 176
product information quality 190
product quality management 121
public enforcement 261

Q

quality 77, 83, 147
quality-extended query 30
quality management 121, 252
quality management practices 252

quality of data (QoD) 23, 25, 81, 105, 113,
    254, 272
quality of service (QoS) 23, 25, 277
quality of service modeling language 26

R

radio frequency identification (RFID) 222
Rand index 11
reliability 194
resource input (RI) 201, 203
resource process (RP) 201
resource output (RO) 201
rule discovery process 56

S

SAP R/3 software package 166
science statistics 257
security 77, 95, 102, 233, 279
social issues in China's IQ management
    257
social statistics 257
State Council Securities Commission
    (SCSC) 261
statistical agencies in enterprises 266
statistical and financial data in China 252
statistical informatics dystem 271
statistical informatics system 271
statistical process control (SPC) 113
statistics of balance of international pay-
    ments 257
supervision of the statistical activities 268
supply chain council 280
supply chain performance 275, 277
surgeon 170, 172
surgery management process 168
symbolic representation 71
system development cycle 79
system of national accounts (SNA) 272

T

technological issues in China's IQ manage-
    ment 270
timeliness 27, 95, 197, 207, 256, 279
tolerance 24

Copyright © 2007, Idea Group Inc. Copying or distributing in print or electronic forms without written permission of
Idea Group Inc. is prohibited.

Copyright © 2007, Idea Group Inc. Copying or distributing in print or electronic forms without written permission
of Idea Group Inc. is prohibited.